THE ROUGH GUIDE TO
BARCELONA

This thirteenth edition updated by
Sally Davies and AnneLise Sorensen

ROUGH
GUIDES

Contents

Introduction to
Barcelona

Barcelona – the past and potentially future capital of the independent nation of Catalunya, and the Mediterranean's most exciting destination – is the very epitome of cosmopolitan panache, hip design and sheer nonstop energy. Time and again the city has reinvented itself, from medieval maritime powerhouse to Olympic city, from neglected Franco-era backwater to trailblazing national force, with its dazzlingly inventive architecture as the most vivid expression of its tireless self-confidence. This is a place whose most famous monument, Antoni Gaudí's Sagrada Família, is an unfinished basilica of rapturous ambition; whose most celebrated street, La Rambla, is a round-the-clock maelstrom of human activity; and whose vibrant restaurants, bars, shops and galleries are at the vanguard of European style and fashion. Whether you're visiting for the first time, expecting a traditional city break, or returning for the fiftieth, thinking you know it inside out, Barcelona never fails to surprise.

The impetus for Barcelona's exuberant self-promotion stems above all from its unique political and cultural identity. Its inhabitants leave you in no doubt that, whatever the map might show, you're not in Spain but in the autonomous province of **Catalunya** (Catalonia in English), which traces its history back as far as the ninth century. This makes Barcelona the capital of what many regard as a nation, and cranks the natural pride that locals feel for their city up an extra notch or two. Galleries and museums, for example, hold "national" collections of Catalan art and history, while the 1992 Olympics – which kickstarted the dynamic rebuilding process – were indisputably Barcelona's Games, and not Spain's. The city fosters an independent spirit, setting itself apart from the rest of the country and single-mindedly pursuing its own social, economic and cultural agenda.

Nowhere is this more perfectly seen than in the otherworldly **modernista** (Art Nouveau) buildings that stud Barcelona's streets, dating from the flamboyant era of

renewal in the late nineteenth century. **Antoni Gaudí** is the most famous of those who have left their mark in this way: his **Sagrada Família** church is rightly revered, but just as fascinating are the (literally) fantastic houses, apartment buildings and parks that he and his contemporaries designed.

Barcelona has at its centre an extensive medieval **old town** – full of landmark monuments from an earlier age of expansion – and a stupendous **artistic** legacy, ranging from exquisite Romanesque treasures to major galleries celebrating Catalan artists Joan Miró and Antoni Tàpies, as well as Pablo Picasso, who spent some of his formative years here. The city is equally proud of its cutting-edge **restaurants**, its late-night bars and clubs, and most of all its football team, the mercurial, incomparable **FC Barcelona**. Add a spruced-up waterfront, 5km of sandy beaches, and swathes of verdant parks and gardens, and even on a lengthy visit you could never see it all.

True, for all its go-ahead feel, Barcelona has its problems, not least the peak-season overcrowding brought on by its well-deserved reputation for welcoming visitors. It's easy enough to escape the congestion, though, if you venture beyond the main tourist sights. Tapas bars hidden down alleys unchanged in centuries, designer boutiques in gentrified old-town quarters, street opera singers belting out arias, bargain lunches in workers' taverns, neighbourhood funicular rides, unmarked gourmet restaurants, craft workshops, restored medieval palaces, suburban walks

BARCELONA ON A PLATE

In a town where lunch can go on until 5pm, and tapas is what you eat *before* dinner, not your dinner itself, dining out is a big deal. Word gets around quick if there's a hot new restaurant or bar, and Barcelona gourmets are pretty discerning customers – not for them La Rambla tourist traps or fast-food chains. Embrace the local tastes and current trends and a whole new world opens up, from no-frills fishermen's favourites in **Can Maño** (see page 188) to inventive, cutting-edge bar snacks at **Gresca** (see page 192). Above all, if it's fresh, seasonal and straight from the market – that's Barcelona on a plate.

and specialist galleries – all are just as much Barcelona as La Rambla or the Sagrada Família.

What to see

Despite being one of the largest cities on the Mediterranean (population 1.7 million, with a further 3.7 million in its metropolitan area), Barcelona is a straightforward place to find your way around. In effect, it's a series of self-contained quarters or neighbourhoods, known as *barris*, stretching out from the harbour, flanked by parks, hills and woodland. The city centre and its major attractions – Gothic cathedral, Picasso museum, markets, Gaudí buildings and art galleries – can be visited on foot, while a fast, cheap, integrated public transport system takes you directly to the peripheral attractions and suburbs.

This Guide starts, as do most visitors, with **La Rambla** (occasionally seen in plural as *Les Rambles* in Catalan or Las Ramblas in Castilian), a kilometre-long, tree-lined avenue – officially five consecutive avenues, hence the plural – of promenading pedestrians, pavement cafés and kiosks that splits the old town in two. East of La Rambla, the **Barri Gòtic** (Gothic Quarter) is immediately recognizable as the medieval nucleus of the city, a labyrinth of twisting streets and historic buildings that include La Seu (the cathedral) and the palaces and museums around Plaça del Rei. A little further east lie the similarly venerable districts of **Sant Pere**, set around the terrific Santa Caterina market, and the fashionable boutique-and-bar quarter of **La Ribera** to the south, home to the Picasso museum. Over to the west of La Rambla, the edgier, artier neighbourhood of **El Raval** contains the city's flagship museum of contemporary art (MACBA) as well as several of its coolest bars and restaurants.

At its southern end, La Rambla reaches the waterfront. Walking east from the spruced-up harbour area here, known as **Port Vell** (Old Port), will take you past the aquarium and marina, through the old fishing and restaurant quarter of **Barceloneta**, beyond the **Parc de la Ciutadella** and out along the promenade to the cafés and restaurants of the **Port Olímpic**. This whole area is where Barcelona most resembles a resort, with city beaches lining the waterfront from Barceloneta all the way to the conference and leisure zone of Parc del Fòrum at **Diagonal Mar**.

The fortress-topped hill of **Montjuïc**, at the southwest corner of modern Barcelona, lay far beyond the city limits originally, and was the site of Roman temples and a medieval Jewish cemetery. It now holds a host of remarkable cultural attractions, including Catalunya's vast and utterly unmissable national art gallery (MNAC), the Joan Miró museum, botanic garden and main Olympic stadium.

At the top of La Rambla, Plaça de Catalunya marks the start of the gridded nineteenth-century extension of the city, known as the **Eixample** and divided into distinct "right" (**Dreta**) and "left" (**Esquerra**) neighbourhoods. A monument to the thrusting expansionism of Barcelona's early industrial age, the Eixample is home to some of Europe's most extraordinary architecture, including Gaudí's astonishing **Casa Batlló** and **La Pedrera**, as well as the ever-growing **Sagrada Família**.

Beyond the Eixample lie the northern suburbs, notably **Gràcia**, with its small squares and lively bars, and the nearby **Park Güell**, while you'll also come out this way to reach the famous **Camp Nou** FC Barcelona stadium. It's worth making for the hills, too, where you can join the crowds at the renowned **Tibidabo** amusement park – or escape them with a walk through the woods in the peaceful **Parc de Collserola**.

The good public transport links also make it easy to head further out of the city. The mountaintop monastery of **Montserrat** makes the most obvious day-trip, not least for the extraordinary ride up to the monastic eyrie by cable car or mountain railway. **Sitges** is the local beach town *par excellence*, while with more time you can follow various trails around Catalunya's **wine country**, head south to the Roman town of **Tarragona** or Gaudí's birthplace of **Reus**, or take a train north to medieval **Girona** or the Salvador Dalí museum in **Figueres**.

When to go

Barcelona is a hugely popular city-break destination with a year-round tourist, business and convention trade. Seasonal attractions range from summer music festivals to Christmas markets, and there's always something going on. In terms of the weather, the best times to visit are late **spring** and early **autumn**, when it's comfortably warm (around 21–25°C) and walking the streets isn't a chore. Evenings might see a chill in the air, but Barcelona in these seasons is often nigh on perfect. However, in **summer** the city can be unbearably hot and humid, with temperatures averaging 28°C but often climbing a lot higher. Avoid August, especially, when the climate is at its most unwelcoming and local inhabitants head out of the city in droves, leaving many shops, bars and restaurants closed. It's worth considering a **winter** break, as long as you don't mind the prospect of occasional rain. Even in December, when temperatures hover around 13°C, it's generally still warm enough to sit out at a café.

Beyond Barcelona, the weather varies enormously. On the coast it's best – naturally enough – in summer, but resorts like **Sitges** are packed from June to September. **Tarragona**, too, can be extremely hot and busy in summer, though **Girona** is much more equable at that time, and escaping from the coast for a few cool days is easy.

BARCELONA BEACH WITH PALM TREES

Author picks

Sant Pol de Mar Trains from Plaça Catalunya run every half hour to this idyllic, seaside village of whitewashed houses (see page 145), where you can expect to find fishing boats, quiet coves, a handful of restaurants and a coastal path that runs for miles in either direction.

Cabinet of Curiosities The attic floor of the Museu Frederic Marès (see page 51) is the cherry on the cake of Barcelona's most charming museum. Known as the Sala de las Diversiones (Hall of Amusements), it's a collection of curios from the eighteenth and nineteenth centuries: lead soldiers, dioramas, puppet theatres, board games, musical boxes and dolls' houses.

Carretera de les Aigües A 10km track overlooking Barcelona from Parc del Collserola (see page 217), the Carretera de les Aigües cuts through woodland of holm oak and pine and is a favourite of runners, cyclists and hikers, with spectacular views of the city and out to sea.

Here be dragons St George is the patron saint of Catalunya, and the dragon is a frequently used motif. As well as the celebrated examples such as Gaudí's dragon at Park Güell (see page 131) and the shimmering dragon hide of the Casa Batlló (see page 108), you'll also spot stone-carved dragons on facades and wrought-iron dragons on gates.

Neighbourhood festes Every barri has its annual festa (see page 211), a rowdy knees-up that involves parades of papier mâché giants, fire-breathing dragons and live music. Barceloneta's festa is also notable for its sea shanties and maritime theme, while Gràcia's is famous for its decorated streets.

Trading plaçes Barcelona is dotted with evocative squares. The central and admittedly touristy Plaça Reial (see page 57) merits a visit for its neo-classical arcades and Gaudí-designed lamp-posts; the Plaça Sant Felip Neri (see page 55) is a hidden and tranquil oasis, pockmarked by Civil War bombs; and the Plaça del Pi (see page 55) thrums with artisanal markets most days.

> Our author recommendations don't end here. We've flagged up our favourite places – a perfectly sited hotel, an atmospheric café, a special restaurant – throughout the Guide, highlighted with the ★ symbol.

SANT POL DE MAR

CORREFOC AT LA MERCÈ FESTIVAL

15

things not to miss

It's not possible to see everything that Barcelona has to offer in one visit – and we don't suggest you try. What follows, in no particular order, is a selective taste of the city's highlights, from glorious modern architecture and world-class art to tapas bars and amusement parks. All entries have a page reference to take you straight into the Guide, where you can find out more.

1 LA PEDRERA
See page 111
Is it an apartment building or a work of art? Both, when the building in question – the undulating Pedrera, or "Stone Quarry" – is designed by Antoni Gaudí.

2 CITY BEACHES
See page 87
Barcelona has a golden seafront, with 7km of sandy beaches stretching from Barceloneta to Diagonal Mar.

3 A TAPAS TOUR
See page 184
Hopping from bar to bar, sampling local specialities, is an ideal way to experience some of Barcelona's finest food.

4 CAMP NOU
See page 136
The magnificent Camp Nou stadium is home to FC Barcelona, one of the world's very greatest football teams, and has a museum full of trophies to prove it.

5 FUNDACIÓ JOAN MIRÓ
See page 99
The adventurous Fundació Joan Miró honours the work of one of Catalunya's greatest artists.

6 LA SEU
See page 49
Marvel at the soaring spaces in one of the greatest Gothic cathedrals in Spain.

7 TRANSBORDADOR AERI
See page 83
Sky-high cable car that whisks passengers right across the harbour to Montjuïc; try keeping your eyes open – the views are superb.

8 TIBIDABO
See page 141
Scale the heights of Mount Tibidabo for fantastic views and a wonderful amusement park.

9 CASA BATLLÓ
See page 108
With its jaw-dropping facade, the "House of Bones" is a *modernista* masterwork by Antoni Gaudí.

10 LA BOQUERIA
See page 44
Barcelona's irresistible central market sells a colourful and mouthwatering array of fresh produce.

10

11 MUSEU NACIONAL D'ART DE CATALUNYA (MNAC)
See page 95
The Catalan National Museum of Art celebrates the grandeur of Catalunya's Romanesque and Gothic heritage and the emergence of *modernisme*.

12 PARK GÜELL
See page 131
The city's most extraordinary park is a fantasyland born of Antoni Gaudí's fertile imagination.

13 MUSEU PICASSO
See page 73
Trace the genesis of genius in the city that Picasso thought of as home.

14 SAGRADA FAMÍLIA
See page 122
The soaring basilica dedicated to the Holy Family is the essential pilgrimage for Gaudí fans.

15 MUSEU D'ART CONTEMPORANI DE BARCELONA (MACBA)
See page 61
Cutting-edge contemporary art exhibitions are at home in El Raval's signature building.

Itineraries

Architectural wonderland, gastronomic trailblazer, sun-kissed playground – Barcelona is all of these things and more. Let these one- to two-day itineraries lead you to its most emblematic sights, as well as those that sparkle below the surface.

FROM A GREAT HEIGHT

You can literally see it all in a couple of days with this jaunt that takes you from the summit of a mountain to the top of the city's culinary scene.

Transbordador Aeri Dangle high above the harbour on a daredevil cable-car ride between the beachside neighbourhood of Barceloneta and the Jardins de Miramar on Montjuïc (173m). See page 83

Tibidabo The journey up to the mountain-top amusement park is part of the fun, but the grand prize is the panorama of city, sea and sky that greets you at the summit of the 550m peak. See page 141

Mirablau Chic bar and restaurant in Tibidabo, where you can enjoy tapas and cocktails as night-time Barcelona glitters and glints in the background. See page 202

Arenas de Barcelona The rooftop terrace on top of this bullring-turned-shopping-centre affords grand views of Plaça d'Espanya and the domed Palau Nacional. See page 118

Santa María del Pi Reached via an ever more constricting stone staircase, this medieval bell tower offers a close-up prospect of the roofscape of the Barrí Gotic. See page 54

Mirador de Colom The precarious platform at the top of this slender iron column, at the foot of La Rambla, may not be the city's highest vantage point, but thanks to its alarming sway it's by far the most terrifying. See page 81

GAUDÍ'S LEGACY

As Antoni Gaudí's landmark Sagrada Família approaches completion, tracing the visionary architect's career has become an ever-greater priority for Barcelona visitors.

Museu Diocesà This small museum provides the ideal introduction to Gaudí's work, and the tools, techniques and beliefs that made it possible. See page 50

Palau Güell From stables to rooftop, the innovative townhouse that Gaudí designed for his greatest patron was an early indication of his genius. See page 66

Casa Batlló With its fearsome facade and snaking curves, acclaimed by surrealists

Create your own itinerary with Rough Guides. Whether you're after adventure or a family-friendly holiday, we have a trip for you, with all the activities you enjoy doing and the sights you want to see. All our trips are devised by local experts who get the most out of the destination. Visit **www.roughguides.com/trips** to chat with one of our travel agents.

including Salvador Dalí, this astonishing apartment block shows just what can happen if you hire Antoni Gaudí to redecorate your house. See page 108

La Pedrera Guarded by eerie sentinels and warriors, and framing the Sagrada Família on the skyline, the hallucinatory rooftop terrace of the "Stone Quarry" is unforgettable. See page 111

Park Güell This hugely ambitious, never completed housing development holds a gloriously colourful mosaic-decorated terrace and an enormous Hall of Columns; the architect's own house stands nearby. See page 131

Gaudí Centre In Gaudí's home town, an enjoyable day-trip 100km southwest of Barcelona, a fascinating gallery explores the roots of his inspiration. See page 161

SAVING THE PENNIES

You can easily spend two to three days taking advantage of these inexpensive, if not free, attractions that are scattered around the city.

The beaches Unfurl a towel, slather on the sunblock and settle in for a relaxing day of golden sand and aquamarine waters at any of the city's eight beaches. See page 87

Mercat de la Boqueria It doesn't cost a thing to browse the colourful displays of fruits, vegetables, seafood and sweets inside Barcelona's most famous market. And who knows? Your stroll might yield a free sample or two. See page 44

La Seu Arrive in the morning or late afternoon, and you can wander around the ornate interior and lush cloister of Barcelona's grand Gothic cathedral for free. See page 49

Els Encants Vells If it's bargains you seek, then bargains you shall find at the city's main flea market, where spirited haggling is the name of the game. See page 125

CaixaForum A superb collection of contemporary art fills the halls of CaixaForum, an arts and cultural complex that's partly free to the public. See page 94

Font Màgica A gorgeous display of music, water and colour that's been attracting oohs and aahs since its debut during the 1929 International Exhibition. See page 94

STRICTLY CATALAN

The following places offer a deeper understanding of what defines Catalunya and its people.

Museu d'Història de Catalunya Journey from prehistoric times to the present day via engaging, interactive exhibits, housed inside a gorgeously renovated warehouse that overlooks Port Vell. See page 84

The sardana Performances of this dance – a graceful symbol of Catalan unity and identity – take place every Sunday afternoon at Plaça de la Seu. See page 204

Lunch at Can Culleretes Said to be the oldest restaurant in Barcelona, this wood-panelled gem serves quintessential Catalan food in a timeless setting. See page 183

Plaça del Pi's farmers' market Purveyors of locally made wine, cheese, pastries and more set up shop in the picturesque Plaça del Pi during this bimonthly farmers' market. See page 55

Palau de la Música Catalana From the music played within its walls to the allegorical decorations found both inside and out, this concert hall designed by *modernista* architect Lluís Domènech i Montaner is Catalan through and through. See page 69

Gràcia To experience small-town Catalunya without leaving the city, head to the charming squares and narrow streets of Gràcia, where the air is filled with the Catalan language. See page 128

Sustainable travel

From green gifts to beach clean-ups, we've rounded up ideas for experiencing the best of Barcelona while being conscious of visitor impact on the city's environment, culture and people.

Barcelona's phenomenal growth as a tourist destination has been both a blessing and a curse for its residents. Around 130,000 *barcelonins* work in the sector, but rent hikes have pushed tenants out from the centre and closed small businesses. The Old City can be choked with tourists in peak season, and a proliferation of 24-hour supermarkets has meant the end of many small, family-run shops. There are, however, steps that visitors can take to mitigate their impact.

WATER WISE

In 2023 Catalunya experienced one of the worst droughts in its history and has implemented water restrictions that include turning off many drinking fountains as well as the showers on the beach. While there are no specific restrictions for individuals, the public has been urged to save water as much as possible. Advice includes keeping showers short and re-using water where possible.

SUSTAINABLE TRANSPORT

More than half of Barcelona's bus fleet is electric or hybrid, the trams are electric, and there are several taxi companies with electric fleets, including Taxi Ecològic (Ⓦ taxiecologic.com). Barcelona is a fantastic city for cycling, with an extensive network of bike lanes (around 300km) and green routes. There are scores of bike rental companies in town, offering both mechanical and electric bikes (including Rent A Bike Barcelona, Ⓦ rentabikebarcelona.com, and Bike Rental Barcelona, Ⓦ bikerentalbarcelona.com) or you can use bike-sharing apps such as Donkey Republic, which allows you to pick up and drop off bikes all over the city.

VOLUNTARY WORK

If you want to get involved with sustainable voluntary work, you can take part in regular beach and park clean-ups in Barcelona: these are organized by Clean Beach Initiative (Ⓦ cleanbeachinitiative.org), the Surfrider Foundation (Ⓦ volunteers.surfrider.eu) and Voluntariat Ambiental a Catalunya (Ⓦ voluntariatambiental.cat). Other initiatives include Espigoladors (Ⓦ espigoladors.cat/en), a non-profit which combats food waste through gleaning (harvesting crops that are unsuitable for market), and either distributing the crops to social enterprises or turning them in sauces, soups or jams, in kitchens staffed by people at risk of social inclusion. Volunteers are always welcome to help glean.

SUSTAINABLE FOOD AND DRINK

The Slow Food movement has long had a strong following in Barcelona. You'll find countless restaurants – among them Rasoterra (see page 183) and Cinc Sentits (see page 192) – which are committed to the 'Kilometre Zero' (or KM0) principle, which advocates sourcing ingredients produced within 100km of where they will be prepared, whenever possible.

RECINTE MODERNISTA DE SANT PAU

Barcelonins are also increasingly conscious of zero waste, and there are now several plastic-free shops where you can fill up your own containers, such as Gra de Gràcia (Ⓦgradegracia.cat) and Yes Future (Ⓦyesfuture.store).

GREEN GIVING

Sabater Hnos. (Ⓦsabaterhnos.com) is one of Barcelona's prettiest shops on one of its prettiest squares, and its beautiful range of natural soaps in every hue and scent are the perfect gift. For designer fashion that is unique, sustainable and locally made, head to Green Lifestyle (Ⓦgreenlifestyle.es), which features on-trend yet timeless women's clothing and accessories, or InfinitDenim (Ⓦinfinitdenim.com), which upcycles denim into unique clothing, bags, homeware and more. At Flor de Barcelona (Ⓦflordebarcelona.info), the famous flower that adorns the city's paving stones is the motif on bags, notepads, mugs and more, all locally and ethically made.

OFF THE BEATEN TRACK

The historic centre of Barcelona can get spectacularly overcrowded, which has caused some friction with residents. If you're visiting one of the most popular sights – such as La Boqueria market, for example – make a purchase rather than simply stopping for a selfie. One historic shop, the Colmado Múrria,

has even taken to charging tourists who "just want to look", perhaps forgetting that the shop has to do business to stay in existence. There are plenty of outlying neighbourhoods – such as Sants, Sarrià and seaside Poblenou – with fewer tourists, which still offer plenty of charm and a more authentic Barcelona experience. You could head to the stunning *modernista* Sant Antoni market, rather than La Boqueria, or visit the Recinte Modernista de Sant Pau, rather than the Palau de la Música Catalana.

ARC DE TRIOMF

Basics

Getting there

It's easy to reach Barcelona by air; budget airlines from regional UK and European airports compete with the Spanish national carrier Iberia to get you directly to the city, quickly and cheaply. There's also a fair amount of choice from North America, though you may well have to fly via Madrid or another European city to get the best fare.

For the very cheapest fares on budget airlines you generally need to book weeks, if not months, in advance. Flights with Iberia and other major airlines tend to be more expensive and seasonal, with the highest fares from June to September, at Christmas, New Year and Easter, and at weekends all year.

When buying **online**, always check terms and conditions; most budget airline tickets are non-changeable and non-refundable, and all sorts of potential extra charges lurk in the small print. For a short city break it can be worth buying an all-in package that covers accommodation as well as flights.

Travelling to Barcelona from elsewhere in Europe by **train** or **bus** inevitably takes longer than flying, and usually works out more expensive, though it makes an increasingly popular, greener alternative. However, if Barcelona and Spain are part of a longer European trip it can be an interesting proposition. **Driving** to Barcelona from the UK is something of an undertaking, and what with motorway tolls in France and Spain, fuel costs, cross-Channel ferry and Eurotunnel fares, it's certainly not cheap.

Flights from the UK and Ireland

More than a dozen **airports** in the UK and Ireland offer flights to Barcelona all year, including all the London airports, plus Belfast, Birmingham, Bristol, Dublin, East Midlands, Edinburgh, Glasgow, Leeds-Bradford, Liverpool, Manchester, Newcastle and Southend, with a **flight time** of something between two and two-and-a-half hours.

Airlines serving Barcelona range from budget operators Ryanair (Wryanair.com), easyJet (Weasyjet.com), Monarch (Wmonarch.co.uk), Jet2 (Wjet2.com) and Vueling (Wvueling.com), to national carriers like Iberia (Wiberia.com), British Airways (Wba.com) and Aer Lingus (Waerlingus.com). You can get a sense of current fares, and a list of relevant airlines, by using comparison sites such as Wskyscanner.net. For most of the year, you can confidently expect to find one-way fares in any specific week starting at less than £50, and often significantly lower than that. Even on the national airlines, however, taking check-in baggage is liable to cost extra, while budget airlines charge hefty penalties if for example your carry-on baggage is the wrong size, or you fail to print your own boarding pass.

With so many Barcelona options, it's only likely to be worth flying to any of Catalunya's other airports if you want to see more of the region than just Barcelona itself. Ryanair do however fly to **Girona**, 90km north of Barcelona, and **Reus**, 110km south of Barcelona, near Tarragona, from several British, Irish and European airports, including smaller UK airports like Bournemouth and Bristol (look on the Ryanair website for "Barcelona Girona" and "Barcelona Reus" respectively). Both Girona and Reus are more than an hour's journey from Barcelona, via bus or train.

Flights from the USA and Canada

While most **direct scheduled services** to Spain from North America are to Madrid, there are a handful of non-stop flights to Barcelona, including American Airlines (Waa.com) from Chicago, New York and Miami; United (Wunited.com) from New York and Washington DC; and Delta (Wdelta.com) from Atlanta and New York. European-based airlines like Iberia and British Airways can also get you to Barcelona, though you'll be routed via their respective European hubs. Flying time from New York is around seven hours to Madrid, eight to Barcelona direct, though with an onward connection it can take up to eleven hours to reach Barcelona.

A BETTER KIND OF TRAVEL

At Rough Guides we are passionately committed to travel. We believe it helps us understand the world we live in and the people we share it with – and of course tourism is vital to many developing economies. But the scale of modern tourism has also damaged some places irreparably, and climate change is accelerated by most forms of transport, especially flying. We encourage all our authors to consider the carbon footprint of the journeys they make in the course of researching our guides.

Return **fares** are as much as US$1400 in summer, though outside peak periods you should be able to fly for under US$800.

Flights from Australia, New Zealand and South Africa

There are no direct **flights** to Spain from Australia, New Zealand or South Africa. However, a number of airlines do fly to Barcelona with a stopover elsewhere in Europe or Asia – flights via Asia are generally cheaper – and you can also fly to Madrid, and pick up a connecting flight or train from there. If your visit to Barcelona is part of a wider trip, it may help to discuss your route and preferences with a flight and travel agent like Flight Centre (Ⓦflight-centre.com.au or Ⓦflightcentre.co.nz).

City breaks and tours

Three-night **city breaks** to Barcelona, flying from London, Manchester or Dublin, start from as little as £300 (€345) per person. For this price, accommodation is likely to be in a two-star hotel, potentially on a room-only basis. For three nights' bed-and-breakfast in a three- or four-star hotel you can usually expect to pay more like £400–525 (€460–610). The bigger US operators, such as American Express and Delta Vacations, can also easily organize short city breaks to Spain on a flight-and-hotel basis.

A few British and Spanish operators offer rather more **specialist holidays** in and around Barcelona, concentrating on themes like art and architecture, cooking classes, wine tours or rural Catalunya. Prices vary widely, according to the standard of accommodation and services provided, from say £150 (€175) for a fully catered day out to several thousand pounds/euros for an all-inclusive luxury holiday. North American **tour companies** also tend to include a couple of days in Barcelona as part of a whirlwind escorted itinerary around Spain, starting from around US$1,750–2,300 for a standard two-week tour.

UK

Martin Randall Travel ⓣ 020 8742 3355, Ⓦmartinrandall.com. Experts lead small groups on annual, all-inclusive quality tours to Spain – tours and themes change each year, though a typical gastronomic tour of Catalunya might cost from £3,040 for seven nights' wining and dining.

SPAIN

Madrid & Beyond ⓣ 917 580 063, Ⓦmadridandbeyond.com. Classy, customized holidays and special experiences, from private gallery tours to expert-led walks through Gaudí's Barcelona.

USA

Petrabax ⓣ 1 800 634 1188, Ⓦpetrabax.com. City breaks, escorted Catalunya tours or self-drive Spanish holidays, plus independent travel services such as accommodation bookings and car rental.
Saranjan Tours ⓣ 1 206 972 1939, Ⓦsaranjan.com. Upscale, fully guided, customized tours concentrating on Barcelona and its nearby wine country.
Spain Tours ⓣ 1 800 770 7148, Ⓦspaintours.biz. An extensive programme of Spanish tours, including trips that combine Barcelona with other regions both near and far.

By rail

Although travelling **by train** to Barcelona can't compete in price with the cheapest budget-airline fares, it can be a real adventure. Your first stop for information should be the amazingly useful Ⓦ**seat61.com**, which provides route, ticket, timetable and contact information for all European train services.

Ultra-fast TGV Duplex now connect Paris with Barcelona in little more than six hours, making it possible to get all the way from London to Barcelona within a single, comfortable day's journey. All year round, you can leave London after 9am, change trains in Paris, and arrive in Barcelona just after 8.30pm. Fares for each individual leg of the trip vary widely, and are of course at their highest during peak times and seasons, so it's hard to predict total costs, but you're unlikely to find a full round-trip fare for under £350. Either book the entire journey at Ⓦloco2.com, or look around for cheaper individual segments by booking the London–Paris **Eurostar** service (Ⓦeurostar.com) separately from the Paris–Barcelona legs (try Ⓦvoyages-sncf.com, Ⓦtrainline.eu or Ⓦrenfe.com). Sadly, overnight sleeper trains no longer connect Paris and Barcelona, though of course it's possible to spend a night in Paris en route.

If you plan to travel extensively in Europe by train, a **rail pass** might prove a good investment. However, if you're simply headed for Barcelona, Interrail (Ⓦinterrail.eu) and Eurail (Ⓦeurail.com) aren't a good deal, and even if you intend to travel around Catalunya by train, rail travel in that part of Spain is fairly limited (and quite cheap), so you probably won't get your money's worth.

By bus

It's still possible to travel by bus between London and Barcelona, though the journey takes at least 22 hours and with typical fares starting at around £65 one way it's likely to be more expensive than flying. The chief UK operator are BlaBlaCar (Ⓦblablacar.co.uk) and Flixbus (Ⓦflixbus.co.uk).

Driving to Barcelona

It takes a good two days, with stops, to drive the 1600km from London to Barcelona. Motoring organizations such as the AA (ⓦtheaa.com) or the RAC (ⓦrac.co.uk) can advise on insurance, documentation and avoiding toll roads. If you're bringing your own car, carry your licence, vehicle registration and insurance documents with you; you must also have two warning triangles, a breatha-lyzer kit, and a fluorescent vest in case of breakdown.

Many drivers use the various ferry links to get from England to France – principally Dover–Calais, though services to Brittany or Normandy can be more convenient – but the quickest way across the Channel is the **Eurotunnel** service (ⓦeurotunnel.com), which operates drive-on-drive-off shuttle trains between Folkestone and Calais/Coquelles.

Alternatively, Brittany Ferries (ⓦbrittany-ferries.co.uk) operates car and passenger ferry services from Portsmouth (2–3 weekly, 24hr) and Plymouth to **Santander** (one weekly; 20hr), which is around 6–7 hours' drive from Barcelona, and from Portsmouth only to **Bilbao** (2 weekly; 24 or 32hr), which is more like 5–6 hours' drive. Be warned that some routes run fewer ferries in winter. Expect to pay at least £300 each way for a car, two passengers and a cabin, and potentially much more in summer.

Once in Barcelona itself, you're unlikely to need a car (see page 28).

Visas and red tape

EU citizens need only a valid national identity card or passport to enter Spain. Other Europeans – including British citizens – as well as citizens of the United States, Canada, Australia and New Zealand, require a passport but no visa and can stay as a tourist for up to ninety days, but from May 2025 will need an ETIAS visa waiver (see ⓦ**schengenvisainfo.com). Other nationalities (including South Africans) must get a visa from a Spanish embassy or consulate before departure. Visa require-ments do change, so check the current situation before you leave home.**

Most EU citizens who want to stay in Spain for longer than three months need to register, and receive a residence certificate, at the **Oficina de Extranjería** (foreigners' office; Passeig de Sant Joan 189–193; ⓜJoanic; Mon–Fri 9am–2pm). You don't need the certificate if you're an EU citizen living and working legally in Barcelona, or if you're legally self-employed and working in the city or a student. US citizens can apply at a police station for one ninety-day extension, at least three weeks before the initial entry period expires. Other nationalities wishing to extend their stay must get a special visa from a Spanish embassy or consulate before departure.

Anyone planning to stay and live in Barcelona also needs a **Número de Identidad de Extranjero** (NIE), an ID number that's essential to open a bank account, sign a utilities, job or accommodation contract, and for many other financial transactions.

A telephone helpline on ☎012 (Mon–Fri 9am–5pm) deals with all aspects of **residency and immigration**, and you can find more information at ⓦgencat.cat.

Embassies and consulates

Most countries have their embassies in Madrid and maintain a consulate in Barcelona. You'll need to contact them if you lose your passport or need other assistance. Most consulates are open for enquiries Monday to Friday, usually 9am–1pm and 3–5pm, though the morning shift is the most reliable.

FOREIGN CONSULATES IN BARCELONA

Australia Avda. Diagonal 433 bis, Esquerra de l'Eixample ☎933 623 792, ⓦspain.embassy.gov.au; ⓜHospital Clinic.

Canada Pl. de Catalunya 9, Dreta de l'Eixample ☎932 703 614, ⓦcanadainternational.gc.ca; ⓜCatalunya.

Republic of Ireland Gran Via Carles III 94, Les Corts ☎934 915 021, ⓦembassyofireland.es; ⓜMaria Cristina/Les Corts.

UK Avda. Diagonal 477, Esquerra de l'Eixample ☎933 666 200, ⓦukinspain.fco.gov.uk; ⓜHospital Clinic.

USA Pg. de la Reina Elisenda 23, Sarrià ☎932 802 227, ⓦbarcelona.usconsulate.gov; FGC Reina Elisenda.

Arrival and departure

Whether you travel to Barcelona by plane, train or bus, it's usually possible to get to a city-centre hotel within an hour of arrival.

By air

Barcelona airport (☎902 404 704, ⓦaena.es), officially known as **Barcelona-El Prat**, is around 15km southwest of the city centre at El Prat de Llobregat. The terminals hold tourist information offices that handle hotel bookings, as well as ATMs, exchange facilities and car-rental offices.

Metered **taxis** wait at the terminals, and charge around €35 for trips to the city centre, including the airport surcharge (further surcharges are added for travel after 8pm and at weekends or on public holidays).

Following the opening of the **L9 Sud** line in 2016, the airport is now connected to Barcelona's **metro** system, though the line is of limited use to visitors. L9 Sud does not run to the centre of the city, but to Zona Universitària; to get to the Catalunya station, for example, you have to change onto the L1 line at Torrassa. A single ticket between the airport and any other metro station costs €5.15, and the T-Casual ticket (see page 27) is not valid.

Most visitors still prefer to use the **airport train service** (daily 5.42am–11.38pm; journey time 20min to Sants; €4.60; ☏ 902 320 320), which runs every thirty minutes to Barcelona Sants station (the main train station) and Passeig de Gràcia (the best stop for Eixample, Plaça de Catalunya and La Rambla). It departs from Terminal T2 – a free shuttle bus to the station from T1 takes around ten minutes. Trains back to the airport run from Barcelona Sants on a similar half-hourly schedule (daily 5.13am–11.14pm). Zone 1 city travel passes (*targetes*), the T-Casual ticket and the Barcelona Card are valid on the airport train service.

Additionally, the **Aerobús** service (daily 5.35am–1.05am; €6.75 one-way, €11.65 return; departures every 5–10min; ☒ aerobusbarcelona.es) from T1 and T2 stops in the city at Plaça d'Espanya, Gran Via–Urgell, Plaça Universitat and Plaça de Catalunya. It takes around 35–40 minutes to reach Plaça de Catalunya, though allow longer in the rush hour. Aerobús departures to the airport from Plaça de Catalunya leave from in front of El Corte Inglés department store (daily 5am–12.30am); note that T1 and T2 are served by separate services.

The cheapest route of all is to use local bus #46, which connects both T1 and T2 with Plaça d'Espanya for a one-way fare of just €2.40, though if you're staying in the city centre you'll need to catch a connecting bus or metro onwards from Plaça d'Espanya.

Anyone flying into **Girona airport**, 90km north of Barcelona, can take the Sagalés Airport Line bus direct to Barcelona Nord bus station (€19.50 one-way, €30 return; journey time 1hr 15min; ☏ 902 130 014, ☒ sagalesairportline.com).

From **Reus airport**, 110km south of Barcelona, there's a connecting Hispano Igualadina bus (☏ 902 292 900, ☒ igualadina.com) to Barcelona Sants (€17.20 one-way, €32.80 return; 1hr 40min).

By train

The main station for domestic and international arrivals – **Barcelona Sants**, 3km west of the city centre – holds a tourist office with an accommodation booking service, plus ATMs, an exchange office, car-rental outlets, a police station and left-luggage facilities. The metro station that's accessed from inside Barcelona Sants is called ⓜ Sants Estació. Line 3 from here runs direct to Liceu (for La Rambla), Catalunya (for Plaça de Catalunya) and Passeig de Gràcia, while line 5 runs to Diagonal.

Some Spanish intercity services and international trains also stop at **Estació de França**, 1km east of La Rambla and close to ⓜ Barceloneta. Other possible arrival points by train are **Plaça de Catalunya**, at the top of La Rambla (for trains from coastal towns north of the city), and **Passeig de Gràcia** (Catalunya provincial destinations).

Barcelona and Madrid are connected by the high-speed **AVE line** (Alta Velocidad Española), which takes between 2hr 30min and 3hr 10min and runs via Tarragona and Zaragoza. Arrivals and departures are for the moment at Barcelona Sants, though at some future and much postponed point a second high-speed station is due to open at **La Sagrera**, east of the centre beyond Glòries.

TRAIN INFORMATION

RENFE ☏ 902 320 320, ☒ renfe.com. For all national rail enquiries, sales and reservations. Barcelona Sants station (Pl. dels Països Catalans, Sants; ⓜ Sants Estació) has train information desks and advance ticket booking counters, some with English-speakers.

By bus

The main bus terminal, used by international, long-distance and provincial buses, is **Barcelona Nord** on C/Ali-Bei (☏ 937 065 366, ☒ barcelonanord.cat; ⓜ Arc de Triomf), four blocks north of Parc de la Ciutadella. There's a bus information desk on the

---

UP AND AWAY – FUNICULARS AND CABLE CARS

Several **funicular rail lines** still operate in the city, up the hills to Montjuïc park, Tibidabo funfair and the suburb of Vallvidrera. Summer and year-round weekend visits to Tibidabo also combine a funicular trip with a fun ride on the clanking antique tram, the **Tramvia Blau** (see page 143).

There are also two dramatic **cable-car** (*telefèric*) rides: from Barceloneta right across the harbour to Montjuïc (see page 93), and then from the top station of the Montjuïc funicular all the way up to the castle. Both are great experiences, with extraordinary views across the city and beyond.

ground floor (daily 7am–9pm), plus a tourist office (daily 9am–7pm), free wi-fi, accommodation agency, ATMs, shops and luggage lockers. Various companies operate services across Catalunya, Spain and Europe – reserve tickets in advance for long-distance routes, either online, or at the station a day before).

Some intercity and international Eurolines services also stop at the bus terminal behind Barcelona Sants station on C/Viriat (Ⓜ Sants Estació). Either way, you're only a short metro ride from the city centre.

By car

Driving into Barcelona is reasonably straightforward, with traffic only slow in the morning and evening rush hours. Parking, however, is a different matter altogether – rarely easy and never cheap. If your trip is just to the city and its surroundings, our advice is not to bother with a car at all, but you'll find some useful pointers in any case in the "City transport" section.

Coming into Barcelona along any one of the motorways (autopistes), head for the Ronda Litoral (B-10), the southern half of the city's ring road. Following signs for "Port Vell" (coming from the south) or "Ciutat Vella" (coming from the north) will take you towards the main exit for the old town, though there is also an exit for Gran Via de les Corts Catalanes (C-31) if uptown Barcelona is your destination.

City transport

Barcelona's excellent integrated transport system comprises the metro, buses, trams and local trains, plus assorted funiculars and cable cars. The local transport authority, Transports Metropolitans de Barcelona (TMB, Ⓦtmb.cat), has a useful website (English-language available) with full timetable and ticket information.

TMB operates customer service centres at Barcelona Sants station, and at Universitat, Diagonal and Sagrada Família metro stations, where you can pick up a free public transport map. The map and ticket information is also posted at major bus stops and all metro and tram stations.

Tickets and travel passes

Although a transit plan divides the province into six zones, the entire metropolitan area of Barcelona (except the airport; see page 26) falls within **Zone 1**, so that's the only zone you'll need to worry about on a day-to-day basis.

On all the city's public transport, including night buses and funiculars, you can buy a single ticket every time you ride (€2.40), but if you're staying for a few days it's much cheaper to buy a *targeta* – a **discount ticket** strip which you pass through the metro or train barrier, or slot in the machine on the bus, tram or funicular. *Targetes* are available at metro, train and tram stations, but not on buses.

The best general deal is the **T-Casual** ("tay kaz-oo-al" in Catalan) *targeta* (€11.35), valid for ten separate journeys other than to or from the airport on metro line L9 Sud, with changes between methods of transport allowed within 75 minutes. The ticket can only be used by one person at a time, but people travelling together can share a T-Familiar (€10 for eight journeys) – just make sure you punch it the same number of times as there are people travelling. It's also available at newsstands and tobacconists.

Other useful (single-person) *targetes* for Zone 1 include the **T-Dia** ("tay dee-ah"; one day's unlimited travel; €10.50); the **Hola BCN!** (three to five days' travel, including to and from the airport; €23.80–38.20, with a ten percent discount on online sales); the **T-Usual** (unlimited trips within a thirty-day period; €20). The Barcelona Card (see box, p.27) also includes city transport for between two and five days.

Heading for Sitges, Montserrat or further **out of town**, you'll need to buy a specific ticket or relevant-zoned *targeta*, as the Zone 1 *targetes* don't run that far. Anyone caught without a valid ticket anywhere on the system is liable to an immediate fine of €100 (or €50 if you pay in cash on the spot or within two working days).

The metro

The quickest way to get around Barcelona is by **metro**, which runs on eight lines. Metro entrances are marked with a red diamond sign with an "M". The **hours of operation** are Monday to Thursday, plus Sunday and public holidays, 5am to midnight; Friday and evenings of public holidays, 5am to 2am; Saturday 24-hour service. There's a metro map at the back of this book, and you can pick up a little foldout one at metro stations (ask for *una guia del metro*).

Trains are fast and efficient, but note that changing from one line to another can involve a very long walk within what's nominally the same station. The system is perfectly safe, but beware of pickpockets.

Buses

Most buses operate daily, roughly from 4 or 5am until 10.30pm, though some lines stop earlier and some run until after midnight. Night bus (*Nit bus*) services fill in the gaps on all the main routes, with services every twenty to sixty minutes between around 10pm and 4am. Many bus routes (including all night buses) stop in or near Plaça de Catalunya, but the full route is marked at each bus stop, along with a timetable.

Trams

The tram system (◍tram.cat) runs on six lines, with departures every eight to twenty minutes throughout the day from 5am up to as late as 2am on some segments. **Lines T1, T2** and **T3** depart from Plaça Francesc Macià and run along the uptown part of Avinguda Diagonal to suburban destinations in the northwest – useful tourist stops are at L'Illa shopping centre and the Maria Cristina and Palau Reial metro stations. **Line T4** operates from Ciutadella-Vila Olímpica (where there's also a metro station) and runs up past the zoo and TNC (the National Theatre) to Glòries before running down Avinguda Diagonal to Diagonal Mar and the Parc del Fòrum. You're unlikely to use suburban lines T5 and T6.

Trains

Barcelona has a cheap and efficient commuter train line, the **Ferrocarrils de la Generalitat de Catalunya** (FGC; ☎932 051 515, ◍fgc.cat), with its main stations at Plaça de Catalunya and Plaça d'Espanya. These go to places like Sarrià, Vallvidrera, Tibidabo, Sant Cugat, Terrassa and Montserrat, and details are given in the text where appropriate. The Zone 1 *targeta* is valid as far as the city limits, which in practice is everywhere you're likely to want to go except for Montserrat, Colònia Güell, Sant Cugat and Terrassa.

The national rail service, operated by **RENFE** (☎902 320 320, ◍renfe.com), runs all the other services out of Barcelona. Local lines – northeast to the Costa Maresme and southwest to Sitges – are designated as **Rodiales/Cercanías**. The hub is Barcelona Sants station, with services also passing through Plaça de Catalunya (heading north) and Passeig de Gràcia (south). Arrive in plenty of time to buy a ticket, as queues are often horrendous, though for all destinations you can use the automatic vending machines instead.

Taxis

Black-and-yellow taxis (with a green roof-light on when available for hire) are relatively inexpensive – most short journeys across town run to around €12. There's a minimum charge of €2.55, after which it's €1.23 per kilometre (€1.51 after 8pm, and on Sat, Sun & hols), with surcharges for pick-ups from Barcelona Sants station (€2.50) and the airport (€4.50). The taxis have meters so charges are transparent – if not, asking for a receipt (*rebut* in Catalan, *recibo* in Spanish) should ensure that the price is fair (and current rates are posted on ◍taxi.amb.cat). Many taxis take credit-card payment. You should tip around five percent.

Taxi ranks can be found outside major train and metro stations, in main squares, near large hotels and along the main avenues. You can call a taxi in advance, for a typical additional charge of €7 on top of the fare, but few cab company operators speak English.

Note that both **Uber** and **Lyft** are currently forbidden to operate in Barcelona.

TAXI COMPANIES

Barna Taxi ☎933 222 222, ◍barnataxi.com.
Radio Taxi 033 ☎933 033 033, ◍radiotaxi033.com.
Servi-Taxi ☎933 300 300, ◍servitaxi.com.

Driving

You don't need a car to get around Barcelona, but you may want to rent one if you plan to see any more of Catalunya. That said, in summer the coastal roads in particular are nightmarish, so if you just want to zip to the beach or wine region for the day, it's far better to stick to the trains. Driving as a means of exploring

---

ADDRESSES

Addresses are written as: C/Picasso 2 4° – which means Picasso street (*carrer*) number two, fourth floor. You may also see *esquerra*, meaning "left-hand" (apartment or office); *dreta* is right; *centro* centre. C/Picasso s/n means the building has no number (*sense número*). In the gridded streets of the Eixample, building numbers run from south to north (ie lower numbers at the Plaça de Catalunya end) and from west to east (lower numbers at Plaça d'Espanya).

The main address abbreviations used in this book are: Avda. (for Avinguda, avenue); Bxda. (for Baixada, alley); C/ (for Carrer, street); Pg. (for Passeig, more a boulevard than a street); Pl. (for Plaça, square); and Ptge. (for Passatge, passage).

the city itself is not recommended either. Parking is notoriously difficult, and vehicle crime is rampant – never leave anything visible in the car.

Most foreign **driving licences** are honoured in Spain – including all EU, US and Canadian ones. Remember that you drive on the right in Spain, and away from main roads you yield to vehicles approaching from the right. Speed limits are posted – maximum on urban roads is 60kph, other roads 90kph, motorways 120kph. Wearing seatbelts is compulsory.

Parking

City-centre display boards indicate which indoor **car parks** have free spaces. Central locations include Plaça de Catalunya, Plaça Urquinaona, Arc de Triomf, Passeig de Gràcia, Plaça dels Angels/MACBA and Avinguda del Paral·lel. Parking in any of these is convenient, but it's also pretty expensive (1hr from around €4, 24hr from €24).

City-owned **long-term car parks**, run by BSM (Barcelona Serveis Municipals, ⓦaparcamentsbsm. cat), are available for residents and visitors, and work out cheaper. The best option is the large Plaça Fòrum car park at Diagonal Mar (Pl. d'Ernest Lluch i Martin; ⓜEl Maresme-Fòrum or tram T4). Parking costs €11 for one day and €16 overnight, while multiple-entry stays cost from €46 for three days. Closer to the centre, the 24-hour BSM car park at Barcelona Nord bus station (C/Ali-Bei 54; ⓜArc de Triomf) charges €16 for an overnight stay.

Street parking is permitted in most areas, but it can be tough to find spaces, especially in the old town and Gràcia, where it's nearly all either restricted access or residents' parking only. The ubiquitous residents' **Área Verda meter-zones** (ⓦareaverda. cat) throughout the city allow pay-and-display parking for visitors, from €3 per hour, with either a one- or two-hour maximum stay. Elsewhere, don't be tempted to double-park, leave your car in loading zones or otherwise park illegally – the **towing fee** is €150, plus a daily €20 charge, and no mercy is shown to tourists or foreign-plated vehicles.

Vehicle rental

Car rental is cheapest arranged in advance through one of the large multinational agencies. In Barcelona, the major chains have outlets at the airport and at, or near, Barcelona Sants station. Inclusive rates start from around €40 per day for an economy car (proportionately less by the week, with good rates often available for a three-day weekend rental, around €150). Drivers need to be at least 21 (23 with some companies) and to have been driving for at least a year. It's essential to take out fully comprehensive insurance and pay for Collision Damage Waiver, otherwise you'll be liable for every scratch. By far the cheapest option is to buy a separate annual insurance policy covering vehicle hire excess, with operators such as Questor Insurance (ⓦquestor-insurance.co.uk).

Some local outlets, like Vanguard (☎934 393 880, ⓦvanguardrent.com), rent out **mopeds and motor-cycles**, though given the traffic conditions and the good public transport system, that's not really recommended as a means of getting around the city.

Cycling

The city council has embraced cycling, and is investing heavily in cycle lanes and schemes such as the much-touted **Bicing** pick-up and drop-off system (ⓦbicing.com). You'll see the red bikes and bike stations all over the city, but Bicing is aimed at encouraging locals to use the bikes for short trips, rather than at tourists. Users can register online or at the **Oficina del Bicing**, Pl. Pi i Sunyer 8–10, Barri Gòtic, between C/ Canuda and C/Duran i Bas (Mon–Fri 8.30am–5.30pm). Once you've paid the annual fee of €47, you only pay for rides that exceed half an hour.

In any case, **bike-rental outfits** all over town are more geared to tourist requirements in that you can take the bike wherever you like – your hotel, for example – and hang on to it for as long as you need it. They typically charge €6–7 for two hours, and €15–17 for a full 24 hours, and double that for an electric bike. Many cycle-tour companies can also fix you up with a rental bike.

BIKE RENTAL

Barceloneta Bikes C/Atlàntida 49, Barceloneta ⓜ Barceloneta ☎931 771 119, ⓦ barcelonetabikes.com.
Biciclot Pg. Marítim 33, Port Olímpic ⓜ Ciutadella-Vila Olímpica ☎933 077 475, ⓦ biciclot.net.
Bike Tours Barcelona Plaça Sant Agustí Vell 16, Sant Pere ⓜ Barceloneta ☎935 480 457, ⓦ biketoursbarcelona.com.

City tours

A bewildering number of tours enable you to see the sights on anything from a bus to a hot-air balloon. Bike tours in particular are hugely popular – at times it seems as if every tourist in the city is playing follow-my-leader down the same old-town alley – while other operators offer tapas-bar crawls, party nights and out-of-town excursions. Highest profile

are the open-top sightseeing bus tours, whose board-at-will services can drop you outside every attraction in the city. Barcelona also has some good walking tours, showing you parts of the old town you might not find otherwise, while sightseeing boats offer a different view.

BIKE TOURS

Baja Bikes ⓦ biketoursbarcelona.com. Three-hour tours start in the Pl. de Sant Jaume in the Barri Gòtic, and visit various places in the Born, followed by some of Gaudí's buildings in the Eixample (11am daily; €32.50).

Fat Tire Bike Tours ⓣ 933 429 275, ⓦ fattiretours.com. English-speaking guides lead the way during these relaxed four-hour pedals past some of the city's most iconic sights (daily: mid-April to Oct 10.30am & 4pm; Nov to mid-April 10.30am; €30). No reservations required; tour meets at Plaça Sant Jaume on the side nearest to La Rambla. They also offer tours of Montjuïc on electrically assisted e-bikes, for which reservations are required (Sat; €44).

BUS TOURS

Bus Turístic ⓦ barcelonabusturistic.cat. The city's official sightseeing service offers three distinct but interconnecting routes for a single ticket, linking all the main tourist sights and making over forty stops (departures every 5–25min). The northern (red) and southern (blue) routes depart from Pl. de Catalunya (daily 9am–7pm; April–Sept 9am–8pm); a full circuit on either takes two hours. The green Forùm route (daily April–Sept 9.30am–8pm) runs from Port Olímpic to Diagonal Mar and back via the beaches, and takes forty minutes. Tickets are valid for all routes, and cost €29.70 for one day, €39.60 for two days (children aged 4–12 €16.20/20.70 respectively, under-4s free). The ticket also gives discounts at various sights, attractions, shops and restaurants. Buy on board the bus, at Barcelona Sants station or any tourist office or TMB customer centre, or online for a ten percent reduction.

WALKING TOURS

Barcelona Walking Tours ⓣ 932 853 832, ⓦ barcelonaturisme. com. The Pl. de Catalunya tourist office coordinates a popular series of walks and tours, including a two-hour historical walking tour of the Barri Gòtic (daily 10am; €23.75). There are also Picasso tours that include an hour walking and an hour in the Picasso museum (3pm, days vary; €33.25, includes museum entry); a two-hour gourmet tour (Mon, Wed & Sat 6.30pm; €110, includes tastings); and many other specialist itineraries. Times given are for the current English-language tours; advance booking essential (discounts for online bookings, and reductions for children/seniors).

My Favourite Things ⓣ 637 265 405, ⓦ myft.net. Highly individual tours that reveal the city in a new light – whether it's where and what the locals eat, contemporary architecture or Barcelona in the movies. Tours (in English) cost €30 per person and last around four hours, and there's always time for anecdotes,

diversions, workshop visits and café visits. Tour numbers are limited to ten, and advance bookings are essential.

Runner Bean Walking Tour ⓣ 636 108 776, ⓦ runnerbeantours. com. Spanish-Irish couple Gorka and Ann-Marie, along with their team of passionate, well-versed guides, offer a couple of free, or rather tip-funded, walking tours (2hr 30min; donations accepted), one devoted to Gaudí and the other to the Old City, plus various specialist tours and private excursions, including night walks (€18).

Spanish Civil War Tour ⓦ thespanishcivilwar.com. Engrossing, four-hour English-language tours devoted to Barcelona and the Spanish Civil War. Led by Civil War expert and author Nick Lloyd and costing €30 per person, they bring to life the city that George Orwell knew so well.

WATER TOURS

Catamaran Orsom ⓣ 667 592 306, ⓦ barcelona-orsom.com. Catamaran trips around the port (May–Sept daily noon or 3.30pm; €17.50), plus jazz cruises (May–Sept daily 3.30pm, 6.30pm €21.50). Both depart from the Moll de Drassanes, opposite the Columbus statue at the bottom of La Rambla (ⓂDrassanes); you can buy tickets there or online, but call ahead to be certain of departures.

Las Golondrinas ⓣ 934 423 106, ⓦ lasgolondrinas.com. Daily sightseeing boats depart from Pl. Portal de la Pau, behind the Columbus monument (July–Sept every 30min; Feb–May, Oct & Nov at least 5 daily; none Dec & Jan; ⓂDrassanes) – trips are either around the port (40min; €8, under-10s €3, under-4s free), or port and coast including the Port Olímpic and Diagonal Mar (90min; €10.50, under-10s €4.50, under-4s free). Bad weather can force cancellations.

Information

The city tourist board, Turisme de Barcelona, is the best first stop for information about Barcelona. Its useful English-language website sells discounted tickets for most city museums and attractions (ⓦbarcelonaturisme.com), while it has offices at Plaça de Catalunya, the airport, Barcelona Sants station and Plaça de Sant Jaume.

There are also **staffed kiosks** in main tourist areas, such as on La Rambla, outside the Sagrada Família and at Plaça d'Espanya, which dispense information and sell discount passes and entrance tickets for attractions.

Information about the wider province of Catalunya can be picked up at either the **Palau Moja** on La Rambla or the **Palau Robert** in the Eixample, while events, concerts, exhibitions, festivals and other cultural diversions are covered at the Institut de Cultura in the **Palau de la Virreina** on La Rambla.

DISCOUNT CARDS

If you're planning to do a lot of sightseeing, you can save money by buying one of the widely available discount cards.

You are in the best position to judge which suits your needs, but the Barcelona Card is likely to be the best deal, as it includes public transport.

The Gaudí Bundle offers fast-track access to the Sagrada Família and Park Güell (**w** barcelonacard.org/tickets/gaudibundle.

• **Barcelona Card** (3 days €48, 4 days €58 or 5 days €63; **w** barcelonacard.org). As well as free public transport, this provides free admission to the following major museums: Blau, Cultures del Món, Disseny, Egipci, Etnòlogic, Frederic Marès, Modernisme, Música, Xocolata, Nacional d'Art de Catalunya, Olimpici de l'Esport; and to the CaixaForum, CCCB, CosmoCaixa, El Born Centre, Fundació Antoni Tàpies, Fundació Joan Miró, Jardí Botànic, MACBA, Monestir de Pedralbes, and all sections of MUHBA; and to the Museu Picasso with advance reservation only. It also offers typical discounts of 20–30 percent at other museums, venues, shops, theatres and restaurants. A two-day version, called Barcelona Card Express, costs €22.50, and includes transport but no free museum admissions, only discounts. All are available at points of arrival, tourist offices and kiosks and other outlets, and there's a ten-percent discount if you buy online, in which case you have to collect your card from any of those same outlets.

• **Articket** (€38, valid three months; **w** articketbcn.org). Free admission into the permanent and temporary exhibitions at six major art centres and galleries (MNAC, MACBA, CCCB, Museu Picasso, Fundació Antoni Tàpies and Fundació Joan Miró). Buy at participating galleries, at Barcelona tourist offices and kiosks or online. For most visitors, the Barcelona Card is a better option.

• **Arqueoticket** (€14.50, valid calendar year). In the same vein as Articket, offers free entry into four historical museums (Museu d'Arqueologia de Catalunya, Egipci, Historia de Barcelona and Maritím). Available at participating museums and tourist offices. It's only worth buying if you plan to visit them all and don't have a Barcelona Card.

• **Ruta del Modernisme** (€12, valid one year, **w** rutadelmodernisme.com). An excellent English-language guidebook, map and discount-voucher package that covers 116 *modernista* buildings in Barcelona and other Catalan towns, offering discounts of up to fifty percent on admission fees, tours and purchases. Accompanying adults who pay a one-off fee of €5 can benefit from the same discounts without buying a separate copy of the book. If you plan to visit several such sites, this will probably prove worth having as well as a Barcelona Card.

The city hall (Ajuntament; **w** bcn.cat) and regional government (Generalitat; **w** gencat.cat) **websites** are mines of information about every aspect of cultural, social and working life in Barcelona, from museum opening hours and festival dates to local politics and council office locations; they both have English-language versions. Also useful is **w** **barcelona-online. com**, with punchy reviews in English of all things Barcelona plus links galore.

For arts and events listings, the websites of local newspapers and magazines (see below) are also useful.

INFORMATION OFFICES

Turisme de Barcelona ☎ 932 853 834, **w** barcelonaturisme. com. Main office, Pl. de Catalunya 17, **M** Catalunya (daily 8.30am– 8.30pm); also at Airport Metro L9 lobby T1 (daily 8.30am–2.30pm); Airport Metro L9 lobby T2 (daily 8.30am–8.30pm); Airport Terminals 1 & 2 (daily 8.30am–8.30pm); Barcelona Sants, Pl. dels Països Catalans, **M** Sants Estació (daily 8am–8pm); Catedral, Col·legi Oficial d'Arquitectes de Catalunya, Pl. Nova 5, **M** Jaume I (daily 9am–5pm); Glòries, Pl. de les Glòries Catalanes, **M** Glòries (Mon, Wed, Fri & Sat 10am–5pm); Mirador de Colom, Pl. Portal de la Pau, **M** Drassanes (daily 8.30am–230pm); Pl. d'Espanya, Avda. Maria Cristina, **M** Espanya (daily 8.30am–2.30pm); Pl. de Sant Jaume, entrance at C/Ciutat 2, Barri Gòtic, **M** Jaume I (Mon–Fri 8.30am–8.30pm, Sat 9am–7pm, Sun & hols 9am–2pm); Rambla-Liceu, Ramblas 51–59, **M** Liceu (daily 9am–6.30pm); Sagrada Família, Pl. Sagrada Família, **M** Sagrada Família (daily 9am–8pm). The main Pl. de Catalunya office is down the steps in the southeast corner of the square, opposite El Corte Inglés. It's always busy and can be frustrating if you just want a quick answer to a question. There's also a money exchange service, separate accommodation desk, tour and ticket sales and a gift shop.

Institut de Cultura Palau de la Virreina, Ramblas 99 ☎ 933 161 000 🌐 barcelonacultura.bcn.cat, Ⓜ Liceu (daily 10am–8.30pm). Cultural information office, with details and ticket sales for everything that's happening in the city, from events and concerts to exhibitions and festivals.

Centre del Modernisme ☎ 933 177 652, 🌐 rutadelmodernisme. com. Offices at Institut Municipal del Paisatge Urbà i la Qualitat de Vida, Ajuntament de Barcelona, Avda. Drassanes 6–8, planta 21, Ⓜ Drassanes (Mon–Fri 9am–2pm), and Pavellons Güell, Avda. de Pedralbes 7, Pedralbes, Ⓜ Palau Reial (daily 10am–4pm). Details of visits to *modernista* buildings and monuments, and sales of the Ruta del Modernisme package.

Palau Moja La Rambla 188 ☎ 933 162 740, 🌐 palaumoja. com; Ⓜ Liceu (daily 10am–9pm). Information on Catalunya in general, plus classes and workshops, ticket sales, and a large souvenir shop.

Centre d'Informació de Catalunya Palau Robert, Pg. de Gràcia 107, Eixample ☎ 932 388 091, 🌐 palaurobert.gencat.cat; Ⓜ Diagonal (Mon–Sat 9am–8pm, Sun & hols 9am–2.30pm). Information about travel in Catalunya, plus maps, guides, details of how to get around and lists of places to stay. Also exhibitions and events relating to all matters Catalan.

Barcelona Informació (Oficina d'Atenció Ciutadana) Pl. de Sant Miquel 3, Barri Gòtic ☎ 010, 🌐 ajuntament.barcelona.cat; Ⓜ Jaume I (Mon–Sat 8.30am–8pm, except Aug Sat 9am–2pm). Citizens' information office, around the back of the Ajuntament in the new building. While not targeted at tourists, it's invariably helpful with all aspects of living in Barcelona (though English won't necessarily be spoken).

The media

You can buy foreign newspapers and magazines at the stalls down La Rambla, and around Plaça de Catalunya, on Passeig de Gràcia, on Rambla de Catalunya and at Barcelona Sants station. If you can't find what you're looking for, try FNAC at El Triangle on Plaça de Catalunya (Ⓜ Catalunya), which has an excellent ground-floor magazine section.

Newspapers and magazines

The best **local newspaper** is the liberal *El País* (🌐 elpais.com), which has a daily Catalunya supplement and is good on entertainment and the arts. The conservative Barcelona paper *La Vanguardia* (🌐 lavanguardia.com) has shifted downmarket in recent years, but still has a good arts and culture listings section on Friday, while *El Periódico* (🌐 elperiodico.com) is more tabloid in style, and also comes in a Catalan edition. *Ara* (🌐 ara.cat) is the chief nationalist paper, printed in Catalan. For wall-to-wall coverage of sport (for which, in Barcelona, read FC Barcelona), seek out specialist daily *Sport* (🌐 sport.es), which has an English option.

English-language publications

Barcelona Metropolitan (🌐 barcelona-metropolitan. com) is a free online magazine for English-speakers living in Barcelona, packed with news features, reviews and listings, while another free monthly, **Miniguide** (🌐 miniguide.co), contains mostly news of upcoming concerts and exhibitions, along with restaurant and bar reviews. You'll find this and other free mags in hotels, hostels, bars and other outlets. For the style scene, look in newsagents for **b-guided** (🌐 b-guided. com), a painfully cool quarterly magazine, while 🌐 **barcelona.lecool.com** is a hip cultural agenda and city guide, available online or as a weekly e-magazine.

Television

In Catalunya you can pick up various **national TV channels**, and a handful of **Catalan-language channels**. Barcelona itself also offers the city-run **BTV**, which is useful for information about local events, and news programmes. TVs in most *pensiones* and small hotels tend to offer these stations, with cable and satellite channels available in higher-rated hotels.

Travel essentials

Accessible travel

Barcelona's tourist office devotes a separate website to the needs of travellers with disabilities (🌐 barcelona-access.com), featuring a full guide to accessible sights and facilities, and detailing all forms of public transport. Barcelona's **airport** and **Aerobús** are fully accessible to travellers in wheelchairs, though the bus gets very busy and can be difficult if you have lots of luggage. **Barcelona Sants** has lifts to the platforms, though not all trains are accessible. There are access ramps at Estació de França and lifts to the platforms at Plaça de Catalunya's FGC and RENFE stations. Almost all metro stations are now accessible – see 🌐 tmb.cat/en/transport-accessible for details. All **city buses** and trams are wheelchair-accessible, as is the sightseeing Bus Turístic. If you need a **wheelchair-accessible taxi** contact Radio Taxi (☎ 933 033 033, 🌐 radiotaxi033. com) or Taxi Amic (☎ 934 208 088, 🌐 taxi-amic-adaptat.com, English rarely spoken).

BUDGET BARCELONA

Boutique hotels, designer stores, gourmet restaurants and hip bars – life in Barcelona can get pretty pricey at times. But here's how to keep costs to a minimum while still having a great time.

- **Cafés and restaurants** Eat your main meal of the day at lunchtime, when the *menú del día* offers fantastic value. Also note that there's usually a surcharge for terrace service.
- **Public transport** Buy a public transport travel pass, which will save you around fifty percent on every ride, or a Barcelona Card.
- **Discount cards** Several useful discount cards offer substantial price reductions, while student, youth or senior citizen cards also entitle bearers to discounts on museum, gallery and attraction charges.
- **Special offers** Take advantage of the discount nights at the cinema (Mon &

sometimes Wed), and at the theatre (Tues), and visit Tiquet Rambles in the Palau de la Virreina for half-price last-minute theatre and show tickets.
- **Museums and galleries** At many museums and galleries, admission is usually free one day a month, and most museums are free on saints' days (see page 37).
- **See the sights for free** Go to La Rambla, Boqueria market, Santa María del Mar, Ajuntament and Generalitat, Parc de la Ciutadella, Parc de Collserola, Port Vell, Port Olímpic, city beaches, Els Encants flea market, Diagonal Mar/Fòrum and Caixa Fórum – all free.

On the streets, the number of acoustic traffic-light signals is slowly growing, while dropped kerbs are being put in place across the city. However, many old-town attractions, including the Museu Picasso, have steps, cobbles or other impediments to access. Fully accessible **sights and attractions** include MNAC, Fundacío Antoni Tàpies, Fundacío Joan Miró, La Pedrera, Caixa Forum, CosmoCaixa, Museu d'Història de Catalunya and the Palau de la Música Catalana.

USEFUL CONTACTS

Institut Municipal de Persones amb Discapacitat C/ de València 344, Eixample ☎ 934 132 775, ⓦ bcn.cat/imd; Ⓜ Verdaguer. Information, some in English, on most aspects of life and travel in the city for disabled residents and visitors.

Admission charges

Admission charges for city attractions vary between €4 and €26, with most museums and galleries costing around €4–10. Many offer free admission on the first or last Sunday of every month, and most museums are free on the saints' days of February 12, April 23 and September 24, plus May 18 (international museum day). There's usually a reduction or free entrance if you show a student, youth or senior citizen card. Several discount cards give heavily reduced admission to Barcelona's museums and galleries (see page 31).

Costs

Barcelona tends to be more expensive than other major cities in Spain. However, it still rates as pretty

good value when compared with the cost of visiting cities in Britain, France or Germany, especially when it comes to dining out or getting around on public transport. Hotel prices are the main drain on the budget. Realistically, you'll be paying from €80 a night for a room in a simple *pensión*, and from €140 for a three-star or budget boutique hotel. Still, once you're there, public transport is very cheap, as is entrance to most museums and attractions (with the exception of Gaudí buildings and the Camp Nou stadium). A set three-course lunch goes for €13–20, and dinner from around €35 a head, though of course the Michelin-starred destination restaurants are much pricier – even so, at around €120 a head, they're still a better deal than the equivalent places in London or Paris.

Crime and personal safety

Catalunya has its own autonomous police force, the **Mossos d'Esquadra** (ⓦ mossos.gencat.cat), dressed in navy-blue uniforms with red trim. They have gradually taken over most of the local duties traditionally carried out by Spain's other police services, namely the **Policía Nacional** (ⓦ policia.es) – the national police, whose uniforms resemble blue combat gear – and the **Guàrdia Urbana** (ⓦ bcn.cat/guardiaurbana), municipal police in blue shirts and high-visibility jackets. There's also the **Guàrdia Civil**, a national paramilitary force in green uniforms, seen guarding some public buildings, and at airports and border crossings.

In theory you're supposed to carry some kind of **identification** at all times, and the police can stop you in the street and demand to see it. In practice they're rarely bothered if you're clearly a tourist, and a photocopy of your passport or a photo-driving licence should suffice.

If you're robbed, you need to go to the police to report it, not least because your insurance company will require a police report. Don't expect a great deal of concern if your loss is relatively small – but do expect the process of completing forms and formalities to take ages.

The easiest place to report a crime is at the **Guàrdia Urbana station** at La Rambla 43, opposite Pl. Reial, Ⓜ Liceu ☎932 562 477 (24hr; English spoken), though there's a Guàrdia Urbana office in each city district (see their website).

However, to get a police report for your insurance you need to go to the **Mossos d'Esquadra station** at C/ Nou de la Rambla 76–80, El Raval, Ⓜ Paral·lel (☎933 062 300). You can fill in a report online (under "Denunciar", then "Denúncies per internet" on Ⓦ mossos.gencat.cat (English option available), but you'll still have to go to the office within 72hr to sign the document.

Electricity

The electricity supply is 220v and plugs come with two round pins – bring an adaptor (and transformer) to use UK and US laptops, cellphone chargers, etc.

Health

The **Global Health Insurance Card** or GHIC (still occasionally known as the European Health Insurance Card) gives British and EU citizens access to Spanish state public health services under reciprocal agreements. While this will provide free or reduced-cost medical care in the event of minor injuries and emergencies, it won't cover every eventuality, so travel insurance (see page 35) is essential.

For minor health complaints, look for the green cross of a **pharmacy** (*farmàcia*), where highly trained staff can give advice (often in English), and are able to dispense many drugs (including some antibiotics) available only on prescription in other countries. Usual hours are weekdays 9am–1pm and 4–8pm. At least one in each neighbourhood is open daily 24 hours (and marked as such), or phone ☎010 for information on those open out of hours – Farmacia Clapes, Ramblas 98, Ⓜ Liceu (☎933 012 843) is a convenient 24-hour pharmacy. A list of out-of-hours pharmacies can be found in the window of any pharmacy store.

Any local **healthcare centre** (Centre d'Atenció Primària, CAP) can provide non-emergency assistance. In the old town, those at Ptge. Pau 1, Barri Gòtic, Ⓜ Drassanes (☎933 436 140), and C/Rec Comtal 24, Sant Pere, Ⓜ Arc de Triomf (☎933 101 421), are open Monday to Friday 8am–8pm, Saturday 9am–5pm. Alternatively, call ☎010 or consult Ⓦ bcn.cat for a full list.

For emergency hospital treatment, call ☎061 or go to one of the following **central hospitals**, which have 24hr accident and emergency (*urgències*) services.

HOSPITALS

Centre Perecamps C/Pieyre de Mandiargues 5, El Raval ☎934 410 600; Ⓜ Drassanes.
Hospital Clínic i Provincial C/Villaroel 170, Eixample ☎932 275 400; Ⓜ Hospital Clínic.
Hospital del Mar Pg. Marítim 25–29, Vila Olímpica ☎932 483 000; Ⓜ Ciutadella-Vila Olímpica.

ROUGH GUIDES TRAVEL INSURANCE

Looking for travel insurance? Rough Guides partners with top providers worldwide to offer you the best coverage. Policies are available to residents of anywhere in the world, with a range of options whether you are looking for single-trip, multi-country or long-stay insurance. There's coverage for a wide range of adventure sports, 24-hour emergency assistance, high levels of medical and evacuation cover and a stream of travel safety information. Even better, ⓦroughguides.com users can take advantage of these policies online 24/7, from anywhere in the world – even if you're already travelling. To make the most of your travels and ensure a smoother experience, it's always good to be prepared for when things don't go according to plan. For more information go to ⓦroughguides.com/bookings/insurance.

Hospital de la Santa Creu i Sant Pau C/Sant Quintí 89, Eixample ⓣ932 919 000; ⓜHospital de Sant Pau.

Insurance

Take out a comprehensive **insurance policy** before you travel to Barcelona, to cover against loss, theft, illness or injury. A typical policy will cover loss of baggage, tickets and – up to a certain limit – cash or travellers' cheques, as well as cancellation or curtailment of your journey. With medical coverage, ascertain whether benefits will be paid as treatment proceeds or only after you return home, and whether there is a 24-hour medical emergency number. When securing baggage cover, make sure the per-article limit covers your most valuable possession. Most policies exclude so-called dangerous sports unless an extra premium is paid: in Spain this can mean most watersports are excluded, though seldom things like bike tours or hiking.

If you need to make a claim, keep receipts for medicines and medical treatment, and if you have anything stolen, obtain an official statement from the police (see page 33).

Internet and wi-fi

Wi-fi (pronounced "wee-fee" in Barcelona) is widespread in cafés, bars and hotels, while Barcelona city council operates Spain's largest free public wi-fi network, with more than six hundred hotspots all over the city (ⓦbcn.cat/barcelonawifi). While there are fewer internet shops around these days, a stroll down La Rambla, or through the Barri Gòtic, La Ribera, El Raval and Gràcia will still reveal plenty of possibilities.

Language schools

The Generalitat (the government of Catalonia) offers low-cost **Catalan classes** for non-Spanish

speakers through the Consorci per a la Normalització Lingüística (ⓣ010, ⓦcpnl.cat). Otherwise, you can find great-value **Spanish** or Catalan classes at the Escola Oficial d'Idiomes, Avda. Drassanes 14, El Raval, ⓜDrassanes (ⓣ933 249 330, ⓦeoibd.cat) – expect queues when you sign on. Barcelona University also offers language courses for beginners, at various locations (ⓣ934 021 100, ⓦwww.ub.es).

Laundry

Most youth hostels, and some *pensiones*, offer inexpensive laundry services; hotels charge considerably more. Self-service laundries include LavaXpres, at eighteen city locations, including C/la Junta de Comerç 10, El Raval, ⓜLiceu, and C/Nou de Sant Francesc 5, Barri Gòtic, ⓜDrassanes (daily 8am–10pm; ⓦlavaxpres.com), and Splash, at C/Diputació 199, Esquerra de l'Eixample, ⓜUniversitat, and C/Sicília 348, ⓜSagrada Família (daily 8am–10pm; ⓦsplashlaundry.es).

Left luggage

There are left-luggage offices (*consigna*) at Barcelona Sants train station (daily 5.30am–11pm; €5/day) and Barcelona Nord bus station (daily 6am–11.30pm; €5). **Locker Barcelona**, near Plaça Catalunya at C/Estruc 36, Barri Gòtic, ⓜCatalunya/Urquinaona (daily: July–Oct 8.30am–10.30pm; Nov–June 9am–9pm; €4–13; ⓣ933 028 796, ⓦlockerbarcelona.com), lets you access your belongings throughout the day free of charge, and offers other services such as luggage weighing, boarding pass printing, a changing room and internet access.

Libraries

The **British Council**, C/Amigó 83, Sant Gervasi, FGC Muntaner (ⓣ932 419 700, ⓦbritishcouncil.es), has Barcelona's only English-language lending library, and puts on a full arts and events programme.

The Catalan national library, the **Biblioteca de Catalunya**, is at C/Hospital 56, El Raval, Ⓜ Liceu (Mon–Fri 9am–8pm, Sat 9am 2pm; ☎ 932 702 300, Ⓦ www.bnc.cat). A letter of academic reference or degree certificate is required, but there's a public library in the same building, the **Biblioteca Sant Pau-Santa Creu** (Mon, Wed & Fri 3.30–8.30pm; Tues & Thurs 10am–2pm & 3.30–8.30pm; Sat 10am–2pm). Barcelona's other public libraries are listed on Ⓦ bcn.cat – all have internet and wi-fi, and some have English-language books, international press, etc.

Lost property

Anything recovered by the police, or left on public transport, is sent to the **Oficina de Troballes** (municipal lost property office), at C/de la Ciutat 2, Barri Gòtic, Ⓜ Jaume I/Catalunya (Mon–Fri 9am–2pm; ☎ 010). Most items are kept for three months. You could also try the TMB (public transport) customer service centre at Universitat metro station.

Maps

City tourist offices and kiosks charge for their maps – pick up a good free one instead from the information desk on the ground floor of El Corte Inglés department store, near the main tourist office. With that, and the maps in this book, you'll easily find your way around.

Bookshops, newspaper kiosks and petrol stations stock regional and national Spanish maps. Map and travel shops in your home country should also be able to supply road maps of Catalunya or northern Spain, or you can order from a map specialist like Ⓦ stanfords.co.uk or Ⓦ randmcnally.com.

Money

Spain's **currency** is the euro (€), with notes issued in denominations of 5, 10, 20, 50, 100, 200 and 500 euros, and coins in denominations of 1, 2, 5, 10, 20 and 50 cents, and 1 and 2 euros.

By far the easiest way to get money is to use your bank debit card to withdraw cash from an **ATM**, found all over the city. You can usually withdraw up to €400 a day and instructions are offered in English once you insert your card. Take a note of your bank's emergency contact number in case the machine swallows the card.

All major **credit cards** are accepted in hotels, restaurants and shops, and for tours, tickets and transport, but don't count on being able to use them in every small hotel or backstreet café.

Spanish **banks** (*bancos*) and savings banks (*caixas*) have branches throughout Barcelona, especially along La Rambla and around Plaça de Catalunya. Normal banking hours are Monday to Friday from 8.30am to 2pm, although between October and May most institutions also open Thursday 4pm to 6.30pm (savings banks) or Saturday 9am to 1pm (banks).

Opening hours and public holidays

Basic **working hours** are Monday to Saturday 9.30am or 10am to 2pm and 4pm to 8pm, though many offices and shops don't open on Saturday afternoons. Local cafés, bars and markets open around 7am, while shopping centres, major stores and large supermarkets typically open all day from 10am to 9pm, with some open on Sunday. In the lazy days of summer everything becomes a bit more relaxed, with offices working until around 3pm and many shops and restaurants closing for part or the whole of August.

Most of Barcelona's showpiece **museums and galleries** open all day, from 10am to 8pm, though some smaller collections and attractions close between 1pm and 4pm. On Sundays most are open for shorter periods, and almost all close all day on Mondays. On public holidays, most museums and galleries have Sunday opening hours, while pretty much everything is closed on Christmas Day, New Year's Day and January 6.

Apart from the cathedral (La Seu) and the Sagrada Família – the two churches you're most likely to visit, which have tourist-friendly opening hours – other **churches** tend only to open for worship in the early morning (around 7–9am) and the evening (around 6–9pm).

Not all **public and bank holidays** in Spain are observed in Catalunya, and vice versa. On the days

AVERAGE MONTHLY TEMPERATURES

	Jan	Feb	Mar	Apr	May	Jun	Jul	Aug	Sep	Oct	Nov	Dec
Max/min (°C)	13/6	14/7	16/9	18/11	21/16	25/18	28/21	28/21	25/19	21/15	16/11	13/8
Max/min (°F)	56/42	58/44	61/48	65/52	70/61	77/64	82/70	82/70	77/66	70/59	61/52	56/46

listed below, and during the many local festivals, most shops are closed, though bars and restaurants tend to stay open.

BARCELONA'S PUBLIC HOLIDAYS

January 1 Cap d'Any, New Year's Day
January 6 Epifanía, Epiphany
Variable Good Friday & Easter Monday
May 1 Día del Treball, May Day/Labour Day
June 24 Día de Sant Joan, St John's Day
August 15 L'Assumpció, Assumption of the Virgin
September 11 Diada Nacional, Catalan National Day
September 24 Festa de la Mercè, Our Lady of Mercy (Barcelona's patron saint)
October 12 Día de la Hispanidad, Spanish National Day
November 1 Tots Sants, All Saints' Day
December 6 Día de la Constitució, Constitution Day
December 8 La Imaculada, Immaculate Conception
December 25 Nadal, Christmas Day
December 26 Sant Esteve, St Stephen's Day

Post

The main **post office** in Barcelona is near the harbour in the old town, while each city neighbourhood also has a post office, with far less comprehensive opening hours and services. If you simply need **stamps**, it's usually quicker to visit local tobacconists (look for the brown-and-yellow *estanc* sign), which can also weigh letters and small parcels, advise about postal rates and send express mail (*urgente*). Use the yellow on-street postboxes and put your mail in the flap marked *províncies i estranger* or *altres destins*. Letters or cards take around five days to a week to European countries, a week or two to North America.

POSTAL SERVICES

Main post office (Correus) Pl. de Correus, at the eastern end of Pg. de Colom, Barri Gòtic ☎ 934 868 302, ⊚ correos. es; Ⓜ Barceloneta/Jaume I (Mon–Fri 8.30am–9.30pm, Sat 8.30am–2pm). There's a poste restante/general delivery service here (*llista de correus*), plus express post, mobile phone top-ups, phonecard sales and bill payments.

Smoking

Smoking is forbidden in all Barcelona's public buildings and transport facilities, plus bars, restaurants, clubs and cafés. Since 2023, smoking has also been banned from bar and restaurant terraces.

Taxes

Local sales tax, **IVA**, is ten percent in hotels and restaurants, and 21 percent in shops. It's usually but not always included in the price, so some hotel or restaurant bills can come as a surprise. Quoted prices should always make it clear whether or not tax is included. Note that there is also an additional tax on stays in tourist establishments in Barcelona of €2.75–6.75 (determined by the type of property) per person per night for up to seven days (under-16s exempt).

Telephones

Spanish **telephone numbers** have nine digits. The first two digits of all landline numbers in Barcelona are the regional prefix, 93, which you dial even when calling from within the city. Spanish mobile numbers begin with a 6 or 7, freephone numbers with 900, while other 90-plus- and 80-plus-digit numbers are

CALLING HOME FROM ABROAD

When dialling the UK, Ireland, Australia or New Zealand from abroad, omit the initial zero from the area code.
Australia international access code + 61
New Zealand international access code + 64
UK international access code + 44
US and Canada international access code + 1
Ireland international access code + 353
South Africa international access code + 27

nationwide standard-rate or special-rate services. To **call Barcelona from abroad**, dial your international access number + 34 (Spain country code) + nine-digit number.

Most European **mobile phones** work in Barcelona, though it's worth checking with your provider whether you need to get international access switched on and whether any extra charges are involved. Even though prices have dropped, it's expensive to use your own mobile extensively while abroad, and you may well pay for receiving incoming calls for example.

For **international calls**, it's generally much cheaper to use an internet application such as Skype than a mobile or hotel-room phone.

Ticket agencies

You can buy tickets for concerts, exhibitions, sporting events and tourist attractions online, in English, through **Ticketmaster** (Ⓦticketmaster) or **Ticketea** (Ⓦticketea.com). There's also a concert ticket desk in the **FNAC store**, El Triangle, Plaça de Catalunya, while for advance tickets for all city council (Ajuntament) -sponsored concerts and events visit the **Palau de la Virreina**, La Rambla 99. The official website Ⓦ**barcelonaturisme.com** also offers online ticket purchase for most city museums and attractions (click on "BCNShop"), with a discount of five to ten percent.

Time

Barcelona is one hour ahead of the UK, six hours ahead of Eastern Standard Time, nine hours ahead of Pacific Standard Time, eight hours behind Australia, ten hours behind New Zealand and in the same time zone as South Africa. Clocks in Spain go forward in the last week in March and back in the last week in October.

Tipping

Service in most **bars** is considered to be included in the price. Locals leave only a few cents or round up the change for a coffee or a drink in a bar, and a euro or two for most meals, though fancier restaurants will expect ten to fifteen percent. **Taxi drivers** usually get around five percent, more if they help with bags or are similarly useful, while **hotel porters** should be tipped a euro or two for their assistance.

Toilets

Public toilets are few and far between, and seldom particularly clean. Bars and restaurants are more likely to have proper (and cleaner) toilets, though there's no guarantee, even in the poshest of places. Ask for *els lavabos* or *serveis (los lavabos* or *servicios* in Spanish). Dones or Damas (Ladies) and Homes/Hombres or Caballeros (Gentlemen) are the usual signs.

Water

Water from the tap is safe to drink, but doesn't taste very nice. You'll always be given bottled mineral water in a bar or restaurant.

Women's Barcelona

Ca la Dona, C/Ripoll 25, Barri Gòtic, ⓂJaume I (Ⓣ646 355 864, Ⓦcaladona.org), is a women's centre hosting meetings for women's groups, with a library and bar. The Ajuntament's official women's resource centre, the **Centre Municipal d'Informació i Recursos per a les Dones** (CIRD), C/Camèlies 36–38, Gràcia, ⓂAlfons X (Ⓣ932 850 357, Ⓦbcn.cat/dones), publishes a monthly calendar of events online. The **Barcelona Women's Network** (Ⓦbcnwomensnetwork.com) is a social, business and networking club for English-speaking women living and working in the city.

PLAÇA DEL PORTAL DE LA PAU

La Rambla

It's a telling comment on the character of Barcelona that a single street – La Rambla (*Rambles* in Catalan) – can count as a highlight. No day in the city seems complete without a stroll down at least part of what poet Federico García Lorca hailed as "the only street in the world which I wish would never end". Lined with cafés, restaurants, souvenir shops, flower stalls and newspaper kiosks, and thronged by tourists, locals and performance artists, it's at the heart of Barcelona's life and self-image. There are significant buildings and sights along the way, not least the Liceu opera house and the mouthwatering Boqueria food market, but undoubtedly it's the vibrant street life that is the greatest attraction along Spain's most famous thoroughfare.

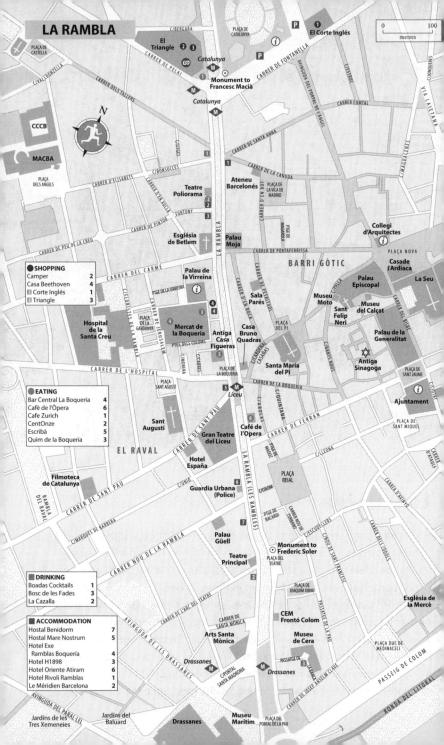

LA RAMBLA

PLAÇA DE CASTELLA

C/BERGARA

PLAÇA DE CATALUNYA

El Triangle

El Corte Inglés

CARRER DE PELAI

Catalunya

CARRER DE FONTANELLA

AVINGUDA DEL PORTAL DE L'ANGEL

CARRER COMTAL

Monument to Francesc Macià

Catalunya

CARRER DELS TALLERS

C/VALLDONZELLA

CCCB

MACBA

PLAÇA DELS ANGELS

CARRER D'ELISABETS

CARRER D'EN XUCLÀ

CARRER DE SANTA ANNA

CARRER DE LA CANUDA

Ateneu Barcelonés

PLAÇA DE LA VILA DE MADRID

Teatre Poliorama

Collegi d'Arquitectes

PLAÇA NOVA

FORTUNY

CARRER DE PINTOR

CARRER DE PEU DE LA CREU

Església de Betlem

Palau Moja

CARRER DE PORTAFERRISSA

BARRI GÒTIC

Casa de l'Ardiaca

La Seu

Palau Episcopal

Museu Moto

Sant Felip Neri

Museu del Calçat

SHOPPING
Camper	2
Casa Beethoven	4
El Corte Inglés	1
El Triangle	3

Palau de la Virreina

CARRER DEL CARME

PTGE DE LA VIRREINA

Sala Parés

PLAÇA DEL PI

Palau de la Generalitat

Antiga Sinagoga

PLAÇA DE SANT JAUME

Hospital de la Santa Creu

PLAÇA DE LA GARDUÑA

Mercat de la Boqueria

Antiga Casa Figueras

Casa Bruno Quadras

Santa Maria del Pi

CARRER DE L'HOSPITAL

PTGE DELS COLOMS

PLAÇA DE LA BOQUERIA

CARRER DE LA BOQUERIA

Ajuntament

PLAÇA SANT AGUSTÍ

Liceu

PLAÇA DE SANT MIQUEL

EATING
Bar Central La Boqueria	4
Cafè de l'Opera	6
Cafe Zurich	1
CentOnze	2
Escribà	5
Quim de la Boqueria	3

Sant Agustí

Gran Teatre del Liceu

Café de l'Opera

CARRER DE FERRAN

EL RAVAL

Hotel España

Filmoteca de Catalunya

CARRER DE SANT PAU

Guardia Urbana (Police)

PLAÇA REIAL

C/JUNTA

Palau Güell

Teatre Principal

CARRER NOU DE LA RAMBLA

Monument to Frederic Soler

PLAÇA DEL TEATRE

DRINKING
Boadas Cocktails	1
Bosc de les Fades	3
La Cazalla	2

PLAÇA DE JOAQUIM XIRAU

Església de la Mercè

ACCOMMODATION
Hostal Benidorm	7
Hostal Mare Nostrum	5
Hotel Exe Ramblas Boqueria	4
Hotel H1898	3
Hotel Oriente Atiram	6
Hotel Rivoli Ramblas	1
Le Méridien Barcelona	2

AVINGUDA DE LES DRASSANES

CARRER DE L'ARC DEL TEATRE

CARRER DE SANTA MÒNICA

CEM Frontó Colom

Arts Santa Mònica

Museu de Cera

PLAÇA DUC DE MEDINACELI

Drassanes

C/PORTAL SANTA MADRONA

PASSEIG DE COLOM

AVINGUDA DEL PARAL·LEL

Jardins de les Tres Xemeneies

Jardins del Baluard

Drassanes

Museu Marítim

PLAÇA DEL PORTAL DE LA PAU

RONDA DEL LLITORAL

0   100
metres

1

La Rambla derives its name from the Arabic *ramla* (sand), which refers to the bed of a seasonal stream that was paved over in medieval times. Benches and decorative trees were added, overlooked by stately balconied buildings, during the nineteenth century, and today – in a city choked with traffic – this wide tree-lined swathe is still given over to pedestrians, with cars forced up the narrow strips of road on either side. You can walk the entire length in about twenty minutes, while there are **metro stops** at Catalunya (top of La Rambla), Liceu (middle) and Drassanes (bottom).

La Rambla splits Barcelona's old-town areas in half, with the Barri Gòtic on the east flank of the avenue and El Raval to the west. Technically, it also comprises **five separate sections** (Les Rambles) strung head to tail – from north to south, Rambla Canaletes, Estudis, Sant Josep, Caputxins and Santa Mònica – though it's rare to hear them referred to as such. However, you may notice changes as you walk down La Rambla, primarily that the streets on either side become a little less polished – even seedy – the closer you get to the harbour. The businesses, meanwhile, reflect the mixed clientele, from patisseries to pizza takeaways, and stores selling handcrafted jewellery to shops full of sombreros, bullfight posters ("your name here") and football shirts.

On the central avenue, stallholders beneath the plane trees peddle ice cream, flowers, plants, postcards and books. You can have your palm read and your portrait painted, or while away time with the buskers and human statues (though if you play cards or dice for money with someone on the street, you've only yourself to blame if you get ripped off). Drag yourself home with the dawn, and you'll rub shoulders with street cleaners, watchful policemen and bleary-eyed stallholders. It's a never-ending show, of which visitors and locals alike seldom tire.

Plaça de Catalunya

Ⓜ Catalunya

The huge **Plaça de Catalunya** square at the top of La Rambla stands right at the heart of Barcelona, with the old town and port below it, and the nineteenth-century Eixample district above and beyond. Laid out in its present form in the 1920s, it centres on a formal arrangement of statues, circular fountains and trees, and serves as the focal point for demonstrations and events, including a mass gathering on New Year's Eve. The most prominent monument is a towering angular slab and bust dedicated in 1991 to **Francesc Macià**, leader of the Republican Left, parliamentary deputy for Barcelona and first president of the Generalitat, who died in office in 1933. It was commissioned from the pioneer of Catalan avant-garde sculpture, Josep María Subirachs, best known perhaps for his work on the Sagrada Família church.

For visitors, an initial orientation point is the white-faced **El Corte Inglés** department store on the eastern side of the square, an amazing behemoth – half Art Deco, half Fascist – where the ninth-floor cafeteria offers stupendous views. The main **tourist office** is just across from here on the square itself, while on the southwest side, across the road from the top of La Rambla, **El Triangle** shopping centre makes another landmark. Incorporated into its ground floor is the anodyne modern incarnation of the **Café Zurich**, a veteran Barcelona rendezvous, whose ranks of outdoor tables are a day-long draw for beggars and buskers.

Rambla Canaletes and Estudis

The top two stretches of La Rambla are **Rambla Canaletes**, with its iron fountain (a drink from which supposedly ensures that you'll never leave Barcelona), and **Rambla Estudis**, named after the university (L'Estudi General) that was sited here

1

until the start of the eighteenth century. This part is also known locally as Rambla dels Ocells, as it was until a few years ago home to a **bird market** (*ocell* being the Catalan for "bird").

Teatre Poliorama

La Rambla 115 • ☎ 933 177 599, ⓦ teatrepoliorama.com • Ⓜ Catalunya

It seems hard to believe now, but La Rambla was a war zone during the Spanish Civil War, when the city erupted into factionalism in 1937. George Orwell (see box, page 44) was caught in the crossfire between the *Café Moka* – the restaurant that now occupies part of the ground floor is a modern replacement – and the Poliorama cinema opposite, now the **Teatre Poliorama**. Built in 1863 as the Royal Academy of Science and Arts, this was restored as a theatre in 1985, and hosts regular tourist-oriented flamenco shows.

Església de Betlem

La Rambla 107 • Daily 8.30am–1.30pm & 6–9pm • Ⓜ Liceu

The **Església de Betlem** was built in 1681 in Baroque style for the Jesuits, but was completely gutted during the Civil War as anarchists sacked the city's churches at will – an activity of which Orwell quietly approved. Consequently, the interior is plain in the extreme, though the main facade on C/Carme sports a fine sculpted portal.

Palau Moja

La Rambla 188 • Daily 10am–9pm • ☎ 933 162 740, ⓦ patrimoni.gencat.cat/en/collection/palau-moja • Ⓜ Liceu

Across La Rambla from the Betlem church, the arcaded **Palau Moja** dates from the late eighteenth century and retains an exterior staircase and elegant great hall. Now officially known as the **House of Catalan Heritage**, it functions as a **tourist office** covering the whole of Catalunya, and hosts evening workshops on subjects such as wine-tasting, while also selling passes and tickets for travel, attractions and events in the city, alongside a wide range of local souvenirs.

Just outside, take a look at the illustrated tiles above the **fountain** at the start of Carrer de la Portaferrissa, which show the medieval gate (the Porta Ferriça) and market that once stood here.

Palau de la Virreina

La Rambla 99 • **Tiquet Rambles** Daily 10am–8.30pm • **Centre de la Imatge** Tues–Sun 11am–8pm • Usually free • ⓦ lavirreina.bcn. cat • Ⓜ Liceu

Commissioned by a Peruvian viceroy, Manuel Amat, and named after his widow, the graceful eighteenth-century **Palau de la Virreina** is set back slightly from La Rambla. Its five street-facing bays are adorned with pilasters and Rococo windows. Today the palace is used by the city's culture department, and has a useful ground-floor **information centre** called "Tiquet Rambles" where you can find out about upcoming events and buy tickets. Under the overall name of **Centre de la Imatge**, various galleries and studios towards the rear present interesting temporary **exhibitions**, with an emphasis on contemporary culture, social studies and photography.

The city's two official **Carnival giants** (*gegants vells*), representing the thirteenth-century Catalan king Jaume I and his wife Violant, are usually displayed behind glass at the back of the courtyard. The origin of Catalunya's outsized (5m-high) wood-and-plaster Carnival figures is unclear, though they probably once formed part of the entertainment at medieval travelling fairs. The first record of specific city giants is in 1601 – later used to entertain the city's orphans, they are now an integral part of Barcelona's festival parades (see box, page 213).

On a more mundane note, the complex also holds free public toilets.

Mercat de la Boqueria

La Rambla 91 • Mon–Sat 8am–8.30pm • ⓦ boqueria.info • Ⓜ Liceu

Barcelona's glorious main **food market**, officially the Mercat de Sant Josep but invariably known as **La Boqueria**, stands immediately west of La Rambla, at the point where a sudden profusion of flower stalls marked the switch to **Rambla Sant Josep** (also known as Rambla de les Flors).

Established outside the city's medieval walls in the thirteenth century, as a spot where farmers could bring produce fresh from the fields, La Boqueria can claim to be the most irresistibly appetizing market in Spain. Today's cavernous hall was erected on the site of a former convent between 1836 and 1840. A riot of noise and colour, it's as popular with locals as with snap-happy tourists. Everything radiates out from the central fish and seafood stalls – bunches of herbs, pots of spices, baskets of wild mushrooms, mounds of cheese and sausage, racks of bread, hanging hams and overloaded meat counters.

Many visitors get waylaid near the entrance by the eye-candy fruit trays and squeezed juices, but the flagship fruit and veg stalls here are pricey. It's better value further in, and also in the small outdoor square just beyond the north side of the market where the local allotment-holders and market gardeners gather. Everyone has a favourite market stall, but don't miss Petras and its array of wild mushrooms (stall 867, at the back by the *Bar Central*) or Frutas y Verduras Jesús y Carmen, which is framed with colourful bundles of exotic chillies (stall 579). And of course, there are some excellent stand-up **tapas bars**.

Plaça de la Boqueria

Ⓜ Liceu

At the halfway point of La Rambla, **Plaça de la Boqueria**, a large round **mosaic by Joan Miró** is set in the middle of the pavement. Something of a symbol for the city, it's one of a number of public works in Barcelona by the artist, who was born just a couple of minutes' walk off La Rambla in the Barri Gòtic; a plaque marks the relevant building on Passatge del Crèdit, off C/Ferran.

Close by, at La Rambla 82, Josep Vilaseca's spectacular **Casa Bruno Quadros** – the lower floor of which is now a bank – was built in the 1890s to house an umbrella store. That explains its delightful facade, decorated with a green dragon and Oriental designs, and scattered with parasols.

On the other side of La Rambla, *modernista* flourishes on a lesser scale adorn the **Antiga Casa Figueras** (1902) at no. 83, an exuberant cascade of stained glass and mosaics that sports a corner relief of a female reaper. It's now home to the renowned bakery-café *Escribà* (see page 182).

Gran Teatre del Liceu

La Rambla 51–59 • See website for current tour schedule • Charge • ⓦ liceubarcelona.cat • Ⓜ Liceu

Barcelona's celebrated opera house, the **Gran Teatre del Liceu**, was founded as a private theatre in 1847. It was rebuilt after a fire in 1861 to become Spain's grandest theatre, regarded as a bastion of the city's late nineteenth-century commercial and intellectual classes – in a nod to its bourgeois antecedents, it still has no royal box. The Liceu

1

GEORGE ORWELL IN BARCELONA

Barcelona is a town with a long history of street-fighting.

Homage to Catalonia, 1938

When he first arrived in Barcelona in December 1936, English journalist **George Orwell** was much taken with the egalitarian spirit that he encountered. Loudspeakers on La Rambla bellowed revolutionary songs, café waiters refused tips, brothels were collectivized and buildings were draped in anarchist flags.

After serving as a militiaman on the Aragonese front, Orwell returned on leave to Barcelona in April 1937 to find that everything had changed. Not only had the city lost its revolutionary zeal, but the various leftist parties fighting for the Republican cause had descended into a "miserable internecine scrap". From the **Hotel Continental** (La Rambla 138), where Orwell and his wife Eileen stayed, he observed the deteriorating situation with mounting despair. When street-fighting broke out in May, Orwell was directly caught up in it. As a member of the Workers' Party of Marxist Unification (POUM), Orwell became a target when pro-Communist Assault Guards seized the city telephone exchange near Plaça de Catalunya and set about breaking up the workers' militias. Orwell left the hotel for the **POUM headquarters** (La Rambla 128) just down the street, sited in the building that's now the *Rivoli Ramblas* hotel – a plaque here by the "Banco Popular" sign honours murdered POUM leader Andrés Nin ("victim of Stalinism"). With the trams on La Rambla abandoned by their drivers as the shooting started, and Assault Guards occupying the adjacent **Café Moka** (La Rambla 126), Orwell holed up with a rifle for three days in the rotunda of the **Teatre Poliorama** (La Rambla 115) opposite, in order to defend the POUM HQ if necessary. Breakfasting sparsely on goat's cheese bought from the Boqueria market (its stalls largely empty), concerned about Eileen and caught up in rumour and counter-rumour, Orwell considered it one of the most unbearable periods of his life.

When the fighting subsided, Orwell returned to the front, where he was shot through the throat by a fascist sniper. That was just the start of his troubles. Recuperating in a sanatorium near Tibidabo, he learned that the POUM had been declared illegal, its members rounded up and imprisoned. He avoided arrest by sleeping in gutted churches and derelict buildings and playing the part of a tourist by day, looking "as bourgeois as possible", while scrawling POUM graffiti in defiance on the walls of fancy restaurants. Eventually, with passports and papers arranged by the British consul, Orwell and Eileen escaped Barcelona by train – back to the "deep, deep sleep of England" and the writing of his passionate war memoir, *Homage to Catalonia*. His presence in the city is commemorated by the small Plaça George Orwell in the Barri Gòtic (see page 58).

was devastated again in 1893, when an anarchist, seeking revenge for the execution of a fellow anarchist assassin, threw two bombs into the stalls during a production of *William Tell*, killing twenty people. The theatre burned down for the third time in 1994, when a worker's blowtorch set fire to the scenery during last-minute set alterations. Following a five-year restoration of its lavishly decorated interior, the Liceu reopened in 1999.

The traditional meeting place for post-performance refreshments for audience and performers alike, the famous **Cafè de l'Òpera** (see page 182) stands just across La Rambla.

Liceu tours

Regular **tours** depart from the Liceu's main entrance and conclude in the modern extension, the **Espai Liceu**, which also houses a music and gift shop and café. Check at the ticket office or consult the website for the current schedule, which varies seasonally, and for the timing of tours in English. Highlights include the classically inspired **Saló dels Miralls** (Salon of Mirrors), unaffected by any of the fires and thus largely original in decor, and the impressive gilded **auditorium**, which contains 2,300 seats and makes this one of the world's largest opera houses.

You'll learn more on one of the more expensive 45-minute tours, which also visit the **Cercle del Liceu**, the opera house's private members' club. The burnished rooms here feature tiled floors and painted ceilings, and culminate in an extraordinary *modernista* games room, illuminated by a celebrated series of paintings by Ramon Casas representing Catalan music and dance. For most of its history, membership of the Cercle was restricted to men, until **Montserrat Caballé** – Spain's greatest soprano, born in Barcelona in 1933 – won a court battle to become one of the first women to join.

Teatre Principal and around

Ⓜ Drassanes

Historically a theatre and red-light district, the bottom stretch of La Rambla, the **Rambla de Santa Mònica**, still has a rough edge or two. Across from the **Teatre Principal** a statue of **Frederic Soler** (1839–95) – shown seated, with one leg casually crossed over the other – commemorates the playwright, impresario and founder of modern Catalan theatre, better known as Serafí Pitarra.

Back across La Rambla, street-walkers and theatre-goers alike drink stand-up shots and coffee at **La Cazalla** (La Rambla 25), a famous hole-in-the-wall bar (really just a street counter), just off the street beneath the arch at the start of C/Arc del Teatre, that's straight out of sleaze-era central casting.

Arts Santa Mònica

La Rambla 7 • Tues–Sun 11am–8.30pm • Free • Ⓦ artssantamonica.cat • Ⓜ Drassanes

The Augustinian **convent of Santa Mònica** dates from 1636, making it the oldest building on La Rambla. Remodelled in the 1980s, and given an extensive glass facade, it's now a contemporary **arts centre**, hosting changing exhibitions in its grand, echoing galleries – there's usually something worth seeing, from an offbeat art installation to a show of archive photographs.

In season, pavement artists, caricaturists and palm readers set up stalls outside the centre on La Rambla, and they're augmented on weekend afternoons by a **street market** selling jewellery, beads, bags and ornaments.

UNDER THE ARCH AND INTO THE SHADOWS

One early summer morning in 1945, 10-year-old Daniel Sempere and his father walk under the arch of C/Arc del Teatre, "entering a vault of blue haze … until the glimmer of La Rambla faded behind us". And behind a carved wooden door, Daniel is shown for the first time the "Cemetery of Forgotten Books", where he picks out an obscure book that will change his life.

So begins Carlos Ruiz Zafón's mega-successful novel **Shadow of the Wind**, a gripping mystery set in postwar Barcelona that uses the old town to great atmospheric effect. With copy in hand you can trace Daniel's early progress, from the street where he lives (C/Santa Anna) to the house of the beautiful, blind Clara Barceló on Plaça Reial, as well as a score of other easily identifiable locations across the city, from the cathedral to Tibidabo. Make sure, though, to keep a wary eye out for a pursuing stranger with "a mask of black scarred skin, consumed by fire".

1 Museu de Cera

La Rambla 4–6, entrance on Ptge. de Banca • July–Sept daily 10am–10pm; Oct–June Mon–Thurs 10am–8pm, Fri & Sat 10am–9pm • Charge • Ⓦ museocerabcn.com • Ⓜ Drassanes

Housed in an impressive nineteenth-century bank building at the foot of La Rambla, Barcelona's wax museum, the **Museu de Cera**, is no Madame Tussaud's – it's something stranger and more unsettling than that, and in its own way it's rather wonderful.

In recent years, an effort has been made to replace dusty old politicians and historical figures with current celebrities, singers and actors. Pose next to the Beatles as they sit side by side, or gaze into the eyes of Billie Eilish or Leonardo de Caprio. Whole rooms are given over to Star Wars or to Spanish TV show Money Heist. Some of the old characters remain: climb the marble stairs, echoing with doomy music, to encounter a bullfighter's deathbed scene, and the whole thing culminates in a delirious succession of cheesy underwater tunnels, space capsules and a deeply unpleasant "Terror" room. Before you leave, though, don't miss the museum's extraordinary neighbouring grotto-bar, the **Bosc de les Fades** (see page 196).

Barri Gòtic

Spreading east from La Rambla, the Barri Gòtic, or Gothic Quarter, forms the very heart of the old town. Its buildings date principally from the fourteenth and fifteenth centuries, the era when Barcelona reached the height of medieval commercial prosperity, and culminate in the extraordinary Gothic cathedral, La Seu. It takes the best part of a day to see everything; highlights include the Roman remains at the Museu d'Història de Barcelona, the Gaudí Exhibition Center in the Museu Diocesà and the collections of the Museu Frederic Marès. Other quirks and diversions range from exploring the old Jewish quarter to touring the grand salons of the Ajuntament. That said, sauntering through the narrow alleys, shopping for antiques, tracing the long-lost Roman walls, or simply sitting at a café in one of the lovely squares is every bit as enjoyable.

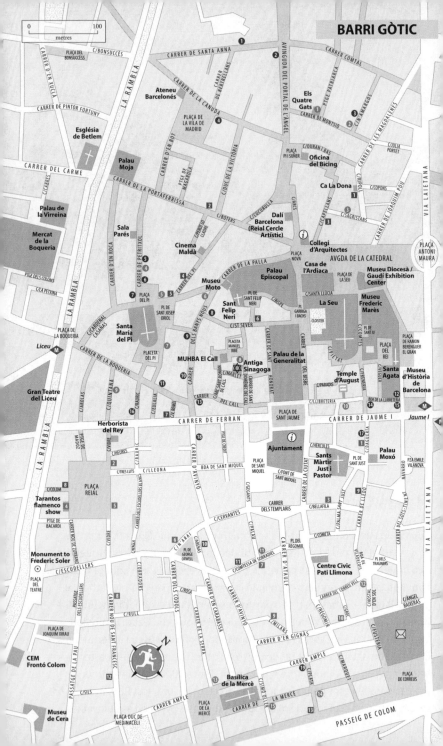

BARRI GÒTIC

0 ——————— 100
metres

The picture-postcard images of the Barri Gòtic are largely based on the streets north of C/Ferran and C/Jaume I, where tourists throng the boutiques, bars, restaurants, museums and galleries. Even here, the district is not entirely preserved and prettified, and the occasional modern block sticks out unapologetically amid the medieval splendours. Further south, from Plaça Reial and C/Avinyó to the harbour, the Barri Gòtic is less gentrified and sometimes just plain run-down. This district may lack specific sights or museums, but it does hold great shops, cafés, tapas bars and restaurants – just watch out for unsavoury characters who may be lurking in the poorly lit streets at night.

2

La Seu

Pl. de la Seu • Mon–Fri 9.30am–6.30pm, Sat 9.30am–5.15pm, Sun 2–5pm • Charge • ⓦ catedralbcn.org • ⓜ Jaume I

Barcelona's mighty cathedral, **La Seu**, whose high, intricate facade and soaring towers dominate the core of the Barri Gòtic, ranks among the great Gothic buildings of Spain. Located on a site previously occupied by a Roman temple and then an early Christian basilica, it was begun in 1298 and finished in 1448, save for the neo-Gothic main facade, added in the 1880s.

The cathedral is dedicated to the city's second patroness, **Santa Eulàlia** (known as Laia in Barcelona), a young girl brutally martyred by the Romans in 304 AD for daring to prefer Christianity. Her remains were initially placed in the original harbourside church of Santa María del Mar in La Ribera, which explains why she's also patron saint of local sailors and seafarers. In 874 Laia was reinterred in the basilica, and her remains later placed in an ornate alabaster tomb that rests in a crypt beneath the high altar.

The cathedral interior

The admission charge includes entry to all sections, including the beautifully carved choir, the cloister, the **museum**, filled with glittering church treasure, the roof terrace and various chapels not otherwise open to the public.

Beyond the ornate fifteenth-century **choir**, sealed off in the centre of the nave, which confronts you the moment you enter the church, all eyes are drawn to the raised altar. Broad steps descend in front of it to the gated **crypt** that contains the venerated **tomb of Santa Eulàlia**. The marble tomb itself (1327–29) is always visible through the grating, while on Laia's saint's day, February 12, the crypt is thrown open for visits and a choir sings in her honour.

La Seu is also known for the richness of its 29 **side-chapels**, which contain splendidly carved, painted and gilded tombs. Halfway up the wall east of the altar, look for the curious wooden caskets that supposedly belong to Ramon Berenguer I (count of

◼ ACCOMMODATION					
Hostal Fernando	7	Hotel Neri	6		
Hostal Rembrandt	2	Hotel Racó del Pi	4		
Hotel Arai	10	Itaca Hostel	1		
Hotel Barcelona Catedral	3	Mercer Hotel	9		
Hotel Cantón	12	Pensió Alamar	11		
Hotel DO	8	Serras Hotel	13		
Hotel El Jardí	5				

◼ DRINKING AND NIGHTLIFE					
L'Ascensor	3	Milk	10		
Harlem Jazz Club	7	Oviso	6		
Jamboree	4	Sidecar	2		
Karma	5	Zim	1		
La Macarena	8				
Milans Cocktail Bar	9				

● EATING				
Bar Celta Pulpería	15	Els Quatre Gats	1	
Bar del Pi	5	El Salón	12	
Bidasoa	13	Rasoterra	11	
Bodega La Plata	14	Shunka	3	
Caelum	6	La Sosenga	2	
Can Culleretes	9	Taller de Tapas	7	
Dulcinea	4	La Viñatería del Call	8	
Mesón del Café	10			

● SHOPPING				
Almacenes del Pilar	11	Ganivetería Roca	6
Alonso	1	Germanes Garcia	9
L'Arca	8	El Ingenio	16
Casa Carot	17	Espai Quera	5
Centre Artesania Catalunya	10	La Manual Alpargatera	18
Cereria Subirà	12	Marionetas Travi	3
La Colmena	15	Obach Sombrería	13
El Corte Inglés	2	Papabubble	19
Custo Barcelona	7	Papirum	14
Decathlon	4		

2

BOHO BARCELONA AND THE FOUR CATS

There may not be much to see these days in the shopping zone north of the cathedral, but just over a century ago a tavern called **Els Quatre Gats** (The Four Cats; C/Montsió 3, ⓦ 4gats. com) burned brightly and briefly as the epicentre of Barcelona's bohemian in-crowd. Opened by Pere Romeu and other *modernista* artists in 1897, the building itself is gloriously decorated inside and out in exuberant Catalan Art Nouveau style – this was architect Josep Puig i Cadafalch's first commission.

Els Quatre Gats soon thrived as the birthplace of *modernista* magazines, and the venue for poetry readings, shadow-puppet theatre and cultural debate. A young Picasso designed the menu and, in 1900, the café provided the setting for his first public exhibition. *Els Quatre Gats* has always traded on its reputation – a place where "accountants, dreamers and would-be geniuses shared tables with the spectres of Pablo Picasso, Isaac Albéniz, Federico García Lorca and Salvador Dalí" (*The Shadow of the Wind*, Carlos Ruiz Zafón). Today, a modern restoration displays something of its former glory, and the – frankly overpriced – bar-restaurant is watched over by a copy of Ramon Casas' famous wall painting of himself and Pere Romeu on a tandem bicycle (the original is in MNAC).

Barcelona from 1035 to 1076) and his wife Almodis; in fact, they hold the remains of an earlier count and Petronila, the Aragonese princess whose betrothal to Ramon Berenguer IV united the crowns of Aragón and Barcelona.

Ride the elevator up to the **roof terrace**, or *terrats*, and you're rewarded with intimate views of the cathedral towers and surrounding Gothic buildings and spires. It's by no means the highest vantage point in town, but nowhere else do you feel so at the heart of medieval Barcelona.

The cloister

The cathedral's magnificent fourteenth-century **cloister**, entered directly from Plaça de Garriga i Bachs on its western side, looks over a lush tropical garden complete with soaring palm trees and – more unusually – a gaggle of plump, honking **geese**. If they disturb the tranquillity of the scene, they do so for a purpose. White geese have been kept here for over five hundred years, either, depending on which story you believe, to reflect the virginity of Santa Eulàlia, or as a reminder of the erstwhile Roman splendour of Barcelona, as geese were kept on the Capitoline Hill in Rome.

Plaça de la Seu

Ⓜ Jaume I

The square immediately in front of the cathedral, **Plaça de la Seu**, is flanked by tourist cafés and generally awash with a milling crowd. Take a moment to stand back and look at the cathedral buildings, and it's still easy to pick out the line of fortified Roman towers that stood here until they were incorporated into the medieval fabric.

Plaça de la Seu is a regular weekly venue for the dancing of the *sardana*, the Catalan national dance (usually Sun at noon, plus Easter–Nov every Sat at 6pm) – anyone can join in, though it's not as simple as it looks (see box, page 204). Meanwhile, in front of the cathedral, the wide, pedestrianized Avinguda de la Catedral hosts an **antiques market** every Thursday, and a **Christmas craft fair**.

Museu Diocesà / Gaudí Exhibition Center

Pl. de la Seu 7 • Daily: March–Oct 10am–8pm; Nov–Feb 10am–6pm • Charge • ⓦ museudiocesa.esglesia.barcelona • Ⓜ Jaume I

The ancient tower immediately to the left (east) of the cathedral's main facade, which once formed part of its almshouse (La Pia Almoina), has long been home to the **Museu Diocesà**. Following a recent overhaul, however, the museum is now almost entirely devoted to celebrating the life, works and spirituality of Antoni Gaudí, and brands itself the **Gaudí Exhibition Center**. Even those ecclesiastical treasures that it continues to display are now cast in terms of their influence on Gaudí.

In many ways it has become the Gaudí museum that Barcelona needed, providing a readily accessible overview of the architect's inspirations and achievements before you visit his actual creations. As well as items he owned, ranging from his wooden workbench and tools to his personal copy of Jacint Verdaguer's Catalan epic *L'Atlàntida*, it displays photos, newspapers and black and white footage of Barcelona a century ago. Successive galleries upstairs explain and illustrate each of Gaudí's "Masterpieces", culminating of course with the Sagrada Família. As if that weren't enough, you can also buy a squeaky Gaudí toy.

2

Casa de l'Ardiaca and Palau Episcopal

Two late medieval buildings closely associated with the cathedral stand on its right, western, flank. The **Casa de l'Ardiaca**, originally the archdeacon's residence, encloses a tiny cloistered and tiled courtyard with a small fountain. Entered via C/Santa Llúcia, it's now used for small-scale temporary exhibitions of local interest, and also holds the city archives, which are not open to visitors. Look for the curious carved swallow-and-tortoise postbox to the right of its badly worn Renaissance gateway.

The **Palau Episcopal**, just beyond at the western end of C/Santa Llúcia, was the bishop's palace and built on a grander scale altogether. Visitors are not allowed inside, but you can go as far as the entrance to see the fine outdoor stairway; there's a patio at the top with Romanesque wall paintings.

Plaça Nova

Ⓜ Jaume I

Plaça Nova, which is effectively the western portion of the main cathedral square, marks one of the medieval entrances to the old town – head north from here, and you'll swiftly find yourself amid the wider streets and more regular contours of the modern city. Designed in 1960 from sketches supplied by Picasso, the frieze that surmounts the modern College of Architects, the **Col·legi d'Arquitectes**, on its northern side has a crude, almost graffiti-like quality. Picasso refused to come to Spain to oversee the work, unwilling to return to his home country so long as Franco remained in power.

Museu Frederic Marès

Museu Frederic Marès Pl. de Sant Iu 5–6, off C/Comtes • Tues–Sat 10am–7pm, Sun & hols 11am–8pm • Charge • ☎ 932 563 500, Ⓦ museumares.bcn.cat • Ⓜ Jaume I

Occupying a wing of the old royal palace, and entered off C/Comtes on the cathedral's eastern side, the **Museu Frederic Marès** celebrates the diverse passions of sculptor, painter and restorer Frederic Marès (1893–1991). His beautifully presented collection of ancient and medieval sculpture does little to prepare visitors for Marès' true obsession – a kaleidoscopic array of curios and collectibles. In addition, the large arcaded courtyard, studded with orange trees, is one of the most romantic spots in the old town, and occasionally holds a pop-up café

2

CORPUS CHRISTI AND THE DANCING EGG

One of Barcelona's biggest annual religious festivals, **Corpus Christi** (late May/early June), is celebrated with the dancing of the *sardana*, parades of *gegants* (festival giants) and a big procession from the cathedral. It also incorporates a unique feature– the *l'ou com balla*, the **dancing egg**, which bubbles atop the water-jets of public fountains across the old town.

Although the origins of the tradition are obscure, it clearly makes sense to see an egg (or rather a hollowed-out, weighted eggshell), gaily dancing on spurts of water and surrounded by colourful flowers, as representing not only the Eucharist but rebirth, renewal and even a celebration of spring. The city council's festival programme lists where you can see this oddity for yourself – most old-town courtyard fountains put on a show, including those of La Seu and the Museu Marès.

Sculpture collection

Frederic Marès trained as a sculptor at Barcelona's La Llotja (School of Fine Arts) and became known for his monumental sculpture, including grand works now on display in Plaça de Catalunya. His later focus, however, was on the restoration of Catalunya's decaying medieval treasures, many of which are preserved in the galleries on the **ground** and **basement floors**.

Marès' personal collection of medieval sculpture includes a comprehensive and utterly transfixing series of polychrome wooden crucifixes showing the stylistic development of the form from the twelfth to the fifteenth century. Look out in particular for the *Appearance of Jesus to His Disciples*, by the Master of Cabestany, in room 2.

There are also antiquities, from Roman busts to Hellenistic terracotta lamps, while the large room downstairs celebrates the intricate craftsmanship of medieval masons in a stunning series of carved doorways, cloister fragments, sculpted capitals and alabaster tombs. Up on the **first floor**, intriguing Baroque and Mannerist pieces complete a remarkable ensemble.

Collector's Cabinet

The upper floors showcase Frederic Marès' extraordinary **Collector's Cabinet** (Gabinet del Col.leccionista). Convinced that "charming objects that lived their lives well loved" should not simply be thrown away, Marès gathered an astonishing array of everyday items during fifty years of travel.

Entire rooms are devoted to keys and locks, carved pipes snugly cradled in cases, cigarette cards and snuffboxes, fans, gloves and brooches, playing cards, draughtsmen's tools, walking sticks, Japanese *netsuke*, dolls' houses, toy theatres, old gramophones and archaic bicycles, to list just a sample of what's on show. Everything is so beautifully and harmoniously displayed that it's an absolute joy to spend an hour or so here.

In the **artist's library** on the second floor, Marès' own reclining nudes, penitent saints and bridling stags offer an insight into his more orthodox work.

Plaça del Rei

Ⓜ Jaume l

The harmonious enclosed square of **Plaça del Rei**, behind the cathedral apse, was once the courtyard of the palace of the counts of Barcelona, which later became the residence of the count-kings of Aragón. The palace buildings themselves are steeped in history, and include the romantic Renaissance Torre del Rei Martí, the main hall, known as the Saló del Tinell, and the fourteenth-century **Santa Agata chapel** – there's no public access to the tower, though there's a fine view of it from the square, while you can usually see inside both hall and chapel by visiting the Museu d'Història de Barcelona (see page 53).

It was in Plaça del Rei that Ferdinand and Isabella received Christopher Columbus on his triumphant return from the Americas in 1493. With the old-town streets packed, Columbus advanced in procession with the monarchs to the palace, where he presented the queen with exotic birds, sweet potatoes and six Haitians who were taken on board during his trip.

Museu d'Història de Barcelona (MUHBA)

Pl. del Rei, entrance on C/Veguer • Tues–Sat 10am–7pm, Sun 10am–8pm• Charge • ⓦ museuhistoria.bcn.cat • Ⓜ Jaume I

The excellent **Museu d'Història de Barcelona** (Barcelona History Museum) not only extends through the labyrinth of buildings that surround the Plaça del Rei – known as the "Conjunt Monumental" or monumental ensemble – but also, crucially, burrows beneath them to reveal the extensive remains of the Roman city of Barcino.

Descend in the lift (the floor indicator spins back to "12 BC"), and you're deposited on a network of underground metal walkways which have been laid over excavations that extend for 4000 square metres, and stretch under the streets as far as the cathedral.

EXPLORING ROMAN BARCELONA

What's now the Barri Gòtic was originally entirely enclosed by **Roman walls and towers**, dating from the fourth century AD. Most were pulled down during the nineteenth century, to create more space for the expanding city, but extensive traces of Roman **Barcino** survive. The complete circuit of walls can easily be followed on an hour-long stroll, and is readily discernible from such vantage points as the bell tower of the Església de Santa María del Pi. At ground level, brown information boards show the route at various points.

Outside the cathedral, in Plaça Nova, metal letters a metre high, spelling out the word "Barcino", stand in front of a restored tower and a reconstructed segment of the Roman **aqueduct**. More of the aqueduct, set into the facade of a building, can be seen a short way north on C/Duran i Bas, while a large area of **Plaça de la Vila de Madrid** nearby has been excavated to reveal a row of sunken Roman tombs, known as the Via Sepulcral, slightly below the modern street level.

The line of the wall itself runs past the cathedral and the Museu Diocesà/Gaudí Exhibition Center, with the next surviving section visible at **Plaça de Ramon Berenguer el Gran** (at Via Laietana). Some of the walls and towers here stand over 13m high, and back onto the Capella de Santa Agata on Plaça del Rei. There's more wall to see if you cross C/Jaume I and walk down **C/Sots-Tinent Navarro**, while the most romantic section is the truncated Roman tower in the sunken **Plaça dels Traginers**, planted with a solitary olive tree. Along nearby **C/Correu Vell**, part of the wall and defence towers were incorporated into a medieval palace – this section is visible in the courtyard of a civic centre (through a gate, opposite C/Groc).

A right turn after here, up C/Regomir, leads to the **Centre Cívic Pati Llimona**, constructed on top of the remains of a gate that led through the Roman wall into inner Barcino. Assorted ancient stones can be seen through a glass window from C/Regomir, and you can wander inside for a closer look (usually Mon–Sat 10am–10pm; free).

Next, head up C/Ciutat and cross Plaça de Sant Jaume to reach the **Temple d'August**, where four impressive **Roman columns** and the architrave of a temple make an incongruous spectacle, tucked away in the green-painted interior courtyard of the **Centre Excursionista de Catalunya** (C/Paradís 10; Mon 10am–2pm, Tues–Sat 10am–7pm, Sun 10am–8pm, hols 10am–3pm; free).

From here it's just a short walk back to the cathedral, though no Roman enthusiast should miss the nearby **Museu d'Història de Barcelona**, where the underground excavations have left several of Barcino's ancient structures exposed to the eyes of visitors.

The archeological remains range from the first century BC up to the sixth century AD. Little now stands above chest height, so you'd struggle to know what you were looking at without the audio-guide and display panels, but they reflect the transition from Roman to Visigothic rule and beyond. Thus an almost complete factory where the Romans once manufactured the fish sauce *garum* was topped by a Christian church at the end of the sixth century, itself later replaced by the Episcopal Palace. Huge ceramic jars, half-embedded in the earth, mark the site of an ancient cellar from which wine was shipped all over the Mediterranean.

While the displays on the upper levels inevitably lack the visceral impact of actually seeing the ancient city laid out at your feet, they do illuminate Barcelona's subsequent history, including its spell as a Muslim city under the caliphate of Damascus, and explore its medieval growth as a major trading port. The complex also incorporates the beautiful **Capella de Santa Agata** (also known as the Capella Palatina) and the impressive **Saló del Tinell**, in which temporary exhibitions may incur an extra admission charge. A fine example of secular Gothic architecture, with interior arches that span 17m, the Saló del Tinell was the seat of the Catalan parliament from 1370 onwards, and was also where Christopher Columbus delivered his report to Ferdinand and Isabella in 1493. Later on, the Spanish Inquisition met here, taking advantage of the popular belief that the walls of the hall would move if a lie was spoken.

Església de Santa María del Pi and around

Ⓜ Liceu

With the cathedral area and Plaça del Rei sucking in every visitor at some point during the day, the third focus of attraction in the Barri Gòtic is to the west, around the church of **Santa María del Pi** – five minutes' walk from the cathedral or just two minutes off La Rambla.

Església de Santa María del Pi

Pl. Sant Josep Oriol • Mon–Sat 10am–6pm, tower tours Mon–Sat 11am, 12.30pm, 2pm, 3.30pm, 4.45pm • Charge • Ⓦ basilicadelpi.com • Ⓜ Liceu

The **Església de Santa María del Pi** stands at the intersection of three delightful little squares. Originally dating from the eleventh century – hence its Romanesque door – it was rebuilt three hundred years later at much the same time as Santa María del Mar (see page 75), in a similarly homogeneous Catalan-Gothic style. Anti-clerical activists set the place alight in July 1936, during the Civil War, but it was restored in the 1960s. It essentially consists of a single enormous nave, with small side chapels – one of which is dedicated to St Pancras – set between the buttresses. The overall plainness of its interior only serves to set off some marvellous **stained glass**, at its most impressive in a 10m-wide rose window.

Daily **guided tours** lead visitors up the 260 steps of the church's octagonal **bell tower**, which doubled in the Middle Ages as a watchtower and defensive refuge. The long steep climb up a series of ever-narrowing spiral staircases is rewarded at the very top – above the bells – with magnificent views over the Barri Gòtic and beyond, although the Sagrada Família remains for the moment obscured behind intervening buildings.

Plaça Sant Josep Oriol and around

The Santa María del Pi church flanks **Plaça Sant Josep Oriol**, the prettiest of the three adjacent squares, which makes an ideal spot to take an outdoor coffee, listen to buskers or browse the weekend **artists' market** (Sat 11am–8pm, Sun 11am–2pm). The statue

JEWISH BARCELONA

Barcelona was home to a Jewish population well before the ninth century, while a specifically Jewish district was documented in the city by the eleventh. Later, as elsewhere in Spain, Barcelona's **medieval Jewish quarter** lay nestled in the shadow of the cathedral, under the careful scrutiny of the Church. During the thirteenth and early fourteenth centuries, some of the realm's greatest and most powerful administrators, tax collectors and ambassadors hailed from here, but reactionary trends sparked persecution and led to the community being sealed off in these narrow, dark alleys. Nevertheless, a prosperous settlement persisted until the pogrom and forced conversion of 1391 and exile of 1492 (see box, page 238).

These days little except the street name and the synagogue survive as reminders of the Jewish presence – after their expulsion, most of the buildings used by the Jews were torn down and used for construction elsewhere in the city. With the demise of the Franco regime, a small community was again established in Barcelona, and recent years have seen a revival in interest in Barcelona's Jewish heritage. As well as the synagogue, the sites of the butcher's, baker's, fishmonger's and Jewish baths have all been identified. The Jewish cemetery was located over on the eastern side of Montjuïc – according to some, the name means "Jewish Mountain" – where the castle now displays around thirty tombstones that were recovered in the early twentieth century.

2

here is of Àngel Guimerà, nineteenth-century Catalan playwright and poet, who had a house on the square.

Meanwhile, off Plaça Sant Josep Oriol, the old town's **antiques trade** is concentrated in shiny galleries and stores along C/Palla and C/Banys Nous.

Plaça del Pi and Carrer de Petritxol

The church of Santa María del Pi is named – like the squares on either side, **Plaça del Pi** and Placeta del Pi – after the pine trees that once stood here (a solitary specimen still stands in Plaça del Pi). A **farmers' market** spills across Plaça del Pi on the first and third Friday, Saturday and Sunday of each month, while the characteristic cafés of narrow **Carrer de Petritxol** (off Plaça del Pi) are the places to head to for a cup of hot chocolate – *Dulcinea* at no. 2 is the traditional choice – and a browse around the street's commercial art galleries. The most famous is at C/Petritxol 5, where the **Sala Parés** was already well established when Picasso and Miró were young.

Plaça Sant Felip Neri

Ⓜ Liceu

In the narrow streets close to the cathedral, behind the Palau Episcopal, it's a pleasure to stumble upon the pretty little **Plaça Sant Felip Neri**, scarred by Civil War bombing and now a school playground. Antoni Gaudí would walk to this charming square every evening after work at the Sagrada Família to hear Mass at the eighteenth-century **Església de Sant Felip Neri**. Many of the buildings that now surround it were brought here from other parts of the city. In summer you can eat outside at candlelit tables, set out by the restaurant of the boutique *Hotel Neri* (see page 173).

El Call Major and the Antiga Sinagoga

What was once the medieval **Jewish quarter** of Barcelona lies south of Plaça Sant Felip Neri, centred on C/Sant Domènec del Call. The city authorities have erected plaques to mark points of interest in what's known as **El Call Major** (*Call* being the Catalan word for a narrow passage).

Antiga Sinagoga

C/Marlet 5, corner with C/Sant Domènec del Call • Mon–Fri 10.30am–6.30pm, Sun 10.30am–3pm • Charge • ⓦ sinagogamayor.com • ⓜ Liceu

The most notable surviving landmark of the Jewish quarter is the main synagogue, the **Antiga Sinagoga**. There was a synagogue here, on the edge of the Roman forum, from the third century AD until the pogrom of 1391. Even after that, though, the building survived in various guises – the sunken dye vats from a family business of fifteenth-century New Christian (forcibly converted Jews) dyers are still visible, alongside some original Roman walling. Not many people stop by; if you do, you'll get a personalized tour of the small room, courtesy of a member of the local Jewish community.

MUHBA El Call

Pl. Manuel Ribé • Wed 11am–2pm, Sat & Sun 11am–3pm & 4–7pm • Charge • ⓦ museuhistoria.bcn.cat • ⓜ Liceu

Apart from the Antiga Sinagoga, most of Barcelona's Jewish buildings have long since vanished. Behind a modern facade in Plaçeta Manuel Ribé, however, a house that originally belonged to a veil-maker now serves as a small museum, **MUHBA El Call**. Inside, wordy educational displays (translated into English), along with a handful of artefacts, shed light on the city's fascinating Jewish heritage. Rooms upstairs celebrate medieval luminaries such as astronomer Abraham bar Hiyyah (1065–1137) and rabbi Solomon ben Adret (1235–1310).

Plaça de Sant Jaume

ⓜ Jaume I

The spacious **Plaça de Sant Jaume**, at the end of the main C/Ferran, marks the very centre of the Barri Gòtic. Once the site of Barcelona's Roman forum and marketplace, it's now at the heart of city and regional government, containing two of Barcelona's most significant buildings, the **Ajuntament**, or City Hall, and the **Palau de la Generalitat**. Whistle-happy local police try to keep things moving in the *plaça*, while taxis and bike-tour groups weave between the pedestrians. The square is also the time-honoured site of demonstrations and festivals.

Ajuntament de Barcelona

Pl. de Sant Jaume • Public admitted Sun 10am–1pm, entrance on C/Font de Sant Miquel • Free • ⓦ ajuntament.barcelona.cat • ⓜ Jaume I

Although parts of Barcelona's City Hall, the **Ajuntament** on the south side of Plaça de Sant Jaume (also known as Casa de la Ciutat), date from as early as 1373, its Neoclassical facade was added when the square was laid out in the nineteenth century. You can get a much better idea of the grandeur of the original structure by nipping around the corner, to see its previous main entrance on C/Ciutat. It's a typically exuberant Catalan-Gothic facade, but was badly damaged during the nineteenth-century renovations.

Visitors are allowed into the building on Sundays, to take a self-guided tour around its rather splendid marble halls, galleries and staircases – an English-language leaflet is provided. There are also guided tours in English at 11am. The highlights are the magnificent, restored fourteenth-century council chamber, the **Saló de Cent**, and the dramatic historical murals by Josep María Sert in the **Saló de les Cròniques** (Hall of Chronicles), while the ground-floor courtyard features sculptural works by celebrated Catalan artists.

Palau de la Generalitat

Pl. de Sant Jaume, entrance on C/Sant Honorat • 1hr tours on second Sunday of the month (except Aug), 10am; online bookings essential; public also admitted without reservation on April 23, Sept 11 & Sept 24 10am–6pm • Free, ID required • Ⓦ presidencia.gencat.cat/es/ ambits_d_actuacio/palau-de-la-generalitat • Ⓜ Jaume I

It was from the **Palau de la Generalitat**, the traditional home of the Catalan government opposite the Ajuntament, that the short-lived Catalan Republic was proclaimed in April 1931. The oldest part of the building is the fifteenth-century facade on C/Bisbe, which sports a spirited medallion portraying St George and the Dragon. A beautiful cloister with superb coffered ceilings is located on the first floor inside, opening off which are the chapel and salon of Sant Jordi (St George, patron saint of Catalunya as well as England) and an upper courtyard planted with orange trees and peppered with presidential busts.

Incidentally, the enclosed Gothic bridge across the narrow C/Bisbe – the so-called **Bridge of Sighs** – is an anachronism, added in 1928, though it features on many a postcard of the "Gothic" quarter. It connects the Generalitat with the former canons' houses across the street, now used as the official residence of the president.

Aside from the guided tours on alternate weekends, the Generalitat is also open to the public on **Dia de Sant Jordi**, or Saint George's Day (April 23; expect a 2hr wait), as well as **Diada Nacional de Catalunya** (National Day; Sept 11) and **La Mercè** (Sept 24).

Plaça de Sant Just

Ⓜ Jaume I

East of the Ajuntament, down C/Hercules, **Plaça de Sant Just** is a handsome little corner of the old town, and a particularly nice spot for coffee on one of the bar terraces. The square also boasts a medieval **church** and restored fourteenth-century fountain, as well as a remarkable Baroque palace, the **Palau Moxó**, which sadly is no longer open to visitors.

Basílica dels Sants Màrtirs Just i Pastor

Pl. de Sant Just • Mon, Thurs–Sat 10am–8.30pm, Tues & Wed 10am–6pm, Sun 10am–1pm • Charge • Ⓦ basilicasantjust.cat • Ⓜ Jaume I

The very plain stone facade of the **Basílica dels Sants Màrtirs Just i Pastor**, whose name commemorates the city's earliest Christian martyrs, belies the rich stained glass and elaborate chapel decoration within. What claims to be the oldest parish church site in Barcelona is held to have first supported a foundation at the start of the ninth century; the restored interior, though, dates from the mid-fourteenth century.

Plaça Reial and around

Ⓜ Liceu

Of all the old-town squares, perhaps the least typical of Barcelona but these days the most popular with visitors is the grand, arcaded **Plaça Reial**, hidden behind an archway, just off La Rambla. Laid out in around 1850 in a deliberate echo of the great *places* of France, this elegant square is studded with tall palm trees and decorated iron lamps (made by the young Antoni Gaudí), bordered by high, pastel-coloured buildings, and centres on a fountain depicting the Three Graces. Taking in the sun at one of the benches puts you in the company of bikers, buskers, beggars and backpackers, not to mention more affluent tourists drinking a coffee at one of the pavement cafés. As recently as the 1980s, Plaça Reial used to have a reputation for violence and drug-dealing, but the unsavoury characters have largely been driven away, and nowadays predatory menu-toting waiters tend to be the biggest nuisance. The surrounding bars and restaurants are generally upmarket, but don't expect to see too many locals until night falls.

On Sunday morning Plaça Reial hosts a long-standing **coin and stamp market** (10am–2pm). Otherwise, the arcaded passageways connecting the square with the surrounding streets throw up a few interesting sights, like the quirky **Herborista del Rei** (C/Vidre; closed Mon), an early nineteenth-century herbalist's shop, which stocks more than 250 medicinal herbs that purport to combat any complaint you can imagine.

2

Carrer dels Escudellers and Plaça de George Orwell

The alleys on the south side of Plaça Reial emerge on C/Escudellers, where the turning spits of grilled chicken at **Los Caracoles** restaurant make a good photograph. **Carrer dels Escudellers** itself was once a thriving red-light street, and still has a late-night seediness about it, while teetering on the edge of respectability.

Bars and restaurants around here attract a youthful clientele, nowhere more so than those flanking **Plaça de George Orwell**, at the eastern end of C/Escudellers. Named in honour of the English writer in 1996, the wedge-shaped square was created by levelling an old-town block – a favoured tactic in Barcelona to let in a bit of light.

Carrer d'Avinyó

Ⓜ Liceu

Carrer d'Avinyó, running south from C/Ferran towards the harbour, cuts through the most atmospheric part of the southern Barri Gòtic. It used to be a red-light district of some renown, littered with brothels and bars, and frequented by the young Picasso, whose family moved into the area in 1895. It still looks the part – a narrow thoroughfare lined with dark overhanging buildings – but the cafés, streetwear shops and boutiques tell the story of its creeping gentrification. The locals aren't overly enamoured of the influx of bar-crawling fun-seekers – banners and notices along the length of this and neighbouring streets plead with visitors to keep the noise down.

La Mercè

Ⓜ Drassanes

During the eighteenth century, the harbourside neighbourhood known as **La Mercè** was home to the nobles and merchants enriched by Barcelona's maritime trade. After most took the opportunity to move north to the more fashionable Eixample later in the nineteenth century, the streets of La Mercè took on an earthier hue. Since then, C/Mercè and the surrounding streets (particularly Ample, d'en Gignas and Regomir) have been home to a series of old-style **taverns** known as *tascas* or *bodegas* – a glass of wine from the barrel in *Bodega la Plata*, or some similar joint, is one of the old town's more authentic experiences.

Basílica de la Mercè

Pl. de la Mercè • Mon, Tues, Thurs, Fri & Sun 10am–8pm, Wed & Sat 10am–1pm & 6–8pm; Guided tours Sun 1pm • Free, guided tours charge • Ⓦ basilicadelamerce.com • Ⓜ Drassanes

The eighteenth-century **Basílica de la Mercè** is the focus every September of the city's biggest annual celebration, the Festes de la Mercè. Dedicated to the co-patroness of Barcelona, the Virgin of Mercè, whose image is paraded from here, it's the excuse for a week of intense merrymaking, culminating in spectacular fireworks along the seafront. The church itself was burned out in 1936, but the gilt side-chapels, stained-glass medallions and apse murals have been restored, while the statue of Virgin and Child sits behind glass above the altar – a staircase allows you a closer look.

Palau Martorell

C/Ample 11 • Daily 10am–8pm • Ⓦ palaumartorell.com • Ⓜ Drassanes

This grand neoclassical building, sitting on the Plaça de Mercè, has opened to the public as an art museum. Its stated aim is to house temporary exhibitions by international artists, such as Alphonse Mucha, Basquiat, Alexander Calder and Tamara de Lempicka. The three-storeyed interior, lit by a vast stained-glass skylight, is worth a visit in its own right.

2

PALAU GÜELL ROOF

El Raval

Known as El Raval (from the Arabic word for "suburb"), the old-town area west of La Rambla has always formed a world apart from the nobler Barri Gòtic. Until the fourteenth century, it was primarily agricultural and responsible for growing the city's food. It then became the site of hospitals, churches, monasteries and various noxious trades, while later still it acquired a reputation as a major centre for prostitution and vice, known to all (for obscure reasons) as the Barri Xinès – China Town. El Raval has changed markedly, particularly in the "upper Raval" around Barcelona's contemporary art museum, MACBA. Now cutting-edge galleries, designer restaurants and fashionable bars are all part of the scene, while the "lower Raval" holds the neighbourhood's two other outstanding buildings, namely Gaudí's Palau Güell and the church of Sant Pau del Camp.

According to the Barcelona writer Manuel Vázquez Montalbán, El Raval once housed "theatrical homosexuals and anarcho-syndicalist, revolutionary meeting places; women's prisons … condom shops and brothels which smelled of liquor and groins." Even today in the backstreets between C/Sant Pau and C/Nou de la Rambla visitors may run the gauntlet of cat-calling prostitutes and petty drug dealers, while a handful of atmospheric old bars trade on their former reputations as bohemian hangouts.

Yet the combination of the Olympics and subsequent EU funding achieved what Franco never could, and cleaned up large parts of the neighbourhood almost overnight. North of C/Hospital, the development of the MACBA, the adjacent CCCB culture centre and new university faculty buildings saw entire city blocks demolished and remodelled. To the south, between C/Hospital and C/Sant Pau, former tenements and alleys were bulldozed away to allow an entire boulevard – the **Rambla del Raval** – to be gouged through, creating a huge pedestrianized area where none existed before, while the **Filmoteca de Catalunya** has polished away some of Plaça Salvador Seguí's grit.

At the same time the area's older, traditional residents have gradually been supplanted by more affluent incomers, and there's also been a growing influx of migrants from the Indian subcontinent and North Africa. Alongside the surviving spit-and-sawdust bars, and the recent crop of restaurants, galleries and boutiques, you'll find specialist grocery stores, curry houses, halal butchers and hole-in-the-wall phone and internet offices.

All that said, you'd hesitate to call El Raval gentrified; it clearly still has its rough edges. You needn't be unduly concerned during the day as you make your way around, but it's as well to keep your wits about you at night, particularly when wandering in the southernmost streets.

Museu d'Art Contemporani de Barcelona (MACBA)

Pl. dels Àngels 1 • Mon & Wed–Fri 11am–7.30pm, Sat 10am–8pm, Sun & hols 10am–3pm • Charge • Ⓦ macba.cat • Ⓜ Catalunya/Universitat

The iconic **Museu d'Art Contemporani de Barcelona**, which opened in 1995 and is universally known as the **MACBA**, anchors the upper reaches of El Raval. The contrast between this huge, white, almost luminous, structure and the buildings that surround it could hardly be starker. Its American architect, Richard Meier, set out to make as much use of natural light as possible, and to "create a dialogue" between the museum and its neighbours; this is reflected in the front of the building, constructed entirely of glass.

The open concrete **square** outside is usually filled with careering skateboarders by day; by night, unfortunately, it turns into a vast public urinal. On a more salubrious note, the western wall is adorned by a long AIDS-awareness **mural** painted by **Keith Haring** in 1989; this is a tracing, as the original, executed in Plaça de Salvador Seguí to the south, deteriorated beyond repair within ten years.

Once inside the museum, you ascend from the ground floor to the fourth up a series of swooping ramps that afford continuous views of the square below. While the **permanent collection** represents the main movements in contemporary art since 1945, focusing largely but not exclusively on Catalunya and Spain, only a small selection is on show at any one time, in changing themed exhibitions. There are always two or three other temporary exhibitions and installations as well, so, depending on when you visit, you may catch works by major names such as Joan Miró, Antoni Tàpies or Eduardo Chillida. Joan Brossa, leading light of the Catalan Dau al Set group of the late 1940s and 1950s, also has work here, as do contemporary multimedia and installation artists like Antoni Muntadas and Francesc Torres. A good museum **shop** sells everything from designer espresso cups to art books.

EL RAVAL

ACCOMMODATION	
Barceló Raval	6
Casa Camper	4
Hostal Centric	1
Hostal Grau	3
Hotel Curious	5
Hotel España	9
Hotel Onix Liceo	10
Hotel Peninsular	8
Hotel Sant Agustí	7
Market Hotel	2

Centre de Cultura Contemporània de Barcelona (CCCB)

Museu d'Art Contemporani de Barcelona (MACBA)

PL DE LES DONES

PLAÇA DE JOAN COROMINES

PLAÇA DELS ÀNGELS

PLAÇA DELS CARAMELLES

Reial Acadèmia de Medicina

Hospital de la Santa Creu

Jardins Dr Fleming

Miscelànea

Teatre Poliorama

Església de Betlem

Palau de la Virreina

Palau Moja

Renoir Floridablanca

Mercat de Sant Antoni

Café Teatre Llantiol

Universitat

Sant Antoni

PLAÇA DE CASTELLA

PLAÇA DE VICENÇ MARTORELL

PLAÇA DEL PEDRO

PLAÇA DEL DUBTE

CARRER DE PELAI

CARRER DELS TALLERS

CARRER DE LES RAMBLES

CARRER D'EN XUCLÀ

CARRER DEL CARME

CARRER DEL HOSPITAL

RONDA DE SANT ANTONI

RONDA DE SANT PAU

CARRER DE SEPÚLVEDA

CARRER DE FLORIDABLANCA

CARRER DE TAMARIT

CARRER DEL COMTE D'URGELL

CARRER DE VILLARROEL

CARRER DE JOAQUÍN COSTA

CARRER DE PEU DE LA CREU

CARRER DELS ÀNGELS

C/JOVELLANOS

C/VALLDONZELLA

CARRER DE MONTALEGRE

C/BONSUCCES

FORTUNY

C/SITGES

LA RAMBLA

FLORISTES DE LA RAMBLA

PIGE DE LA VIRREINA

C/CARBRES

RAMBLA DE LES FLORS

PIGE ELISABETS

C/NOTARIAT

C/ELISABETS

CARRER DEL DOCTOR DOU

CARRER DEL TIGRE

CARRER DE LA PALOMA

CARRER DEL LLEÓ

CARRER DE LA LLUNA

CARRER DE FERLANDINA

CARRER DE CARDONA

CARRER DE SANT VICENÇ

CARRER DE SANT GIL

CARRER DE LA RIERA ALTA

C/ERASME DE JANER

C/BISBE LAGUARDA

C/NOU DE LA DULCE

C/SANT JERONIM

PLAÇA DE VIANA

CARRER DE LA CENDRA

C/LLEBREGÒS

C/SANT ANTONI ABAT

CARRER DE SANT ANTONI ABAT

CARRER DELS SALVADOR

CARRER DE LA CERA

C/SANT CLIMENT

CARRER DE VISTALEGRE

CARRER DE L'HOSPITAL

M/AURÈLIA CAPMANY

C/RIERA BAIXA

C/PICALQUERS

CARRER D'EN ROIG

C/DE LES EGIPCÍAQUES

CARRER DE PEU DE LA CREU

CÉGUTÈRE

MONTJUÏC DEL CARME

CARRER DE PINTOR

CARRER D'EN XUCLÀ

PIGE ELISABETS

C/CANUDA

PL DE GOBO

GRAVINA

C/VALLDONZELLA

C/D'JOORES LAMAT

C/CASANOVA

C/PRINCEP DE VIANA

C/BOTELLA

C/ERASME

C/BOTELLA

Sala

PLAÇA DE LA

EATING

A Tu Bola	12
Bar Cañete	16
Biocenter	8
Ca l'Estevet	1
Café de les Delícies	13
Cera 23	11
Dos Palillos	5
Dos Pebrots	6
Elisabets	4
Federal	10
Fonda España	14
Frankie Gallo Cha Cha Cha	17
Granja M. Viader	9
Kasparo	3
Sésamo	7
Suculent	15
Teresa Carles	2

DRINKING & NIGHTLIFE

23 Robadors	8
Betty Ford's	2
Casa Almirall	4
La Concha	13
La Confitería	12
Fàbrica Moritz	1
La Llibertària	3
Marmalade	5
Marsella	11
Moog	14
Pesca Salada	7
Resclis	6

LGBTQ+ DRINKING

La Casa de la Pradera	9
Madame Jasmine	10

SHOPPING

La Central del Raval	7
Discos Paradiso	5
Fantàstik	2
Flamingos Vintage Kilo	3
Holala! Plaza	1
Museu d'Art Contemporani de Barcelona	4
Revólver Records	6
Teranyina	8
Wah Wah Discos	9

Map labels:

Casa Bruno Quadros
Antiga Casa Figueras
Café de l'Òpera
Gran Teatre del Liceu
Liceu
Palau Güell
Teatre Principal
Hotel España
Arts Santa Mònica
Sant Agustí
Teatre Romea
La Capella
Filmoteca
Plaça de Sant Agustí
Plaça de Salvador Seguí
Plaça de Vázquez Montalbán
Plaça de Josep Maria Folch i Torres
Plaça Reial
Plaça del Teatre
Església de Sant Pau del Camp
Mossos d'Esquadra (Police)
Jardins de les Voltes d'en Cires
Funicular de Montjuïc
Paral·lel

Streets:

C/MARQUES DE CAMPO SAGRADO
C/NOU DE SANT FRANCESC
CARRER DE FERRAN
C/QUINTANA
CARRER DE LA BOQUERIA
LA RAMBLA
CARRER DE LA UNIÓ
CARRER DE L'HOSPITAL
CARRER DE LA JUNTA DE COMERÇ
C/PENEDIDES
CARRER LANCASTER
CARRER DE GUARDIA
CARRER DE MONTSERRAT
CARRER DE L'EST
AVINGUDA DE LES DRASSANES
CARRER D'EN ROBADOR
CARRER DE SANT RAFAEL
C/SANT JOSEP ORIOL
CARRER DE SANT PAU
CARRER DE SANT OLEGUER
RAMBLA DEL RAVAL
CARRER DE LA RIERETA
CARRER DE SANT MARTI
CARRER DE SANT BARTOMEU
L'AURORA
CARRER DE SANT RAFAEL
C/SANT PACIÀ
C/SANTA ELENA
CARRER DE LES CARRETES
CARRER DE LA REINA AMÀLIA
CARRER DE SANT PAU
CARRER DE LES FLORS
CARRER DE L'OM
CARRER DE SANTA MADRONA
AVINGUDA DEL PARAL·LEL
C/L'HORT DE ST PAU
CARRER DE LES TÀPIES
CARRER DE VILA I VILA
CARRER DE CABANES
CARRER DE PIQUER
CARRER DEL ROSER
CARRER DE LA FONTRODONA
CARRER DE SADURNÍ
CARRER DE L'ARC DEL TEATRE
CARRER NOU DE LA RAMBLA
C/MARQUÉS DE BARBERÀ
PASSATGE DELS ESCUDELLERS
PTGE DE MADOZ
PTGE DE BACARDÍ

0 100 metres

Centre de Cultura Contemporània de Barcelona (CCCB)

C/Montalegre 5 • **CCCB** Tues–Sun 11am–8pm; **La Terracccita bar/restaurant** Mon–Fri 9am–9pm, Sat & Sun 10am–9.30pm • Charge • Ⓦ cccb.org • Ⓜ Catalunya/Universitat

As well as hosting excellent (and often challenging) art and city-related exhibitions ranging from photography to architecture, the **Centre de Cultura Contemporània de Barcelona**, adjoining the MACBA, supports a varied cinema, concert and festival programme. This imaginatively restored building is a prime example of the juxtaposition of old and new; originally built in 1714 on the site of an Augustinian convent, it was once an infamous workhouse and lunatic asylum. The main courtyard, now called the Plaça de les Dones, still retains its old tile panels and presiding statue of Sant Jordi, the patron saint of Catalunya.

The CCCB's **bar/restaurant**, *La Terracccita*, spreads across a sunny *terrassa* on the modern square that connects it to the MACBA.

Plaça de Vicenç Martorell

Ⓜ Catalunya

The Raval's nicest traffic-free square, the arcaded **Plaça de Vicenç Martorell**, lies just a few minutes' walk towards La Rambla from the MACBA. Tables in its first-rate café, the *Kasparo*, overlook a popular children's playground. Meanwhile, around the corner, the narrow Carrer del Bonsuccés, Carrer de les Sitges and Carrer dels Tallers house a concentrated selection of the city's best independent **music stores** and urban and streetwear shops.

Hospital de la Santa Creu

Entrances on C/Carme and C/Hospital • **Garden** Daily 8am–dusk • Free • **La Capella** C/Hospital 56 • Tues–Sat noon–8pm, Sun & hols 11am–2pm; temporary closures between each exhibition • Ⓦ lacapella.bcn.cat • Ⓜ Liceu

The most historic relic in El Raval, the **Hospital de la Santa Creu** occupies a large site between C/Carme and C/Hospital. This attractive complex of Gothic buildings was founded as the city's main hospital in 1402, a role that it assumed for over five hundred

---

HIGH SOCIETY AT THE HOTEL ESPAÑA

A hidden gem is tucked around the back of the Liceu opera house, on the otherwise fairly shabby C/Sant Pau. Here, in the lower reaches of El Raval, some of the most influential names in Catalan architecture and design came together at the start of the twentieth century to transform the **Hotel España** (C/Sant Pau 9–11, Ⓦ hotelespanya.com; Ⓜ Liceu) – built as a simple boarding house in 1860 – into one of the most lavish addresses in the city (see page 174).

With a wonderfully tiled dining room designed by Lluís Domènech i Montaner, a bar featuring an amazing marble fireplace by Eusebi Arnau, and a bathing area with glass roof (now the breakfast room) whose marine murals were executed by Ramon Casas, the hotel was the fashionable sensation of its day. Over a century later it's back in vogue, since a remarkable restoration has highlighted its classy *modernista* public spaces and brought the rooms up to scratch. Lunch or dinner here is a real in-the-know treat, with the original *modernista* dining room (known as the Fonda España) under the helm of Michelin-starred Basque chef Martín Berasategui, while the classy bar welcomes passing visitors.

years. Antoni Gaudí, knocked down by a tram in 1926, was brought here for treatment but died three days later.

After the hospital shifted to Domènech i Montaner's new creation in the Eixample in 1930 (see page 124), the spacious fifteenth-century wards were converted for cultural and educational use; they now hold the Royal Academy of Medicine, an art and design school and two libraries, including the Catalan national library, the Biblioteca de Catalunya.

Visitors can wander freely through a charming medieval cloistered **garden** (access from either street), while inside the C/Carme entrance (on the right) are some superb seventeenth-century decorative tiles of various religious scenes. There's also the hospital's former chapel, **La Capella** (entered separately from C/Hospital), an exhibition space for new contemporary artists.

Reial Acadèmia de Medicina

Hospital de la Santa Creu, C/Carme 47 entrance • Guided tours Wed & Sat 10.30am, 11.30am & 12.30pm; closed Aug • Charge • Ⓦ ramc.cat • Ⓜ Liceu

Behind the firmly locked door of the **Reial Acadèmia de Medicina** (Royal Academy of Medicine) – even on the few days it's open, you'll probably have to ring the bell to gain admittance – lies a remarkable eighteenth-century **anatomical theatre**. Guided tours lead visitors into the ornate and beautifully preserved circular chamber, where students would gather around the marble slab to observe the four-hour **dissections** of corpses that were often simply abandoned outside overnight. Up on the balcony, beneath the gilded cupola, four latticed screens enabled women visitors to watch proceedings without being seen.

The tours are conducted in Catalan or Spanish only – though the free audio-guide offers a much shorter English version – and dwell rather too long on the Academy grandees whose portraits hang in the "Hall of Presidents" upstairs. Much the most popular time to come is on Friday evening – reservations are essential – when the increased price includes a glass of cava and a short, entertaining **illusionist show**.

Rambla del Raval and around

Ⓜ Liceu

Perhaps the most obvious manifestation of the changed character of El Raval is the **Rambla del Raval**, a palm-lined boulevard driven through the heart of the district between C/Hospital and C/Sant Pau. The *rambla* has a distinct character that's all its own, mixing kebab joints and grocery stores with an ever-increasing number of fashionable cafés and bars. The signature building, halfway down, is the glowing, cylindrical tower of the **Barceló Raval hotel**, while children find it hard to resist a clamber on the massive, bulbous Botero cat sculpture. A weekend **street market** (selling anything from samosas to hammocks) adds a bit more character, while at the bottom end, off **Carrer de Sant Pau**, the *barri*'s remaining prostitutes accost passers-by heading towards La Rambla. The top end, by contrast, leads straight into the streets of the "upper Raval", flush with boutiques, bars and galleries.

HIDDEN GEMS: EL RAVAL

Weekend market on Rambla del Raval See page 65
Terrace of Palau Güell See page 66
Music shopping See page 228
Bar Cañete See page 184
Art shows at La Capella See page 208
Summer drinks on Barceló Raval's 360° Terrace See page 174

Carrer de la Riera Baixa

Just off the north end of Rambla del Raval, the narrow **Carrer de la Riera Baixa** is at the centre of the city's secondhand and vintage clothing scene. A dozen funky little independent clothes shops provide the scope for an hour's browsing, while the *Bar Resolis* (no. 22) makes the best place to take a break in between.

Plaça del Pedró and Carrer d'en Botella

In **Plaça del Pedró** (junction of C/Carme and C/Hospital) a cherished statue of Santa Eulàlia (co-patron of the city) stands on the site of her supposed crucifixion, facing the surviving apse of a Romanesque chapel. Carrer d'en Botella, just off the square, is unremarkable, save for the plaque at no. 11 that records the **birthplace of Manuel Vázquez Montalbán**, probably the city's most famous writer, whose likes and prejudices found expression in his favourite character, detective Pepe Carvalho (see box, page 66).

3

Filmoteca de Catalunya

Pl. de Salvador Seguí 1–9 • **Cinema** Tues–Fri 5–10pm, Sat & Sun 4.30–10pm • Charge • ⓦ filmoteca.cat • ⓜ Liceu

The 2012 opening of the Josep Lluís Mateo-designed **Filmoteca de Catalunya**, a colossus of concrete and glass in Plaça de Salvador Seguí (long known for its pickpockets and prostitutes), marked yet another step in the push to revitalize El Raval. As well as two below-ground cinemas, Sala Chomón and Sala Laya, the building holds a film library, a bookshop and spaces for cinema-related exhibitions. The thematic programming ranges across topics such as Tim Burton's monsters or the silent films of Fritz Lang, and children's movies are screened on Saturdays and Sundays. All films are shown in their original language, with Spanish or Catalan subtitles, and ticket prices are exceptionally low.

Palau Güell

C/Nou de la Rambla 3–5 • Tues–Sun & hols: April–Sept 10am–8pm; Oct–March 10am–5.30pm; English guided tour Sat 10am, no extra charge • Charge, includes audio-guide • ⓦ palauguell.cat • ⓜ Liceu

Between 1886 and 1890, the young **Antoni Gaudí** designed the extraordinary **Palau Güell** as a townhouse for the wealthy ship owner and industrialist **Eusebi Güell i**

SNOOPING AROUND THE RAVAL

Barcelona-born author, journalist, critic and poet, **Manuel Vázquez Montalbán** (1939–2003) was one of Spain's most popular writers. His shabby, fast-living fictional detective **Pepe Carvalho** – ex-Communist and CIA agent – investigated foul deeds in the city in a series of terrific novels that spanned thirty years.

By no accident, Montalbán's own passions – for Barcelona itself, and for politics, markets, cooking, food and drink – rubbed off on his detective, and Pepe Carvalho's cases took him around easily identifiable parts of the city, particularly the earthy streets of the Raval. With an office on La Rambla, the gourmand detective is often picking out groceries in the Boqueria market or grabbing a bite at *Pinotxo*, the classic stand-up market bar, while both Montalbán and Carvalho found their spiritual home in the *Casa Leopoldo* restaurant, sadly now closed forever, at C/Sant Rafael 24, off Rambla del Raval. The remodelled square nearby, by the *Barceló Raval* hotel, was re-named in honour of the author, while an annual crime fiction prize bears the name of his celebrated detective; winners include Henning Mankell, Ian Rankin and Donna Leon.

Bacigalupi. Commissioned as an extension of the Güell family's house on La Rambla, to which it's connected by a corridor, it was the first modern building to be declared a World Heritage Site by UNESCO. Restored, complete with remarkable roof terrace, to its original state, it's now one of Barcelona's major architectural showpieces.

Steered by a helpful audio-guide, visitors explore the astonishing edifice from top to bottom, at their own pace. At a time when architects sought to conceal the iron supports within buildings, Gaudí turned them to his advantage, displaying them as decorative features in the grand rooms on the **main floor**. Columns, arches and ceilings are all shaped, carved and twisted in an elaborate style that was to become the hallmark of Gaudí's later works. No expense was spared on the materials used, which ranged from dark marble hewn from the Güell family quarries to the opulent hardwoods seen in the coffered ceilings and marquetry floors. The vast **central hall** is topped with a parabolic dome pierced with holes to allow natural light, in emulation of the night sky, and echoes to a thunderous organ that's played throughout the day and also used for regular recitals.

Even the basement **stables** bear Gaudí's distinct touch, a forest of brick capitals and arches that, with a touch of imagination, become mushrooms and palms. Displays in the supremely light spaces of the attic trace the painstaking twenty-year restoration programme, while tours culminate on the spectacular **roof terrace**, adorned with a fantastical series of chimneys decorated with swirling patterns made from fragments of glazed tile, glass and earthenware. The family rarely ventured up here – it was the servants instead who were exposed to the fullest flight of Gaudí's fantasy as they hung the washing out on lines strung from chimney to chimney.

3

Església de Sant Pau del Camp

C/Sant Pau 101 • Mon–Sat 10am–6pm, Sun (guided tour only) 12.45pm • Charge • ☎ 934 410 001 • Ⓜ Paral·lel

Carrer de Sant Pau cuts west through El Raval to the church of **Sant Pau del Camp**, whose name – St Paul of the Field – is a graphic reminder that it once stood in open fields beyond the city walls. A Benedictine foundation of the tenth century, Sant Pau was constructed, on a Greek cross plan, after its predecessor was destroyed in a Muslim raid of 985 AD. It was renovated again at the end of the thirteenth century; the curious, primitive carvings of fish, birds and faces above the main entrance date from that period, while other animal forms adorn the twin capitals of the charming twelfth-century cloister. Inside, the church is dark and rather plain, enlivened only by tiny arrow-slit windows and small stained-glass circles high up in the central dome.

Mercat de Sant Antoni

C/Comte d'Urgell 1 • Mon–Sat 8am–8.30pm Ⓦ mercatdesantantoni.com • Ⓜ Sant Antoni

The stunning **Mercat de Sant Antoni** stands at the neighbourhood's western edge, where the Ronda de Sant Pau meets the Ronda de Sant Antoni. Built in 1876 with considerable input from the Catalan engineer Josep Cornet i Mas, a pioneer of using iron in construction, it became the major produce market for El Raval. Following extensive reconstruction and renovation that became delayed when archeologists unearthed medieval remains on the site, it reopened to the public in 2018.

A weekly **book and coin market** takes place around the perimeter of the market building (Sun 8.30am–2.30pm), with collectors and enthusiasts arriving early to pick through the best bargains.

THE PALAU DE LA MÚSICA CATALANA CONCERT HALL

Sant Pere, La Ribera and Ciutadella

The two easternmost old-town neighbourhoods of Sant Pere and La Ribera
sit one above the other, divided by Carrer de la Princesa. Both medieval in
origin, they are often thought of as a single district (the Born), but each has a
distinct character. Sant Pere – once the least visited part of the old town but
increasingly lively as gentrification takes hold – holds two remarkable buildings:
the *modernista* concert hall known as the Palau de la Música Catalana and the
stylishly designed market, the Mercat de Santa Caterina. By way of contrast,
the old artisans' quarter of La Ribera is always busy with tourists, due to the
hugely popular Museu Picasso, and the graceful church of Santa María del Mar.
If you fancy time out from the old town's labyrinthine alleys, you can retreat
to the city's favourite park, Parc de la Ciutadella, on La Ribera's eastern edge.

Both neighbourhoods have seen considerable regeneration in recent years, particularly Sant Pere, where new boulevards and community projects sit alongside DJ bars and designer shops. La Ribera's cramped, narrow streets, on the other hand, were at the heart of medieval industry and commerce, and it's still the location of choice for many contemporary designers, craftspeople and artists. Galleries and applied art museums occupy the mansions of Carrer de Montcada – the neighbourhood's most handsome street – while the *barri* is at its hippest in the area around the **Passeig del Born**, whose cafés, restaurants and bars make it one of the city's premier nightlife centres.

To walk through both neighbourhoods you can start at Ⓜ Urquinaona, close to the Palau de la Música Catalana, or Ⓜ Arc de Triomf over to the east, while Ⓜ Jaume I marks both the southern end of Sant Pere and the most direct access point to La Ribera.

Palau de la Música Catalana

C/Sant Pere Més Alt • Guided tours (in English on the hour) daily: Sept–June 10am–3.30pm; Easter week & July 10am–6pm; Aug 9am–6pm • Charge • Tour tickets available online or at the box office • Ⓦ palaumusica.cat • Ⓜ Urquinaona

Commissioned from *modernista* architect Lluís Domènech i Montaner by the Orfeo Català choral group, the stupendous **Palau de la Música Catalana** was completed in 1908. This extraordinary concert hall made an immediate statement of nationalistic intent. Smothered in tiles and mosaics typical of *modernisme*, the highly elaborate facade rests on three great columns, resembling elephant legs, while the corner sculpture represents Catalan popular song, its allegorical figures protected by a strident Sant Jordi (St George).

Stumble upon it from the narrow C/Sant Pere Més Alt, and the Palau barely seems to have enough space to breathe. Domènech i Montaner had no say in choosing the location; the choir bought this confined site, squeezed in between tall existing buildings, to be as close as possible to the homes of its members. Determined to make the interior a veritable "box of light", the architect capped the second-storey auditorium with a mighty bulbous stained-glass skylight – something contemporary critics considered an engineering impossibility.

Successive extensions and interior remodelling have opened up and expanded the original site. To the side, an enveloping glass facade provides the main public access to the box office, terrace restaurant and foyer bar, while the complex also now incorporates a smaller underground auditorium, the **Petit Palau**. It's still privately owned, incidentally, although the Orfeo has moved to L'Auditori in Plaça de las Glòries.

To see the Palau at its best, try to join the 2000-plus audience at a performance in the main auditorium, ideally in daylight – the **concert season** runs from September until June (see page 205). Otherwise, it's well worth taking a daytime tour of the interior.

Touring the concert hall

As numbers are limited on the hour-long **guided tours** of the Palau de la Música Catalana, it's best to buy a ticket in advance. Each tour begins with a short video extolling the virtues of the building, shown in the Petit Palau, then moves on to take a close-up look at the decorated facade columns and visit the two floors of the main concert hall. Sculptures of the Muses erupt from the backdrop of the main stage, while allegorical decoration is everywhere, from the sculpted red and white roses in the colours of the Catalan flag to the representations of music and nature in the glistening stained glass.

Plaça de Sant Pere

Ⓜ Arc de Triomf/Urquinaona

Sant Pere neighbourhood extends around three parallel medieval streets, *carrers* de Sant Pere de Més Baix (lower), Mitjà (middle) and Alt (upper), which contain the bulk of the district's most characteristic buildings and shops – a mixture of boutiques, textile firms, groceries and old family businesses.

The three streets converge upon the original neighbourhood square, the pleasant **Plaça de Sant Pere** – more of a trapezoid, actually – where the foursquare **Església de Sant Pere de les Puel·les** flanks one side, overlooking a flamboyant iron drinking fountain and a few cafés with outdoor tables. Although the church has been destroyed and burned too many times to retain any interior interest, it's among the oldest in the

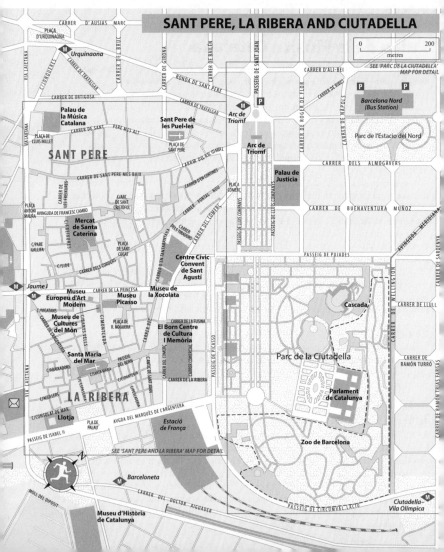

city, rebuilt in 1147 on tenth-century foundations. Despite its medieval appearance, the high-walled facade is a twentieth-century renovation.

Mercat de Santa Caterina

Avda. de Francesc Cambò 16 • Aug Mon–Thurs & Sat 7.30am–3.30pm, Fri 7.30am–8pm; Sept– July Mon, Wed & Sat 7.30am–3.30pm, Tues, Thurs & Fri 7.30am–8.30pm • ⓦ mercatsantacaterina.com • Ⓜ Jaume I

The splendid restoration of the **Mercat de Santa Caterina**, at the very heart of Sant Pere, has retained its original nineteenth-century balustraded market walls while adding slatted wooden doors and windows and a dramatic multicoloured undulating roof designed by Enric Miralles, architect behind the Scottish parliament building. This is one of Barcelona's best places to shop for food or grab a snack, and the market restaurant and bar are worth a visit in any case. The foundations of a medieval convent discovered here during the renovation work are visible at the rear.

Plaça de Sant Agusti Vell and around

Ⓜ Jaume I

The pretty, tree-shaded **Plaça de Sant Agusti Vell** sits at the centre of Sant Pere's most ambitious regeneration project, which transformed crowded alleyways into landscaped boulevards. To the north, locals tend organic allotments in the middle of the **Pou de la Figuera** *rambla*, while south down **Carrer de l'Allada Vermell** you'll find overarching trees, a children's playground and plenty of outdoor cafés and bars.

Meanwhile, running down from Plaça de Sant Agusti Vell, **Carrer dels Carders** – once "ropemakers' street" – is now a retail quarter mixing grocery stores and cafés with shops selling streetwear, African and Asian arts and crafts and contemporary jewellery. The little Romanesque chapel at the end of the street, the **Capella d'en Marcus** (usually locked), dates back to the twelfth century, but was stripped of interest during the Civil War.

Centre Cívic Convent de Sant Agustí

C/Comerç 36, entrance on C/Tantarantana • Mon–Fri 9am–10pm, Sat 10am–2pm & 4–9pm • Charge, some events free • ⓦ conventagusti.com • Ⓜ Jaume I/Arc de Triomf

A driving force behind many of the neighbourhood improvements in Sant Pere is the community centre installed inside the revamped **Convent de Sant Agustí**, where a thirteenth-century cloister provides a unique performance space. There's a full cultural programme here, from workshops to concerts, with a particular emphasis on electronic and experimental music and art, and don't miss lunch at the excellent *Bar del Convent*, with seats in the cloister (see page 186).

Museu de la Xocolata

C/Comerç 36 • Tues–Sat 10am–7pm (until 8pm mid-June to mid-Sept), Sun 10am–3pm • Charge • ⓦ museuxocolata.cat • Ⓜ Jaume I/Arc de Triomf

Perhaps the most exciting thing about the **Museu de la Xocolata**, housed in sections of the Convent de Sant Agustí, is that your entrance ticket is a little bar of **chocolate**. Inside, the museum does a rudimentary job of tracing the history of chocolate back to its origins as a sacred and medicinal product in ancient Central America (the topic has some local relevance, in that the Bourbon army, when quartered in this building, demanded the provision of chocolate for its sweet-toothed troops). Whether you

4

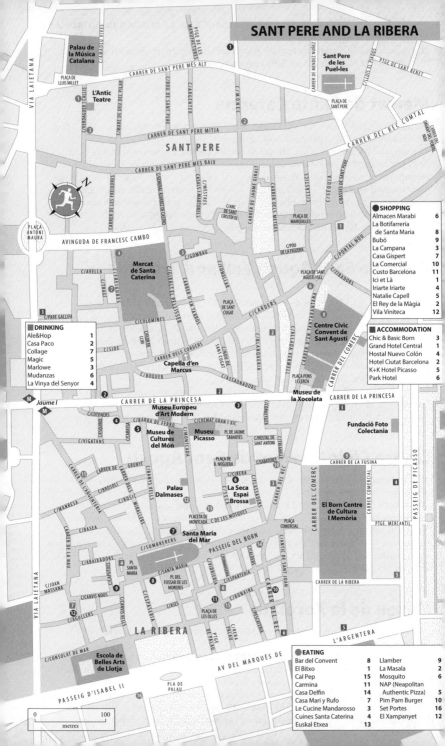

actually go in or not, however, will depend on how keen you are to relish a baffling array of endless chocolate models. Proudly displayed like precious objects are Gaudí buildings and religious icons, Komodo dragons and bullfights – there's even a Lionel Messi, his shorts, boots and sturdy limbs magnificently gleaming with a cocoa-rich sheen. Some are rather wonderful, while others, like Don Quixote and his dopey horse, are the height of kitsch. The chocolate artistes are individually credited, and you can put names to faces at the sculptors' Hall of Fame.

Chocolates are available to buy, of course, and a small café serves hot chocolate. At the adjacent Escola de Pastisseria, you can look through huge picture windows to watch students learning their craft in the kitchens. Note, though, that the various **workshops** detailed on the museum website, largely targeted at children, are conducted in Catalan and Castilian only.

Museu Picasso

C/Montcada 15–23 • Tues, Wed & Fri–Sun 10am–7pm • Permanent collection charge • Free guided tours in English Tues 3pm & 4pm, Sun 11am; advance bookings essential • ⓦ museupicasso.bcn.cat • ⓜ Jaume I

Although the celebrated **Museu Picasso** ranks among the world's most important collections of Picasso's work, some visitors are disappointed to find it contains few of his best-known pictures, and few in the Cubist style. Nonetheless, the permanent collection holds almost 4000 works, displayed in five adjoining medieval palaces, which provide a fascinating opportunity to trace Picasso's development from his early paintings as a young boy to the major works of later years. The whole place is extremely well laid out, with abundant space and natural light.

It might often seem as if every visitor to Barcelona is trying to get into the museum at the same time, but you can hardly come to the city and not make the effort. Arriving when it opens offers the best chance of beating the crowds. A **café** with a courtyard *terrassa* offers refreshments, and there is of course a **shop**, stuffed full of Picasso-related gifts.

PICASSO IN BARCELONA

Although he was born in Málaga, **Pablo Picasso** (1881–1973) spent much of his youth – from the age of 14 to 23 – in Barcelona. He maintained close links with the city and his Catalan friends long after he left for Paris in 1904, and is said to have always thought of himself as Catalan rather than *andaluz*. The time Picasso spent in Barcelona encompassed the whole of his Blue Period (1901–04) and provided many of the formative influences on his art.

While the major goal for visitors is of course the Museu Picasso, sites throughout the old town carry echoes of the great artist. Not too far from the museum, you can still see many of the buildings in which Picasso lived and worked, notably the **Escola de Belles Arts de Llotja** (C/Consolat del Mar, near Estació de França), where his father taught drawing and where Picasso himself absorbed an academic training. The **apartments** where the family lived when they first arrived in Barcelona – Pg. d'Isabel II 4 and C/Reina Cristina 3, both near the Escola – can also be seen, though only from the outside, while Picasso also worked opposite the spanking-new Palau Güell, and had his first real **studio** (in 1896) on C/Plata at no. 4. A few years later, many of his Blue Period works were finished at a studio at C/Comerç 28. His first **public exhibition** was in 1900 at *Els Quatre Gats* tavern (see box, page 50). The other place to retain a link with Picasso is **C/Avinyó** in the Barri Gòtic, which cuts south from C/Ferran to C/Ample. Large houses along here were converted into brothels at the end of the nineteenth century, and Picasso used to haunt the street sketching what he saw. Some accounts of his life – based on Picasso's own testimony, it has to be said – claim that he had his first sexual experience here at the age of 14, and certainly the women at one of the brothels inspired his seminal Cubist work, *Les Demoiselles d'Avignon*.

The collection

When the museum opened in 1963, its collection was largely based on the donations of Jaume Sabartés, longtime friend and former secretary to the artist – you'll see him pictured as a "poeta decadente" in 1900, in a ruff and hat in 1939, and as a faun in 1946. Following Sabartés' death in 1968, Picasso himself added a large number of works – above all, those in the Meninas series – and in 1970 he donated a further vast number of watercolours, drawings, prints and paintings.

The **early drawings**, particularly, are fascinating, in which Picasso – still signing with his full name, Pablo Ruiz Picasso – attempted to copy the nature paintings in which his father specialized. Far from what might be considered juvenilia, they show the experimentation and learning of an emergent genius. Works from his **art school** days in Barcelona (1895–97) offer tantalizing glimpses of the city the young Picasso knew – the Gothic old town, the cloisters of Sant Pau del Camp, Barceloneta beach. Even at the ages of 15 and 16 he was producing serious works, including knowing self-portraits and a closely observed study of his father from 1896. Works in the style of Toulouse-Lautrec, like the menu Picasso did for *Els Quatre Gats* tavern in 1900, reflect his burgeoning interest in Parisian art, while other sketches, drawings and illustrations (many undertaken for competitions and magazines) demonstrate the development of his unique personal style. Paintings from the **Blue Period** (1901–04), ranging from moody Barcelona roofscapes to the cold face of *La Dona Morta*, burst upon you. Subsequent galleries only make the barest nods to Picasso's Cubist (1907–20) and Neoclassical (1920–25) stages, though his return to the city with the Ballets Russes in 1917 is commemorated by *Harlequin*. Another large jump brings us to 1957, and the 44 interpretations of **Las Meninas**, brilliantly deconstructing the individual portraits and compositions that make up Velázquez's masterpiece, which Picasso completed between August and December that year. A separate room displays nine gorgeous light-filled Mediterranean scenes, inspired by the pigeons and dovecotes of his Cannes studio, which Picasso painted within a week during that same period, and are regarded as part of the same set.

Vibrantly decorated dishes and jugs donated by Picasso's wife Jacqueline highlight his work as a **ceramicist**. There are various portraits of Jacqueline here, too, though it's the seventy-year friendship that Picasso shared with Jaume Sabartés, reflected in mature portraits, character studies and jokey sketches by one friend of another, that offers the clearest expression of endearment. Further rooms display changing exhibitions of **prints**, culled from the museum's 1500-plus engravings and lithographs.

Along Carrer de Montcada

Ⓜ Jaume I

The street on which the Museu Picasso stands – **Carrer de Montcada** – ranks among the best looking in the city. Laid out in the fourteenth century, it was, until the Eixample was planned almost five hundred years later, home to most of the city's leading citizens. They occupied spacious mansions built around central courtyards, from which external staircases climbed to the living rooms on the first floor; the facades facing the street were all endowed with huge gated doors that could be swung open to allow coaches access to the interior. Today, almost all the mansions and palaces along La Ribera's showpiece street serve instead as museums, private galleries and craft and gift shops, sucking up trade from Picasso-bound visitors.

Museu de Cultures del Món

C/Montcada 12 • May–Sept Tues–Sun 10am–8pm; Oct–April Tues–Sat 10am–7pm, Sun 10am–8pm • Charge • Ⓦ museuculturesmon. bcn.cat • Ⓜ Jaume I

Housed in two medieval palaces directly across from the Picasso museum, the **Museu de Cultures del Món** – Museum of World Cultures – opened in 2015. It showcases objects of phenomenal beauty and power from the world beyond Europe, not necessarily ancient but mostly imbued by their creators with deep spiritual significance. Drawn partly from the Museu Etnòlogic on Montjuïc, which now focuses exclusively on Catalunya itself (see page 97), and partly from two substantial private collections, it's a somewhat haphazard assortment, but there's no disputing its overall quality or impact.

Downstairs, the African section ranges from the Christian art of Ethiopia to reliquary statuettes, helmets and masks, some credited to specific twentieth-century sculptors. On the higher levels, the Oceania segment includes actual remodelled human skulls from New Guinea, belonging to enemies and revered ancestors alike, and carved *moai* figures from Easter Island, while the extensive Asian galleries hold everything from Japanese Noh theatre masks and Korean ceramics to jewelled knives from Indonesia and bronze Krishna statuettes from India, with touch-screen displays to explain whatever catches your eye. The pre-Columbian artefacts from the Americas on the top floor belong to hotelier Jordi Clos, the collector responsible for the Museu Egipci (see page 110).

Museu Europeu d'Art Modern

C/Barra de Ferro 5 • Tues–Sun 11am–7pm • Charge • ⓦ meam.es • ⓜ Jaume I

Shamelessly trading on its enticing location, in a renovated eighteenth-century palace facing the Museu Picasso, the **Museu Europeu d'Art Modern** is reviewed here only because its high visibility and vigorous self-promotion might tempt you to pay good money to visit. In fact, though, its permanent collection, while genuinely contemporary in that it's all the work of artists active in the twenty-first century, is mostly of an abysmally low standard. For what it's worth, the emphasis is on figurative rather than abstract art, and it abounds in hyper-photorealistic paintings.

To see the building itself, come instead for the **concerts** that take place on Fridays (blues) and Saturdays (classical) either in the palace's sculpture-peppered courtyard or beneath the high ceiling of its grand, Neoclassical main room.

Basílica de Santa María del Mar

Pl. de Santa María • Daily 10am–8.30pm; Mass Mon–Sat 7.30pm, Sun noon & 7.30pm • 45min guided tours Fri 4pm, Sat 11.15am, Sun 3pm • Charge • ⓦ santamariadelmarbarcelona.org • ⓜ Jaume I

La Ribera's flagship church of **Santa María del Mar** is the city's most exquisite example of pure Catalan-Gothic architecture. Much dearer to the heart of the average local than the overpowering cathedral, La Seu, it was conceived as thanks for the Catalan conquest of Sardinia in 1324. Work began in 1329 and was finished in just over half a century, which explains the consistency of style. It may not be obvious today, but, when built, Santa María *del Mar* (ie, of the sea) stood much closer to the seashore (hence the title of Ildefonso Falcones' medieval blockbuster novel *Cathedral of the Sea*, which relates its construction).

Set foursquare at the heart of Barcelona's trading district, the church came to embody the commercial supremacy of the Crown of Aragón, of which the city was capital. Its wide nave, narrow aisles, massive buttresses and octagonal, flat-topped towers are typical Catalan-Gothic features, while it's arguably all to the good that its later Baroque trappings were destroyed during the Civil War (the blackened ceiling still bears witness to the ten-day fire that blazed here). Subsequent long-term restoration work has concentrated on showing off the simple bare spaces of the interior, and the stained glass is especially beautiful.

Rather than exploring the church itself, the bilingual **guided tours** of Santa María del Mar, conducted in Catalan and English, take visitors up to a small platform that has been erected on the rooftop, for views over the city.

Plaça del Fossar de les Moreres

The modern brick-lined square known as **Plaça del Fossar de les Moreres** lines the southern flank of Santa María del Mar church. It was opened in 1989 to mark the spot where, following the defeat of Barcelona on September 11, 1714, Catalan martyrs fighting for independence against the king of Spain, Felipe V, were executed. An enormous red steel scimitar, arching almost to touch the church, is topped by an eternal flame that commemorates the fallen.

Passeig del Born

Ⓜ Jaume I/Barceloneta

Once the site of medieval fairs and tournaments – *born* means tournament – the fashionable **Passeig del Born** fronting the church of Santa María del Mar is now an avenue lined with plane trees shading a host of classy bars, delis and shops.

At night the Born becomes one of Barcelona's biggest bar zones, as spirited locals frequent the drinking haunts, from old-style cocktail lounges to thumping music bars. Shoppers and browsers, meanwhile, scour the narrow, vaulted medieval alleys to either side for boutiques and **craft workshops** – carrers Flassaders, Vidreria and Rec in particular are noted for clothes, shoes, jewellery and design galleries.

El Born Centre de Cultura I Memòria

Pl. Comercial 12, at Pg. del Born • Tues–Sun: March–Oct 10am–8pm, Nov–Feb 10am–7pm • Free access to the centre, charge for exhibitions (includes audio-guide) and guided tours (Tues–Sun 4pm) • Ⓦ elborncentrecultural.cat • Ⓜ Jaume I/Barceloneta

The largest of Barcelona's nineteenth-century market halls, the handsome **Antic Mercat del Born**, was built between 1873 and 1876, and spent a century as the city's main wholesale fruit and veg market before closing in 1971. Spared demolition thanks to local protest, it languished empty for decades, and finally reopened in 2013. Now, beneath a renovated canopy of sparkling glass and intricate wrought iron, **El Born Centre de Cultura I Memòria** looks back over three centuries of Catalan history, from the siege of 1714 to the present day. The transformation took so long partly because excavations revealed that the market stood directly on the remains of eighteenth-century shops, factories, houses and taverns that predate the Ciutadella fortress and the Barceloneta district – a fascinating discovery that's been put on full display.

HIDDEN GEMS: SANT PERE, LA RIBERA AND CIUTADELLA

Lunch at Bar del Convent See page 186
Picasso's re-creations of Velázquez's Las Meninas See page 74
Boutique-lined Carrer dels Flassaders See page 222
Concerts at Museu Europeu d'Art Modern See page 75
Rowing boats in Parc Ciutadella See page 78
Beers at Ale&Hop See page 198
L'Antic Teatre See page 207

From the freely accessible ground floor, visitors can look down on the painstakingly preserved ruins, which for their size, condition and era are unique in Europe. Display panels provide historical context, while if you're intrigued you can also pay to inspect choice artefacts in the **permanent gallery** or to join various **themed tours** down on the lower level, where raised walkways offer close-up views. Additional charges are levied for temporary exhibitions.

Outside the market, a swathe of Carrer del Comerç has been turned into a pedestrian zone, creating a channel that leads from Passeig del Born, through the market (and directly above the ruins) and towards the Parc de la Ciutadella.

Foto Colectània

Pg. de Picasso 14 • Tues–Sat 11am–8pm, Sun 11am–3pm • Charge • ⓦ fotocolectania.org • Ⓜ Jaume I/Barceloneta

A non-profit photography gallery that houses small but high-quality exhibitions from Catalan, Spanish and international photographers. Run by a foundation that promotes local photographers abroad, it also houses a library comprising thousands of images.

Parc de la Ciutadella

Daily 10am–dusk • Park entrance free • Entrances on Pg. de Picasso (Ⓜ Barceloneta, or a short walk from La Ribera) and Pg. de Pujades (Ⓜ Arc de Triomf); use Ⓜ Ciutadella-Vila Olímpica for direct access to the zoo

While you might escape to Montjuïc or the Collserola hills for the air, there's no beating the spacious **Parc de la Ciutadella** for a quick break from the downtown bustle. Most of its showcase buildings, which include Catalunya's legislative assembly, the **Parlament**, are not open to the public, but it's still a nice place to spend a lazy summer afternoon strolling the garden paths or rowing a boat across the ornamental lake.

The park's name refers to the Bourbon citadel that Felipe V erected here, to quell the local population following Barcelona's spirited resistance during the War of the Spanish Succession. A great part of La Ribera neighbourhood was brutally destroyed to make way for the fortress, and this symbol of authority survived uneasily until 1869, when the military moved base. Its only surviving portion is the much-altered Arsenal, which since 1980 has housed the Catalan parliament building. The surrounding area subsequently became a park, and hosted the 1888 **Universal Exhibition** – hence the eye-catching buildings and monuments erected by pioneering *modernista* architects.

Arc de Triomf

Pg. de Lluís Companys • Ⓜ Arc de Triomf

The giant brick **Arc de Triomf**, at the inland end of the Parc de la Ciutadella, announces the architectural splendours to come in the park itself. Roman in scale, and conceived as a bold statement of Catalan intent, it's studded with ceramic figures and motifs, and topped by two pairs of bulbous domes. Reliefs on its main facade show Barcelona welcoming visitors to the 1888 Universal Exhibition.

Cascada

Parc de la Ciutadella • Ⓜ Arc de Triomf

The first of the major projects undertaken inside the Parc de la Ciutadella, the monumental **Cascada** fountain in its northeast corner was designed by Josep Fontseré i Mestrés, the architect chosen to oversee the conversion of the former citadel grounds into a park. His assistant in the task was Antoni Gaudí, then a young student, and its Baroque extravagance is suggestive of the flamboyant decoration that was to become

Gaudí's trademark. Gaudí worked on the hydraulic system for the fountain, and is thought to have had a hand in the design of the iron park gates.

Near the small open-air **café-kiosk** that makes the ideal vantage point from which to contemplate the fountain's tiers and swirls, you can **rent a rowing boat** on the lake and paddle about among the ducks.

Castell dels Tres Dragons and Museu Martorell

Pg. de Picasso • Ⓜ Arc de Triomf

The **Castell dels Tres Dragons** (Three Dragons Castle), a whimsical red-brick confection at the park's northwest corner, was designed by Lluís Domènech i Montaner for use as a café-restaurant for the Universal Exhibition. Home for many years to the

local zoology museum, it's not currently in use. Along with the similarly defunct Neoclassical **Museu Martorell**, which opened in 1882 as Barcelona's first public museum and long housed the city's geological collections, it's slated for restoration at some point.

Umbracle and Hivernacle

Pg. de Picasso • Under renovation at time of writing • Ⓜ Arc de Triomf

The twin unsung glories of Ciutadella are its plant houses, arranged either side of the Museu Martorell. Both are currently closed to visitors and looking somewhat dilapidated, though the plants within are sufficiently tended to cling to life. The imposing **Umbracle** (palm house) is a handsome structure with a barrelled wood-slat roof supported by cast-iron pillars, which allows shafts of light to play across the palms and ferns, while the enclosed greenhouses of the larger **Hivernacle** (conservatory) are separated by a soaring glass-roofed terrace.

Zoo de Barcelona

Main entrance on C/Wellington • Daily: Jan to late March & late Oct to Dec 10am–5.30pm, last admission 5pm; late March to mid-May & mid-Sept to late Oct 10am–7pm, last admission 6pm; mid-May to mid-Sept 10am–8pm, last admission 7pm • Charge • Ⓦ zoobarcelona. cat • Signposted from Ⓜ Ciutadella-Vila Olímpica, or tram T4 stops outside

The **Zoo de Barcelona** occupies the entire southeastern portion of Ciutadella park. Still essentially nineteenth century in character, its tiny enclosures squeezed into the formal grounds of a public park, it boasts over two thousand animals, including such endangered species as Komodo dragons, Iberian wolves and Sumatran tigers.

In 2016, the zoo was obliged to close its dolphinarium, which failed to meet minimal legal requirements. Despite ongoing renovation work that is of course said to be aimed at improving conditions for the rest of its captive creatures, and despite the obvious enthusiasm of local families, it cannot in good faith be recommended.

4

The waterfront

Perhaps the greatest transformation in Barcelona in recent decades has taken place along the waterfront. Dramatic changes have shifted the cargo and container trade away to the south, opened up the old docksides as promenades and entertainment areas, and landscaped the beaches to the north – it's as if a theatre curtain has been raised to reveal that, all along, Barcelona had an urban waterfront of which it could be proud. The glistening harbourside merges seamlessly with the old town, with the museums and attractions of Port Vell just steps from the bottom of La Rambla. No visit to the city is complete without a seafood meal in the eighteenth-century fishing quarter of Barceloneta, followed by a stroll along the beachfront promenade as far as the showpiece Port Olímpic.

Barcelona's **beaches** extend for 7km along the waterfront, from Barceloneta in the centre out to the River Besòs, which defines the northeastern city limits. Locals make use of the sands in a big way – jogging, cycling and skating their length, and descending in force at the weekend for leisurely lunches or late drinks in scores of restaurants and bars. Though the main development is around the Port Olímpic, there are also spruced-up beaches further north, on either side of the old working-class neighbourhood of **Poblenou**, whose pretty *rambla* makes for an off-piste diversion. Beyond here, the **Diagonal Mar** business district might appear to be a journey too far for most visitors, but there's much to be admired in its bold urban scale.

Plaça del Portal de la Pau

Ⓜ Drassanes

The **Plaça del Portal de la Pau** marks the seaward end of a stroll along La Rambla, coming up hard against the teeming traffic that runs along the harbourfront road. The landmark Columbus monument is straight ahead in the middle of the traffic circle, with the quayside square beyond flanked by the **Port de Barcelona** (Port Authority) and **Duana** (Customs House) buildings. An **antiques market**, where you can find dusty treasures, fills the square at the weekend (10am–8pm). To the south, a landscaped wharf known as the **Moll de Barcelona** leads to the Torre de Jaume I **cable-car station** and the **Estació Marítima**, departure point for ferries to the Balearics (Ⓦ trasmediterranea.es). The large, bulbous building perched in the centre of the wharf is the city's **World Trade Centre**, housing a deluxe hotel, plus offices, convention halls, shops and restaurants.

Mirador de Colom

Pl. del Portal de la Pau • Daily 8am–8pm • Charge • ☎ 932 853 834 • Ⓜ Drassanes

Inaugurated just before the Universal Exhibition of 1888, the striking **Mirador de Colom** commemorates the visit made by Christopher Columbus (known locally as Cristòfol Colom) to Barcelona in 1493, bringing the news of his transatlantic voyage to the monarchs Ferdinand and Isabella (see page 81). The explorer tops a grandiose iron column, 52m high, guarded by lions at the base, around which unfold reliefs telling the story of his life and travels – here, if nowhere else, the old mercenary is still the "discoverer of America". A lift whisks you up to the enclosed *mirador* at Columbus's feet for terrific 360-degree city views – the narrow viewing platform, which tilts perceptibly outwards and downwards, is emphatically not for those who lack a head for heights.

ANOTHER WRONG TURN FOR COLUMBUS?

When the Italian-born navigator **Christopher Columbus** sailed into Barcelona harbour in June 1493, he was received in style by Ferdinand and Isabella. Seeking new and profitable trading routes, they had financed his voyage of exploration a year earlier, when Columbus had set out to chart a passage west to the Orient. Although he famously failed in that objective, just as he also failed to reach the North American mainland (instead "discovering" the Bahamas, Cuba and Haiti), Columbus did enough to enhance his reputation, and made three more voyages by 1504. Later, nineteenth-century Catalan nationalists took the navigator to their hearts – if he wasn't exactly Catalan, he was the closest they had to a local Vasco da Gama – and so they put him on the pedestal they thought he deserved. The statue is actually pointing in the general direction of Libya, not North America, but as historian Robert Hughes puts it, at least "the sea is Catalan".

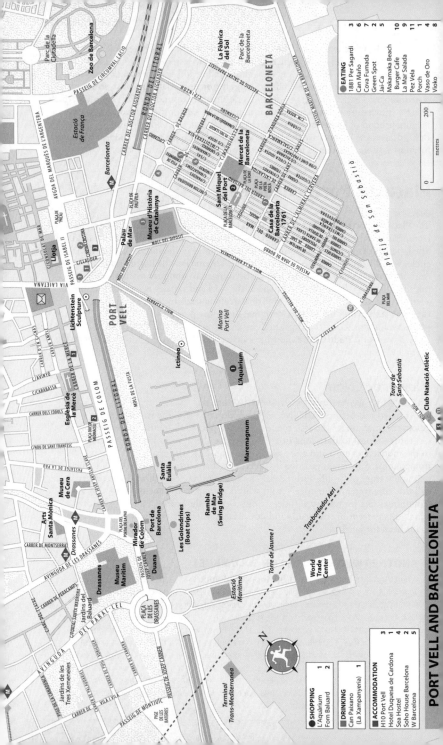

PORT VELL AND BARCELONETA

BARCELONETA

La Fàbrica del Sol

Parc de la Barceloneta

Parc de la Ciutadella

Zoo de Barcelona

PASSEIG DE CIRCUMVAL·LACIÓ

RONDA DEL DOCTOR AIGUADER

Estació de França

Platja de Sant Sebastià

Mercat de la Barceloneta

Sant Miquel del Port

Museu d'Història de Catalunya

Palau de Mar

Casa de la Barceloneta 1761

PLAÇA DE LA BARCELONETA

PASSEIG DE JOAN DE BORBÓ

PLAÇA DEL MAR

Torre de Sant Sebastià

Club Natació Atlètic

Trasbordador Aeri

PORT VELL

Marina Port Vell

Ictineo

L'Aquàrium

Maremagnum

Santa Eulàlia

Rambla de Mar (Swing Bridge)

Les Golondrines (Boat trips)

Port de Barcelona

Mirador de Colom

Duana

Museu de Cera

Arts Santa Mònica

Drassanes

Museu Marítim

Lichtenstein Sculpture

Església de la Mercè

VIA LAIETANA

Llotja

PASSEIG DE COLOM

RONDA DEL LITORAL

Torre de Jaume I

World Trade Center

Estació Marítima

Terminal Trans-Mediterranea

PLAÇA DE LES DRASSANES

Jardins de les Tres Xemeneies

AVINGUDA DEL PARAL·LEL

PASSEIG D'ISABEL II

N

0   200
metres

EATING

1881 Per Sagardi	3
Can Maño	6
Cova Fumada	7
Green Spot	2
Jai-Ca	5
Makamaka Beach Burger Cafe	10
La Mar Salada	9
Pez Vela	11
Porch	4
Vaso de Oro	1
Vioko	8

SHOPPING

L'Aquàrium	1
Forn Baluard	2

DRINKING

Can Paixano (La Xampanyeria)	1

ACCOMMODATION

H10 Port Vell	3
Hotel Duquesa de Cardona	1
Sea Hostel	4
Soho House Barcelona	2
W Barcelona	5

Museu Marítim   5

Avda. de les Drassanes • Daily 10am–8pm • Charge • ⓦ mmb.cat • Ⓜ Drassanes

Barcelona's medieval shipyards, or **Drassanes**, at the foot of La Rambla, date back
to the fourteenth century. They remained in continuous use – fitting and arming
Catalunya's war fleet or trading vessels – until well into the eighteenth century, when
the imposing central cluster of stone-vaulted buildings was taken over for use as
military barracks and an arsenal. Now they make a superb location for the **Museu
Marítim** (Maritime Museum), which celebrates the city's role as a naval base, trading
centre, and port of passage for generations of migrants and visitors.

The permanent collection focuses on seven specific vessels, beginning with a
Greek merchant ship from the fourth century BC, as a means to trace the history of
navigation. Delicate model boats and gorgeous antique maps illuminate the story, with
actual shipping containers serving as display cases. The real showpiece comes in the
vast central gallery, in the form of a full-size replica of the magnificent, 60m-long *Royal
Galley*, which was built right here in 1568, and fought as the Spanish flagship when the
Holy League defeated the Ottoman fleet in the Battle of Lepanto three years later.

The huge, high-ceilinged halls offer plenty of space for interesting, high-tech
temporary exhibitions, and also hold a good shop and café, while the admission fee also
provides access to the **Santa Eulàlia** schooner on the nearby waterfront.

Santa Eulàlia

Tues–Sun & hols: April–Oct 10am–8.30pm, Nov–March 10am–5.30pm; sailing excursions Sat 10am–1pm (reservations essential) •
Charge • ⓦ mmb.cat • ⊜ reserves@mmb.cat

The pride and joy of the Maritime Museum, the three-masted ocean schooner **Santa
Eulàlia** is moored over on the Moll de la Fusta (beyond the harbour's swing bridge).
Built using pine and olive wood in 1918, as the *Carmen Flores*, she originally sped
around the Mediterranean, and also made the run between Barcelona and Cuba. She
was acquired and restored by the museum in 1997, and a short tour lets you walk the
deck and view the interior.

Port Vell

Ⓜ Drassanes/Barceloneta

While Barcelona's remodelled inner harbour, known as **Port Vell** (Old Port), has its local
critics – it's undoubtedly touristy and expensive – there's no denying the improvement

---

HARBOUR RIDES BY SKY AND SEA

Barcelona's most thrilling ride has to be the **Transbordador Aeri** cable car, which sweeps
passengers all the way across the inner harbour between the top of the Torre de Sant Sebastiá,
near the tip of Barceloneta, and the hill of Montjuïc (departures every 15min; daily: March, April
& mid-Sept to Oct 10.30am–7pm; June to mid-Sept 10.30am–8pm; Nov–Feb 11am–5.30pm;
€11 one-way, €16.50 return; ☎934 304 716, ⓦ telefericodebarcelona.com). As you dangle high
above the water, you can enjoy superb views over the city. There's an additional stop in the
middle, at the 100m-tall Torre de Jaume I in front of the World Trade Centre in Port Vell. As the
cable car can only carry nineteen people at a time, you can expect queues – and potential
disappointment – in summer and at weekends. Strong winds can close the ride altogether.

From the quayside just beyond the foot of the Mirador de Colom, **Las Golondrinas**
sightseeing boats and the *Catamaran Orsom* depart on regular trips throughout the year
along the waterfront (see page 30).

5

to what was formerly a decaying harbourside. The city's old timber wharf, for example, the **Moll de la Fusta**, re-emerged as a landscaped promenade with a note of humour injected by the addition of a giant fibreglass crayfish by Catalan designer Javier Mariscal and, further on, **Roy Lichtenstein**'s totem-pole sculpture known as *El Cap de Barcelona* (*Barcelona Head*).

From the Columbus statue end of the wharf, the wooden **Rambla de Mar** swing bridge strides across to the **Moll d'Espanya**, whose main features are the Maremagnum mall and aquarium. From here, it's only a ten-minute walk around the **marina** to the Palau de Mar and the Catalan history museum.

Maremagnum

Moll d'Espanya • Daily 10am–9pm • ⓦ maremagnum.es • ⓜ Drassanes

The **Maremagnum** mall is a typically bold piece of Catalan design, its soaring glass lines tempered by the surrounding undulating wooden walkways. Inside are two floors of gift shops and boutiques, plus assorted cafés and fast-food outlets (restaurants are open until 1am); outside, benches and park areas provide fantastic views back across the harbour to the city.

L'Aquàrium

Moll d'Espanya • April–June & Oct daily 10am–8pm; June & Sept daily 10am–9pm; July & Aug daily 10am–9pm; Nov–March daily 10am–7pm • Charge • ⓦ aquariumbcn.com • ⓜ Drassanes/Barceloneta

Anchoring Moll d'Espanya, **L'Aquàrium** drags in families and school parties year-round to see "a magical world, full of mystery". Or, to be more precise, to see eleven thousand fish and sea creatures in 35 themed tanks representing underwater caves, tidal areas, tropical reefs and other maritime habitats. It's vastly overpriced and, despite the claims of excellence, it offers few new experiences, save perhaps the 80m-long walk-through underwater tunnel which brings you face to face with gliding rays and cruising sharks. Some child-centred displays and activities and a nod towards ecology and conservation issues pad things out before you're tipped out into the aquarium shop to be relieved of even more of your money.

The marina

ⓜ Barceloneta

The walk from Port Vell to Barceloneta takes you around the packed **marina**, where Catalans park their yachts like they park their cars – impossibly tightly and with plenty of gesticulation. Hawkers spread blankets on the marina promenade, selling jewellery and sunglasses, while a line of seafood restaurants behind overlooks the water.

For a sundowner drink overlooking the harbour, head to the *terrassa* bar of rooftop restaurant *1881 per Sagardi* (see page 188), above the Museu d'Història de Catalunya.

Museu d'Història de Catalunya

Pl. de Pau Vila 3 • Tues & Thurs–Sat 10am–7pm, Wed 10am–8pm, Sun 10am–2.30pm • Charge • ⓦ mhcat.net • ⓜ Barceloneta

The absorbing **Museu d'Història de Catalunya** (Catalunya History Museum) occupies the upper levels of the one warehouse that survives on the Port Vell harbourside, the beautifully restored **Palau de Mar**, poised above the shops and seafood restaurants in its lower arcade. This exhaustive museum traces the history of Catalunya from the Stone Age to the present day, with its spacious exhibition areas wrapped around a wide atrium.

The permanent displays start with a mocked-up Bronze Age dwelling and the arrival of Greek settlers at Empúries around 600 BC, and swiftly move on to the Romans, with a cross-section model of a small Roman cargo ship. From there on in, as you pass through Catalunya's golden years and the Industrial Revolution and enter the modern era, there's plenty to get your teeth into; not every caption is translated into English, but English notes are available throughout.

A dramatic section on the Civil War features music, footage and a replica hide-out, while a 1940s cinema shows contemporary newsreels. Other fascinating asides shed light on matters as diverse as housing in the 1960s, the rival nineteenth-century architectural plans for the Eixample, and the origins of the design of the Catalan flag.

Barceloneta

Ⓜ Barceloneta

An eighteenth-century neighbourhood of tightly packed streets, **Barceloneta** squeezes between the harbour on one side and the **beach** on the other. It was laid out in 1755, on a site that previously consisted of nothing but mudflats, primarily to re-house inhabitants of the Ribera district to the north, whose homes had been destroyed to make way for the Ciutadella fortress. Its long, narrow streets, broken at intervals by small squares, are lined with small, tall and abundantly windowed

MONTURIOL AND THE CATALAN SUBMARINE

Barcelona's connection to the sea goes deeper than you think: it was in its harbour waters in 1859 that the first **man-powered submarine** made its maiden voyage. This "fish-boat", the **Ictineo**, was the work of self-taught scientist, engineer and inventor **Narcís Monturiol i Estarriol** (1819–85). Born in Figueres, Monturiol fell in with radicals as a student in Barcelona. He set up a publishing company in 1846, espousing his beliefs in feminism, pacifism and utopian communism – radical ideas that saw him forced briefly into exile during the heady revolutionary days of 1848. This was a period in which scientific progress and social justice appeared as two sides of the same coin to utopians like Monturiol – indeed, his friend, the civil engineer Ildefons Cerdà, would mastermind the building of Barcelona's Eixample on socially useful grounds.

Inspired by the harsh conditions in which Catalan coral fishermen worked, Monturiol conceived the idea of the **Ictineo**. At 7m long, it could carry four or five men, and made more than fifty dives at depths of up to 20m before being destroyed in an accident. Construction began on an improved version in 1862 – the 17m-long *Ictineo II*, which was intended to be propelled by up to sixteen men. When trials showed that human power wasn't sufficient for the job, Monturiol installed a steam engine. Thus the world's first **steam-powered** submarine was launched on October 22, 1867, diving up to 30m on thirteen separate runs (the longest lasting for over seven hours). However, the sub never managed to pay its way, and when Monturiol's financial backers withdrew their support, the *Ictineo II* was seized by creditors and sold for scrap – the engine ended up in a paper mill.

Undaunted, Monturiol continued to come up with new inventions. With the submarines he had pioneered the use of the double hull, a technique still used today, while he also made advances in the manufacture of glues and gums, copying documents, commercial cigarette production and steam engine efficiency. Even so, he died in relative obscurity in 1885 and was buried in Barcelona, though his remains were later transferred to his home town. A memorial to Monturiol stands on the main *rambla* in Figueres, while he's remembered in Barcelona not only by a simple plaque at the Cementiri de Poblenou, but by replicas of his two amazing vessels, the **Ictineo I** and the **Ictineo II**, at the Museu Marítim and Port Vell respectively.

5

houses, designed to give the sailors and fishing folk who originally lived here plenty of sun and fresh air.

Though this remains very much a workaday community, some original houses feature a decorative flourish here, a sculpted balcony or a carved lintel there, while an eighteenth-century fountain and the Neoclassical church of **Sant Miquel del Port** survives in **Plaça de la Barceloneta**. A block over, in Plaça de la Font, the beautifully refurbished local food market, **Mercat de la Barceloneta** (Mon–Thurs 7am–2pm, Sat 7am–3pm, Fri 7am–8pm), boasts a couple of excellent bars and restaurants.

Barceloneta is renowned for its **seafood restaurants**, which can be found all over the neighbourhood. They're especially concentrated along the harbourside **Passeig Joan de Borbó**, where for most of the year you can eat at an outdoor table, though if you'd rather escape the traffic the restaurants along the nearby marina are preferable.

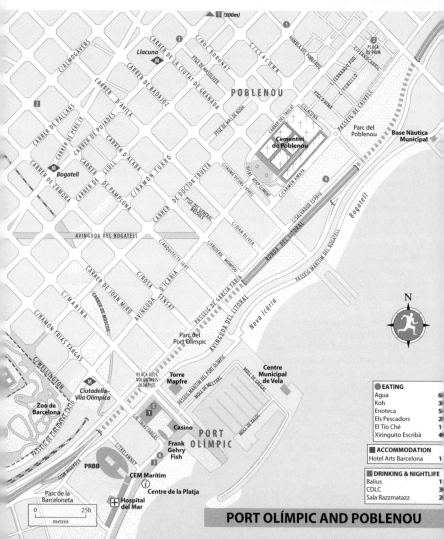

● EATING	
Agua	6
Koh	3
Enoteca	5
Els Pescadors	2
El Tío Ché	1
Xiringuito Escribà	4

■ ACCOMMODATION	
Hotel Arts Barcelona	1

■ DRINKING & NIGHTLIFE	
Balius	1
CDLC	3
Sala Razzmatazz	2

PORT OLÍMPIC AND POBLENOU

Casa de la Barceloneta 1761

C/Sant Carles 6 • Tues–Fri 10.30am–1.30pm & 4–8pm, Sat 10am–2pm • Free • ⓦ casadelabarceloneta1761.bcn.cat • Ⓜ Barceloneta

The two-storey **Casa de la Barceloneta 1761** has seen its fair share of change over the centuries. Constructed, much as its name might lead you to surmise, in 1761, the Baroque-style building, which faces three streets, was home to one of the neighbourhood's maritime families before being divided into smaller units, turned into a grocery store and then converted into a restaurant. Subsequently falling into disrepair, it was restored and transformed into a cultural and interpretive centre. Inside, you'll find a small yet informative (for those who read Catalan) exhibition about the evolution of the neighbourhood, as well as an upstairs gallery space.

La Fàbrica del Sol

Pg. Salvat Papasseit 1 • Mon–Thurs 9am–6.30pm, Fri 9am–2.30pm • Free • ⓦ bcn.cat/lafabricadelsol • Ⓜ Barceloneta

A yellow-painted, red-brick building on the edge of the Parc de la Barceloneta that used to be the city's gas works is now home to **La Fàbrica del Sol**, a sustainable eco-centre designed to take a close look at green living in all its guises, from recycling to transport. You can expect to see displays, gadgets and exhibits on assorted eco-themes. Head up to the roof to admire the building's garden and solar thermal system, and you'll also get a view of the park's whimsical *modernista* water tower (1905), rising like a minaret above the palms.

Platja de Sant Sebastià and Passeig Marítim

Ⓜ Barceloneta

Barceloneta's beach, **Platja de Sant Sebastià**, is the first in the series of sandy city beaches that stretches northeast along the coast all the way to the River Besòs. It curves out past the indoor and outdoor swimming pools of the *Club Natació* (see page 219) to the landmark, sail-shaped **W Barcelona** hotel, designed by Catalan architect Ricardo Bofill.

Meanwhile, at the Barceloneta end you'll encounter a plethora of beach bars, outdoor cafés and public sculptures, while a double row of palms backs the **Passeig Marítim** esplanade that parallels the beach as far as the Port Olímpic (a 10min walk). Sunbathers sprawl on the sands, swimmers venture into the water, and there's a surfing break immediately offshore. Rickshaw tours weave through the strolling pedestrians, and itinerant vendors patrol the strands offering snacks and drinks including mojitos and samosas.

Just short of Port Olímpic, a dramatic latticed funnel of wood and steel marks the **Parc Recerca Biomèdica de Barcelona (PRBB)**, the city's biomedical research centre.

Port Olímpic

Ⓜ Ciutadella-Vila Olímpica

As you approach the Olympic port along the Passeig Marítim, a shimmering golden mirage above the promenade slowly resolves itself into a **huge copper fish**, courtesy of Frank Gehry, architect of Bilbao's Guggenheim. The emblem of the huge seafront development that was constructed for the 1992 Olympics – and hosted many of the watersports events – it's backed by the city's two tallest buildings, the **Torre Mapfre** and the steel-framed **Hotel Arts Barcelona**, both 154m high.

The bulk of the Port Olímpic action is contained within two wharves: the **Moll de Mestral** and the **Moll de Gregal**. Previously home to two tiers of fairly tacky bars and seafood restaurants, and a hotspot for crime, the area has been overhauled for the 2024 Americas Cup, with upmarket restaurants and various maritime enterprises.

5

The beaches beyond Port Olímpic

From Port Olímpic (ⓂCiutadella-Vila Olímpica) it's a 15min walk along the promenade to Bogatell beach, or around 1hr all the way to Parc del Fòrum

Northeast along the coast from Port Olímpic, the city **beaches** continue right the way up to Parc del Fòrum and Diagonal Mar, split into separate named sections **Nova Icària**, **Bogatell**, **Mar Bella**, **Nova Mar Bella** and **Llevant**, each with showers, playgrounds and open-air café-bars (Mar Bella offers an area for nudists). It's a pretty extraordinary leisure facility to find so close to a city centre – the water might not be as clean as it could be, but the sands are regularly swept and replenished, while joggers, cyclists and bladers have one of the Med's best views for company.

Poblenou

ⓂPoblenou (at the junction of C/Pujades and C/Bilbao, one block east of Rambla del Poblenou), or bus #36 from Port Olímpic

The next neighbourhood along from Port Olímpic, **Poblenou** (New Village), is a largely nineteenth-century industrial area that has been in the throes of redevelopment since before the millennium, and continues to change year upon

BEACH BUSINESS

On Port Olímpic's boardwalk arcade, in front of the Hospital del Mar, the city council operates a beach visitor centre, the **Centre de la Platja** (March–May Tues–Sun 10am–2pm; June–Sept Tues–Sun 10am–7pm; ⓦ bcn.cat/platges), as a kind of one-stop shop for information and activities along the seafront. There's a programme of seafront walks and activities, a small summer lending library for beach reading, and Frisbees, volleyball and beach tennis gear available for pick-up games on the sand.

year. Under the suitably contemporary rubric of **22@** (ⓦ 22barcelona.com), the authorities are slowly and hopefully transforming 500 acres of land into "the innovation district".

You can come here directly on the metro, but it's far nicer to walk along the promenade from Port Olímpic (15min) to Poblenou's spruced-up **beaches** before crossing the main highway to reach the neighbourhood's main spine, Rambla del Poblenou.

Rambla del Poblenou

ⓜ Poblenou

Poblenou may be in the throes of change, but the main avenue still ticks along largely unaffected. Pretty, tree-lined **Rambla del Poblenou** remains entirely local in character – no cardsharps or human statues here – with a run of modest shops, cafés and restaurants, including the classic milk and juice bar of *El Tío Ché* (see page 189).

Cementiri de Poblenou

Avda. d'Icaria • Daily 8am–6pm; free guided tours on first and third Sun, 10.30am & 12.30pm (Catalan & Spanish) • ⓦ cbsa.cat • ⓜ Llacuna or buses #H16 or #V27

The vast nineteenth-century **Cementiri de Poblenou** has its tombs set in walls 7m high – the families that tend them have to climb great stepladders to reach the uppermost tiers. With traffic noise muted by the high walls, and birdsong accompanying a stroll around the flower-lined pavements, quiet courtyards, sculpted angels and tiny chapels, this village of the dead is a rare haven in contemporary Barcelona.

Diagonal Mar

ⓜ El Maresme-Fòrum or tram T4 to Fòrum via Glòries and Avda. Diagonal

Developed in the wake of 2004's Universal Forum of Cultures event, the waterfront district north of Poblenou is promoted as **Diagonal Mar**. It's anchored by the Diagonal Mar shopping mall, with business hotels, convention centres and exhibition halls grouped nearby.

Everything here is on a grand scale, starting with the showpiece **Museu Blau**, which houses the main exhibitions of the Natural History Museum, while the vast landscaped area beyond is a showpiece urban leisure project, the **Parc del Fòrum**. The district can still seem a bit soulless much of the time – hot as Hades in summer, buffeted by biting winds and all but devoid of pedestrians in winter– but for anyone stirred by heroic-scale public projects it's worth the metro ride. The tram comes down here too, so you could always glide there or back via Avinguda Diagonal and Glòries to see more of Barcelona in transformation.

5

Museu Blau

Pl. Leonardo da Vinci 4–5, Parc del Fòrum • March–Sept Tues–Sat 10am–7pm, Sun & hols 10am–8pm; Oct–Feb Tues–Fri 10am–6pm, Sat 10am–7pm, Sun & hols 10am–8pm • Charge • Ⓦ museuciencies.bcn.cat • Ⓜ El Maresme-Fòrum, or tram T4 to Fòrum

A dazzling blue biscuit tin of a building, hovering seemingly unsupported above the ground, the dramatic **Museu Blau** (Blue Museum) was designed by **Jacques Herzog** to hold the Natural Science Museum's state-of-the-art reboot of its heritage collections. Inside, the permanent Planeta Vida (Planet Life) exhibition plots a journey through nothing less than the history of life on earth. Starting logically enough with the Big Bang, it draws on a million-strong array of rocks, fossils, plants and animals, ranging from the smallest microbe to a giant whale skeleton. It's heavily focused on evolutionary, whole-earth, Gaia principles, with plenty of entertaining, interactive bells and whistles to guide you through topics as diverse as sex and reproduction and conservation of the environment.

Parc del Fòrum

Ⓜ El Maresme-Fòrum, or tram T4 to Fòrum via Glòries and Avda. Diagonal

The claim of Diagonal Mar's main open space, the **Parc del Fòrum**, to be at 150,000 square metres the second-largest square in the world after Beijing's Tiananmen Square, is palpably not true – several other squares are actually bigger than both. Unquestionably, though, it's an immense, undulating expanse, spreading towards the sea and culminating in a giant solar-panelled canopy that overlooks the marina, beach and park areas. In summer, temporary bars, dancefloors, open-air cinema and chill-out zones are established, while the city authorities have shifted some of the larger annual music festivals and events down here to inject a bit of life outside convention time.

MUSEU NACIONAL D'ART DE CATALUNYA IN BARCELONA

Montjuïc

It takes at least a day to see Montjuïc, the steep hill and park that rises over Barcelona to the southwest. The Romans built a shrine to Jupiter here and knew it as Mons Iovis, which may well be the root of its modern name, though it's often also explained as deriving from the siting of a Jewish cemetery on these slopes. Modern Montjuïc is essentially a cultural leisure park, anchored around the magnificent collection of Catalan treasures in the Museu Nacional d'Art de Catalunya (MNAC). Two further galleries, one devoted to Catalan artist Joan Miró, and the other, the CaixaForum, showcasing changing exhibitions of international contemporary art, are similarly unmissable. In addition, Montjuïc holds separate archeological, ethnological, military and theatrical museums, as well as structures and stadiums from the 1992 Olympics.

6

From the Roman era right up until the 1950s, Montjuïc was quarried to provide the stone that built much of Barcelona. As late as the 1890s, the hill was nothing more than a collection of private farms and woodland on the edge of the old town, though some landscaping had already taken place by the time Montjuïc was chosen to host the **International Exhibition** of 1929. The slopes were then laid with gardens, terraces and fountains, while monumental Neoclassical buildings, many of which later became museums, were added to the north side. The **Poble Espanyol** (Spanish Village) is the most extraordinary relic, while assorted lush **gardens** still offer respite from the crowds. Above all, perhaps, Barcelona's most favoured hill offers city and ocean views to savour: from the steps in front of the Museu Nacional, from the castle ramparts, from the Olympic terraces or from the cable cars that zigzag up the steepest slopes.

ARRIVAL AND GETTING AROUND   MONTJUÏC

By metro For easy access to Caixa Forum, Poble Espanyol and the Museu Nacional d'Art de Catalunya (MNAC) use Ⓜ Espanya (follow exit signs for "Fira/Exposició").

By funicular The Funicular de Montjuïc departs from inside the metro station at Ⓜ Paral·lel and takes a couple of minutes to ascend the hill (every 10 min: Mon–Fri

7.30am–10pm, Sat, Sun & public hols 9am–10pm, Nov–March till 8pm; €2.40, transport tickets and passes valid; Ⓦ tmb.cat). From the upper station on Agda. de Miramar, you can switch to the Montjuïc cable car or bus services, or walk in around 5min to the Fundació Joan Miró, more like 20min to the MNAC.

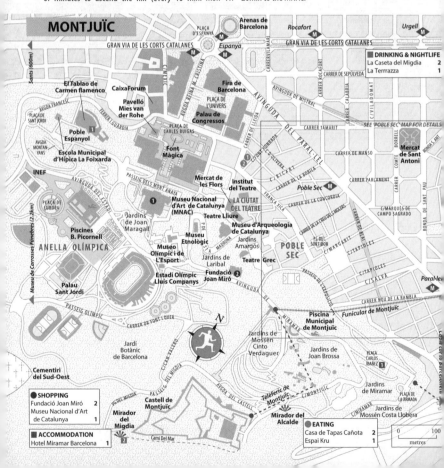

Telefèric de Montjuïc The Telefèric de Montjuïc cable car, which starts from Avda. de Miramar just across from the higher Funicular de Montjuïc station, and serves as a complement to the funicular, carries passengers in automated eight-seater gondolas up to the castle (daily: March–May & Oct 10am–7pm; June–Sept 10am–9pm; Nov–Feb 10am–6pm; charge; ⊛ telefericdemontjuic.cat).

Transbordador Aeri The cross-harbour Transbordador Aeri cable car crosses high above Barcelona's harbour, all the way from Barceloneta to the Jardins de Miramar (departures every 15min; daily: March–May & mid-Sept to Oct 10.30am–7pm; June to Sept 10.30am–8pm; Oct–Feb 11am–5.30pm; charge ⊛ telefericodebarcelona.com). From there it's a 10min walk to the Montjuïc cable car and funicular stations, and another 5min to the Fundació Joan Miró.

By bus City bus #150 (transport tickets and passes valid) covers a circular route around the main Montjuïc attractions, departing from a stop on Avda. de la Reina María Cristina, outside Ⓜ Espanya. The sightseeing, hop-on-hop-off Bus Turístic follows a similar route.

6

INFORMATION

Timing your visit Montjuïc covers a wide area, so to cover everything you might prefer to make two separate visits, perhaps seeing MNAC, Poble Espanyol and the Olympic area on one day, and Fundació Joan Miró, the cable car and the castle on the other. From Ⓜ Espanya, it takes a good hour to walk on the road around the hill, past Poble Espanyol, the Olympic area and Fundació Joan Miró to the cross-harbour cable-car station at the far end of Montjuïc. Escalators up from MNAC to the Olympic area cut out the worst of the slog. Walking up the steep hill all the way to the castle is not advised in hot weather (though steps climb through the gardens and between the roads) – use the cable car.

Tickets The Barcelona Card, Articket and Arqueoticket (see box, page 31) and Bus Turístic pass (see page 30) provide discounted entry into Montjuïc's museums, galleries and attractions.

Eating and drinking Places to eat are thin on the ground, though there are good cafés in Caixa Forum, Fundació Joan Miró and MNAC, outdoor snack bars at the castle and on the slopes below MNAC, and a restaurant with outdoor terrace at the Font del Gat in the Jardins de Laribal, below the Fundació Joan Miró. Decent restaurants and bars also abound in the neighbouring *barri* of Poble Sec.

Plaça d'Espanya

Ⓜ Espanya

The vast **Plaça d'Espanya**, laid out to plans drawn up by architect Josep Puig i Cadafalch, was completed in 1929 to serve as the gateway to that year's International Exhibition. Arranged around a huge Neoclassical fountain, the square is unlike any other in Barcelona, a radical departure from the *modernisme* then in vogue.

Landmark structures surrounding the square include the majestic former bullring, now reincarnated as the Arenas de Barcelona shopping and leisure centre (see page 118), and the striking twin towers, 47m high, that stand at the foot of the imposing **Avinguda de la Reina María Cristina**. This avenue spears up towards Montjuïc, and is lined by huge exhibition halls used for trade fairs. From Plaça de Carles Buïgas at its upper end, monumental steps, fortunately paralleled by escalators, ascend the hill to the Palau Nacional (home of MNAC), past water cascades and under the flanking walls of two grand Viennese-style pavilions. The higher you climb, the better the views, while a few café-kiosks put out seats on the way up to MNAC.

FLYING THE FLAG

Architect Josep Puig i Cadafalch's simplest idea for the ceremonial gateway to Montjuïc at Plaça d'Espanya saw **four 20m-high columns** erected in 1919 on a raised site below the future Palau Nacional. Who could possibly object? The authoritarian government of General Primo de Rivera, of course, which knew perfectly well that as a Catalan nationalist Puig i Cadafalch intended the columns to represent the four stripes of the *senyera*, the Catalan flag. Down they came in 1928, to be replaced by the Magic Fountain. Not until 2010 were the columns seen again, reconstructed using the original plans and erected across from the fountain by the city government as both "an act of memory" and a symbol of freedom and democracy.

Font Màgica

Pl. de Carles Buïgas • Temporarily closed • Free • W bcn.es/fontmagica • M Espanya

Things were certainly different in 1929, when mere whooshing water was enough to wow the crowds that flocked to the International Exhibition. The **Font Màgica** (Magic Fountain) at the foot of the Montjuïc is temporarily closed due to a long period of drought, but ordinarily does its stuff several evenings each week, forming the centrepiece of what is now an impressive, if slightly kitsch, sound-and-light show, with sprays and sheets of brightly coloured water dancing to the strains of Holst and Abba. The fountain is also the site of a spectacular firework, music and laser show every September, at the close of the annual Mercè festival.

Caixa Forum

Avda. de Francesc Ferrer i Guàrdia 6–8 • Daily 10am–8pm • Charge • W caixaforum.es • M Espanya

A terrific arts and cultural centre, the **Caixa Forum** stands within a magnificent *modernista* edifice. Originally built as the Casaramona textile factory by Josep Puig i Cadafalch in 1911, this remarkable building reopened in 2002, following a fifty-year hiatus as a headquarters for police horses and subsequent renovation and expansion under the auspices of the Fundació La Caixa. While its essential external structure was left untouched, with girders, pillars, brickwork and crenellated walls at every turn, twin iron-and-glass canopies representing spreading trees were added at the front, beneath which visitors now descend to enter below street level.

Up on the main floor, a permanent exhibition covers the history and design of the former factory, while the next level up offers access to several distinct pavilion-like gallery spaces. Each usually holds a separate temporary exhibition, on themes ranging from film or fashion to medieval history, though at times they're combined to stage a single major event. The Fundació La Caixa has sufficient clout, or money, to borrow artefacts from big-name international outfits like the British Museum or the Musée d'Orsay, so you can expect a very high standard.

Riding the elevators one level higher – follow signs to "terrats" – brings you to the factory's undulating brick-paved **roof**, which offers views up to Montjuïc. There's no access however to its tall, emblematic Casaramona **tower**, etched in blue and yellow tiling.

The complex also includes the Mediateca multimedia space, as well as an arts bookshop, an area devoted to kids' activities, and a four-hundred-seat auditorium for music, art and literary events, while its indoor-outdoor **café** serves breakfast and light meals.

Pavelló Mies van der Rohe

Avda. de Francesc Ferrer i Guàrdia 7, opposite CaixaForum • Daily: March–Oct 10am–8pm; Nov–Feb 10am–6pm • Charge • W miesbcn.com • M Espanya

The German contribution to the 1929 International Exhibition, a groundbreaking pavilion designed as a reception room by Ludwig Mies van der Rohe, was dismantled a year later. Considered a masterpiece of modern rationalist architecture, the **Pavelló Mies van der Rohe** was reconstructed in 1986 by Catalan architects.

Standing opposite and slightly uphill from the Caixa Forum, the pavilion is small and easily overlooked. Spare a moment, though, to admire its startlingly beautiful conjunction of hard straight lines with watery surfaces, and dark-green polished onyx alternating with shining glass. While it's open to visitors, unless a temporary exhibition is in place, there's little to see inside save Mies van der Rohe's iconic, tubular steel *Barcelona Chair*. Still, you can always buy postcards and books from the small shop.

Poble Espanyol

Avda. de Francesc Ferrer i Guàrdia 13 · Mon 10am–8pm, Tues–Sun 10am–midnight · Charge · ⓦ poble-espanyol.com · Ⓜ Espanya and 800m walk, or bus #150 or #13 from Avda. de la Reina María Cristina

An inspired concept for 1929's International Exhibition, the **Poble Espanyol**, or Spanish Village, is a homogeneous self-contained enclave, built in old stone, where various streets and squares hold reconstructions of famous or characteristic buildings from all over Spain. Each little district is dedicated to a specific region, starting with the fairy-tale medieval walls of Ávila through which you enter. "Get to know Spain in one hour" is the promise; it's all hugely enjoyable, and nothing like as cheesy as you might imagine. You could easily believe, in fact, that it had been here for hundreds of years, an impression helped of course by the fact that it's now almost a century old.

The echoing main square is lined with cafés, while the surrounding alleys and courtyards contain regionally themed restaurants and bars. There's also a gallery of twentieth-century art, the **Museu Fran Daurel** (free, same hours; ⓦ fundaciofrandaurel. com), which holds a handful of Miró prints plus a fair assortment of etchings, drawings and ceramics by Picasso. Workshops scattered through the village demonstrate crafts like engraving, weaving and glass-blowing, and there are plenty of family activities. Children, who can run free in the absence of traffic, will love it.

Inevitably, the whole place is riddled with shopping opportunities – you can buy everything from castanets to Lladró porcelain, religious icons to Barcelona soccer shirts – but no more so than the original destinations it celebrates.

Arrive early to enjoy the village relatively crowd-free – once the tour groups arrive, it becomes a bit of a scrum. You could always come instead at the other end of the day, when venues such as *Tablao de Carmen*, which puts on flamenco shows (see page 205), keep the action going well into the night.

Museu Nacional d'Art de Catalunya (MNAC)

Palau Nacional · May–Sept Tues–Sat 10am–8pm, Sun 10am–3pm; Oct–April Tues–Sat 10am–6pm, Sun 10am–3pm · Charge · ⓦ museunacional.cat · Ⓜ Espanya/Poble Sec, or bus #150 from Avda. de la Reina María Cristina, or bus #55 from C/Lleida

The towering, domed **Palau Nacional**, set proud on Montjuïc at the top of the long climb up from the Font Màgica, was the flagship building of Barcelona's 1929 International Exhibition. Used for the opening ceremony, the palace was due to be demolished once the expo was over, but gained a reprieve and ultimately became home to one of Spain's greatest museums – the **Museu Nacional d'Art de Catalunya** (**MNAC**), showcasing a thousand years of Catalan art in stupendous surroundings.

In such a wide-ranging museum, it can be hard to know where to start. If your time is at all limited, be sure not to miss the **medieval** collection, which is split into two main sections. One is dedicated to **Romanesque** art, the other to **Gothic**; both were periods during which Catalan artists were pre-eminent in Spain. MNAC also has impressive holdings of European **Renaissance and Baroque** art, as well as an unsurpassed collection of **nineteenth- and twentieth-century Catalan art** (up until the 1950s; subsequent periods are covered by the MACBA in the Raval). In addition, there's a changing roster of blockbuster exhibitions and special shows based on the museum's archives. You'll also find a **café-bar** and gift shop and art **bookshop** in the gloriously restored oval hall, a kiosk on the front terrace, and a separate museum restaurant with more sweeping views over the city.

The Romanesque collection

From the eleventh century onwards, as the Christian Reconquest spread across the Iberian peninsula, great numbers of sturdy **Romanesque** churches were built in the high Catalan Pyrenees. Medieval Catalan studios decorated these churches with extraordinary biblical **frescoes**, and even the most remote Pyrenean valleys boasted lavish masterpieces. By the nineteenth century, however, many of these churches either lay abandoned or had been ruined by renovations. Finally, in 1919, a concerted effort was made to preserve the frescoes for future generations, by removing them to a museum where they could be better displayed.

Today, the frescoes are magnificently presented in meticulously proportioned nest-like reconstructions of the original interiors, enabling visitors to see exactly where they would have been placed in the church buildings. Most possess a vibrant, raw quality that's best exemplified by those taken from churches in the Boí valley in the Catalan Pyrenees.

The highlight of the whole astonishing collection comes in **room 7**, where the extraordinarily powerful *Christ in Majesty*, painted by the so-called **Master of Taüll** for the apse of the early twelfth-century church of Sant Climent in Taüll, combines a Byzantine hierarchical composition with the imposing colours and strong outlines of contemporary manuscript illuminators. Look out for details such as the leper, to the left of the altar, patiently allowing a dog to lick his sores. The matching **room 9** holds a much larger set of frescoes from the neighbouring church of Santa Maria in Taüll, which rather amazingly was consecrated just one day later, in 1123.

Frescoes from other churches illustrate various themes, from heaven to hell, with the displays complemented by sculptures, altar panels, woodcarvings, religious objects and furniture retrieved from the mouldering churches.

The Gothic collection

The evolution from the Romanesque to the **Gothic** period was marked by a move from murals to painting on wood, and by the depiction of more naturalistic figures in scenes showing the lives of the saints, and later in portraits of kings and patrons of the arts.

THE BRILLIANT FLOWERING OF CATALAN ART

Between around 1850 and 1940, Catalan art enjoyed a modern golden age. The break-out artist, **Marià Fortuny i Marsal**, is often regarded as the earliest *modernista* artist, and was certainly the first Catalan painter to be known widely abroad, thanks to acclaimed exhibitions in Paris and Rome. He specialized in minutely detailed pictures, often of exotic subjects – the showpiece *Battle of Tetuan* in the MNAC, for example, was the result of his 1859 trip to observe the war in Morocco. The main name in contemporary Catalan Realism was **Ramon Martí i Alsina**, while the master of nineteenth-century Catalan landscape painting was **Joaquim Veyreda i Vila**, founder of the "Olot School", whose members were influenced both by the work of the early Impressionists and by the distinctive volcanic scenery of the Olot region in northern Catalunya.

However, only with the emergence of **Ramon Casas i Carbó** (whose famous picture of himself and Pere Romeu riding a tandem, as displayed at MNAC, once hung on the walls of *Els Quatre Gats*) and **Santiago Rusiñol i Prats** did Catalan art acquire its first contemporary art superstars. They took their cue from the very latest in European styles, whether the symbolism of Whistler or the vibrant social observation of Toulouse-Lautrec. Hot on their heels came a new generation of artists – Josep María Sert, Marià Pidelaserra i Brias, Ricard Canals i Llambí and others – who were strongly influenced by the scene in contemporary Paris. The two brightest stars of the period, though, were **Joaquim Mir i Trinxet**, whose highly charged landscapes tended towards the abstract, and **Isidre Nonell i Monturiol**, who from 1902 until his early death in 1911 painted sombre naturalistic studies of impoverished Gypsy communities.

The other dominant contemporary trend was *noucentisme*, a style at once more classical and less consciously flamboyant than *modernisme* – witness the portraits and landscapes of **Joaquim Sunyer i Miró**, perhaps the best known *noucentista* artist, and the work of sculptors like **Pau Gargallo i Catalán**.

TEATRE GREC AND THE BARCELONA FESTIVAL

Montjuïc takes centre-stage each year during Barcelona's annual summer cultural festival (⚙ barcelonafestival.com), known locally as the Grec, when arias soar from the open-air stage of the **Teatre Grec**, a Greek theatre cut into a former quarry on the Poble Sec side of the hill. Running from late June until the end of August, the festival incorporates drama, music and dance, with the opening sessions and many atmospheric events staged in the theatre, from Shakespearean productions to shows by avant-garde performance artists. These can be magical nights – a true Barcelona experience – though you'll need to be quick off the mark for tickets, which usually go on sale in May.

6

At first, the Catalan and Valencian schools in particular were influenced by contemporary Italian styles, and you'll see some outstanding altarpieces, tombs and church decoration. Later came the International Gothic or "1400" style, in which the influences became more widespread; the important figures of this movement were the artists **Jaume Huguet** (1412–92) and **Lluís Dalmau** (active 1428–61). Works from the end of this period show the strong influence of contemporary Flemish painting, in the use of denser colours, the depiction of crowd scenes and a concern for perspective.

The last Catalan artist of note here, the so-called **Master of La Seu d'Urgell**, is represented by several works, including a fine series of six paintings (Christ, the Virgin Mary, saints Peter, Paul and Sebastian and Mary Magdalene) that once formed the covers of an organ.

The Renaissance and Baroque collections

Many of MNAC's **Renaissance** and **Baroque** works have come from private collections bequeathed to the museum, notably by conservative politician Francesc Cambó and Madrid's Thyssen-Bornemisza. Selections from these bequests are shown in their own rooms within the Renaissance and Baroque galleries, while the other rooms in this section trace artistic development from the early sixteenth to the eighteenth century. Major European artists displayed include Peter Paul Rubens, Giovanni Battista Tiepolo, Jean Honoré Fragonard, Francisco de Goya, El Greco, Lucas Cranach, Francisco de Zurbarán and Diego Velázquez, though the museum is of course keen to play up Catalan works of the period, by the likes of Barcelona artist Antoni Viladomat (1678–1755). However, more familiar to most will be the masterpieces of the Spanish Golden Age, notably Velázquez's *Saint Paul* and Zurbarán's *Immaculate Conception*.

The modern art collection

MNAC ends on a high note with its unsurpassed **nineteenth- and twentieth-century Catalan art** collection, which is particularly good on *modernista* and *noucentista* painting and sculpture (see box, page 96), the two dominant schools of the period. Rooms highlight individual artists and genres, shedding light on the development of art in an exciting period of Catalunya's history. The works provide a rich, varied experience, ranging from intricate Barcelona street scenes to *modernista* interior design (including furniture by Gaudí), while there are also fascinating diversions into avant-garde sculpture and historical photography. Salvador Dalí is represented by a couple of paintings, including a portrait of his father from 1925, and there's a fascinating array of graphic art from the Civil War era.

Museu Etnològic

Pg. de Santa Madrona 16–22 • May–Sept Tues–Sun 10am–8pm; Oct–Apr Tues–Sat 10am–7pm, Sun 10am–8pm • Charge •
⚙ www.museuetnologic.bcn.cat • Ⓜ Espanya/Poble Sec, or bus #55 from C/Lleida

In recent years, Barcelona's ethnological museum, the **Museu Etnològic**, has divided into two sections. Most of its extensive collection of art and artefacts from around the globe is now on show in the Museu de Cultures del Món in the old town (see page 74). Its original home, on Montjuïc not far from MNAC, is now dedicated exclusively to artefacts from **Catalunya**.

While the main open-plan hall holds plenty of rural relics, ranging from huts to handlooms, much of its attention is focused on urban traditions that have grown up in Barcelona itself. Prize exhibits include everything from modern *gegants* – festival giants – to accordions.

6

The Olympic area

Ⓜ Espanya, then either walk via the hillside escalators behind MNAC or take bus #13 from Avda. de la Reina María Cristina or #55 from C/Lleida

The principal area used for the 1992 Olympics, sometimes known as the **Anella Olímpica** (Olympic Ring), stands high on Montjuïc, well above the Museu Nacional d'Art de Catalunya. These were actually the second Olympics to be planned for this location. The first, in 1936 – the "People's Olympics" – were organized as an alternative to the Nazis' infamous Berlin games of that year, but the day before the official opening, Franco's army revolt triggered the Civil War and scuppered the Barcelona games. Some of the 25,000 athletes and spectators who had turned up stayed on to join the Republican forces.

As well as the **stadium** itself, and the **sports museum**, signature buildings in the "Ring" include the steel-and-glass **Palau Sant Jordi**, a 17,000-seat sports and concert hall, Catalan architect Ricardo Bofill's **Institut Nacional d'Educació Física de Catalunya** (**INEF**; a sports university) and – one building you can visit as a general punter – the impressive **Piscines Picornell** (see page 219).

Museu Olímpic i de l'Esport

Avda. de l'Estadi 60 • April–Sept Tues–Sat 10am–8pm, Sun & hols 10am–2.30pm; Oct–March Tues–Sat 10am–6pm, Sun & hols 10am–2.30pm • Charge, under-7s free • ☎ 932 925 379, ⓦ museuolimpicbcn.com • Ⓜ Espanya then 25min walk, or bus #13 or #150 from Avda. de la Reina María Cristina

Just across the road from the Olympic stadium, the **Museu Olímpic i de l'Esport** is fronted by a walk of fame featuring footprints from the likes of Nadia Comaneci, Jack Nicklaus and Martina Navratilova. As Barcelona's moment in the sun recedes into history, it's become less a celebration of the 1992 games than a general museum of sport itself.

As well as tracing the entire story of the Olympics, including the 1169-year period of the ancient games, it covers everything from bull-jumping in Minoan Crete to cricket in modern Pakistan. It also includes a sizeable section on the Catalan administrator Juan Samaranch, who as President of the International Olympic Committee brought the games to Barcelona; should you wish, you can admire his personal collection of chestnuts. Much more fun are the interactive displays in which you can set your own records in the long or high jump.

The Olympic Stadium

Estadi Olímpic Lluís Companys, Avda. de l'Estadi • No public access, except during events • ⓦ estadiolimpic.barcelona

Built for the 1929 Exhibition, the **Olympic Stadium** atop Montjuïc was entirely refitted for the 1992 Barcelona Olympics, while retaining its original Neoclassical facade. Although seventy thousand spectators packed in for the opening and closing ceremonies, its current capacity is around 54,000. Now officially named the **Estadi Olímpic Lluís Companys**, in honour of the Generalitat president executed on Montjuïc after the Civil War, it's still used for various sporting events, as well as concerts by the likes of Bruce Springsteen.

A vast *terrassa* on the west side of the stadium provides one of the finest vantage points in the city. Long water-fed troughs break up the concrete and marble expanse, while the confident space-age curve of Santiago Calatrava's **communications tower** dominates the skyline.

6

Fundació Joan Miró

Parc de Montjuïc • Tues–Sat 10am–8pm, Sun 10am–7pm • Charge • ⓦ fmirobcn.org • Ⓜ Paral·lel, then Funicular de Montjuïc and 5min walk, or bus #150 from Avda. de la Reina María Cristina, or #55 from C/Llieda

Barcelona's most adventurous art museum, the **Fundació Joan Miró**, celebrates the life's work of the great Catalan artist Joan Miró (1893–1983), who established an international reputation while always retaining links with his homeland. The stark white modernist museum, designed by Miró's architect friend Josep Lluís Sert, and set amid lovely gardens, lies just a few minutes' walk from both the Olympic stadium and the Montjuïc funicular and cable-car stations.

Born in Barcelona in 1893, Miró showed a childlike delight in colours and shapes and developed a free, highly decorative style – his paintings and drawings are instantly recognizable, and are among the chief links between Surrealism and abstract art. Miró had his first exhibition in 1918; met Picasso in Paris during the 1920s; and subsequently spent his summers in Catalunya and the rest of the time in France, before moving to Mallorca in 1956, where he died.

Largely donated by Miró himself, the museum's huge collection of paintings, graphics, tapestries and sculptures ranges from 1914 up to 1978. Aside from the permanent displays, the Fundació sponsors excellent temporary exhibitions, film shows, lectures and children's theatre, as well as summer music nights (usually June and July). Young experimental artists have their own space in the **Espai 13** gallery, and there's also a contemporary art **library**, a **bookshop** and a pleasant open-air **café** on the Carob Tree Patio that's accessible whether or not you pay to get into the museum itself.

The collection

The museum's two-hundred-plus paintings are largely drawn from Miró's later years – by the time he started to set works aside for the museum in the 1960s, he had been painting for almost half a century. However, the collection does include early Realist works dating from before he decided to "assassinate art" and abandon figurative painting in the mid-1920s, like his landscapes from Mont.roig in Tarragona, where he

---

ON THE MIRÓ TRAIL

Once you've seen one Miró, well, you start to spot them everywhere in Barcelona, whether it's T-shirts for tourists or branding for businesses. There's the large ceramic mural on the facade of Terminal B at the **airport**, for a start, or the circular pavement mural at **Plaça de la Boqueria** that catches your attention every time you stroll down La Rambla.

Miró also designed the starfish logo for the **Caixa de Pensións** savings bank and the **España logo** on Spanish National Tourist Board publications. Then there's his towering *Dona i Ocell* ("Woman and Bird'") in the **Parc Joan Miró**, near Barcelona Sants train station, while a smaller *Dona* stands with other Catalan works in the courtyard of the **Ajuntament** (city hall). In many ways, Barcelona's a Miró city, whatever Picasso fans might think.

returned repeatedly after convalescing from typhoid fever in 1911, and the effervescent *Portrait of a Young Girl* (1919).

Other gaps are filled by a collection donated by Miró's widow, Pilar Juncosa, which demonstrates Miró's preoccupations in the 1930s and 1940s. This was the period when he started his **Constellations** series, introducing the colours, themes and symbols that, eventually pared down to the minimalist basics, came to define his work: reds and blues; women, birds and tears; the sun, moon and stars. That same period also saw the fifty black-and-white lithographs of the **Barcelona Series** (1939–44), executed in the immediate aftermath of the Civil War. They are a dark reflection of the turmoil of the period, all snarling faces and great black shapes and shadows.

Elsewhere you'll find several of Miró's enormous, dense and very shaggy **tapestries**; his **pencil drawings**, particularly of misshapen women and gawky ballerinas; **film footage** of the artist at work on, and setting light to, a canvas in 1973; and **sketches and notes** including doodles on scraps of newspaper. His **sculptures** are displayed outdoors, both in the gardens and on the spacious roof terrace.

Castell de Montjuïc

Carretera de Montjuïc 66 • **Castle** Daily: March–Oct 10am–8pm; Nov–Feb 10am–6pm • Charge • **Grounds** Daily: March–Oct 9am–9pm; Nov–Feb 9am–7pm • Free • ⊕ bcn.cat/castelldemontjuic • Direct access by Telefèric de Montjuïc, or bus #150 from Avda. de la Reina María Cristina

The best way to reach the **castle** at the very top of Montjuïc is via the Telefèric de Montjuïc (see page 93). The cable car tacks up the hillside before depositing you just outside the forbidding red-brick walls of the eighteenth-century fortress itself. It's worth coming up here simply to admire the dramatic location, and to enjoy the superb views out over the port from the grounds, which are free to enter.

Paying admission to the castle buys you marginally better views, especially from its surprisingly broad ramparts, but more importantly gives access to fascinating displays on its history and significance. Finally handed over to the city in 2008, the fortress had long been a symbol of Barcelona's occupation by a foreign power – the Spanish state. After all, it had served for decades as a military base and prison, with its mighty cannon trained on the city down below, and it was here that the last president of the prewar Generalitat, **Lluís Companys i Jover**, was executed on Franco's orders on October 15, 1940. Companys had been in exile in Paris after the Civil War, but was handed over to Franco by the Germans upon their capture of the French capital; he's buried in the nearby Cementiri del Sud-Oest. Small wonder, therefore, that the captions in the castle's interpretation centre refer to it as "hated for centuries".

Camí del Mar and Mirador del Migdia

Below the castle ramparts, a panoramic pathway – the **Camí del Mar** – has been cut from the cliff edge, providing further magnificent views, first across to Port Olímpic and the northern beaches, and then southwest as the path swings around the castle. This is an unfamiliar view of Barcelona, of the sprawling docks and container yards, with cruise ships and tankers usually visible negotiating the busy sea lanes.

Just over 1km long, the path ends at the back of the castle battlements near the **Mirador del Migdia**, where there's a great open-air bar, *La Caseta del Migdia* (see page 199). Down through the trees is the *mirador* itself, a balcony with extensive views over the Baix Llobregat industrial area. You can see across to the Olympic stadium from here, while in the immediate foreground the **Cementiri del Sud-Oest** stretches along the ridge below, with its tombs stacked like apartment blocks along great conifer-lined avenues.

Jardí Botànic de Barcelona

C/Dr Font i Quer 2 • Daily: April, May, Sept & Oct 10am–7pm; Feb–March 10am–6pm; June–Aug 10am–8pm; Nov–Jan 10am–5pm •
Charge • ⓦ museuciencies.bcn.cat • ⓜ Espanya, then 20min walk via escalators, or bus #150 from Avda. de la Reina María Cristina or #55
from C/Lleida

Principal among Montjuïc's many gardens is the **Jardí Botànic de Barcelona**, laid
out on terraced slopes that offer fine views across the city. It's a beautifully kept,
contemporary botanical garden, where wide, easy-to-follow paths (fine for buggies,
strollers and wheelchairs) wind through landscaped zones representing the flora of the
Mediterranean, Canary Islands, California, Chile, South Africa and Australia. Just don't
come in the full heat of summer, as there's very little shade. Guided tours in Spanish/
Catalan every weekend (except Aug) show you the highlights, but an English-language
booklet is included in the entry fee.

6

Museu de Carrosses Fúnebres

C/Mare de Déu de Port 56–58 • Sat & Sun 10am–2pm • Free • ⓦ cbsa.cat/colleccio • Bus #21 from Paral·lel

Unfortunately open on weekends only, for limited hours, the esoteric **Museu
de Carrosses Fúnebres** (Funerary Carriage Museum) stands at the entrance to
Montjuïc cemetery. The horse-drawn carriages on display were used for city funeral
processions from the 1830s until the service was mechanized in the 1950s, when the
silver Buick that's also on show came into use. Most of the carriages and hearses are
extravagantly decorated in gilt, black or white; some, such as the Grand Doumont
and the Stove, carried dignitaries, politicians and big-name bullfighters to their final
resting places. There are also plenty of old photographs, alongside antique uniforms,
mourning wear and formal riding gear. Free guided tours start at noon on Saturdays
(Spanish/Catalan).

THE GARDENS OF MONTJUÏC

Botanical gardens aside, Montjuïc holds plenty of places where you can roll out a picnic rug or
let the children scamper around safely.

Signposted off Avinguda de Miramar, west of (and below) the Fundació Joan Miró, the
terraces, clipped hedges and grottoes of the **Jardins de Laribal** (daily 10am–dusk; free)
date from 1918. They surround the spring of **Font del Gat**, which has been a picnic site since
the nineteenth century. A little higher up, between the Ethnology and Sports museums,
the verdant **Jardins de Joan Maragall**, open on weekend afternoons only (Sat & Sun
10am–3pm), surround the grand Neoclassical Palauet Albéniz, which was built as the official
Barcelona residence of the Spanish royal family.

Further east, the Montjuïc cable car passes over the **Jardins de Mossèn Cinto Verdaguer**
and adjacent **Jardins de Joan Brossa** (both daily 10am–dusk; free), which tack up the
hillside to the castle. Walking down through the gardens from the castle makes a pleasant way
to return to the lower slopes of Montjuïc, through the site of the former Montjuïc amusement
park, now fully landscaped with children's play areas. Halfway down, the **Mirador de
l'Alcalde** offers sweeping city views.

Outside the upper cross-harbour cable-car station, you'll find the formal **Jardins de
Miramar** (always open; free), plus more fine views from the cable-car station café-*terrassa*.
Steps nearby lead down into the precipitous cactus gardens of the **Jardins de Mossèn
Costa i Llobera** (daily 10am–dusk; free), which look out over the port. The flourishing stands
of Central and South American, Indian and African cacti, some over 6m high, make a dramatic
scene experienced by few visitors to Montjuïc, though as the crowds lounging on the steps
and in the shade of the bigger specimens suggest, it's an open secret among locals.

Museu d'Arqueologia de Catalunya

Pg. de Santa Madrona 39–41 • Tues–Sat 9.30am–7pm, Sun 10am–2.30pm • Charge • Ⓦ mac.cat • Ⓜ Espanya/Poble Sec, or bus #55 from C/Lleida

Though it's somewhat off the beaten track, down near the foot of Montjuïc at the edge of Poble Sec, the **Museu d'Arqueologia de Catalunya** is something no one interested in the early and classical-era history of what's now known as Catalunya should miss. Spanning the centuries from the Stone Age to the time of the Visigoths, its rich collection centres on dramatic finds from the region's most famous archeological sites.

As few captions are translated from Catalan, it's well worth picking up the free audio-guide before you begin. The human story kicks off forty thousand years ago, with early highlights including stunning cave paintings, and continues with reconstructed

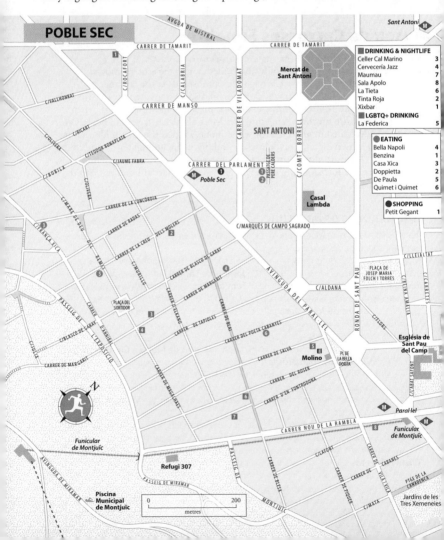

POBLE SEC

DRINKING & NIGHTLIFE
Celler Cal Marino	3
Cervecería Jazz	4
Maumau	7
Sala Apolo	8
La Tieta	6
Tinta Roja	2
Xixbar	1

LGBTQ+ DRINKING
La Federica	5

● EATING
Bella Napoli	4
Benzina	1
Casa Xica	3
Doppietta	2
De Paula	5
Quimet i Quimet	6

● SHOPPING
Petit Gegant	1

burial sites such as the megalithic Dolmen del Collet de Su and the Bronze Age cave of Montanisell, discovered in 2004.

One section traces the rise and fall of the original Iberian culture, which flourished between 660 BC and 200 AD; look out for the gruesome human skull with a nail driven through it, thought to have been displayed on the walls of some ancient settlement. There's also some fine Egyptian glassware and Roman mosaic work, while the upper floor records life in Roman **Barcino** itself, via tombstones, statues, inscriptions and friezes found all over the city.

6

La Ciutat del Teatre

C/Lleida • Ⓜ Poble Sec

At the foot of Montjuïc, on the eastern slopes, the theatre area known as **La Ciutat del Teatre** occupies a back corner of the old working-class neighbourhood of Poble Sec. Direct steps descend the hillside, while Passeig de Santa Madrona runs down here from MNAC, passing the archeological museum.

The theatre buildings that make up La Ciutat del Teatre sit in a tight huddle off C/Lleida. Here you'll find the **Mercat de les Flors** (see page 205) – once a flower market, now a centre for dance and the "movement arts" – and progressive **Teatre Lliure** (see page 206), "Free Theatre", occupying the spaghetti-western-style Palau de l'Agricultura premises built for the 1929 Exhibition.

Walk through the terracotta arch from C/Lleida, and off to the left is the far sleeker **Institut del Teatre** (see page 206), which brings together the city's major drama and dance schools, along with various conservatories, libraries and study centres. The sheer walls of the gleaming Theatre City form a marked contrast with the neighbourhood's low-cost housing just metres away, draped with hanging laundry.

Poble Sec

Ⓜ Poble Sec/Paral·lel

Lying immediately below Montjuïc, confined by the hill on one side and the busy Avinguda del Paral·lel on the other, the neighbourhood of **Poble Sec**, or "Dry Village",

---

A CITY UNDER SIEGE

During the Civil War, Poble Sec – like many inner-city neighbourhoods – suffered grievously from Nationalist bombing raids, a foretaste of what was to come elsewhere in Europe during World War II. From 1936 onwards, the city authorities oversaw the construction of communal **air-raid shelters**, many of which were ready by the time the first raids hit Barcelona early in 1937. Most were constructed in working-class areas like Poble Sec, Barceloneta and Gràcia, where locals hadn't been able to leave the city or couldn't reach the relative safety of either the metro tunnels or the Collserola hills.

Altogether, around 1400 shelters were built in Barcelona, plus another two thousand across Catalunya. While some were as simple as reinforced cellars, many, like **Refugi 307**, were larger efforts that featured vaulted brick-lined tunnels, ventilation, water supplies and even infirmaries and play areas. The raids were particularly savage in March 1938, and by the end of the war had killed three thousand inhabitants, with many more injured and thousands of buildings destroyed. Even so, the shelters undoubtedly saved many lives. In the wake of Republican defeat, after the war, many shelters were forgotten, but these days the city authorities are keen to raise their profile in remembrance of Barcelona's often overlooked wartime history.

is so-called because it had no water supply until the nineteenth century. It's a complete contrast to the landscaped slopes that rise above – a grid of contoured narrow streets, down-to-earth grocery stores, bakeries, local shops and good-value restaurants. Asian immigrants have stamped their mark on many of the neighbourhood stores and businesses, while Poble Sec is also emerging as an "off-Raval" nightlife destination, with its bars and music clubs – pedestrianized **Carrer de Blai** is the focal point of the scene, and lined with increasingly touristed tapas bars.

Refugi 307

C/Nou de la Rambla 175 • Guided visits Sun 10.30am (English), 11.30am (Spanish) & 12.30pm (Catalan) • Charge •
Ⓦ museuhistoria.bcn.cat • Ⓜ Paral·lel

Many visitors never set foot in Poble Sec, though one of the city's old Civil War air-raid shelters provides a compelling reason to make the short journey across town. **Refugi 307** was dug into the Montjuïc hillside by local people from 1936 onwards, and its 200m of tunnels could shelter up to two thousand people from Franco's bombing raids. With no radar to protect the city, they had two minutes from the first sound of the sirens to get underground. To take a tour, you can simply turn up on Sunday morning. Photographic storyboards at the start of the tour provide a bit of background, and then it's hard hat on to follow your guide into the labyrinth, all to the sound of screaming sirens and droning warplanes.

Dreta de l'Eixample

Now Barcelona's main shopping and business district, the nineteenth-century street grid north of Plaça de Catalunya was laid out as part of a revolutionary urban plan. Dubbed the Eixample in Catalan – pronounced *ey-sham-pla*, it means the "Extension" or "Widening" – the scheme divided the area into regular blocks, whose characteristic wide streets and shaved corners survive today. Two parallel avenues, Passeig de Gràcia and Rambla de Catalunya, form its backbone, with everything to the east known as the Dreta de l'Eixample. It's here that the bulk of Barcelona's famous *modernista* buildings is found, along with an array of classy galleries and fashionable hotels, shops and boutiques. You won't be able to see everything here on a single outing, but the Dreta does contain many of the city's most stylish, show-stopping buildings.

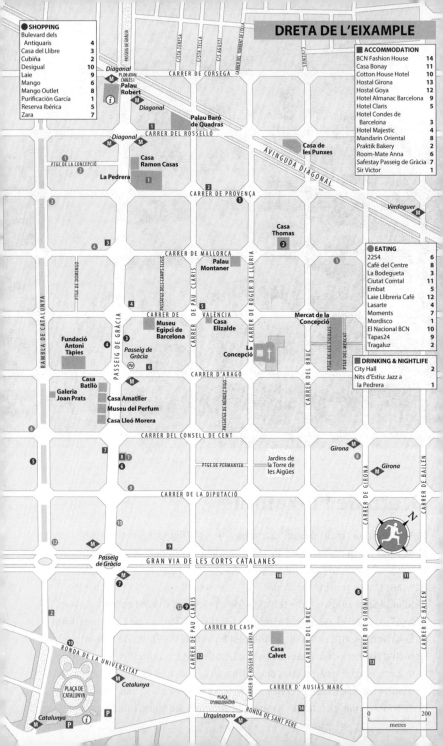

DRETA DE L'EIXAMPLE

● SHOPPING
Bulevard dels Antiquaris	4
Casa del Llibre	3
Cubiña	2
Desigual	10
Laie	9
Mango	6
Mango Outlet	8
Purificación García	1
Reserva Ibérica	5
Zara	7

■ ACCOMMODATION
BCN Fashion House	14
Casa Bonay	11
Cotton House Hotel	10
Hostal Girona	13
Hostal Goya	12
Hotel Almanac Barcelona	9
Hotel Claris	5
Hotel Condes de Barcelona	3
Hotel Majestic	8
Mandarin Oriental	4
Praktik Bakery	2
Room-Mate Anna	6
Safestay Passeig de Gràcia	7
Sir Victor	1

● EATING
2254	6
Café del Centre	8
La Bodegueta	3
Ciutat Comtal	11
Embat	5
Laie Llibreria Café	12
Lasarte	4
Moments	7
Mordisco	1
El Nacional BCN	10
Tapas24	9
Tragaluz	2

■ DRINKING & NIGHTLIFE
City Hall	2
Nits d'Estiu: Jazz a la Pedrera	1

Acting as a sort of open-air museum, Dreta de l'Eixample features the masterworks of a new class of *modernista* architects, who changed the look of Barcelona from 1880 onwards. These extraordinary edifices – notably by Antoni Gaudí i Cornet, Lluís Domènech i Montaner and Josep Puig i Cadafalch – were commissioned by status-conscious merchants and businessmen. Constructed as private houses and apartments, many of the buildings are now open to the public. Most are enclosed in a triangle formed by the Passeig de Gràcia, Avinguda Diagonal and the Gran Via de les Corts Catalanes, within a few blocks of each other.

The standout sights are Gaudí's **La Pedrera** apartment building, and the so-called **Mansana de la Discòrdia**, or "Block of Discord" (Pg. de Gràcia, between carrers del Consell de Cent and d'Aragó), which gets its name because the three adjacent houses, casas **Lleó Morera**, **Amatller** and **Batlló** – erected within a decade of each other by three different architects – show off wildly varying manifestations of the *modernista* style and spirit. The Dreta also holds the not-to-miss gallery dedicated to Catalunya's most eminent postwar artist **Antoni Tàpies**, and a great neighbourhood **market**.

7

Casa Lleó Morera

Pg. de Gràcia 35 • Currently closed • ⓦ casalleomorera.com • Ⓜ Passeig de Gràcia

Designed by Lluís Domènech i Montaner and completed in 1905, the six-storey **Casa Lleó Morera** is the least obviously extravagant building in the "Block of Discord", and has suffered the most from depredations wrought by subsequent owners. The original arches and sculptures have long since been removed from its ground floor – Salvador Dalí bought some – which is now occupied by the luxury leather goods store Loewe. In the words of Robert Hughes, "No one who cares for architecture should ever buy anything from Loewe, on principle".

Until recently, the wonderful Art Nouveau interior could be seen on regular guided tours – its sheer scale and opulence are quite extraordinary – but, for now, the only option is a virtual visit on the website.

Museu del Perfum

Pg. de Gràcia 39 • Mon–Fri 10.30am–2pm,• Charge • ⓦ museodelperfume.com • Ⓜ Passeig de Gràcia

There's no missing the **Museu del Perfum**; walk anywhere near the Regia perfume store in which it's sited, and you'll be overwhelmed by the cloying pong. They'll probably have to turn the lights on for you to enter the museum itself, though, located in a back room and devoted to an exquisite collection of perfume vessels and containers rather than to their contents. These range from tiny ceramic and alabaster jars from ancient Egypt and Carthage, via Roman glass, up to Turkish filigree-and-crystal ware and bronze and silver Indian elephant flasks. More recent eras are represented by scents made for Grace Kelly and Elizabeth Taylor, and if you're diligent enough to scan all the shelves you should spot the "Sun King" bottles designed by Salvador Dalí.

Casa Amatller

Fundació Amatller, Pg. de Gràcia 41 • Daily 10am–6pm, 50min tours 11am (English), noon (Catalan) & 5pm (Spanish); reservations advised • Charge • ⓦ amatller.org • Ⓜ Passeig de Gràcia

Josep Puig i Cadafalch's striking **Casa Amatller** apartment block (c.1900) was designed for Antoni Amatller, a Catalan chocolate manufacturer, art collector, photographer and traveller. It's a triumph of decorative detail, particularly the facade, which rises in steps to a point, studded with ceramic tiles and heraldic sculptures. Inside, the hallway's twisted

DESIGN A CITY...DESIGNER CITY

As Barcelona grew more industrialized throughout the nineteenth century, the old town became overcrowded and unsanitary. In 1851, the Spanish state finally gave permission to knock down the encircling walls and allow the city to expand beyond its medieval limits.

When it came to building what amounted to an entire new town, Barcelona then, as now, didn't do things by halves. The city authorities championed a fan-shaped plan by popular municipal architect **Antoni Rovira i Trias**, whose design radiated out from the existing shape of the old town. (His statue sits on a bench in Gràcia's Pl. Rovira i Trias, with his Eixample plan set in the ground beneath him.) However, much to local chagrin, Rovira's elegant if conventional plan was passed over by the Spanish government in favour of a revolutionary blueprint drawn up by utopian engineer and urban planner **Ildefons Cerdà i Sunyer**. This was defiantly modern in style and scale – a massive grid marching off to the north, intersected by broad avenues cut on the diagonal. Districts would be divided into wide, spacious blocks, with buildings limited in height, and central gardens, schools, markets, hospitals and other services provided for the inhabitants.

Cerdà lived to see most of his more radical social proposals ignored, as the Eixample rapidly became a fashionable area in which to live and speculators developed buildings on the proposed open spaces. Even today though, the underlying fabric of his plan is always evident, while in certain quiet corners and gardens the original emphasis on social community within grand design lives on.

stone columns are interspersed with dragon lamps. Much of the house is now given over to the library and archive of the Amatller Institute of Hispanic Art, but it's also open to the public, allowing you to admire its original Art Nouveau furniture and interior design, take a peep at Amatller's photographic studio and at certain times sample hot chocolate in the kitchen.

Casa Batlló

Pg. de Gràcia 43 • Daily 9am–8pm • Charge; buy tickets in advance, in person or online • ⓦ casabatllo.es • Ⓜ Passeig de Gràcia

The most extraordinary creation on the "Block of Discord", Antoni Gaudí's **Casa Batlló** (pronounced *by-o*) was designed for the industrialist Josep Batlló. The original apartment building, built in 1877, was considered dull by contemporaries, so Gaudí was hired to give it a face-lift, and completed the work by 1907. This time, the result was very far from dull, as indicated by nicknames that include "House of Bones", "House That Yawns" and "House That Breathes". Salvador Dalí called it "a house of sea-shapes, representing the waves on a stormy day". Its most conspicuous feature is its undulating street facade, adorned with balconies that might be carnival masks or the teeth-laden jaws of fish, and pockmarked higher up with circular ceramic buttons laid on a bright mosaic background. The interior, however, is every bit as compelling, meaning that despite the crowds and high prices, the **self-guided audio tours** should absolutely not be missed.

There's barely a straight line in the entire building, which resembles some great organism, threaded through by sinuous polished-wood banisters and complete with snakeskin-patterned walls, plus curving window frames, fireplaces and doorways. Every room is bathed in natural light, while gratings in the doors and elsewhere, modelled perhaps on the gills of fish, allow outside air to circulate.

For once, the audio-guides are excellent, pointing out details you might otherwise miss and providing all the necessary context, and offering "augmented-reality" views of how the place looked when new and first lived in. They steer you up from the main floor, including the gloriously light salon that overlooks Passeig de Gràcia, via the patio and rear terrace, into the attic, supported by Gaudí's trademark catenary arches, and culminate when you emerge on the rooftop to find yourself surrounded by colourful **chimneys**, crusted with mosaics and broken tiles. Commentators, echoing what little explanation Gaudí ever gave of his intentions, have described this scaly roofscape as representing the spine of the dragon killed by Sant Jordi (St George), and the small tower holding a three-dimensional cross as the knight's lance, plunged into the dragon's back.

Fundació Antoni Tàpies

C/Aragó 255 • Tues–Sat 10am–7pm, Sun 10am–3pm • Charge • ⓦ fundaciotapies.org • Ⓜ Passeig de Gràcia

The definitive collection of the work of Catalan abstract artist **Antoni Tàpies** is housed in Lluís Domènech i Montaner's first important building, the **Casa Montaner i Simon** (1880),

MODERNISME – WHO'S WHO AND WHAT'S WHAT

Modernisme – the Catalan equivalent of Art Nouveau – was the expression of a renewed upsurge in Catalan nationalism. Catalunya's economic recovery in the early nineteenth century provided the initial impetus, while the subsequent cultural renaissance – the Renaixença – led to fresh stirrings of a Catalan awareness and identity (see box, page 96). Three architects in particular came to prominence in Barcelona, and introduced a building style that has given the city a look like no other.

ANTONI GAUDÍ I CORNET

Born in Reus, near Tarragona, to a family of artisans, **Antoni Gaudí i Cornet** (1852–1926) brought much more than *modernisme* to his creations, but the imaginative impetus he provided was incalculable. Fantasy, spiritual symbolism and Catalan pride are evident in every building he designed, while his architectural influences were Moorish and Gothic, embellished with elements from the natural world. These themes are visible in projects as diverse as his extraordinary suburban industrial estate, Colònia Güell, and his masterpiece church, the Sagrada Família. Yet Gaudí rarely wrote a word about the theory of his art, preferring to leave it to the buildings to provoke a reaction– no one stands mute in front of an Antoni Gaudí masterpiece.
Key buildings and works:
Casa Batlló See page 108; **Colònia Güell** See page 153; **Palau Güell** See page 66; **Park Güell** See page 131; **La Pedrera** See page 111; **Sagrada Família** See page 122

LLUÍS DOMÈNECH I MONTANER

While Gaudí may be in a class of his own, arguably the greatest pure *modernista* architect was **Lluís Domènech i Montaner** (1850–1923). Drawing on the rich Catalan Romanesque and Gothic traditions, his work combined traditional craft methods with modern technological experiments – with spectacularly innovative results.
Key buildings and works:
Casa Lleó Morera See page 107; **Hospital de la Santa Creu i de Sant Pau** See page 124; **Palau de la Música Catalana** See page 69; **Castell dels Tres Dragons** See page 78

JOSEP PUIG I CADAFALCH

The work of **Josep Puig i Cadafalch** (1867–1957) is characterized by a wildly inventive use of ceramic tiles, ironwork, stained glass and stone carving. His first commission, the **Casa Martí**, housed the famous *Els Quatre Gats* tavern for the city's avant-garde artists and hangers-on, while in uptown mansions built for the newly enriched Barcelona bourgeoisie, he brought distinct Gothic and medieval influences to bear.
Key buildings and works:
Casa Amatller See page 107; **Casa de les Punxes** See page 113; **Els Quatre Gats** See page 50

7

originally constructed for the publishing firm of Montaner i Simon. Converted in 1990 to house the **Fundació Antoni Tàpies**, it's now capped by Tàpies's own striking sculpture, **Núvol i Cadira** ("Cloud and Chair"; 1990), a tangle of glass, wire and aluminium.

While the building itself is a beauty, with its Moorish-style flourishes, cast-iron columns and lack of dividing walls, Tàpies's art polarizes opinion. It's not immediately accessible (in the way of, say, Miró), and most visitors seem either to love or hate the gallery. Expect to see a selection of works from the permanent collection, while constantly changing temporary exhibitions highlight works and installations by contemporary artists. The foundation also includes a peerless archive on Tàpies's work, held in the gorgeous **library** on the upper floor, fashioned from the original shelves of the publisher's warehouse.

Museu Egipci de Barcelona

C/València 284 • Early June to late Sept Mon–Sat 10am–8pm, Sun 10am–2pm; late Sept to early June Mon–Fri 10am–2pm & 4–7.30pm, Sat 10am–3pm & 4–7.30pm, Sun 10am–2pm • Charge • Guided tours Sat at 11am (Catalan) & 5pm (Spanish) • ⓦ museuegipci.com • ⓜ Passeig de Gràcia

7

The **Museu Egipci de Barcelona**, half a block east of Passeig de Gràcia, holds an exceptional private collection of artefacts from ancient Egypt – Spain has nothing else quite like it. Founded by hotelier and antiquity collector Jordi Clos – whose deluxe *Hotel Claris*, a block away, has its own museum of pre-Columbian art – it displays a remarkable gathering of over a thousand objects, ranging from amulets to sarcophagi. Everything is beautifully presented, over three floors, with an emphasis on exploring the shape and character of Egyptian society.

The real pleasure here is a serendipitous wander, turning up items like a wood-and-leather bed from the First and Second Dynasties (2920–2649 BC); a magnificent pectoral adornment that once belonged to costume designer Natacha Rambova, the second wife of Rudolph Valentino; some remarkable flint knives and bronze axes; and

ANTONI TÀPIES

Born on C/Canuda in the Barri Gòtic, **Antoni Tàpies i Puig** (1923–2012) initially studied law at the University of Barcelona, but left without completing his degree. Drawn to art from an early age, and largely self-taught (though he did study briefly at Barcelona's Acadèmia Valls), he became in 1948 a founding member of the influential Dau al Set ("Die at Seven"), a group of seven artists that produced an eponymous avant-garde magazine that ran until 1956. His first major paintings date from as early as 1945, by which time he was already interested in collage (using newspaper, cardboard, silver wrapping, string and wire) and engraving techniques.

During the Dau al Set period, having come into contact with Miró among others, **Tàpies** went through a brief Surrealist phase. However, following a stay in Paris he found his feet with an **abstract style** that matured in the 1950s, when he held his first major exhibitions, including shows in New York and Europe. His large works are deceptively simple, though underlying messages and themes are signalled by the collage-like inclusion of everyday objects and a wide use of symbols on the canvas. He also continually experimented with unusual materials, such as oil paint mixed with crushed marble, or by employing sand, clay, cloth or straw in his collages.

Tàpies's work became increasingly **political** during the 1960s and 1970s: *A la memòria de Salvador Puig Antich, 1974* commemorates a Catalan anarchist executed by Franco's regime, while slogans splashed across his works, or the frequent use of the red bars of the Catalan flag, leave no doubt about his affiliations. The works preceding his death were more sombre still, featuring recurring images of earth, shrouds and bodies, as echoes of civil war and conflict. Meanwhile, he had left a string of important outdoor pieces across the city, including the mysterious glass box that is his *Homenatge a Picasso* (1983), on Passeig de Picasso, outside the gates of the Parc de la Ciutadella.

cat mummies from the Late Period (715–332 BC). There's also a good bookshop and a terrace café, plus a programme of study sessions, children's activities and evening events.

Jardins de la Torre de les Aigües

C/Roger de Llúria 56, between C/Consell de Cent and C/Diputació • Daily 10am–dusk, Aug & Sept Sat & Sun until 3pm • Free • Ⓜ Girona

The nineteenth-century Eixample urban plan was drawn up with local inhabitants very much in mind. Space, light and social community projects were integral to the grand design, and something of the original municipal spirit can be seen in the **Jardins de la Torre de les Aigües**, an enclosed square (reached down a herringbone-brick tunnel) that centres on a Moorish-style water tower. It has been handsomely restored by the city council, though the wide paddling pool has been allowed to dry up.

Another example of the old Eixample lies directly opposite, across C/Roger de Llúria, where the cobbled **Passatge del Permanyer** cuts across an Eixample block, lined by candy-coloured single-storey townhouses.

7

Mercat de la Concepció and around

Between C/València and C/Aragó • Aug Mon–Sat 8am–3pm; Sept–July Mon & Sat 8am–3pm, Tues–Fri 8am–8pm • Ⓦ laconcepcio.cat • Ⓜ Girona

The Dreta's finest neighbourhood market, the **Mercat de la Concepció**, was inaugurated in 1888, its iron-and-glass tram-shed structure reminiscent of others in the city. Flowers, shrubs, trees and plants are a Concepció speciality, and the florists on C/València stay open 24 hours a day. As well as a couple of good snack bars inside the market, there are a few outdoor cafés to the side.

La Concepció

C/Aragó 299, entrance on C/Roger de Llúria • Daily Mon–Sat 7.30am–1pm & 5–9pm, Sun 7.30am–2pm & 5–9pm • Free • Ⓜ Girona

The quiet cloister of the church of **La Concepció**, a block west of its namesake market, is a surprising haven of slender columns and orange trees. Part of a fifteenth-century Gothic convent that originally stood in the old town, the church was transferred here brick by brick during the 1870s, along with the Romanesque belfry from another old-town church.

Palau Montaner

C/Mallorca 278 • Occasional guided tours; check website for updates Ⓦ rutadelmodernisme.com • Ⓜ Passeig de Gràcia

The **Palau Montaner** was built in 1896 for the Montaner i Simon publishing family. After the original architect quit, *modernista* architect Lluís Domènech i Montaner took over halfway through construction, which explains why the top half of the facade is more elaborate than the lower part. Meanwhile, the period's most celebrated craftsmen were set to work on the interior, which sports rich mosaic floors, painted glass, carved woodwork and a monumental staircase. Now the seat of the Madrid government's delegation to Catalunya, the building is only open via occasional guided tours.

La Pedrera

Pg. de Gràcia 92, entrance on C/Provença • Daily: March–Oct 9am–8.30pm; Nov–Feb 9am–6.30pm • Charge • Ⓦ lapedrera.com • Ⓜ Diagonal

The weird and wonderful apartment building that was constructed by Antoni Gaudí as the **Casa Milà** between 1905 and 1911, but is universally known as **La Pedrera** – "The

Stone Quarry" – deservedly ranks among Barcelona's most popular tourist attractions. It was declared a UNESCO World Heritage Site in 1984. Curving around the street corner, its hulking, rippled facade is said to have been inspired by the mountain of Montserrat just outside the city, while the apartments themselves, whose balconies of tangled metal drip over the facade, resemble eroded cave dwellings. It's all so seamlessly sinuous that Gaudí's contemporaries joked that the new tenants would only be able to keep snakes as pets.

Gaudí himself described the building as "more luminous than light". This was his final secular commission, even here he was injecting religious motifs and sculptures until its owners told him to remove them. Alarmed by the anti-religious fervour of the "Tragic Week" in 1909, when anarchist-sponsored rioting destroyed churches and religious foundations – and the disinterred corpses of nuns were deposited on the doorstep of Palau Güell – they forbade him to add the sculpture of the Virgin Mary with which he planned to complete the roof. Gaudí, by now working full-time on the Sagrada Família, was appalled, and resolved to use his skills exclusively for religious purposes in future.

La Pedrera is always busy with visitors, so at peak periods it's essential to book ahead. Ordinarily you have to reserve for a specific date and time, but booking an "open date" ticket means you can visit at any time within a month of whatever date you choose.

In addition, the whole place reopens in the evening for various after-dark tours and events, including occasional jazz concerts on the rooftop. Other ways to visit La Pedrera include a tour with VR glasses, access to "unseen" spaces with a paid supplement or a joint ticket with the Recinte Modernista de Sant Pau (check the website for details).

Note that the building's grand main entrance on Passeig de Gràcia also provides access to an **exhibition hall** run by the Fundació Caixa de Catalunya (⊚fundaciocatalunya-lapedrera.com), which hosts temporary art shows by international artists, plus a full programme of children's and family activities, concerts and events.

Touring La Pedrera

Visitors to La Pedrera only get to see a small proportion of the building, as most of the apartments are still privately occupied. Entering the complex, you step first into the larger of two oval interior courtyards. You're directed into an elevator that climbs straight up to its crowning glory, the extraordinary **terrat** or roof terrace (which may be closed if it's raining). Those among the bizarre structures up here that most resemble chimneys, albeit crusted with broken tiles, tend in fact to stand atop ventilation shafts, while others mark the top of stairwells; by and large it's what look like clusters of helmeted sentinels or warriors that truly are chimneys. Stroll around the rooftop and take in the superb views.

An excellent exhibition on Gaudí's life and work has been installed beneath the 270 curved brick arches of the **attic** immediately below. All his major Barcelona buildings are covered, in displays that illustrate how he drew his inspiration from natural forms like python skeletons, pumpkins and seashells.

The one apartment included on the tour itineraries, **El Pis** (simply, "the apartment") on the fourth floor, re-creates the design and style of a *modernista*-era bourgeois apartment in a series of extraordinarily light rooms that flow seamlessly each to the next. They're

---

A NIGHT ON THE TILES

Gaudí fans can get closer to the great man's work at a unique venue – and enjoy a night out in the process. At **Nits d'estiu: Jazz a la Pedrera** (see page 200), Gaudí's amazing ceramic-tiled rooftop at La Pedrera is the evening backdrop for a glass of cava and live jazz.

filled with period furniture and effects, while the moulded door and window frames, and even the brass door handles, bear witness to Gaudí's ergonomic sense of design.

Casa Ramon Casas

Pg. de Gràcia 96 • **Massimo Dutti** Mon–Sat 10am–9pm • ☎ 932 177 306 • Ⓜ Diagonal

Next to La Pedrera, the **Casa Ramon Casas** (1899) was built as a house and studio for the wealthy Barcelona artist Ramon Casas i Carbó (1866–1932). He had found early success in Paris with friends Santiago Rusiñol and Miquel Utrillo, and the trio were later involved in *Els Quatre Gats* tavern, which Casas largely financed.

For 75 years, it was occupied by the prestigious furniture and design store Vinçon. In 2015, it was taken over by the fashion store Massimo Dutti and restored to show off its *modernista* glories. An open-air terrace on the second floor offers views of La Pedrera, while the original studio holds a **gallery** that puts on excellent temporary exhibitions.

7

Palau Robert

Pg. de Gràcia 107 • Mon–Sat 10am–8pm, Sun & hols 10am–2.30pm • Free • Ⓦ palaurobert.gencat.cat • Ⓜ Diagonal

Catalunya's regional information centre, inside the **Palau Robert** at the top of Passeig de Gràcia, hosts changing **exhibitions** on all matters Catalan. Both the main palace – built as a typical aristocratic residence in 1903 – and its former coach house hold exhibition spaces, while the centre is also an important **concert venue** for recitals and orchestras. The pretty gardens around the back make a popular meeting point for local nannies.

Palau Baró de Quadras

Avda. Diagonal 373 • Guided tour Fri 10am • Charge • Ⓦ llull.cat/monografics/palaubaroquadras • Ⓜ Diagonal

Neo-Gothic palace or *modernista* apartment building? How you categorize the beautifully detailed **Palau Baró de Quadras** – a Josep Puig i Cadafalch structure from 1904 that's home to the Institut Ramon Llull, promoting the Catalan language – depends on how you approach it. With intricate carvings, an ornate balcony and mansard roof, the Avinguda Diagonal facade takes a cue from northern European palaces. The building's Carrer del Rosselló side is decorated in a more subdued, but very lovely, *modernista* style. The only way to see the interior is by guided tour.

Casa de les Punxes

Avda. Diagonal 420 • Daily 9am–8pm • Charge • Ⓦ casalespunxes.com • Ⓜ Verdaguer

Architect Josep Puig i Cadafalch's largest work, the soaring Casa Terrades, is thanks to its red-tiled turrets and steep gables more usually known as the **Casa de les Punxes** (House of Spikes). Built in 1903 for three sisters, and converted from three separate houses, the crenellated structure is almost northern European in style, reminiscent of a Gothic castle.

Sadly, successive occupants stripped the interior of almost all original furnishings and embellishments. The ground floor now simply holds a gift shop, while **self-guided tours** of the empty apartments above start with an inane multi-media retelling of the legend of **St George** and the dragon.

Eventually, you reach informative panels about Cadafalch and his work, and can then ride the elevator to the **roof terrace**, where the individual turrets contain further displays. The St George theme owes to the fact that Cadafalch crowned one facade – on C/del Rosselló – with a painted-tile image of Catalunya's patron saint.

Esquerra de l'Eixample

The long streets of the Esquerra de l'Eixample start west of Rambla de Catalunya and reach as far as Barcelona Sants train station. With the major architectural highlights found on the right side of the Eixample, the Esquerra or left-hand side was primarily intended by its nineteenth-century planners to hold public buildings, institutions and industrial concerns, many of which remain in place. However, the district does hold significant cultural interest, including a couple of art galleries and an eye-catching public park or two, while the former Arenas bullring has been restyled as a leisure and shopping complex. This is also one of Barcelona's hottest night-out destinations, featuring some of the city's best restaurants, bars and clubs, particularly in the LGBTQ+-friendly streets of the so-called Gaixample district, behind the university.

Universitat de Barcelona

Gran Via de les Corts Catalanes 585, at Pl. de la Universitat • ⓜ Universitat

Erected in the 1860s, the grand Neoclassical main building of the **Universitat de Barcelona** is now largely used for ceremonies and administrative purposes, but no one will mind if you stroll through the doors. There's usually an exhibition in the echoing main hall, while two fine arcaded courtyards beyond, plus extensive gardens with a pond, a fountain and some of the city's oldest trees, provide a welcome escape from the traffic hereabouts.

Museu del Modernisme Barcelona

C/Balmes 48 • Mon–Sat 11am–7pm • Charge • ⓦ mmcat.cat • ⓜ Passeig de Gràcia

Barcelona's traditional "gallery district", around C/Consell de Cent, makes a fitting location for the *modernista* treasures of the small **Museu del Modernisme Barcelona**. The private enterprise of the celebrated local Gothsland antiques gallery, it displays a collection that was forty years in the making. Craftsman Eusebi Arnau's famous marble decorative vase, which served as the symbol of the Gothsland gallery for over thirty years, is just one of 350 works on show across two exhibition floors, in a restored building that originally served as a textile warehouse.

The ground floor is largely devoted to *modernista* furniture, from screens to sofas, with a Univers Gaudí section that includes sinuous mirrors and tables created by Antoni Gaudí for the casas Batlló and Calvet. Downstairs, the grand vaulted basement holds paintings, sculptures and huge stained-glass panels. Above all, this is a rare opportunity to examine extraordinary Art Nouveau fixtures and fittings by artists with whom you may not be familiar: wonderful creations by pioneering cabinet-maker Joan Busquets i Jané (1874–1949), for example; the dramatic carved mahogany headboards of Gaspar Homar i Mezquida (1870–1955); or the expressive terracotta sculptures of Lambert Escaler i Milà (1874–1957), which include several busts of women floating on seas of swirling hair. As a crash course in the varied facets of Catalan *modernisme*, beyond the iconic buildings themselves, it's invaluable.

8

Mercat del Ninot and around

C/Mallorca 133 • Mon–Fri 8am–9pm, Sat 8am–6pm • ⓦ mercatdelninot.com • ⓜ Hospital Clinic

One of the oldest markets in the city, the colossal **Mercat del Ninot** takes up a large area between carrers Villaroel and Casanova. Built in 1892, it has recently reopened following major refurbishment. Everything is gleaming and spotless, with stalls and cafés at street level and a Mercadona supermarket downstairs. While it's not really a tourist destination and is mostly visited by locals, it's a great spot to pick up a snack or have a drink at the wine stand.

Escola del Treball

Corner of C/Comte d'Urgell and C/Rosselló • ⓦ escoladeltreball.org • ⓜ Hospital Clinic

West of the Mercat del Ninot, around the back of the massive Hospital Clinic, it's worth taking a look at the **Escola del Treball**, converted in 1908 from buildings of the former Batlló textile mill. It occupies four entire Eixample blocks, with later academic buildings added in the 1920s, including a chapel by Joan Rubió i Bellvér, who worked with Antoni Gaudí. Students usually fill the courtyards, and you're free to take a stroll through to view the highly decorative buildings.

Museu i Centre d'Estudis de l'Esport

C/Buenos Aires 56–58 • Currently closed for restoration • ☎ 934 192 232 • Ⓜ Hospital Clínic

The quirky **Museu i Centre d'Estudis de l'Esport**, a low-key museum devoted to the sporting history of Catalunya, is at the time of writing undergoing refurbishment. Assuming it reopens in similar shape, it's primarily of interest for the building in which it stands – a villa that was built as a private house by Josep Puig i Cadafalch in 1911, and has the incongruous look of an Alpine inn.

CONTEMPORARY ARCHITECTURE

It's easy to get sidetracked by the *modernista* architecture of the Eixample, and to forget that Barcelona also boasts plenty of contemporary wonders. Following the death of Franco, there was a feeling among architects that Barcelona had a lot of catching up to do. Subsequently, though, the city has taken centre-stage in matters of urban design and renewal, and now the world looks to Barcelona for inspiration.

Even during the Franco years, exciting work had taken place, particularly among the Rationalist school of architects working from the 1950s to the 1970s, such as **José Antonio Coderch**. From the latter part of this period, too, dates the earliest work by the Catalan architects – among them **Oriol Bohigas**, **Carlos Buxadé**, **Joan Margarit**, **Ricardo Bofill** and **Frederic Correa** – who later transformed the very look and feel of the city.

The impetus for change on a substantial level came from hosting the **1992 Olympics**. Nothing less than the redesign of entire city neighbourhoods would do, with decaying industrial areas either swept away or transformed. While Correa, Margarit and Buxadé worked on the refit of the **Estadi Olímpic**, Bofill was in charge of **INEF** (the Sports University) and had a hand in the airport refit. Down at the harbour, Bohigas and others were responsible for creating the visionary **Vila Olímpica** development, carving residential, commercial and leisure facilities out of abandoned industrial spots. New city landmarks appeared, like **Norman Foster's Torre de Collserola** tower at Tibidabo, and the twin towers of the *Hotel Arts* and **Torre Mapfre** at the Port Olímpic.

Attention later turned to other neglected areas, with signature buildings announcing a planned transformation of the local environment. Richard Meier's contemporary art museum, **MACBA**, in the Raval, and Helio Piñon and Alberto Viaplana's **Maremagnum** complex at Port Vell anchored those neighbourhoods' respective revivals. Ricardo Bofill's Greek-temple-style **Teatre Nacional de Catalunya** was an early indicator of change on the eastern side of the city, and several major projects focused on the area. Anchored by the eye-catching 142m-high **Torre Agbar**, a giant glowing cigar of a building by Jean Nouvel, the **Plaça de les Glòries Catalanes** has undergone radical restructuring as a public plaza. Work continues on a new transport interchange, and it's also home to the **Disseny Hub**, the sleek, zinc-plated "Stapler" that holds the city's applied arts collections (see page 126).

At the foot of Avinguda Diagonal, down on the shoreline, the former industrial area of Poblenou was transformed by the works associated with the Universal Forum of Cultures held in 2004. **Diagonal Mar**, as the area is now known, sits at the heart of a new business and commercial district linking Barcelona with the once-desolate environs of the River Besòs. Meanwhile, on the other side of the city, Richard Rogers revitalized the city's old bullring, at Plaça d'Espanya, now the **Arenas de Barcelona**, incorporating a domed promenade and viewing platform atop a shopping and leisure centre.

Plans to build the city's second AVE (high-speed train) station at **La Sagrera**, however, stalled when recession hit in 2010 and had only just got going again when grounded by a corruption scandal in 2016, while it looks very unlikely that Frank Gehry's proposed 34-storey Torre Sagrera will ever materialize.

8

Parc de l'Espanya Industrial

C/Muntades 37 • Daily 10am–11pm • Free • Ⓜ Sants Estació

If you have time to kill at Barcelona Sants station, nip around the south side to Basque architect Luis Peña Ganchegui's urban park, the **Parc de l'Espanya Industrial**. Built on the site of an old textile factory, it has a line of red-and-yellow-striped lighthouses at the top of glaring white steps, with an incongruously classical Neptune in the water below. Altogether, six sculptors are represented – Andrés Nagel was responsible for the enormous dragon – and, along with the boating lake, café-kiosk, playground and sports facilities provided, the park takes a decent stab at reconciling local interests with the mundane nature of the surroundings.

Parc Joan Miró

C/Tarragona 74 • Daily 10am–11pm • Free • Ⓜ Tarragona

Laid out on the site of Barcelona's nineteenth-century municipal slaughterhouse, **Parc Joan Miró** features a raised piazza whose only feature is Joan Miró's gigantic, 22m-tall mosaic sculpture **Dona i Ocell** ("Woman and Bird"), towering above a shallow reflecting pool. It's a familiar symbol if you've studied Miró's other works, but the sculpture is known locally by several other names – all of them easy to guess when you consider its erect, helmeted shape.

The rear of the park is given over to games areas and landscaped sections of palms and firs, with a kiosk café and outdoor tables among the trees. The children's **playground** here is among the best in the city, with a climbing frame and aerial runway as well as swings and slides.

Arenas de Barcelona

Gran Via de les Corts Catalanes 373–385, at Pl. d'Espanya • Daily 10am–10pm • Ⓦ arenasdebarcelona.com • Ⓜ Espanya

The landmark building on the north side of Plaça d'Espanya is the fabulous Moorish-style bullring, the **Arenas de Barcelona**, originally constructed in 1900 but reopened as a shopping and leisure centre in 2011. Conceived by architect **Richard Rogers** as a gateway to the city centre, and preserving the beautiful brick exterior, the various retail levels at Arenas are hung in sweeping circular galleries, while right on top, outside, a wide walk-around promenade circles the **dome** that offers 360-degree views of the western side of the city. An express elevator whisks you up here from street level, or you can take the glass lifts or escalators inside, through four floors of shopping and entertainment that include a cinema, gym and health centre, and several restaurants, some of which are on the top-floor promenade.

Casa de la Papallona

C/Llançà 20 • No public access • Ⓜ Espanya

It's worth walking around the Arenas de Barcelona and craning your neck up to the top of the six-storey Casa Fajol, universally known as the **Casa de la Papallona** (1912). The work of architect Josep Graner i Prat (1844–1930), it's crowned by a huge ceramic **butterfly** (*papallona*) made using the favoured *modernista* technique of *trencadís*, or broken coloured tiles formed to make a picture.

Sagrada Família and Glòries

Many visitors simply make the necessary pilgrimage by metro to see Antoni Gaudí's great church of the Sagrada Família, out in the eastern reaches of the Eixample, and then head straight back into the centre. It's well worth checking out the lesser-known *modernista*-era buildings nearby, though, and the enchanting pavilions of the Hospital de la Santa Creu i de Sant Pau (now known as the Recinte Modernista de Sant Pau). A few blocks south, the area known as Glòries is home to the city's main concert hall, music and design museums, and the flagship national theatre building. Glòries was originally conceived as the nucleus of the nineteenth-century city expansion plan. That never materialized, but the neighbourhood is destined for dramatic redevelopment, as the city council breathes new life into its peripheral urban areas.

SAGRADA FAMÍLIA AND GLÒRIES

EATING
Bardeni	3
Casa Rafols	7
Firo Tast	1
Gorria	6
Granja Petitbo	4
Parking Pizza	5
La Taqueria	2

ACCOMMODATION
Barcelona Urbany	1
Hotel Eurostars	
Monumental	2

DRINKING & NIGHTLIFE
JazzMan	2
Pipa Club	1

SHOPPING
Norma Comics	2
Westfield Glòries	1

Westfield Glòries

C/GREENWICH
C/DEL PERÚ
AVINGUDA DIAGONAL
GRAN VIA DE LES CORTS CATALANES
C/ROC BORONAT
C/CABANYAL
C/ESQUIROL COMTAL
PLAÇA DEL MERCAT
C/CORONEL SANFELIÚ
C/HERNÁN CORTÉS
C/CLOT
C/DELS
C/RABÍ RUBEN
Parc del Clot
AVINGUDA MERIDIANA
PTGE DEL VINTRÓ
C/CORUNYA

Torre Agbar
Glòries
Museu del Disseny & Disseny Hub
C/CIUTAT DE GRANADA
C/GRANADA
C/BADAJOZ
C/BOLÍVIA
CARRER DE TÀNGER
CARRER DE SANCHO DE ÁVILA
CARRER D'ÁVILA
CARRER D'ÁLABA
PLAÇA DE LES GLÒRIES CATALANES
CARRER DEL DOS DE MA
CARRER DELS ALMOGÀVERS
CARRER DE PALLARS

Els Encants Vells
AVINGUDA DIAGONAL
CARRER DEL CONSELL DE CENT
CARRER D'ENAMORATS
CARRER D'ARAGÓ
Teatre Nacional de Catalunya
PLAÇA DE LES ARTS
CARRER DE PADILLA
AVINGUDA MERIDIANA
C/PAMPLONA
C/ZAMORA
L'Auditori (Museu de la Música)
CARRER DE LEPANT
CARRER DE LA MARINA
Marina

Plaça de Toros
Monumental
GRAN VIA DE LES CORTS CATALANES
CARRER DE LA DIPUTACIÓ
CARRER DE SARDENYA
CARRER DE SICÍLIA
CARRER DE RIBES
CARRER D'ALÍ-BEI
C/SARDENYA
Barcelona Nord (Bus Station)
Parc de L'Estació del Nord
CARRER DE BUENAVENTURA MUÑOZ

Skating Pista del Gel
CARRER DE NÁPOLS
CARRER DE CASP
CARRER D'AUSIÀS MARC
CARRER DE ROGER DE FLOR
Plaça Tetuan
PASSEIG DE SANT JOAN
CARRER DE BAILÉN
Arc de Triomf
C/TRAFALGAR

0   100   200
metres

9 Basilica de la Sagrada Família

C/Mallorca 401 • Daily: March & Oct Mon–Fri 9am–7pm, Sat 9am–6am, Sun 10.30am–6pm; April–Sept Mon–Fri 9am–8pm, Sat 9am–6pm, Sun 10.30am–8pm; Nov–Feb Mon–Sat 9am–6pm, Sun 10.30am–6pm • Charge • six guided 50min tours in English daily; see website for current schedule • Ⓦ sagradafamilia.cat • Ⓜ Sagrada Família

Encountering the **Basilica de la Sagrada Família** for the first time has a breathtaking visceral impact on every visitor. As work on Gaudí's masterpiece races towards completion, and its extraordinary towers climb ever closer towards the heavens, the glorious, overpowering church of the "Holy Family" is now more than ever a symbol

ANTONI GAUDÍ AND THE SAGRADA FAMÍLIA

Begun in 1882 by public subscription, the **Sagrada Família** was originally intended by its progenitor, the Catalan publisher Josep Bocabella, as an expiatory building to atone for the increasingly revolutionary ideas then at large in Barcelona. Bocabella signed up the architect Francesc de Paula Villar, and his plan was to build a modest church in an orthodox neo-Gothic style. Two years later, however, after arguments between the two men, the 31-year-old **Antoni Gaudí** took over as Architect Director. He changed the direction and scale of the project almost immediately, seeing in the Sagrada Família an opportunity to reflect his own deepening spiritual and nationalist feelings.

Initial work on the church was slow. It took four years, until 1901, to finish the crypt – which thereupon functioned, as it still does, as the local parish church – and the first full plan of the building was only published in 1917. Gaudí himself vowed after completing Park Güell in 1911 that he'd never work on secular projects again, and he devoted the rest of his life to the Sagrada Família. What may seem paradoxical to modern sensibilities, though, is that the more rigid his devotion to his **Catholic faith** grew, the more unfettered his architectural imagination became. That said, no matter what flights of fantasy his church design displayed, it remained always rooted in functionality and strict attention to detail.

Antoni Gaudí eventually moved to live in a small studio on the Sagrada Família site, and ceaselessly adapted the plans until he was run over by a tram on the Gran Via on June 7, 1926. Initially unrecognized, as he had largely withdrawn from the public eye, he **died** in hospital three days later. His death was treated as a Catalan national disaster, and all of Barcelona turned out for his funeral procession. Following papal dispensation, he was buried in the Sagrada Família crypt, a fitting resting place for an architect whose masterpiece was designed, in his words, to show "the religious realities of present and future life…man's origin, his end". Everything from the Creation to Heaven and Hell, in short, was incorporated into one magnificent sacred ensemble.

Only one facade of the Sagrada Família was then complete, and work stalled with the coming of the Civil War. Most of Gaudí's plans and models were destroyed amid the turmoil – indeed, George Orwell called the Sagrada Família "one of the most hideous buildings in the world", and described the anarchists as showing "bad taste in not blowing it up when they had the chance".

Construction restarted, amid great controversy, during the 1950s, and has continued ever since. Some argued that the Sagrada Família should be left incomplete as a memorial to Gaudí, though the architect himself always saw the project as requiring centuries to complete. Financed by private funding and ticket sales, rather than government or church, the work has long been overseen by chief architect **Jordi Bonet I Armengol**, the son of one of Gaudí's assistants. While Gaudí's own plans have been followed wherever possible, both Bonet and sculptor **Josep María Subirachs** (1927–2014), who worked for decades on the Passion facade, have been accused by critics of infringing his original spirit.

Computer-aided design and high-tech construction techniques have so greatly speeded up the processes involved, however, that the debate is effectively over. Even if the builders fail to meet their current target, of finishing the church to mark the centenary of Gaudí's death in **2026** – an anniversary that may also be marked by Gaudí's elevation to nothing less than official sainthood – no doubt now remains that the Sagrada Família will indeed be completed in the near future.

9

for Barcelona, speaking volumes about the Catalan urge to embrace uniqueness and endeavour. By no coincidence, the most fantastic expression of the architectural creativity in which the city excels was one of the few churches left untouched during the 1909 "Tragic Week" church-burnings and the 1936 revolution, and even the coldest hearts continue to find the Sagrada Família inspirational in both form and spirit.

The Sagrada Família passed perhaps the most crucial milestone in its history in 2010, when, with the nave finally roofed over, it was consecrated as a **basilica** by Pope Benedict. Contrary to popular belief, it's not, and was never intended to be, a cathedral; that word only applies to the seat of a bishop. It is, however, now a fully functioning church, complete with altar, pews, organ, stained-glass windows and regular Masses. Not that it's necessarily a peaceful place to visit – it's also a **building site**, with all the cacophony of cranes, drills and general clatter that suggests.

Work is progressing so fast that it's impossible to predict exactly how the building may look when you visit. At the time of writing, out of its planned eighteen spires, the smallest eight, in the form of four "Apostles" grouped on each of the Nativity and Passion facades; the four Evangelists; and the spire for the Virgin Mary, had been completed. That leaves four Apostles still to build on the Glory facade and the central Jesus Christ spire. Surmounted by a giant cross, this will be the tallest of all, at 172.5m, thereby making the Sagrada Família the tallest building in Barcelona, and the tallest church in the world.

Visiting the Basilica

All tickets to enter the Sagrada Família are for a specific date and time. Buy yours online as far in advance as possible; in summer, you've very little chance of simply turning up and being able to get in. And if you want to go up one of the towers, book that as well – numbers are even more restricted, and even when tickets to the church itself are available at the gate, you may have to wait several hours for the next available slot for the towers.

Aim to visit as early in the day as possible, to beat the crowds. If you're lucky, you may coincide with an English-language tour. Failing that, you can get substantially the same information on the audio-guides. Whether you visit with a guide or by yourself, you'll start by circling the outside of the church. The eastern **Nativity facade**, facing C/ Marina, was the first to be completed and is alive with fecund detail, its very columns resting on the backs of giant tortoises, and a green, almost-kitsch Christmas tree, flecked with white doves, adorning its apex. Contrast this with the Cubist austerity of Subirachs' work on the western **Passion facade** (C/Sardenya), where the brutal story of the Crucifixion is played out across the harsh mountain stone, each scene with the relevant Bible verse inscribed immediately below.

The **interior** of the Basilica is an immense, peaceful and uncluttered space which thanks to Gaudí's innovative use of hyperboloids is every bit as "luminous" as he dreamed. Gaudí envisaged it as essentially a forest, filled with the light that streams through its stained-glass windows, with its columns as the trees that bear the weight of the structure down to the foundations. At the heart of it all, the main altar is positively drenched in natural light.

Separate elevators climb the **towers** on the Passion and Nativity facades. As well as a close-up look at the spires themselves, you'll be rewarded by partial views of the city through an extraordinary jumble of latticed stonework, ceramic decoration, carved buttresses and sculpture.

The museum

Tickets to the Sagrada Família also offer access to the excellent **museum** that extends through most of its lower level, and traces Gaudí's career, with models and diagrams to explain the construction and symbolism of the church. Some of Gaudí's original

9

drawings are displayed in dim light, as well as photos of him escorting various dignitaries around the site, and of his funeral. You can also peer down at his actual tomb in the crypt, and watch sculptors and model-makers at work in the plaster workshop.

Recinte Modernista de Sant Pau

C/Sant Antoni María Claret 167, at C/Independència • April–Oct daily 9.30am–6.30pm; Nov–March daily 9.30am–5pm • Charge • Ⓦ santpaubarcelona.org • Ⓜ Hospital de Sant Pau

Lluís Domènech i Montaner's *modernista* public hospital, the **Hospital de la Santa Creu i de Sant Pau**, is possibly Barcelona's one piece of architecture that can rival the Sagrada Família for size and invention. A huge precinct of dazzling Art Nouveau imagination, devoted to secular rather than spiritual ends, it has its own metro stop, but it's much better to approach by walking up the four-block Avinguda de Gaudí from the Sagrada Família, which gives terrific views back over the spires of the church.

Domènech i Montaner started work on the project in 1902, with the brief of replacing the medieval Santa Creu hospital in the Raval. He created an astonishing complex of pavilions, at once practical and playful, topped by golden-tiled domes, festooned with turrets and towers, and covered with sculpture, mosaics, stained glass and ironwork. They're set just far enough apart not to overshadow each other, in what was originally a botanic garden and is now a single precinct replete with orange and lavender trees.

The hospital finally closed in 2009, with its patients moving to an adjoining new hospital, and the complex reopened to visitors in 2014. Of the 48 pavilions Domènech i Montaner originally envisaged, 27 were completed; twelve now constitute a World Heritage Site, of which six have so far benefited from a €100 million restoration programme. While still primarily noteworthy for their exterior decoration, they're being progressively filled with display panels and exhibits, some of which are devoted to explaining the details and history of the ensemble. The pick of the bunch is what was the main administration building, which has an ornate Gothic-style chapel upstairs, kitted out with Art Nouveau tiles and floral mosaics, and is also used for conferences and concerts.

There's also a good café/restaurant alongside the main entrance.

MODERNISME'S CRAFTY COLLABORATORS

Despite the overwhelming noise of the big-gun architects of the period, *modernisme* was often a true collaborative effort between the architects and their craftsmen and artisans. Lluís Domènech i Montaner, in particular, recognized the importance of ensemble working, and established a pioneering craft workshop in the Castell dels Tres Dragons, which he designed initially as a restaurant for the Universal Exhibition of 1888. Antoni Gaudí, too, always worked with skilled craftsmen, including his longtime collaborator – a master of mosaic decoration – **Josep María Jujol i Gilbert** (1879–1949).

Another significant figure, **Eusebi Arnau i Mascort** (1864–1933), provided meticulous carvings for all the main *modernista* architects – much loved are his quirky figures adorning Josep Puig i Cadafalch's Casa Macaya and the tour-de-force carved fireplace in the Raval's *Hotel Espanya*.

Some projects brought together the cream of craft talent. Thus the glorious stained glass by Antoni Rigalt and elaborate facade sculpture by Miquel Blay form an integral part of Domènech i Montaner's Palau de la Música Catalana. Meanwhile, the stunning private houses built for wealthy captains of industry looked as good on the inside as they did on the outside, filled with furniture by *modernista* craftsmen like cabinet-maker extraordinaire **Joan Busquets i Jané** (1874–1949) and artist and interior designer **Gaspar Homar i Mezquida** (1870–1955).

TREASURE-HUNTING AT ELS ENCANTS VELLS

A treasure trove of dusty delights, Barcelona's flea market, **El Encants Vells**, is adjacent to the Teatre Nacional de Catalunya at Avda. Meridiana 69 (Mon, Wed, Fri & Sat 9am–8pm, plus public auctions Mon, Wed & Fri 7.15–8.30am; ⓦencantsbcn.com; ⓜGlòries). Several levels of open-air treasure-hunting action are protected by a gleaming metallic canopy.

Despite its recent move into this shiny new home, the market retains its street-bazaar vibe. You name it, you can buy it: old sewing machines, cheese graters, photograph albums, cutlery, lawnmowers, clothes, shoes, CDs, antiques, furniture and out-and-out junk. It's best in the early morning, and haggling for any "old charms" (*encants vells*) you might fancy is *de rigueur*, but you're up against experts.

Palau Macaya

Pg. de Sant Joan 108 • Courtyard access only • Mon–Fri 9am–2pm & 4–8pm • Free • ⓦ caixaforum.org/es/macaya • ⓜ Verdaguer

Josep Puig i Cadafalch's palatial **Palau Macaya**, four blocks west of the Sagrada Família, dates from 1898–1900. It's a superbly ornamental building with an attractive Gothic-inspired courtyard and canopied staircase from which griffins spring. Pause as you pass by to view the unusual exterior carvings by *modernista* craftsman **Eusebi Arnau i Mascort**, including the angel with a "box" Brownie camera and the sculptor himself cycling to work. Today the Palau is run as a cultural centre by the Fundació La Caixa, and hosts conferences and classes as well as, usually free, exhibitions.

Casa Planells

Avda. Diagonal 332 • No public access • ⓜ Monumental/Sagrada Família

Built in 1923–24, the **Casa Planells** apartment block – a sinuous solution to an acute-corner building – simplifies many of the themes that Gaudí emphasized in his work. It's actually by **Josep María Jujol i Gilbert**, who was one of Gaudí's early collaborators, responsible not only for La Pedrera's iconic undulating balconies but also much of Park Güell's celebrated mosaic work.

Plaça de les Glòries Catalanes

ⓜ Glòries

All Barcelona's major avenues meet at the **Plaça de les Glòries Catalanes**, a glorified roundabout that's dedicated to the "Catalan glories", from architecture to literature. Long a focal point for the city's regeneration plans, it's been undergoing work for several years now, with the ultimate intention being to tunnel traffic underground, and open up a grand pedestrianized park centring on the **Museu del Disseny**.

Glòries is already positioned as a gateway to the Diagonal Mar district, with **trams** running there down Avinguda Diagonal. Meanwhile, the roundabout also holds French architect **Jean Nouvel**'s cigar-shaped **Torre Agbar** (142m), erected in 2005 as the headquarters of the local water company (Aigües de Barcelona). A highly distinctive aluminium-and-glass tower that has no fewer than four thousand multicoloured windows, and glows blue and orange at night, its shape is reminiscent of London's "Gherkin", but was inspired by the rocky protuberances of Montserrat.

The huge Glòries shopping mall lies across the Diagonal from here, while further across the Gran Via the park and play areas of the tree-shaded **Parc del Clot** show what can be achieved in an urban setting within the remains of a razed factory site.

9 # Museu del Disseny

Pl. de les Glòries Catalanes 37–38 • **Museu del Disseny** Tues–Sun 10am–8pm • **Disseny Hub** Mon 3.30–9pm, Tues–Sun 9am–9pm • Museum charge, entrance to Hub free • ⓦ dissenyhub.barcelona • Ⓜ Glòries

Barcelona's showpiece **Museu del Disseny** (Design Museum) gathers what used to be the separate collections of the city's decorative arts, ceramics, textile and clothing, and graphic arts museums into a single, stunning new building, the **Disseny Hub**. Nicknamed La Grapadora ("The Stapler") after its shape, the building consists of two parts: a narrow, zinc-plated above-ground section whose topmost floors cantilever over the motorway; and a wide base housing temporary exhibitions, a library, a cafeteria and, below street level, the headquarters of local design institutions.

As for the exhibits, it's effectively several distinct museums in one. Of the four upper floors, the first most closely corresponds to what you might expect of a design museum, displaying everyday objects, largely of Catalan origin, that range from chairs, tables and bicycles to toilets and, yes, staplers. The second floor holds a rather random but unarguably beautiful assortment of decorative arts from the third century onwards, starting with Coptic textiles from Egypt and winding up with ceramic works by Picasso and Miró. Next comes a floor devoted to fashion, illustrating how clothing has successively increased, reduced, accentuated and revealed various body shapes over the past five centuries, while the top floor traces the history of graphic design in twentieth-century Barcelona.

Teatre Nacional de Catalunya

Pl. de les Arts 1 • Guided tours Wed & Thurs 11am & 12.30pm; charge • ⓔ visites@tnc.cat • ⓦ tnc.cat • Ⓜ Glòries or tram T4

Designed by local architect Ricardo Bofill and inaugurated in 1997, the **Teatre Nacional de Catalunya** – Catalunya's national theatre, southwest of Glòries – is a soaring, postmodern glass box, encased within a faux-Greek temple on a raised dais. Reserve in advance by phone or email, and you can take an hour-long guided backstage **tour**, while the bar and restaurant are open in the evening – a summer evening's drink on the open-air *terrassa* is a nice way to take in the grandiose surroundings.

L'Auditori and the Museu de la Música

L'Auditori C/Lepant 150 • ⓦ auditori.cat • **Museu de la Música** C/Padilla 155 • Tues, Wed & Fri 10am–6pm, Thurs 10am–9pm, Sat & Sun 10am–7pm • Charge • ⓦ visitmuseum.gencat.cat/es/museu-de-la-musica-de-barcelona • Ⓜ Glòries/Marina

Forming a sort of cultural enclave with the national theatre, one block over, **L'Auditori** is the city's contemporary concert hall, an unlovely modern building whose concrete and metal exterior has seen better days. Housed within the same complex, the **Museu de la Música** displays a remarkable collection of instruments and musical devices from around the world, from serpentine seventeenth-century horns to reel-to-reel cassette decks.

It's all very impressive, with soaring glass-walled cases letting you view the pieces from all sides, and the objects themselves are undeniably beautiful. For the non-expert, however, it struggles to engage, partly because of the sheer number and variety of instruments and partly because of the impenetrable commentary, with sections called things like "The humanist spirit and the predominance of polyphony". Still, there's a bit of big-screen Elvis here and African drumming there, and if you've ever wanted to pluck tunelessly at a harp without anyone shouting at you to stop, this is your chance.

Gràcia, Park Güell and Horta

Before it was finally annexed as a city suburb in the late nineteenth century, Gràcia had long maintained its identity as a village. It retains a genuine small-town atmosphere, distinct from the old-town neighbourhoods, while its cultural scene and nightlife counter the notion that Barcelona begins and ends on La Rambla. The one unmissable attraction, though, is the surreal Park Güell, created by architectural genius Antoni Gaudí. Meanwhile, nearby Horta ("garden"), so-called thanks to the gardens and country estates that once characterized the area, holds two further distinctive parks – Creueta del Coll, a prime example of the new urban projects that have revitalized forgotten corners of the city, and the eighteenth-century Parc del Laberint, where a renowned maze speaks of a very different era.

Gràcia

Still very much the liberal, almost bohemian, stronghold it was in the nineteenth century, the northern neighbourhood of **Gràcia** feels set apart from the city in many ways. Its traditional annual summer festival, August's **Festa Major** – a solid week of concerts, parades, fireworks and parties – has no peer in any other neighbourhood, and although actual sights in Gràcia are few and far between, it's well known for its cinemas, bars and restaurants. Wander the gridded streets, park yourself on a bench under a plane tree, catch a film, grab a beer or otherwise take time out from the rigours of city-centre life – you'll soon get the feel of a neighbourhood that, unlike some in Barcelona, has a genuine soul.

ARRIVAL AND DEPARTURE   GRÀCIA

By bus Buses #22 or #24 from Pl. de Catalunya run to Gràcia, stopping on the main C/Gran de Gràcia.

By metro and train The most convenient metro stations are Ⓜ Diagonal (south), Ⓜ Fontana (north) or Ⓜ Joanic (east),

or take the FGC train from Pl. de Catalunya to Gràcia station.

On foot Gràcia is a 30min walk from Pl. de Catalunya. From any of the neighbourhood stations, it's around a 500m walk to Gràcia's central squares.

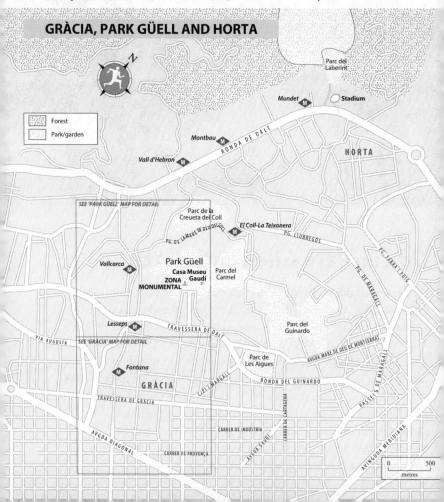

Mercat de la Llibertat

Pl. Llibertat 27 • Mon–Fri 8am–8.30pm, Sat 8am–3pm • Ⓦ mercatllibertat.cat • Ⓜ Fontana or FGC Gràcia

It's only logical to start a visit to Gràcia where the locals start, first thing in the morning – shopping for bread and provisions in the **Mercat de la Llibertat**, a block west of C/Gran de Gràcia. The building was first revamped in 1893 by a former pupil of Gaudí, **Francesc Berenguer i Mestrès**, who sheltered its food stalls beneath a *modernista* wrought-iron roof. It's since been beautifully restored once more, and is always worth a walk through, especially if you fancy the breakfast of champions – oysters, grilled razor clams and a glass of cava – available from one of the classy stand-up café counters.

10

Casa Vicens

C/Carolines 24 • Apr–Oct daily 9.30am–8pm; Nov–Mar daily 9.30am–6pm; guided tours (English) 9.30pm & 2.30pm • Charge •
Ⓦ casavicens.org • Ⓜ Fontana

Antoni Gaudí's first major private commission, the **Casa Vicens** (1883–85), stands on the northern edge of Gràcia. Here he took inspiration from the Moorish style, covering the facade in linear green-and-white tiles with a flower motif. The decorative iron railings are a reminder of Gaudí's early training as a metalsmith, while to further prove

GRÀCIA

■ ACCOMMODATION
Casa Gracia 2
Generator Hostel
 and Hotel 3
Hotel Casa Fuster 1

● EATING
L'Arrosseria Xàtiva 2
Cal Boter 7
Deliziosa
 Gelateriaitaliana 3
Flash Flash 5
Goliard 8
La Nena 4
Nou Candanchu 6
La Pepita 9
San Kil 1

● SHOPPING
A Casa Portuguesa 1
Entre Latas 4
Hibernian Books 3
Oslo 2

■ DRINKING & NIGHTLIFE
Bobby Gin 10
Café del Sol 7
Canigó 6
Centre Artesà
 Tradicionàrius (CAT) 3
La Cervesera Artesana 11
El Col·leccionista 5
Elephanta 4
Heliogàbal 8
Otto Zutz 1
Vinilo 9
Virreina 2

0   200
metres

10

THE THREE SQUARES BAR CRAWL

Three squares tucked away in the middle of Gràcia (ⓂFontana/Diagonal), within a few blocks' walk of each other, contain many of the best neighbourhood cafés and bars. Any night out in Gràcia invariably entails passing through them at some point.

Traditionally, **Plaça del Sol** has been the beating heart of the district's nightlife, though it was redesigned rather soullessly in the 1980s and is not quite so appealing during the day. Far more in keeping with Gràcia's overall village-like tenor is the mouthful that is **Plaça de la Revolució de Setembre de 1886**, just east of Plaça del Sol, and especially **Plaça Vila de Gràcia**, to the south across Travessera de Gràcia. The 30m-high clocktower in the latter (known as Plaça Rius i Taulet until 2008) was a rallying point for nineteenth-century radicals. Their twenty-first-century counterparts prefer to meet for brunch at the popular café *terrassas*.

his versatility – and how Art Nouveau cuts across art forms – Gaudí also designed much of the mansion's furniture.

Until 2014, the house remained a private residence, but after extensive renovation – including the reconstruction of the building's long-vanished original staircase – is now open to the public.

Plaça de la Virreina

Ⓜ Fontana

Pretty **Plaça de la Virreina**, backed by the parish church of Sant Joan, is one of Gràcia's favourite squares, with the *Virreina* bar and others providing drinks and a place to rest and admire the handsome houses, most notably **Casa Rubinat** (1909), C/Or 44, the last major work of Francesc Berenguer. Children and dogs, meanwhile, scamper around the small drinking fountain. Nearby streets, particularly **Carrer de Verdi**, contain many of the neighbourhood's most fashionable boutiques, galleries, cinemas and cafés.

10

Park Güell

Set on the hillside above Gràcia, Antoni Gaudí's extraordinary **Park Güell** was, with the exception of the Sagrada Família, his most ambitious project. Commissioned by Eusebi Güell (patron of Gaudí's Palau Güell, off La Rambla), it was originally planned as a private housing estate of sixty dwellings, furnished with ornamental paths, recreational areas and decorative monuments. The idea was to build a "Garden City" of the type then popular in England – that's why the official name follows Gaudí in using the English spelling of "Park". Gaudí worked on the project from 1900 until 1914, but in the end only two houses were actually built, and the park was opened to the public instead in 1922.

Park Güell ranks among Barcelona's most popular tourist attractions, receiving millions of visitors each year. As a result, you now have to pay for access to the area that holds its most iconic sites, the **Zona Monumental**. A maximum of four hundred visitors is allowed in every half-hour, and each ticket is only valid for a specific half-hour time-slot (once inside, you can stay as long as you like). Tickets can be reserved online up to three months in advance. You can also buy them at ticket offices or ATMs in the park itself – in summer, check online to see whether they're the day you plan to visit is already sold out – but you may have to wait for the next available time-slot.

Access to the rest of the park remains free. The wooded, landscaped gardens make a nice spot for a picnic, but other than to enjoy the sweeping views from the very highest point – the **Turó de les Tres Creus**, where three stone crosses atop a stepped tumulus mark the spot where Gaudí had planned to place a chapel – it's unlikely to hold your interest for long. There's a large outdoor **café** immediately above the Zona Monumental, but it's usually filled with visitors killing time before they're allowed to go in.

ARRIVAL AND DEPARTURE   PARK GÜELL

As the park straddles a steep hill, all approaches involve an ascent on foot to reach the main entrance on C/Olot. Leaving the park, you'll have to walk back down C/Larrard to Travessera de Dalt for bus or metro connections back to the city, though taxis do hang about the gates on C/Olot.

By bus Bus #24 from Pl. de Catalunya, Pg. de Gràcia or C/ Gran de Gràcia, drops passengers on Carretera del Carmel at the eastern side of the park. The Bus Turístic stops at the foot of C/Larrard.

By metro Marginally the closest station to the Zona Monumental is Ⓜ Lesseps in Gràcia; the 15min walk from there heads right along Travessera de Dalt and then left up steep C/Larrard. Alternatively, get off at Ⓜ Vallcarca and walk a few hundred metres down Avda. de Vallcarca, to find mechanical escalators on your left that ascend Bxda. de la Glòria to the park's western entrance, from where footpaths lead back down to the Zona Monumental.

Zona Monumental

Daily: April, Sept & Oct 8am–8.30pm; May–Aug 8am–9.30pm; Nov–March 9.30am–5.30pm, last entry 1hr before closing • Charge • Ⓦ parkguell.barcelona

Spreading across the slopes, the core of Park Güell, sealed off as the **Zona Monumental** and looking down across the city to the Mediterranean, is an almost hallucinatory swirl of ideas and excesses. You can use your timed ticket to enter at any of three points, but it makes sense to approach it via the original main entrance, on C/Olot. The porter's lodge to the right hosts an informative exhibit that places the park in the context of its times, but it's so small that it usually entails a long wait in line to get in.

Ahead, a monumental stairway climbs past a giant mosaic salamander known as **el drac** (dragon) to reach the vast **Hall of Columns**, where 84 Doric columns soar at disconcertingly irregular angles to enclose a space that Gaudí intended to be the estate's market. Art critic Sacheverell Sitwell described it as "at once a fun fair, a petrified forest, and the great temple of Amun at Karnak, itself drunk, and reeling in an eccentric earthquake".

Perhaps the best-known element of the park is the long, meandering **ceramic bench** that snakes along the edge of the terrace that forms the roof of the Hall of Columns. Entirely covered with a brightly coloured, broken tile-and-glass mosaic (a technique known as *trencadís*), it forms a dizzying sequence of abstract motifs, symbols, words and pictures.

Casa Museu Gaudí

Park Güell, outside Zona Monumental • Daily: April–Sept 9am–8pm; Oct–March 10am–6pm • Charge • ⓦ casamuseugaudi.org

One of Gaudí's collaborators, Francesc Berenguer, designed and built a turreted house for the architect. Now known as the **Casa Museu Gaudí**, it stands within the park, immediately east of the Zona Monumental. Gaudí was persuaded to live here from 1906 until 1925, when he left to camp out at the Sagrada Família for good.

The downstairs rooms celebrate Gaudí's work as a designer, via a diverting collection of furniture he created for other projects – a typical mixture of wild originality and brilliant engineering – while upstairs his ascetic study and bedroom have been kept much as he knew them. Religious texts and images offer some inkling of his personality, while various plans and artefacts explain more about the park.

Parc de la Creueta del Coll

Pg. de la Mare de Deu del Coll 77 • Daily 10am–dusk • Free • Bus #22 from Pl. de Catalunya, via Pg. de Gràcia, stops 100m from the park, or ⓜ El Coll/La Teixonera

There could be no greater contrast with Park Güell than Horta's **Parc de la Creueta del Coll**, a contemporary urban park laid out on the site of an old quarry by Olympic architects Martorell and Mackay. At the top of the park steps is an Ellsworth Kelly metal spike, while suspended by steel cables over a reflecting pool is a massive 50-tonne concrete claw, "In Praise of Water", by Basque artist Eduardo Chillida. There's a stand of palm trees by an artificial lake, and concrete promenades and picnic areas under the sheer quarry walls.

Combining the park with a visit to Park Güell is easy, though you'll need a keen sense of direction. It's easiest to visit Parc de la Creueta del Coll first, then walk back down the main Passeig de la Mare de Deu del Coll until you see the signpost pointing down C/Balears (on your left). From there, signposts guide you into Park Güell the back way.

Parc del Laberint

Pg. dels Castanyers 1–17 • Daily 10am–dusk • Charge • ⓜ Mundet: use the Pg. Vall d'Hebron (Muntanya) exit, walk up the main road and against the traffic flow for 1min (past the sports pitches) and turn left into the grounds of the Velòdrom (cycle stadium)

Just a couple of minutes' walk from Mundet metro station brings you to the gates of the **Parc del Laberint**, behind the cycle stadium. The former estate mansion is used by Barcelona's parks and gardens department, while the late eighteenth-century gardens (the oldest in the city) make an enchanting spectacle. A series of shady paths, terraces, pavilions and water features embrace the hillside. The topiary **maze** at the heart of the park, **El Laberint**, was created for the Marquis de Llupià i Alfarràs in 1792 and designed as an Enlightenment puzzle concerning the forms of love. A statue of Eros serves as the reward for reaching the centre.

FC BARCELONA CAMP NOU STADIUM AND OFFICIAL STORE

Les Corts, Pedralbes and Sarrià-Sant Gervasi

Northwest of Barcelona city centre, what was once the village of Les Corts is now seamlessly integrated into the modern city, and noteworthy primarily for holding the hallowed precincts of Camp Nou, FC Barcelona's stupendous football stadium. Nearby, across Avinguda Diagonal, the Palau de Pedralbes is home to serene public gardens, while a half-day's excursion can be made by walking from the palace, past the Pavellons Güell and Gaudí's dragon gate, up to the calm cloisters of the Gothic monastery of Pedralbes. Complete the day by returning via Sarrià, to the east, with a pretty main street and market to explore. At night the focus shifts to the bars and restaurants of neighbouring Sant Gervasi, in the streets north of Plaça de Francesc Macià.

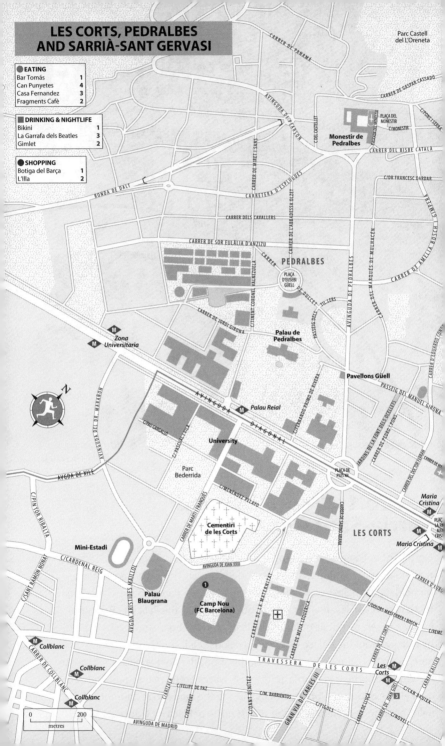

LES CORTS, PEDRALBES AND SARRIÀ-SANT GERVASI

EATING
Bar Tomás	1
Can Punyetes	4
Casa Fernandez	3
Fragments Cafè	2

DRINKING & NIGHTLIFE
Bikini	1
La Garrafa dels Beatles	3
Gimlet	2

SHOPPING
Botiga del Barça	1
L'Illa	2

Parc Castell del L'Oreneta

CARRER DE PANAMA

CARRER DE GASPAR CASSADO

C/PONT I SERRA

PLAÇA DEL MONESTIR

C/MONESTIR

Monestir de Pedralbes

CARRER DEL BISBE CATALÀ

C/DR. FRANCESC DARDER

AVINGUDA DE L'EXÈRCIT

COL·CASTELLET

CARRER DE MIREL I SANS

CARRER DE L'ABADESSA OLZET

CARRETERA D'ESPLUGUES

CARRER DELS CAVALLERS

CARRER DE SOR EULÀLIA D'ANZIZU

CARRER DE L'AMELLADE

CARRER DEL MARQUÈS DE MULHACÉN

PEDRALBES

RONDA DE DALT

C/TINENT CORONEL VALENZUELA

CARRER DE JORDI GIRONA

PLAÇA D'EUSEBI GÜELL

DE DULCET TILLERS

PASSEIG DELS TILLERS

AVINGUDA DE PEDRALBES

Palau de Pedralbes

Pavellons Güell

PASSEIG DEL MANUEL GIRONA

CARRER DE LA FONT DELS OCELLETS

C/FERNANDO PRIMO DE RIVERA

M **Zona Universitaria**

AVINGUDA DEL DR. MARAÑON

AVINGUDA DE XILE

University

C/PAU GARGALLO

C/PASCUAL I VILA

A V I N G U D A   D I A G O N A L

M **Palau Reial**

JARDINS DE PEDRO I PONS

CARRER DEL DOCTOR FERRAN

EMBES DE M

C/PIN TOR RIBATA

Parc Bederrida

C/MENÉNDEZ PELAYO

PLAÇA DE PIUS XII

CARRER DE SACÍNO ABRINA

Maria Cristina

M PLAÇ MA AN CRIS

Cementiri de les Corts

CARRER DE MARTÍ I FRANQUÈS

LES CORTS

Maria Cristina M

AVINGUDA DE JOAN XXIII

CARRER D'EUG

Mini-Estadi

C/CARDENAL REIG

AVGDA ARISTIDES MAILLOL

Palau Blaugrana

❶ **Camp Nou (FC Barcelona)**

CARRER DE LA MATERNITAT

CARRER DE MELIA LUQUERIA

C/DOLORS MASFERRER I BOSCH

C/REME

C/SANT RAMON NONAT

CARRER DE LES CORTS

CARRER GALILEE

M **Collblanc**

CARRER DE COLLBLANC

M **Collblanc**

T R A V E S S E R A   D E   L E S   C O R T S

Les Corts M

M **Collblanc**

CANTUNIA

C/FELIPE DE PAZ

C/M. BARRIENTOS

C/TIGOLS

C/CAN BRUIXA

C/NOVEL

❸

GRAN VIA DE CARLES III

C/DANT BENITEZ

AVINGUDA DE MADRID

0 — 200 metres

N

Uptown Avinguda Diagonal

Ⓜ María Cristina or tram T1, T2 or T3 from Pl. de Francesc Macià

The uptown section of **Avinguda Diagonal** runs through the heart of Barcelona's flashiest business and shopping district. The giant **L'Illa** shopping centre flanks the avenue, its stepped design a prone echo of New York's Rockefeller Center. Designer fashion stores are ubiquitous, particularly around **Plaça de Francesc Macià** and Avinguda de Pau Casals – at the top of the latter, **Turó Parc** (daily 8am–dusk) makes a good place to rest weary feet, with a small children's playground and a café-kiosk. For picnic supplies, the traditional neighbourhood market, **Mercat de Galvany** (C/Santaló 65; Mon–Thurs & Sat 7am–2.30pm, Fri 7am–8pm; ⓦmercatgalvany.com), is just three blocks to the east.

Behind L'Illa, it's worth seeking out **Plaça de la Concordia**, another surprising survivor from the past amid the uptown tower blocks. The pretty little square is dominated by its church belltower and ringed by local businesses (florist, pharmacy, hairdresser). Have a quiet drink at one of the outdoor cafés or head to *Fragments Cafè* (see page 194) for excellent bistro-style food.

Camp Nou and FC Barcelona

Avda. Aristides Maillol • ⓦ fcbarcelona.com • Ⓜ Collblanc/Palau Reial, then a 10min walk, or Bus Turístic stops outside the stadium

Football in Barcelona being a genuine obsession, support for the local giants **FC (Futbol Club) Barcelona** has been raised to an art form. *Més que un club* ("More than just a club") is the proud boast, and certainly during the dictatorship years the club stood as a symbol around which Catalans could rally. Arch-rivals Real Madrid, on the other hand, were always seen as Franco's club. In recent years, culminating in Barcelona's fifth coronation as European champions in 2015, the swashbuckling players in the *blaugrana* (claret and blue) shirts have won hearts worldwide with their elegant *tiki-taka*, pass-and-move style, to become every football fan's second-favourite team.

There's no more invigorating introduction to Catalan passions than to take in a match at the magnificent **Camp Nou** ("New Ground") stadium, sited in the Les Corts neighbourhood, behind the university buildings. Europe's largest stadium was built in 1957, enlarged for the 1982 World Cup semifinal to accommodate 98,000 people, and after a recent revamp, can fit around 105,000. The club reckons on recouping €200 million, a third of the cost, from selling the naming rights to the new stadium.

Camp Nou provides one of the best football-watching experiences in the world. Attending a match here – tickets tend to be readily available for all but the very biggest clashes (see page 218) – serves as an invigorating introduction to Catalan passions. Whether you get to a game or not, the museum and stadium tour is a must, while the entire complex of what claims to be the "World's Top Sports Club", hosting FC Barcelona's sixteen professional and amateur teams, also puts on basketball, handball and hockey games, and holds a public ice rink, souvenir store and café.

Museum and stadium tour

Entrance on Avda. Aristides Maillol • Oct to March Mon–Sat 10am–6pm, Sun 10am–3pm; April to mid-Oct daily 9.30am–7pm; last tour 1hr before closing; on match days, and also on the day before Champions League matches, the museum is open but there are no tours • Charge • ⓦ fcbarcelona.com • Ⓜ Palau Reial

Hundreds of fans daily make the pilgrimage to Camp Nou, where the combined visit to the club's museum and the stadium itself – billed as the "**Camp Nou Experience**" – provides a magnificent celebration of Spain's national sport. Tracing the history of the club from its foundation in 1899, the **museum** gradually shifts from black-and-white photos and battered old boots and balls to a relentless succession of silverware, including the six cups won in 2009 alone, Barcelona's *annus mirabilis*; a cracking multimedia zone profiles historic games and famous players and relives the match-day atmosphere.

Beyond that, the **self-guided tour** winds through the visitors' changing rooms and players' tunnel out onto the pitch, and then leads up to the press gallery and directors' box for stunning views. While it's a poor substitute for attending an actual game, it does give the chance to take a selfie alongside a life-size photo of Lionel Messi. Eventually, you're steered into the **FC Botiga** megastore, which sells everything from replica shirts (prices start at €100-plus) to branded bottles of wine.

Palau de Pedralbes

Avda. Diagonal 686 • Gardens daily 10am–dusk • Free • Ⓜ Palau Reial or tram T1, T2 or T3

11

Opposite the university on Avinguda Diagonal, formal grounds stretch up to the Italianate **Palau de Pedralbes** – basically a large villa with pretensions. Owner Eusebi Güell donated it to the Spanish royal family in 1918, for use on their visits to Barcelona. The king stayed here for the first time in 1926, but within five years he had abdicated, and the palace somewhat lost its role. Franco kept it on as a presidential residence and it later passed to the city.

Although the palace is currently closed to the public, its **gardens** – a breezy oasis of Himalaya cedars, strawberry trees and bougainvillea – are worth a visit. Hidden in a bamboo thicket, to the left-centre of the facade – is the "Hercules fountain" (1884), an early work by Antoni Gaudí. He also designed the parabolic pergola to the right,

---

IT'S ONLY A GAME?

Some people believe football is a matter of life or death… I can assure you it is much, much more important than that.

Bill Shankly

No Catalan football supporter would disagree with Liverpool legend and quip-meister Bill Shankly. These are fans who boo their own team if they think the performance isn't up to scratch, thousands of white handkerchiefs waving along in disapproval. A disappointing season is seen as a slur on the Catalan nation, and if success goes instead to bitter rivals Real Madrid, then the pain is almost too much to bear. When team figurehead and captain **Luís Figo** was transferred to Madrid in 2000 (making him one of only a handful to have played for both clubs), the outrage was almost comical in its ferocity – at a later match between the two sides, a pig's head was thrown onto the pitch as Figo prepared to take a corner. In recent years, though, there has been a lot more cheering than booing, as the team has played with a swagger rarely seen in modern club football.

Under their former coach **Josep "Pep" Guardiola** – one-time Barça player and all-Catalan hero – Barcelona evolved into a team of scintillating beauty, not only running rings around rivals from home and abroad, but also providing the bulk of the side that won the World Cup for Spain for the first time in 2010. The Barcelona style – don't give the ball away, ever, period – is learned at **La Masia**, the club's own training centre and school for young footballers, most of whom are Catalan or come at an early age from elsewhere – many of the current team are graduates, as is Barça coach Xavi. Things change quickly in football, but the production line at La Masia is the best guarantee that boos and white hankies will be absent from the Camp Nou for a while longer yet.

> **HERE BE DRAGONS**
>
> The slavering beast on Gaudí's dragon gate at the Pavellons Güell is not the vanquished dragon of Sant Jordi (St George), the Catalan patron saint, but the one that appears in the **Labours of Hercules** myth, a familiar Catalan theme in the nineteenth century.
>
> Gaudí's design was based on the reworking of the myth by the Catalan renaissance poet **Jacint Verdaguer**, a friend of the Güell family, in his epic poem, *L'Atlàntida*. Thus, the dragon that traditionally guarded golden apples in the Gardens of Hesperides here protects instead an orange tree (a more Catalan fruit). Gaudí's gate indeed can be read as a homage to Verdaguer, with its stencilled roses representing those traditionally given to the winner of the Catalan poetry competition, the Jocs Floral, awarded to the poet in 1877.

which is covered in climbing plants and makes a nice place to sit and rest your feet. In June and July each year, the gardens hold a season of big-name concerts known as the **Alma Festival** (ⓦalmafestival.info).

Pavellons Güell

Avda. de Pedralbes 7 • Daily 10am–4pm, last entry 3.30pm; English tours, no extra charge, 10am, 11am & 3pm • Charge • ⓦ rutadelmodernisme.com • ⓜ Palau Reial, then a 5min walk

As an early test of his capabilities, **Antoni Gaudí** was asked by his patron, Eusebi Güell, to rework the entrance, gatehouse and stables of the Güell summer residence, which was sited on a large working estate well away from the filth and unruly mobs of downtown Barcelona. While the summer house itself was later given to the royal family, and rebuilt as the Palau de Pedralbes, the brick-and-tile stables and outbuildings – known as the **Pavellons Güell** – survive as Gaudí created them. They are frothy, whimsical affairs showing more than a Moorish touch to them, with minaret-like turrets that display Gaudí's first experimentation with *trencadís* (broken tile mosaics), a technique he used ever afterwards on his subsequent, better-known projects.

However, it's the **gate** that's the most famous element. An extraordinary winged dragon made of twisted iron snarls at the passers-by, its razor-toothed jaws spread wide in a fearsome roar: backing up to pose for a photograph suddenly doesn't seem like such a good idea. You can see the gate for free; paying the entry fee entitles you to peep into the dilapidated gatehouse; walk through Gaudí's innovative, parabolic-arched stables, which now hold assorted tools and equipment used in the construction of La Pedrera; and admire the brickwork from the small gardens.

Monestir de Pedralbes

Bxda. del Monestir 9 • April–Sept Tues–Fri 10am–5pm, Sat 10am–7pm, Sun 10am–8pm; Oct–March Tues–Fri 10am–2pm, Sat & Sun 10am–5pm • Charge • ⓦ monestirpedralbes.barcelona • ⓜ Palau Reial and 20min walk, or FGC Reina Elisenda (frequent trains from Pl. de Catalunya) and 10min walk, or bus #64 from Pl. Universitat

Founded in 1326 for the nuns of the Order of St Clare, the Gothic **Monestir de Pedralbes** is, in effect, an entire monastic village preserved on the outskirts of the city, within medieval walls that completely shut out the noise and clamour of the twenty-first century. It took craftsmen a little over a year to prepare Pedralbes (from the Latin *petras albas*, "white stones") for its first community of nuns. The speed of that initial construction and the subsequent uninterrupted habitation by the order helps explain the perfect architectural harmony. After six hundred years of isolation, the monastery was sequestered by the Generalitat during the Civil War and it

---

HIDDEN GEMS: LES CORTS, PEDRALBES AND SARRIÀ-SANT GERVASI

Pavellons Güell See page 138
Sculpture spotting in the Jardins del Palau de Pedralbes See page 137
Plaça de la Concordia See page 136
Ferrer Bassa's stunning murals at Monestir de Pedrables See page 138
Bar Tomás See page 194
A stroll through Sarrià See page 139

---

later opened to the public in 1983 – as part of the deal, a new convent was built alongside, in which the Clare nuns still reside.

The cloisters

The triple tiers of the magnificent **cloisters** of the Monestir de Pedralbes are supported by the slenderest of columns, with the only sound the tinkling water from the fountain. Side rooms and chambers give a clear impression of medieval convent life, from the chapter house and austere refectory to a fully equipped kitchen and infirmary.

The real highlight here, though, is a small chapel to the right of the entrance, the **Capella de Sant Miquel**, which is adorned with remarkably vivid frescoes painted in 1346 by Catalan artist Ferrer Bassa. High-tech displays in rooms nearby explain their symbolism and restoration, while a small room beside the chapel itself holds the carved marble tomb of the monastery's original sponsor, Elisenda de Montcada, wife of Jaume II. Widowed in 1327, six months after she and her husband laid the first stone, Elisenda retired to an adjacent palace, where she lived until her death in 1364.

The nuns' former dormitory, now equipped with a black marble floor and soaring oak-beamed ceiling, houses a selection of the rarer **treasures**. While the nuns themselves eschewed personal trappings, the monastery acquired valuable art and other possessions over the centuries – including pieces of Gothic furniture, paintings by Flemish artists, an impressive series of so-called "factitious" altarpieces from the sixteenth century (made up of sections of different style and provenance), and some outstanding illuminated choirbooks. The monastic **church** alongside, a simple, single-naved structure, retains some of its original fourteenth-century stained glass.

Sarrià

FGC Sarrià (take C/Mare de Deu de Núria exit), or bus #64 from Monestir de Pedralbes/Pl. Universitat

Once a small town in its own right, the **Sarrià** district still looks the part, with a narrow, traffic-free main street – C/Major de Sarrià – at the top of which stands the much-restored church of **Sant Vicenç**. The church flanks the main Passeig de la Reina Elisenda de Montcada, across which lies the neighbourhood market, **Mercat Sarrià**, housed in a 1911 *modernista* red-brick building.

You'll find a few other surviving old-town squares down the main street, prettiest of which is **Plaça Sant Vicenç de Sarrià** (off C/Mañe i Flaquer), where there's a statue of the saint. If you make it this way, don't miss the *Bar Tomás*, just around the corner on C/Major de Sarrià (see page 194), for the world's best *patatas bravas*.

AMUSEMENT PARK AND SAGRAT COR (SACRED HEART) TEMPLE

Tibidabo and Parc de Collserola

The views from the heights of Tibidabo (550m), the peak that signals the northwestern boundary of Barcelona, are legendary. On a clear day you can see across to the Pyrenees, and out to sea even as far as Mallorca. However, although many visitors make the tram and funicular ride up to Tibidabo's wonderfully old-fashioned amusement park, few realize that the Parc de Collserola stretches beyond, peppered with peaks, wooded valleys and hiking paths, and among the city's best-kept secrets. You can walk into the park from Tibidabo, but it's actually better to start from its information centre, across to the west, above the hilltop village of Vallvidrera, which can be reached by another funicular ride. Meanwhile, families won't want to miss the CosmoCaixa science museum, which can easily be seen en route to or from Tibidabo.

CosmoCaixa

C/Isaac Newton 26 • Daily 10am–8pm • Charge • ⓦ cosmocaixa.org • FGC Avda. del Tibidabo (trains from Pl. de Catalunya) and 10min walk, or Tramvia Blau (see page 143) or Bus Turístic stop close by

For anyone travelling with children in tow, Barcelona's enormous, up-to-the-minute science museum is an absolute must-see attraction, which takes at least two hours to explore fully. Originally housed in a converted *modernista* hospice, **CosmoCaixa** now also incorporates a light-filled public concourse and a huge underground extension, which is entered by means of a vast descending staircase that spirals around a desiccated **Acariquara tree** from the Amazon, and symbolizes a journey back to the origin of life on earth.

Hands-on experiments and displays on the lowest of the four subterranean levels range across life, the universe and everything, "from the quark to Shakespeare". Most require a very large thinking cap, so younger children are soon going to be zooming around the open spaces. But there's no denying the overall pull of the two main attractions, namely the hundred tonnes of "sliced" rock in the **Mur Geològic** (Geological Wall) and, best of all, the **Bosc Inundat** – nothing less than a thousand square metres of real Amazonian rainforest, complete with caimans, an anaconda safely ensconced in its own private enclosure, and giant catfish.

Pick up a schedule when you arrive of children's and family activities, at their most frequent during weekends and school holidays. There are also daily 3D shows in the **planetarium**, plus a great gift shop and a café-restaurant with outdoor seating beneath the restored hospital facade.

12

Torre Bellesguard

C/Bellesguard 16 • Tues–Sun 10am–3pm, last entry 2.30pm; English-language tours Sat 11am; reservations advised • Charge • ⓦ bellesguardgaudi.com • FGC Avda. del Tibidabo (trains from Pl. de Catalunya) and 15min walk, or Tramvia Blau and Bus Turístic stop close by

One of Gaudí's least-known works, the **Torre Bellesguard** a few blocks west of CosmoCaixa, has opened its doors to visitors while still serving as a private residence. Built between 1900 and 1909, it's a surprising hybrid of Gothic castle – in reference to the long-vanished castle of Catalunya's King Martí the Humane, which occupied this high eminence in the fifteenth century – and *modernista* manor house, with additional Moorish influences into the bargain, including its smooth white interior spaces and abundant use of tiles.

To explore the place thoroughly, it's best to coincide with a **guided tour** (there's usually one English-language tour every Saturday, at 11am; book ahead if possible), but even if you take the self-guided tour you'll be briefly ushered inside. And be warned that the whole place may **close** to visitors when the owners choose to have a party or private event, so it's always worth checking in advance before making the trek up here.

Parc d'Atraccions Tibidabo

Pl. del Tibidabo • Days and hours vary, but basically March–May & Oct–Dec Sat, Sun & hols only; June–Sept & hols Wed–Sun; park open noon–7/11pm depending on season; closed Jan & Feb • Charge • ⓦ tibidabo.es

Barcelona's self-styled "magic mountain" amusement park, the **Parc d'Atraccions**, has been thrilling its citizens for over a century. It's a mix of traditional rides, plus an influx of high-tech roller-coasters and free-fall drops, laid out around several levels of the mountaintop, and connected by landscaped paths and gardens. Some of the most famous historic attractions are grouped under the discounted "**Skywalk**" ticket, including the aeroplane – spinning since 1928 – the carousel, and the quirky

Museu d'Autòmates, a fully functional collection of coin-operated antique fairground machines. Summer weekends finish with parades, concerts and a noisy *correfoc*, a theatrical **fireworks** display.

Sagrat Cor

Daily 10am–8pm • Charge

The amazing views from everywhere in Tibidabo park become even more extensive if you climb the shining steps of the neighbouring Templo Expiatorio de España, otherwise known as the **Sagrat Cor** (Sacred Heart). Built from 1886 onwards – eleven years after its famous Paris equivalent, the Sacré Coeur – it's topped by a huge statue of Christ. Inside the church, an elevator (*ascensor*) climbs to a sensational viewing platform at the very summit of the mountain, from where the city, surrounding hills and sea shimmer in the distance.

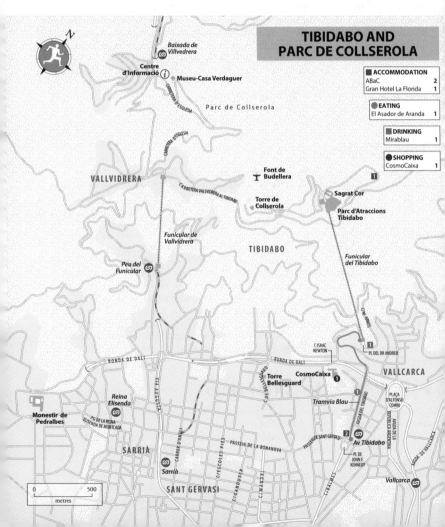

TIBIDABO AND PARC DE COLLSEROLA

■ ACCOMMODATION	
ABaC	2
Gran Hotel La Florida	1

● EATING	
El Asador de Aranda	1

■ DRINKING	
Mirablau	1

● SHOPPING	
CosmoCaixa	1

ARRIVAL AND DEPARTURE

Getting to Tibidabo is a convoluted business, since you have to use several successive forms of transport, but it's also half the fun of a day out. Expect the trip from the city centre to take up to an hour, all told.

By train, tram and funicular Take the FGC train (Tibidabo line #7) from Pl. de Catalunya station to Avda. del Tibidabo (the last stop), where you cross the road to the tram/bus shelter. An antique tram, the Tramvia Blau normally runs you up the hill to Pl. del Doctor Andreu, but, at the time of writing was out of action; there's a bus service instead. By the tram and bus stop on Pl. del Doctor

PARC D'ATRACCIONS TIBIDABO

Andreu (where there are several café-bars and restaurants), you change to the shiny new Cuca de Llum funicular, with connections to Tibidabo at the top (every 15min; operates when the Parc d'Attracions is open; charge).

By bus The Bus Turístic stops at Avda. del Tibidabo, where you can change for the Tramvia Blau replacement bus service. Alternatively, the special Tibibus (T2A) runs direct to Tibidabo from Pl. de Catalunya (from 10.15am every day that the park is open; charge, fare reimbursed with park admission). Local bus #111 runs on a circuit (every 30min; city passes and transport tickets valid) between Tibidabo park and Vallvidrera village.

Torre de Collserola and Vallvidrera

Torre de Collserola: C/Vallvidrera al Tibidabo • March–Dec Sat & Sun noon–2pm • Charge • ⓦ torredecollserola.com • Bus #111 from Tibidabo or Vallvidrera village

Follow the road from the Tibidabo car park and it's only a few minutes' walk to Norman Foster's **Torre de Collserola**, a communications tower soaring high above the tree line, with a glass lift that whisks you up ten floors (115m) for yet more stunning views – 70km, they claim, on a good day.

Afterwards, you could just head back to Tibidabo for the funicular-and-tram ride back to the city, but to complete a circular tour it's more interesting to follow the cobbled path near the tower's car park which brings you out on the pine-clad edges of **Vallvidrera**, a well-to-do suburban village perched on the flank of the Collserola hills – a twenty-minute walk all told from Tibidabo. From here, another **funicular** station (every 6–10min; Mon–Fri 5am–midnight, Sat & Sun 5.36am–2am) connects to Peu del Funicular, an FGC station on the Sabadell and Terrassa line from Plaça de Catalunya.

Vallvidrera's main square is far from obvious – turn left out of the funicular station and walk down the steep steps, and Plaça de Vallvidrera is the traffic roundabout at the bottom.

12

Parc de Collserola

Centre d'Informació daily 9.30am–3pm • ⓦ parcnaturalcollserola.cat • FGC Bxda. de Vallvidrera (on the Sabadell or Terrassa line from Pl. de Catalunya or Gràcia; 15–20min)

Given a half-decent day, bikers, hikers and outdoors enthusiasts alike make a beeline for the ring of wooded hills, known as the **Parc de Collserola**, beyond Tibidabo. The **park information centre** lies in oak- and pine-woods, an easy, signposted ten-minute walk up through the trees from the FGC Baixada de Vallvidrera train station. There's a bar-restaurant here with an outdoor terrace, plus an exhibition on the park's history, flora and fauna; the staff hand out English-language leaflets detailing walks that range from a twenty-minute stroll to the Vallvidrera dam to a couple of hours circling the hills.

Some walks – like the oak-forest hike – swiftly gain height for marvellous views over the tree canopy, while others descend through the valley bottoms to springs and shaded picnic areas. Perhaps the nicest short stroll from the information centre leads to the **Font de la Budellera** (1hr 15min return), a landscaped spring deep in the woods. Follow the signs from the *font* to the Torre de Collserola (another 20min), and you can return to Barcelona instead via the funicular from Vallvidrera, or even take in the views from the Collserola tower or Tibidabo before heading back.

AERIAL VIEW OF SITGES

Out of the city

Catalunya is remarkably diverse, stretching from the Mediterranean coast to the Pyrenees. Within a couple of days, you can see everything from historic villages and fragrant vineyards to medieval churches and seaside nightclubs. Excellent public transport links and well-maintained roads mean that you have multiple options for getting around. Or, opt to rent a car to further discover the area, including Tarragona and beyond, or deep into the verdant inland. Catalunya is also a cycling haven, with over 6000km of bike roads, paths and trails. Girona has emerged as the cycle capital of the region, with numerous services and amenities that cater to cyclists. This chapter is geared towards day-trips; to find out about accommodation in the region, contact the local tourist offices, consult ⓦcatalunya.com, or get hold of the separate *Rough Guide to Spain*.

Although there are plenty of traditional beach getaways close to Barcelona, like Castelldefels to the south or the small towns of the Costa Maresme to the north, such as **Sant Pol de Mar**, unquestionably the best local seaside destination is **Sitges**, on the Costa Daurada half an hour south. This charming resort town has the perfect mix of culture, cocktails and coastline – and it has gained a glittering international reputation, particularly with LGBTQ+ visitors. The other essential excursion is to **Montserrat**, the extraordinary mountain and monastery 40km northwest of Barcelona, reached by a precipitous cable car or mountain railway ride. Besides being a site of great significance for Catalans, it's also a terrific place for a hike in the hills.

If you enjoy Barcelona's varied church architecture, there's more to come, starting with Gaudí's inspired work at the **Colònia Güell**, an idealistic community established by the architect's patron Eusebi Güell. This is a half-day's outing, while a second half-day can be spent visiting the Benedictine monastery at **Sant Cugat del Vallès** and the complex of early medieval churches at **Terrassa**, all largely unsung and utterly fascinating. Another route out of the city, due west, leads through the wine-producing towns of **Sant Sadurní d'Anoia** and **Vilafranca del Penedès**, both of which can be seen in a day's excursion with enough time for a wine-tasting tour.

It's also straightforward to see something of Barcelona's neighbouring cities, all very different from the Catalan capital. South of Barcelona, beyond Sitges, **Tarragona** has a compact old town, a bustling port area and an amazing series of Roman remains, while nearby **Reus**, the birthplace of Antoni Gaudí, features

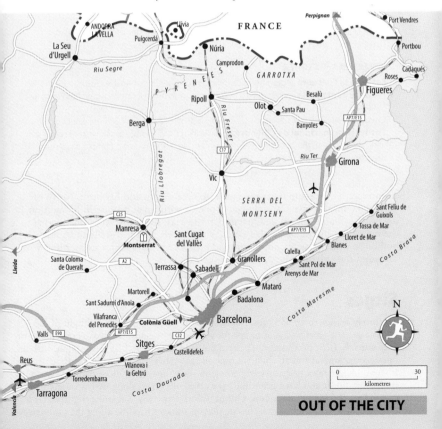

OUT OF THE CITY

13

REGIONAL FESTIVALS

FEBRUARY–MAY

Carnival February or March, dates vary. Sitges has Catalunya's best Carnival celebrations (see box, page 148).

International jazz festival Three weeks in March, Terrassa (ⓦjazzterrassa.org). Acts playing in clubs and old-town squares.

Fires i Festes de la Santa Creu First week in May, Figueres, with processions and music.

Trapezi Third week in May (ⓦtrapezi.cat.en). International circus fair in Reus, with street performances and spectacle.

Festa de Corpus Christi (moveable feast, sometimes falls in early June). Big processions and streets decorated with flowers in Sitges.

JUNE–AUGUST

Dia de Sant Joan June 24. Celebrated everywhere; watch out for things shutting down for a day on either side.

Festa Major de Sant Cugat del Vallès Last week in June.

Festa Major de Sant Pere Last week in June, in Reus. The town's biggest annual bash.

Gay Pride Sitges Second week in July, sometimes held in June (ⓦgaysitgespride.com). Several days of events, parties and street parades.

Festa de Sant Magí August 19 in Tarragona.

Festa Major Last week in August. Festival to honour Sitges' patron saint, Sant Bartolomeu.

Festa Major in Vilafranca del Penedès August 29 & 30 (ⓦfestamajorvilafranca.cat). Dedicated to Sant Felix, with human towers, dancing and processions.

SEPTEMBER–OCTOBER

Festa de la Fil·loxera September 8. Sant Sadurní d'Anoia's big annual festival.

Festa de Santa Tecla September 23, in Tarragona, with processions of *gegants* and human castles.

Cavatast Early October. Cava and gastronomy festival is held in Sant Sadurní d'Anoia.

Festival Internacional de Cinema Fantastic Early October (ⓦsitgesfilmfestival.com). Sitges hosts one of the premier horror and fantasy film fests in Europe, complete with film premieres and zombie walks.

an interpretive museum that's the last word on the man and his work. North of Tarragona unfolds inland Catalunya, peppered with small, wonderfully traditional towns, like Santa Coloma de Queralt. Up the coast sits medieval **Girona**, perhaps the most beautiful of all Catalan cities, with its river, fortified walls and golden buildings, while **Figueres** not far beyond boasts Catalunya's most extraordinary museum, the amazing **Museu Dalí**.

Sitges

The lovely seaside town of **Sitges**, 36km south of Barcelona, is the highlight of the local coast. The great weekend escape for young Barcelonans, who have created a resort very much in their own image, it's also a noted LGBTQ+ holiday destination, with an outrageous carnival and an ebullient nightlife to match – between June and September it seems like there's a nonstop party going on. But Sitges is far more than just cocktails under the sun. It also has a beautifully preserved old town, along with a variety of well-curated art and history museums. Out of season, especially, Sitges is delightful: far less crowded, and with a temperate climate that encourages strolling along the promenade

13

and exploring the narrow central lanes. Note that on Monday, many of the museums and restaurants are closed.

The old town

Old Sitges centres on a tangle of alleyways that climb up and over the knoll, topped by the landmark Baroque **Església Parroquial** (parish church) dedicated to Sant Bartolomeu, which divides the seafront in two. Sweeping views stretch beyond the beaches to either side and along the coast, while a cluster of late medieval whitewashed mansions holds assorted museums and galleries.

Scores of handsome, more recent townhouses were built in Sitges in the nineteenth century by successful local merchants (known as "Americanos") who returned from Cuba and Puerto Rico. A walk along the seafront promenade reveals the best of them, adorned with wrought-iron balconies, stained-glass windows and ceramic decoration. The pedestrianized shopping street, **Carrer Major**, is the best place for browsing boutiques.

Museu Cau Ferrat
C/Fonollar • Tues–Sun: Jan–March & Nov–Dec 10am–5pm; April–Oct 10am–7pm • Charge, includes Museu Maricel • Ⓦ museusdesitges.cat

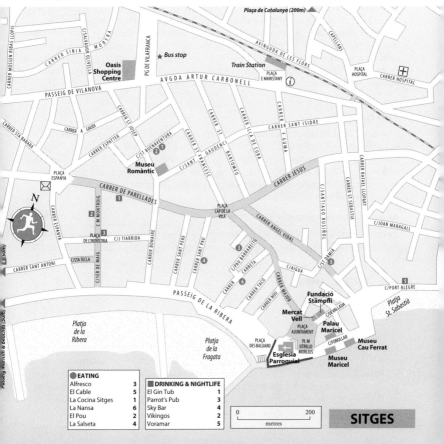

● EATING	
Alfresco	3
El Cable	5
La Cocina Sitges	1
La Nansa	6
El Pou	2
La Salseta	4

■ DRINKING & NIGHTLIFE	
El Gin Tub	1
Parrot's Pub	3
Sky Bar	4
Vikingos	2
Voramar	5

SITGES

13

The gorgeous renovated mansion that overlooks the sea and contains the **Museu Cau Ferrat** served from 1891 onwards as the home and workshop of artist and writer **Santiago Rusiñol i Prats** (1861–1931). Rusiñol organized five *modernista* festivals in Sitges between 1892 and 1899, and the town flourished as a major *modernista* centre under his patronage. Magnificently tiled rooms display an extraordinary array of paintings, artefacts and decorative ironwork gathered by Rusiñol, including works by Rusiñol himself and contemporaries such as Picasso, and even a couple of minor El Grecos that he bought when the painter's reputation was much less elevated than it is today.

Museu Maricel

C/Davallada 12, adjoining Museu Cau Ferrat • Tues–Sun: April–June & Oct 10am–7pm; July–Sept 10am–8pm; Nov–March 10am–5pm • Charge, includes Museum Cau Ferrat • ⓦ museusdesitges.cat

Browse the timeline of Catalan art from the tenth century on, including richly detailed Romanesque and Gothic art, such as altarpieces and ceramics, and the nineteenth-century Luminist School of Sitges, a group of landscape artists who were inspired by the town's beautiful seaside light and open skies.

Fundació Stämpfli

Pl. de l'Ajuntament 13 • Sat & Sun 10–2pm • Charge • ⓦ fundacio-stampfli.org

Housed in Sitges' former fish market and a similarly venerable adjoining building, the **Fundació Stämpfli** is home to the wide-ranging contemporary art collection of Swiss-born artist Peter Stämpfli and his wife, Anna Maria, who have been active members of the local art scene since the 1970s. The works –paintings, sculptures and more by international artists such as Erró, Gérard Fromanger and Stämpfli himself – offer a sweeping view of various art movements from the past fifty years. The renovated space in which the collection is presented is simple but beautiful, with a vaulted, wood-beamed ceiling and gleaming floors.

The beaches

The clean sand **beaches**, located to both east and west of the old-town headland, become extremely crowded in high season. For more space it's best to keep walking west along the promenade, past a series of eight interlinked beaches that runs a couple of kilometres down the coast as far as the *Hotel Terramar*. There are breakwaters, beach bars, restaurants, showers and watersports facilities along the way, with the more notorious nudist beaches found at the far end.

ARRIVAL AND INFORMATION   **SITGES**

By train Trains to Sitges leave Pg. de Gràcia or Barcelona Sants stations roughly every 15min (destination Vilanova or St Vicenç) and take 30–40min depending on the service. The last departure back to Barcelona is at around 10.30pm

---

CARNIVAL TIME

Carnival in Sitges (*Carnestoltes* in Catalan; Feb/March) is a spectacular affair, thanks largely to the strong LGBTQ+ presence. It opens on the so-called Fat Thursday with the arrival of the Carnival King, following which there's a full programme of parades, masked balls, concerts, beach parties and sausage sizzles. The traditional *xatónada* gala dinners are named after the carnival dish, *xató*, a kind of salt-cod salad, which originates in Sitges. Carnival climaxes in Sunday night's **Debauchery Parade** followed by the Tuesday-night **Extermination Parade**, featuring exquisitely dressed drag queens swanning about the streets in high heels. There's also fun, colourful **children's procession**, usually both on Sunday and Tuesday. Bar doors stand wide open, bands play and processions and celebrations go on until dawn. Ash Wednesday itself sees the more traditional Burial of the Sardine.

13

(starting again at around 5am).

By bus Bus Garraf (ⓦbusgarraf.cat) runs services to Sitges from various Barcelona locations, including the Barcelona airport and Plaça Espanya. From Barcelona airport (Mon–Fri once or twice an hour 7.40am–11.40pm, Sat & Sun every 2–3hr), it takes around 35min and stops two blocks from the train station. There are also hourly nightbuses year-round between Pg. de Vilafranca in Sitges and Pl. Espanya in Barcelona. Consult the website for the latest information on ticket prices.

Oficina de Turisme Pl. Eduard Maristany 2, next to the train station (Mon–Sat 10am–2pm & 3.30–6.30pm, until 7pm in summer; Sun 10am–2pm; ☎938 944 251, ⓦsitgestur.cat).

EATING

SEE MAP PAGE 147

Sitges has a huge array of restaurants, and the quality is largely very good, thanks to a discerning, upmarket tourist crowd and well-heeled locals. Every restaurant along the front does a paella with a promenade view, though some of the more interesting places are hidden away in the backstreets. For fresh local produce, stop by the farmers' market in Pl. Catalunya on Saturdays (7am–3pm).

Alfresco C/d'en Pau Barrabeig 4 ⓦalfrescorestaurante. es. Romantic old-town restaurant, tucked away off a stepped alley and and featuring its own trellised patio. The menu matches its charm, with superb Catalan cuisine with Asian touches, such as hoisin-marinated chicken and salmon with stir-fried spinach. Top off the meal with a tangy homemade sorbet. €€

El Cable C/Barcelona 1 ⓦelcable.cat. With its lively social scene, Sitges is a tapas town – and the long-running, amiable El Cable is one of the best. Feast on *patatas bravas*, garlic mushrooms and spicy sausage. €

★ **La Cocina Sitges** C/Sant Bonaventura 19 ⓦlacocina sitges.com. Settle into the lovely outdoor terrace and enjoy innovative fusion seasonal cuisine, which might include tuna tartare with crispy rice and juicy ribeye with chimichurri hollandaise. €€

La Nansa C/Carreta 35 ⓦrestaurantlananasa.com. Family-run fish restaurant – *nansa* means fishing net – where set menus (from €20) may feature everything from *xató*, a bright salad of escarole, cod, tuna and anchovies, to the local variation on the paella, *arròs a la Sitgetana*, complete with a healthy splash of Sitges' Malvasia wine. €€

El Pou C/Sant Bonaventura 21 ⓦelpoudesitges. com. Stylish, welcoming tapas bar, where the Catalan-Japanese-Peruvian fusion menu includes duck carpaccio and meatballs with squid. €€

La Salseta C/de Sant Pau 35 ⓦlasalseta.com. Classic, unpretentious Catalan dishes (cod with garlic and tomato confit, grilled squid with mushrooms and parsley, seafood paella and an excellent array of Catalan cheeses), cooked with slow-food attention and using locally sourced ingredients, keep this cosy little dining room filled with tourists and locals alike. €€

DRINKING AND NIGHTLIFE

SEE MAP PAGE 147

The focus of local **nightlife** is c/Primer de Maig and c/ Montroig, with café-*terrassas* that are busy in summer from morning to night. Call in at *Parrot's* for the lowdown on the LGBTQ+ scene and to find out which clubs are in this year.

El Gin Tub C/Parellades 43 ⓦelgintub.com. Come for the artisanal cocktails, and stay for the rollicking, speakeasy atmosphere, complete with a bathtub you can climb into, and an array of themed events, like Whiskey Wednesdays, karaoke on Thursdays and a regular Cocktail Masterclass, where you can learn how to expertly mix your own libations.

Parrot's Pub Pl. de l'Industria ⓦparrots-sitges.com. The stalwart of the LGBTQ+ bar scene in Sitges, with seats under brightly coloured parasols. The owners also run a number of other bars and restaurants in town, including a Mediterranean hotel and restaurant nearby.

Sky Bar Avda. Sofia 12 ⓦhotelmimsitges.com. Toast the night at this soaring bar that crowns *Hotel Mim Sitges*. The star here is the spectacular view, but the cocktails also hold their own, including tasty mojitos and a creative array of fresh-fruit martinis, from coconut to mandarin and kumquat, as well as top-notch cava.

Vikingos C/Marqués de Montroig 7–9 ⓦlosvikingos. com. Long-standing party-zone bar with an enormous interior and streetside terrace. This and the similar *Montroig* next door serve drinks, snacks and meals from morning until night to a really mixed crowd.

Voramar C/Port Alegre 55 ⓦpub-voramar.com. Charismatic, old-school seafront bar, just right for an ice-cold beer or sundowner cocktail – try the excellent mojitos.

Montserrat

Otherworldly rock formations crown the mountain of **Montserrat**, which looms 40km northwest of Barcelona, off the road to Lleida. Hiking paths that lead to splendid views, tucked-away hermitage caves and, above all, a vast and historic **monastery** make Montserrat one of the most popular day-trips from the city. It's easily reached

13

in around one hour thirty minutes by train and then cable car or mountain railway for the final thrilling ride up. Once there, you can visit the basilica and monastery buildings, and complete your day with a **walk** around the woods and crags, using the two funicular railways that depart from the monastery complex. There are cafés and restaurants at the monastery, but they are relatively pricey, none too inspiring and very busy at peak times – there's a lot to be said for taking your own picnic instead and striking off into the hills for an alfresco lunch.

Legends hang easily upon Montserrat. Fifty years after the birth of Christ, St Peter is said to have deposited an image of the Virgin (known as La Moreneta, the Black Virgin), carved by St Luke, in one of the mountain caves. The icon was lost in the early eighth century after being hidden during the Moorish invasion, but reappeared in 880, accompanied by the customary visions and celestial music. The chapel built to house it was in 976 superseded by a Benedictine monastery, set at an altitude of nearly 1000m. Miracles abounded and the Virgin of Montserrat soon became the chief cult image of Catalunya and a pilgrimage centre second in Spain only to Santiago de Compostela in Galicia., April 27 is the annual feast day of Our Lady of Montserrat, with celebrations and events across the monastery and grounds.

The monastery

Basilica Daily 7am–8pm; access to La Moreneta 8–10.30am & noon–6.25pm • **Boys' choir** Mon–Fri 1pm and in the evening, usually 6.45pm or 7.10pm; Sun at 11am & occasionally in the evening • Free

Of the religious buildings, only the Renaissance **basilica**, dating largely from 1560 to 1592, is open to the public. **La Moreneta** stands above the high altar – reached from behind, by way of an entrance to the right of the basilica's main entrance. The approach to this beautiful icon reveals the enormous wealth of the monastery, as you queue along a corridor leading through the back of the basilica's rich side-chapels. The monastery's various outbuildings – including hotel and restaurant, post office, souvenir shop, self-service cafeteria and bar – fan out around an open square, and there are extraordinary mountain views from the terrace.

Museu de Montserrat

Museu de Montserrat Daily 10am–5.45pm • Charge • ⓦ museudemontserrat.com • **Espai Audiovisual** Mon–Fri 9am–6.45pm, Sat & Sun 9am–7.45pm • Charge

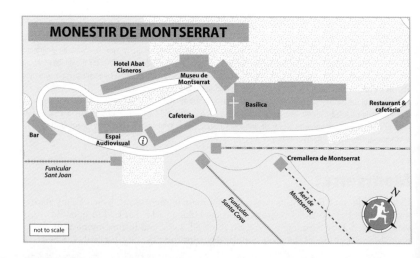

13

MONTSERRAT BOYS' CHOIR

Montserrat is awash in spirituality – but never more so than when the world-famous **boys' choir** sings. Time your visit to hear the boys' soaring voices fill the basilica (Mon–Fri 1pm & in the evening, usually 6.45pm or 7.10pm; Sun at 11am & occasionally in the eve). The choir belongs to the Escolania (**ⓦ** escolania.cat), a choral school established in the fourteenth century and unchanged in musical style since its foundation. One of the oldest boys' choirs in Europe, the Escolania is comprised of boys aged nine to fourteen who receive a rigorous music-focused education at Montserrat. Unlike its famous European counterparts, the choir has rarely toured abroad – that is, until now. After performing in the USA for the first time in 2014, the choir returned in 2017, making appearances on both coasts. In 2023, for the first time in its centuries-long history, girls were admitted, to form a new mixed choral choir that will perform in addition to the traditional boys' choir.

The **Museu de Montserrat**, set in a modernist building by architect Josep Puig i Cadafalch, presents archeological finds brought back by travelling monks, together with paintings and sculpture dating from as early as the thirteenth century, including works by Old Masters, French Impressionists and Catalan *modernistas*. There's also a collection of Byzantine icons, though other religious items are in short supply, as most of the monastery's valuables were carried off by Napoleon's troops who sacked the complex in 1811. For more on the history, and to learn something of the life of a Benedictine community, visit the stimulating **Espai Audiovisual**, near the information office. Additionally, the museum features a regular calendar of temporary exhibitions, many of which focus on contemporary Catalan art and culture.

Mountain walks

Funicular departures vary by season, but mostly every 20min, 10am–5pm • Santa Cova €6 return, Sant Joan €10.40 return • ⓦ cremallerademontserrat.cat

As you follow the mountain tracks that lead from the monastery to the nearby caves and hermitages, you can contemplate Goethe's observation of 1816: "Nowhere but in his own Montserrat will a man find happiness and peace." The going is pretty good on all the tracks and the signposting is clear, but you do need to remember that you're on a mountain – take a bottle of water and keep away from the edges.

Two separate **funiculars** run from points close to the cable-car station; pick up a map with walking notes from the Montserrat tourist office. One drops to the path for **Santa Cova**, a seventeenth-century chapel built where the Moreneta icon is said to have been found. It's an easy walk there and back, which takes less than an hour.

The other funicular rises steeply to the hermitage of **Sant Joan**, from where it's a tougher 45-minute walk to the **Sant Jeroni** hermitage, and another fifteen minutes to the Sant Jeroni summit at 1236m. This is an excellent place to watch for peregrines, crag martins and black redstarts; in summer you may also spot alpine swifts, while Iberian wall lizards emerge from the crevices to bask on the rockfaces. Several other walks are also possible from the Sant Joan funicular, perhaps the nicest being the 45-minute circuit around the ridge that leads all the way back down to the monastery.

ARRIVAL AND DEPARTURE   MONTSERRAT

There are two ways to reach Montserrat by public transport – cable car and mountain railway – but in the first instance you need to take the **FGC train** (line R5, direction Manresa), which leaves Barcelona's Pl. d'Espanya (**ⓦ** Espanya) daily (hourly intervals 8.36am–4.36pm; extra departures March–Oct Mon–Fri 11.56am–4.56pm).

By cable car Get off the train at Montserrat Aeri (1hr) for the connecting cable car, the Aeri de Montserrat (every 15min: March–Oct daily 9.40am–7pm; Nov–Feb Mon–Fri 10.10am–5.45pm, Sat, Sun & hols 9.40am–6.15pm; €8.60 one-way, €13 return; **ⓦ** aeridemontserrat.com). Queues are possible at busy times. Returning to Barcelona,

13

the R5 trains depart hourly from Montserrat Aeri (from 9.45am to around 7pm).

By mountain railway The Montserrat mountain railway, the Cremallera de Montserrat (hourly and daily, generally from morning to late afternoon; ⓦ cremallerademontserrat. cat; see ticket information below), departs from Monistrol de Montserrat (the next stop after Montserrat Aeri, another 4min), and takes 20min. Returning to Barcelona, the R5 trains depart hourly from Monistrol de Montserrat (from 8.15am).

Tickets You can purchase tickets online or at the Pl. d'Espanya station. There are two combination tickets:

the Trans Montserrat (€45), which includes all transport services, including unlimited use of the mountain funiculars and monastery museum entry; and the Tot Montserrat (€65.50), which includes the same plus a self-service lunch of Catalan dishes.

By car Take the A2 motorway as far as the Montserrat exit, and then follow the BP-1103 to the Montserrat turn-off – or park at either the cable-car or the mountain-railway station and take the rides up instead. All-in cable car/Cremallera/ Montserrat attraction combo tickets are available at the station for drivers who park and ride.

INFORMATION

Visitor centre At the monastery (Mon–Fri 9am–6.30pm, Sat & Sun 9am–7.30pm; ⓦ montserratvisita.com). You can pick up maps of the complex and mountain, and they can

also advise about accommodation, from camping to staying at the three-star *Abat Cisneros* hotel (ⓦ hotelabatcisneros montserrat.com-hotel.com).

Sant Cugat and Terrassa

A series of remarkable churches lies on the commuter train line northwest of Barcelona, the first in the town of **Sant Cugat del Vallès** – just 25 minutes from the city – and the second (actually a group of three) another fifteen minutes beyond in the industrial city of **Terrassa**. You can easily see all the churches in a morning, but throw in lunch and this just about stretches to a day-trip, and it's not a bad ride in any case – after Sarrià, the train emerges from the city tunnels and chugs down the wooded valley into Sant Cugat.

Sant Cugat del Vallès

Reial Monestir Mon–Sat 8am–noon & 6–8pm, Sun open for Mass from 9am • Free • **Museu del Monestir** June–Sept Tues–Sat 10.30am–1.30pm & 4–7pm, Sun & hols 10.30am–4.30pm; Oct–May Tues–Sat 10.30am–1.30pm & 5–8pm, Sun & hols 10.30am–4.30pm • Free • **Torre de la Muralla** Generally open in the summer • Free • **Celler Modernista** Sat 10.30am–1.30pm & 4–7pm, 5–8pm in summer, Sun 10.30am–2.30pm • Free • ⓦ museu.santcugat.cat • **Casa Aymat. Espai de Creació** Mon–Fri 9am–9.30pm • Free • ⓦ centresculturals.santcugat.cat

The Benedictine **Reial Monestir** (Royal Monastery) at **Sant Cugat del Vallès** was founded as far back as the ninth century, though most of the surviving buildings date from three or four hundred years later. Its fawn stone facade and triple-decker bell tower make a lovely sight as you approach from the square outside, through the gate, past the renovated Bishop's Palace and under a splendid rose window. Finest of all, though, is the beautiful twelfth-century Romanesque **cloister**, with noteworthy capital carvings of mythical beasts and biblical scenes. Their unusual homogeneity owes to the fact that all were completed by a single sculptor, Arnau Gatell.

The monastery complex encompasses the **Museu de Sant Cugat**, which includes the restored dormitory, kitchen and refectory of the monastery, and holds exhibitions about its history and monastic life. What were once the monastery's kitchen gardens lie across from the Bishop's Palace, though the formerly lush plots that sustained the brothers are now mere dusty gardens, albeit with views over the low walls to Tibidabo and the Collserola hills. The Torre de la Muralla, a lookout tower on the grounds, is also accessible in the summer. Near the monastery rises the **Celler Modernista** (Modernist Winery), a handsome, high-ceilinged 1921 winery designed by Cèsar Martinell, who had a mentor in Antoni Gaudí. Now a museum, exhibitions trace the history of the winery and the vinification process. The **Casa Aymat. Espai de Creació** (Contemporary Tapestry Museum), a cultural centre near the museum and monastery, is set in the 1926 Casa Aymat, once the workshop and factory of textile artist Tomàs

Aymat. The centre offers a wide range of art and textile classes, and workshops, and has more information on creative arts and culture exhibitions around the city.

ARRIVAL AND INFORMATION   SANT CUGAT DEL VALLÈS

By train FGC trains on the S1 line connect Pl. de Catalunya in Barcelona with Sant Cugat, which is in Zone 2, every 10–15min (W fgc.cat). Once in Sant Cugat, walk straight ahead out of the train station and down the pedestrianized C/ Valldoreix, taking the first right and then the first left (it's still C/Valldoreix), and then keep straight along the shopping street (C/Santa María and then C/Santiago Rusiñol) until you see the monastery bell tower (10min walk).

Oficina de Turisme Sant Cugat del Vallès, Pl. Octavia 10, inside the main doorway of the monastery (April–Oct Tues–Sat 10.30am–2pm & 5–7pm, Sun 10am–2pm; Nov–March Tues–Sun 10am–2pm W turisme.santcugat.cat).

Terrassa

Terrassa, a large city with a population of 200,000 located 25km northwest of Barcelona, was an important textile producer in the nineteenth century, and retains many fine *modernista*-style factories, mills and warehouses that now enjoy protected status. But Terrassa has a much longer history, and its true treasures stand on the edge of the city centre, built on the site of the Roman town of Ègara – three pre-Romanesque churches, dating from the fifth to the tenth centuries.

La Seu d'Ègara

La Seu d'Ègara, Pl. del Rector Horns 1 • Tues–Sat 10am–1.30pm & 4–7pm, Sun & hols 11am–2pm • Charge, under-6s free; free entry on 1st weekend of the month • W seudegara.cat

Known as **La Seu d'Ègara**, Terrassa's fully restored ecclesiastical complex centres on its largest church, **Sant Pere**, which sports a badly faded Gothic mural and a tenth-century mosaic fragment within its walls. The church of **Santa María** is far better endowed, featuring a mosaic pavement outside and sunken baptismal font inside, both of which date from the fifth century. Much later Gothic (fourteenth- and fifteenth-century) murals and altarpieces – one by Catalan master Jaume Huguet – are also on display. But it's the fifth-century baptistry of **Sant Miquel** that's the most fascinating – a tiny, square building of rough masonry, steeped in gloom, with eight assorted columns supporting the dome, each with a carved Roman or Visigothic capital. Underneath sits the partially reconstructed baptismal bath, while steps lead down into a simple crypt.

ARRIVAL AND INFORMATION   TERRASSA

By train FGC trains from Barcelona (S1 line from Pl. de Catalunya; W fgc.cat) depart every 20–30min – get off at Terrassa-Rambla, the last stop, which is in Zone 3. The churches are a 25min walk from the station – turn right from the Rambla d'Ègara exit, then immediately right again into Pl. de Clavé, follow C/Major up to Pl. Vella, cross the square, turn up C/Gavatxons and follow C/Sant Pere, C/Nou de Sant Pere and C/Creu Gran, finally crossing a viaduct to arrive at the entrance. There is a more convenient Renfe mainline train station in Terrassa (direct trains from Barcelona Sants every 20–30min; W renfe.com) – a straight 10min walk down C/Mas Adel to the churches – but only the FGC line connects both Sant Cugat and Terrassa.

Oficina de Turisme Masia Freixa, Plaça Freixa i Argemí 11 (April–Sept Mon 9am–2pm, Tues–Fri 9am–2pm & 5–7pm, Sat & Sun 10am–2pm; Aug open mornings only; Oct–March Mon 9am–2pm, Tues–Fri 9am–2pm & 4–6pm, Sat & Sun 10am–2pm; T 937 397 019, W visitaterrassa. cat). Organizes guided tours throughout the city, including many of its historic buildings.

Colònia Güell

Before work at Barcelona's Park Güell got under way (see page 131), Antoni Gaudí had already been charged with the design of parts of Eusebi Güell's earliest attempts to establish a Utopian industrial estate, or *colònia* (colony), on the western outskirts of the city. The **Colònia Güell** (W gaudicoloniaguell.org) at Santa Coloma de Cervelló was very much of its time – more than seventy similar colonies were established along Catalan

13

rivers in the late nineteenth century, using water power to drive the textile mills. The concept was also familiar in Britain, where enlightened Victorian entrepreneurs had long created idealistic towns (Saltaire, Bournville) to house their workers.

The Colònia Güell was begun in 1890, and by 1920 incorporated over one hundred houses and public buildings, plus the chapel and crypt for which Gaudí was responsible. The Güell company was taken over in 1945 and the whole complex closed as a going concern in 1973, though the buildings have since been restored – and, indeed, many are still lived in today. There are rows of terraced houses, with front gardens tended lovingly by the current inhabitants, while brick towers, ceramic panels and stained glass elevate many of the houses above the ordinary. It's a working village, so you'll also find a bank and pharmacy, as well as several cafés and restaurants, and on Saturdays (9am–2pm) there is a farmers' market, with fresh fruit and vegetables from the Baix Llobregat area.

Gaudí's church

Mon–Fri 10am–5pm, Sat & Sun 10am–3pm; generally closed for visits during Mass on Sun (11am & 1pm) • Charge • ⓦ gaudicoloniaguell.org

Gaudí's **church** – built into the pine-clad hillside above the colony – is a masterpiece. While you can see the angular exterior from the outside for free, to see the far more dramatic interior you'll first have to buy a ticket at the visitor centre. The **crypt** was designed to carry the weight of the chapel above, its palm-tree-like columns supporting a brick vault, and the whole lot resembling a labyrinth of caves fashioned from a variety of different stone and brick. Several of Gaudí's more extraordinary flights of fancy – like the original scalloped pews, the conch shells used as water stoups, the vivid stained glass and the window that opens up like the wings of a butterfly – presage his later work on the Sagrada Família. Despite appearances, the church was never actually finished, and Gaudí stopped work on it in 1914. Ongoing restoration aims to maintain the outer walls, though Gaudí's planned 40m-high central dome is unlikely ever to be realized.

ARRIVAL AND INFORMATION   **COLÒNIA GÜELL**

By train Take the FGC train S4, S8 or S33 (direction Martorell; departures every 15–25min; ⓦ fgc.cat) from Pl. d'Espanya to the small Colònia Güell station; the ride takes 20min. From the station, follow the painted blue footprints across the highway and into the *colònia*; they lead directly to the visitor centre (10min).
Centre d'Acollida de Visitants (Mon–Fri 10am–5pm,

Sat & Sun 10am–3pm; ☎ 936 305 807, ⓦ gaudicoloniaguell. org). The visitor centre has an exhibition (with English notes).
Guided tours Tours of the church and Colònia Güell are available daily throughout the year; admission €13. An audio-guide (€10, including admission) is also offered; audio-guide with train trip included to and from Barcelona is €14.80.

EATING AND DRINKING

Ateneu Unió Pl. Joan Güell 5 ☎ 936 613 111. The big, old-fashioned, if a bit faded, bar-restaurant on the quiet

central square is good for sandwiches, tapas and a decent *menú del dia* served on the sunny *terrassa*. €

L'Alt Penedès wine region

L'Alt Penedès wine region (ⓦ enoturismepenedes.cat), roughly halfway between Barcelona and Tarragona, is the largest Catalan producer of still and sparkling wines – as becomes increasingly clear the further the train heads into the region, with vines as far as the eye can see on both sides of the track. Both the two main towns to visit can easily be seen in a single day: **Sant Sadurní d'Anoia**, closer to Barcelona, is the self-styled "Capital del Cava", home to fifty-plus producers of sparkling wine, while **Vilafranca del Penedès**, ten minutes down the line, is the region's administrative capital and produces mostly still wine, red and white.

If you're serious about **visiting vineyards**, the trip is better done by car, as many of the more interesting boutique producers lie out in the countryside. Either of the towns' tourist offices can provide a good map pinpointing all the local vineyards as well as the rural farmhouse restaurants. However, even by train you'll be able to visit a winery or two, including one of the most famous of Catalan wine names. The region is also tailor-made for pedalling, with accessible, relatively flat bike trails that unfold through the lush, rolling terrain. **Penedès 360** (ⓦpenedes360.cat) covers a variety of routes, as well as amenities along the way, including bike hire, luggage transfer, accommodation and more.

Sant Sadurní d'Anoia

The small town of **Sant Sadurní d'Anoia** (population 12,000), built on land watered by the Riu Noya, has been an important centre of wine production since the eighteenth century. When, at the end of the nineteenth century, French vineyards suffered heavily from phylloxera, Sant Sadurní prospered, though later it too succumbed to the same wasting disease – something remembered still in the annual September festival by the parade of a representation of the feared phylloxera parasite. The production of cava, for which the town is now famous, began only in the 1870s – an industry that went hand in hand with the Catalan cork business, established in the forests of the hinterland. Today, a hundred million bottles a year of cava are turned out by dozens of companies, many of which are only too happy to escort you around their premises, show you the fermentation process and let you taste a glass or two. The Sant Sadurní tourist office offers a map featuring the *caves* or cellars in and around town.

Freixenet

Daily tours and tastings, lasting 1hr 30min; usually Mon–Sat 9.30am–4.30pm, Sun 10am–1pm; check website for variations; reservations required • Charge • ⓦ freixenet.es

Most people never get any further than the famous **Freixenet** – producer of those distinctive black bottles – whose building is right outside the train station. Freixenet also has a *Cava Bar*, where you can enjoy a light meal of Iberian ham, local cheese and, of course, glasses of cava.

Codorniu

1.7km north of Sant Sadurní d'Anoia • Daily tours; check website for times; English tours generally once or twice daily on the weekend; reservations required • Charge • ⓦ codorniu.com

The region's earliest cava producer showcases an elegant building by *modernista* architect Josep Puig i Cadafalch. Codorniu offers an array of tours, which includes an

---

CAVA

Cava is a naturally sparkling wine made using the *méthode champenoise*, the traditional method for making champagne. The basic **grape** varieties of L'Alt Penedès are *macabeu*, *xarel.lo* and *parellada*, which are fermented to produce a wine base and then mixed with sugar and yeast before being bottled: a process known as **tiratge**. The bottles are then sealed hermetically – the **tapat** – and laid flat in cellars – the **criança** – for up to nine months to ferment for a second time. The wine is later decanted to get rid of the sediment before being corked.

The cava is then **classified** according to the amount of sugar used in the fermentation: either Brut (less than 20g a litre), Sec (20–30g), Semisec (30–50g) or Dolç (more than 50g). This is the first thing to take note of before buying or drinking: Brut and Sec are to most people's tastes and are excellent with almost any food, or as an aperitif; Semisec and Dolç are better consumed as dessert wines.

13

in-depth exploration of the art and architecture of the winery, from the traditional tour to one that includes lunch with starters, main course and dessert.

Jean Leon

In Torrelavit, 7km west of Sant Sadurní d'Anoia • Regular tours offered, generally on the weekend • Charge, reservations required • Ⓦ jeanleon.com

This boutique winery is as colourful as its founder – Jean Leon. Born Ceferino Carrión in Santander, Jean Leon ambitiously struck out for New York and then Hollywood, where, with James Dean, he opened the famous *La Scala* restaurant in Beverly Hills. But Leon's love of Spain – and wine – brought him back to the Penedès region, where he launched the eponymous winery in the early 1960s. Today, it's owned and managed by Torres (see page 156), and features an American-modernist-inspired visitor centre set in particularly bucolic surroundings. Lively themed tours include tastings of Jean Leon's signature single-vineyard wines, many named after key phases in Leon's life, as well as superb local cuisine.

Juvé & Camps

Daily tours; check website for times; English tours generally 2–3 times daily; reservations required • Charge • Ⓦ juveycamps.com

This historic winery, with century-old cellars surrounded by verdant vineyards, offers a variety of tours, including the Gran Reserva tour, with a guided tour through the cellars, plus a tasting of Gran Reserva cava; and the Terroir Tour, with a guided walk through the cellars and vineyards and a picnic with local nibbles and premium cavas.

Vilafranca del Penedès

As a town, **Vilafranca del Penedès** is rather more interesting than Sant Sadurní. Founded in the eleventh century in a bid to attract settlers to land retaken from the expelled Moors, it became a prosperous market centre. That character remains evident today, in a compact old town at whose heart lie narrow streets and arcaded squares adorned with restored medieval mansions.

From the train station, walk up to the main Rambla de Nostra Senyora and cut to the right up C/Sant Joan to the enclosed Plaça de Sant Joan, which has a small daily produce **market**. A rather larger affair takes place every Saturday, when the stalls also stock clothes, household goods, handicrafts and agricultural gear. The **Festa Major**, meanwhile, at the end of August and the first couple of days in September, brings the place to a standstill: dances and parades clog the streets, while the festival is renowned for its display of *castellers* – teams of people competing to build human towers (see box, page 212).

Vinseum

Pl. Jaume I 5 • May–Sept Tues–Sat 10am–7pm, Sun & hols 10am–2pm; Oct–April Tues–Sat 10am–2pm & 4–7pm, Sun & hols 10am–2pm • Charge • Ⓦ vinseum.cat

Vilafranca's town museum, the **Vinseum**, is housed in a medieval mansion in the centre, and is the best place to get to grips with the region's wine industry. Exhibitions range far and wide, with the emphasis as much on local traditions and culture as wine. Visits culminate with a tasting in the museum's own tavern, which is open daily until 11pm on weekdays and until midnight at the weekend.

Torres

3km northwest of Vilafranca • Regular tours of varying lengths, some with food as well • Charge; reservations required • Ⓦ torres.es

The vineyards of Vilafranca are all out of town, though the largest and best-known winery, **Torres**, is only a short taxi ride away, on the Sant Martí de Sarroca road. Launched in 1870 by Jaime Torres, this family-run behemoth is one of Spain's most recognizable wine brands – and offers a superb array of tours, including a stroll through the Mas Plana vineyards. Also owned by Torres is **Jean Leon** at Torrelavit, closer to Sant Sadurní (see page 156).

Parés Baltà
Masia Can Baltà, Pacs del Penedès, just west of Vilafranca • Regular tours; reservations necessary • Charge • ⓦ paresbalta.com

This is one of the smaller family-run wineries in L'Alt Penedès, which offer a unique alternative to the biggies. Parés Baltà, helmed by two women winemakers, focuses on organic wines, and offers a variety of tours around its lovely property. In some parts, the vineyards grow amid wild parkland – Parés Baltà is one of the few producers in Spain with vineyards in a natural park, the Parc del Foix. Pick up a bottle of the award-winning rosé Parés Baltà Ros de Pacs.

ARRIVAL AND DEPARTURE

L'ALT PENEDÈS

By train Renfe services from Pl. de Catalunya or Barcelona Sants (Mon–Fri every 30min, Sat & Sun every 1hr, ⓦrenfe.com) run west into L'Alt Penedès, calling at Sant Sadurní d'Anoia (40min) and Vilafranca del Penedès (50min).

INFORMATION AND TOURS

L'ALT PENEDÈS
Spanish Trails Adventures (ⓦ spanish-trails.com) offers full-day, small-group escorted Penedès wine tours (from €105, transport and lunch included), including a cycling and wine tour option that lets you bike the quiet country lanes while visiting two or three wineries.
Penedès Ecotours (ⓦ penedesecotours.com) offers a variety of engaging bike and e-bike tours (from €72), taking in wineries, tastings and local snacks along the way.

SANT SADURNÍ D'ANOIA
Oficina de Turisme C/Hospital 26 (Tues–Fri 9.15am–

2.30pm & 4–6pm, Sat 10am–2pm & 4–6pm, Sun 10am–2pm; ⓦ turismesantsadurni.com). The office is in the centre of town – a 15min walk from the train station – at the CIC Fassina Cava Welcome Center, which offers visitors an introduction to the bubbly stuff (€6 entry; see website for tour schedule).

VILAFRANCA DEL PENEDÈS
Oficina de Turisme C/Hermenegild Clascar 2 (Mon–Sat 9.30am–1.30pm & 3–6pm, Sun & hols 10am–1pm; ⓦ turismevilafranca.com).

EATING AND DRINKING

VILAFRANCA DEL PENEDÈS
La Fàbrica C/Hermenegild Clascar 4 ⓦrestaurantla fabrica.com. This Japanese-Mediterranean fusion spot inside an old pasta factory serves up a creative variety of dishes, from prawn skewers with yucca chips to home-

made pastas (try the duck ravioli), to tempura and sushi. €
Inzolia C/Palma 21, off C/Sant Joan ☎938 181 938, ⓦinzolia.com. The most agreeable place in town to sample the local wines – a range of cavas and wines is sold by the glass, and there's a good wine shop attached. €

Tarragona

Majestically sited on a rocky hill, perched directly above the sea 100km southwest of Barcelona, **TARRAGONA** is an ancient place: settled originally by Iberians and then Carthaginians, it was later used as the base for the Roman conquest of the peninsula, which began in 218 BC with Scipio's march south against Hannibal. The fortified city became an imperial resort and, under the Emperor Augustus, who lived here for two years, "Tarraco" was the most elegant and cultured city of Roman Spain, boasting at its peak a quarter of a million inhabitants.

Tarragona today is still a very handsome city – especially the upper town, with the sweeping Rambla Nova at its heart, lined with cafés and restaurants, which leads to the suitably named Balcó del Mediterrani viewpoint. The parallel Rambla Vella marks the start of the old town, while to either side of the *ramblas* is scattered

13

a profusion of relics and monuments from Tarragona's Roman past. The city also holds a wide range of museums, dedicated among other things to modern art, the port and harbour, and the noble Castellarnau family – the city highlight is the archeology museum. Note that most of the sights are **closed on Mondays**, though the Catedral, old town and the exterior of certain Roman remains can still be seen.

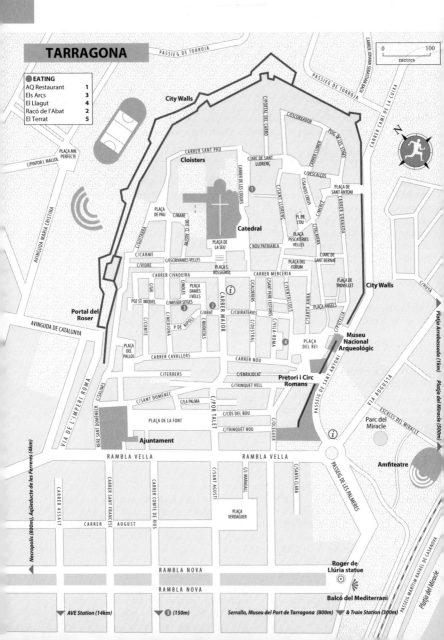

TARRAGONA

PASSEIG DE TORROJA

0 100
metres

EATING
AQ Restaurant	1
Els Arcs	3
El Llagut	4
Racó de l'Abat	2
El Terrat	5

City Walls

Cloisters

Catedral

City Walls

Portal del Roser

AVINGUDA DE CATALUNYA

Museu Nacional Arqueológic

Pretori i Circ Romans

Parc del Miracle

Ajuntament

RAMBLA VELLA

RAMBLA VELLA

Amfiteatre

PLAÇA VERDAGUER

RAMBLA NOVA

RAMBLA NOVA

Roger de Llúria statue

Balcó del Mediterrani

Necropolis (800m), Aqüeducte de les Ferreres (4km)

AVE Station (14km)

(150m)

Serrallo, Museu del Port de Tarragona (800m) & Train Station (300m)

Platja del Miracle

Catedral

Pl. de la Seu • Mid-March to mid-June & mid-Sept to Oct Mon–Sat 10am–7pm; mid-June to mid-Sept Mon–Sat 10am–8pm; Nov to mid-March Mon–Fri 10am–5pm, Sat 10am–7pm • Charge, includes entry to Museu Diocesà • ⓦ catedraldetarragona.com

The focal point of the medieval old town, the **Catedral** is a site of great antiquity; the Christian church was built over the provincial Roman forum. Sitting at the top of a broad flight of steps, the main facade presents a soaring Gothic portal framed by Romanesque doors, surmounted by a cross and an elaborate rose window. Other than during services, entrance to the cathedral is through the lovely **cloisters** (*claustre*; signposted up a street to the left of the facade), where among several oddly sculpted capitals is one representing a cat's funeral being directed by rats. The ticket also gives access to the **Museu Diocesà**, piled high with ecclesiastical treasures, including impressive altarpieces and detailed goldwork.

Museu Nacional Arqueològic

Pl. del Rei 5 • May still be closed for renovations • Charge • ⓦ mnat.cat

The huge collection of the modern **Museu Nacional Arqueològic**, on the seaward edge of the old town, is largely devoted to the Roman era, and serves as a marvellous reflection of the richness of imperial Tarraco. Thematic displays cover the various remains and buildings around the city, as well as whole rooms devoted to statues, inscriptions, ceramics, jewellery, mosaics – including a colourful floor mosaic depicting dozens of species of fish – and some remarkable glass vessels. The museum may still be closed for renovations, but key pieces from the museum can be viewed at Tinglado 4 at the Port of Tarragona. Inquire at the tourist office for more information.

Museum tickets also include admission to Tarraco's ancient **necropolis** – a twenty-minute walk from the centre, down Avinguda Ramon i Cajal, off Rambla Nova – where both pagan and Christian tombs have been uncovered.

Roman Tarragona: Museu d'Història de Tarragona

April–Sept Tues–Fri 9.30am–8pm, Sat 10am–8pm, Sun & hols 10am–3pm; Oct–March Tues–Fri 9am–8pm, Sat 9.30–6.30, Sun & hols 9.30am–2.30pm • Charge • ⓦ tarragona.cat

Most of Tarragona's Roman sites are grouped under the umbrella of the **Museu d'Història de Tarragona** (Tarragona History Museum), and share the same opening hours. These start most spectacularly with the **Pretori i Circ Romans** (entered from Pl. del Rei), built at the end of the first century AD to hold chariot races. The vaults and chambers have been restored to spectacular effect, while a lift takes you up to the roof of the Pretorium Tower – which chillingly still served as a prison in the post-Civil War years – for the best view in Tarragona, looking down over the nearby **Amfiteatre**. There may only be scant remains of the ceremonial provincial forum (Pl. del Fòrum), but the **Fòrum Local** (C/Lleida, a short walk west of Rambla Nova, near the central market) is far more impressive, where the evocative remains of a temple, shops, Roman road and house foundations can still be seen.

Aqüeducte de les Ferreres

Off N240, Lleida road • Open access • Free • Take the bus marked "Sant Salvador" (every 30–45min; 10min) from the stop outside Av. Prat de la Riba 11 (western end of Rambla Nova and off Av. Ramon i Cajal)

Arguably Tarragona's most remarkable monument, the **Roman aqueduct** that brought water to the city from the Riu Gayo, some 32km distant, stands 4km outside the original city walls. Its most impressive surviving section, nearly 220m long and 26m high, lies in an overgrown valley, off the main road, in the middle of nowhere, and is popularly known as the *Pont del Diable* ("Devil's Bridge").

13

Museu del Port Tarragona

Pg. de l'Escullera • June–Sept Tues–Sat 10am–2pm & 5–8pm, Sun 11am–2pm; Oct–May Tues–Sat 10am–2pm & 4–7pm, Sun 10am–2pm • Free • ⓦ porttarragona.cat

A highlight of the revitalized port area, this museum traces Tarragona's formidable seafaring past and the evolution of the port and the Serrallo fishing district with engaging exhibitions. Near the museum is a signed heritage route of the Port of Tarragona, which meanders past historical sights, including the 1860 **Far de la Banya (Banya Lighthouse)**.

Local beaches

The rocky coastline below Tarragona conceals a couple of reasonable beaches. The closest to town is the long **Platja del Miracle**, over the rail lines below the amphitheatre, but **Platja Arrabassada**, a couple of kilometres further up the coast, is nicer by far, and holds a smattering of beach bars. Reach it on a pleasant thirty-minute walk by taking Via Augusta off the end of Rambla Vella.

ARRIVAL AND INFORMATION · TARRAGONA

By train Hourly AVE (high-speed) trains from Barcelona Sants take just 35min, but tickets are expensive and the Camp de Tarragona AVE station is a 10min drive from the centre of town, which adds on the price of a taxi. Otherwise, normal trains from Estació França, Pg. de Gràcia and Barcelona Sants (every 30min; ⓦ renfe.com) take just over an hour: turn right out of the station, and climb the steps ahead of you to reach Rambla Nova, by the statue of Roger de Llúria (10min).

Oficina de Turisme C/Major 39 (July–Sept Mon–Sat 10am–8pm, Sun & hols 10am–2pm; Oct–June Mon–Sat 10am–2pm & 3–6pm, Sun & hols 10am–2pm; ☎ 977 250 795, ⓦ tarragonaturisme.cat).

EATING · SEE MAP PAGE 158

The pretty old-town squares, like Pl. del Rei, Pl. del Fòrum and Pl. de la Font, are the best places for outdoor drinks and meals. The last in particular features more than a dozen **cafés**, **bars and restaurants** serving everything from *pintxos* to pizzas. Otherwise, for a tasty paella lunch it's worth heading down to Tarragona's fishermen's quarter and revitalized port, **Serrallo**, a 15min walk west along the industrial harbourfront from the train station.

AQ Restaurant C/Coques 7 ⓦ aq-restaurant.com. This handsome restaurant – done up in gleaming blonde wood and sleek furnishings – has impressive cuisine to match. Husband-and-wife team Quintín and Ana (after whom the restaurant is named) serve up seasonal food with flair, including superb fresh fish and shellfish (try the excellent variety of oysters) and grilled meats. Note that the restaurant is closed on the weekends.

Els Arcs Misser Sitges 13 ⓦ restaurantarcs.com. Ancient, graceful stone arches preside over a cosy dining room. Fresh Mediterranean dishes include roasted seasonal vegetables with a guacamole ice cream, sautéed squid with spring onions and artichokes, and succulent duck with hibiscus. €€

El Llagut C/Natzaret 10, at Pl. del Rei ☎ 977 228 938. A top town-centre spot for seafood and rice dishes (try the rice with Tarragona sardines), with a quiet *terrassa* opposite the archeological museum. €€

Racó de l'Abat C/Abat 2 ☎ 977 780 371. Beamed ceilings

CULINARY DAY-TRIP TO THE CAMPS SISTERS

Catalunya is justly famous for its wildly progressive cuisine, but this culinary stardom was born in the region's traditional dishes, many of which reveal Catalunya's natural bounty. For a taste, turn to *les germanes Camps* (the Camps sisters) at **Hostal Colomí** (C/Raval de Jesús 12, ☎ 977 880 653; Tues–Sun 1–4pm) in the lovely historical town of Santa Coloma de Queralt, about 50km northwest of Tarragona. For many, *Hostal Colomí*, which was founded in 1948, isn't just the best traditional Catalan cuisine in the Tarragona region. It's the best in the country. The meal starts with two large *porrons* (pitchers) of wine – one white, one red – and a platter of *pa amb tomàquet* (bread smeared in tomato and drizzled in olive oil). The feast continues, including local cheeses, warm ham croquettes, cod and platters of grilled meat and asparagus from the open-air grill, culminating in dessert – *crema Catalana*, of course. Best of all: the set lunch menu is an excellent deal, at around €20.

13

and crimson plaster walls give this Catalan restaurant – located in a former palace dating from the sixteenth century – an intimate, heritage vibe – a perfect setting for excellent local seafood and grilled meats €€

El Terrat C/Pons d'icart 19 ⓦelterratrestaurant.com. Helmed by the talented chef Moha Quach, this elegant, warmly lit restaurant showcases reinvented Mediterranean cuisine influenced by Quach's Moroccan roots. Splurge on the tasting menu, which might include shrimp with toasted almonds or a honey-date tart with veal and Moroccan spices. €€

Reus

The charming little city of **Reus**, 100km southwest of Barcelona and 14km northwest of Tarragona, was the birthplace in 1852 of architect Antoni Gaudí, though there was little in his early life to indicate what was to come. He was born to a humble family of boilermakers and coppersmiths, and left for Barcelona when he was 16 years old. Even though there are no Gaudí buildings in Reus, however, it does hold a fascinating

13

interpretive centre dedicated to its most famous son. The Gaudí Centre forms part of the city's **Ruta del Modernisme**, a marked trail around the many buildings and mansions erected in the *modernista* style at the end of the nineteenth century and start of the twentieth, when Reus ranked as Catalunya's second city after Barcelona, and was home to a merchant class made wealthy by the trade in wine and olive oil and, later, textiles, fabrics and ceramics. You can easily see all of Reus's sights in a day out from Barcelona – it's full of pretty squares, good restaurants and handsome pedestrianized shopping streets, with almost everything of note lying within a clearly defined circuit of boulevards.

Gaudí Centre

Pl. del Mercadal 3 • July to mid-Sept Mon–Sat 10am–8pm, Sun & hols 10am–2pm; June 10am–2pm & 4–8pm, Sun & hols 10am–2pm; Sept to end-May Mon–Sat 10am–2pm & 4–7pm, Sun & hols 10am–2pm • Charge, under-8s free • ⓦ reusturisme.cat

The **Gaudí Centre**, a gleaming building on the main square, throws considerable light on the inspiration, methodology and craftsmanship behind Gaudí's work.

It's not really a museum as such, though exhibits include copper vessels made by his father; school reports announcing the young Gaudí to be "outstanding" at geometry; his only surviving manuscript notebook; and a reconstruction of his study-workshop at the Sagrada Família. Instead, the centre cleverly investigates the architectural techniques pioneered by Gaudí, with meticulous hands-on models and audiovisual aids that explain, for example, how he created wave roofs and spiral towers. If you ever wondered why none of Gaudí's door frames is straight, or what trees, ferns and snails have to do with architecture, this is undoubtedly the place to find out.

Casa Navàs

Pl. del Mercadal 5 • 3–5 tours daily, check with Oficina de Turisme; reservations required • Charge, under-7s free; includes Gaudí Centre

Antoni Gaudí may never have built in Reus, but his contemporary, Lluís Domènech i Montaner, was responsible for Reus's finest townhouse, the magnificently decorated **Casa Navàs** (1901), across Plaça del Mercadal from the Gaudí Centre. It's still privately owned, but is open for pre-booked tours of the virtually intact period interior, which you shuffle around in overshoes to protect the floor. In addition to traditional tours, they offer dramatized tours, with actors playing historical roles.

Plaça del Mercadal itself used to be the site of the general market – the numbers you can see etched in the square's paving indicated the position of the stalls.

Sant Pere and around

Pl. de Sant Pere • Daily 10.30am–1pm & 4.30–8pm • Free

Reus's main church, dedicated to its patron saint, **Sant Pere**, is a couple of minutes' walk from the Gaudí Centre. This is where Gaudí was baptized (there's a plaque by the baptismal chapel) and the church also boasts the heart of Reus's number-two son, *modernista* artist Marià Fortuny i Marsal (the plaque here reads "he gave his soul to heaven, his fame to the world, and his heart to his country").

The arcaded square with cafés behind the church, **Plaça de les Peixateries Velles**, was once the local fish market.

Gaudí's birthplace

C/de Sant Vicenç 4

Divert a few minutes from the commercial centre to see **Gaudí's birthplace**. The house is not original, but a plaque marks the site itself, and there's a rather touching sculpture of the young Gaudí playing marbles outside a school just down the street.

ARRIVAL AND INFORMATION REUS

By plane Reus Airport, 3km east of town and served by Ryanair flights from the UK, offers connecting buses direct to Barcelona, while local bus #50 runs hourly into town, via the train station.

By train There are hourly Renfe services (ⓦ renfe.com) to Reus (via Tarragona) from Pg. de Gràcia and Barcelona Sants; the journey takes 1hr 40min. Taxis wait outside the station, or you can walk to the centre in 15min – head down Pg. Sunyer, turn left at Pl. de les Oques, and follow C/Sant Joan to Pl. del Prim.

Oficina de Turisme Pl. del Mercadal, inside the Gaudí Centre (mid-June to mid-Sept Mon–Sat 10am–8pm, Sun & hols 10am–2pm; mid-Sept to mid-June Mon–Sat 9.30am–8pm, Sun & hols 10am–2pm; ☎ 977 010 670, ⓦ reusturisme.cat). You can pick up a good map of town, and ask about guided tours (not always in English).

EATING SEE MAP PAGE 161

Restaurants are plentiful, with a particular concentration around Pl. del Mercadal and along nearby C/Santa Anna. The daily market (Mon–Sat) takes place at the **Mercat Central** on C/Sant Joan, not far from the train station.

★ **El Circol de Reus** Pl. de Prim 4 ⓦ elcircoldereus. cat/restaurant. The grand *El Circol*, in the heart of town, is a Reus landmark, home to a cultural society founded in 1852. In 2021, acclaimed chefs Joan Urgellès and Xavi Martí

Macarrilla teamed up to manage the restaurant, where they serve up excellent Mediterranean cuisine with classic French touches. €€

Ferran Cerro Pl. del Castell 19 ⓦ ferrancerro.com. Small spot, huge flavours. This charming restaurant features innovative, seasonal cuisine, like hake with dashi cream and seaweed, tomato ceviche with corn, tender lamb with curry and an array of rice dishes. €€

Girona

The ancient walled city of **GIRONA** stands on a fortress-like hill, high above the Riu Onyar, 100km northeast of Barcelona but now barely forty minutes by train. Fought over in almost every century since this site held the Roman fortress of Gerunda, it has been rebuilt and added to many times: following the Moorish conquest of Spain, Girona was an Arab town for over two centuries, and there was also a continuous Jewish presence for six hundred years – which resulted in El Call, one of the best-preserved Jewish quarters in Europe. In short: Girona is an overwhelmingly beautiful medieval city, with old and new towns divided by the river, which is crisscrossed by footbridges, with pastel-coloured houses reflected in the waters below. The compact wedge of land that comprises the old town contains all the sights and monuments, making historic Girona an easy and very enjoyable day-trip from Barcelona.

Catedral

Pl. de la Catedral • mid-March to mid-June & mid-Sept to Oct Mon–Fri 10am–6pm, Sat 10am–7pm, noon–6pm; mid-June to mid-Sept Mon–Fri 10am–7pm, Sat 10am–8pm, Sun noon–7pm; Nov–mid-March Mon–Sat 10am–5pm, Sun noon–5pm • Charge, under-7s free • ⓦ catedraldegirona.org

The centrepiece of old Girona, its mighty Gothic **Catedral**, is approached by a magnificent flight of seventeenth-century Baroque steps. Inside, there are no aisles, just one tremendous Gothic nave vault with a span of 22m. Such emphasis on width and height is a defining feature of Catalan-Gothic "hall churches", of which this is the ultimate example. The cathedral treasures include the famous eleventh-century "Creation Tapestry", the finest surviving specimen of Romanesque textile. But it's the exquisite Romanesque **cloisters** (1180–1210) that make the strongest impression, boasting minutely carved figures and scenes on double columns.

Banys Àrabs

C/Ferran el Catòlic • Mon–Sat 10am–6pm, Sun & hols 10am–2pm • Charge • ⓦ banysarabs.org

The intact remains of Girona's **Banys Àrabs**, reached via the twin-towered Portal de Sobreportas below the cathedral, are the best-preserved ancient baths in Spain after

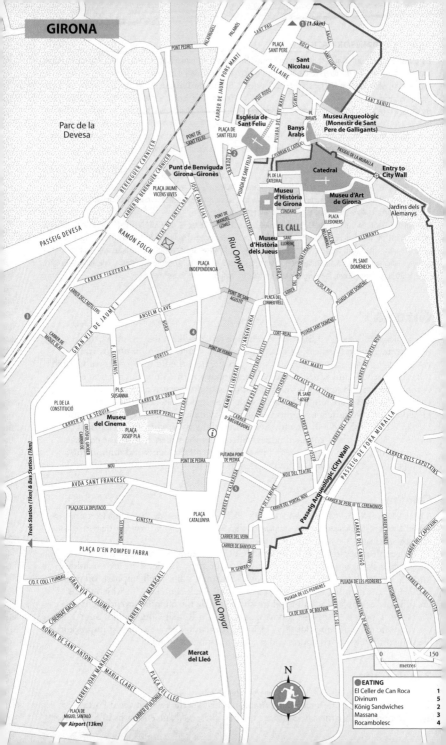

GIRONA

Parc de la Devesa

Sant Nicolau

Església de Sant Feliu

Banys Àrabs

Museu Arqueològic (Monestir de Sant Pere de Galligants)

Punt de Benviguda Girona–Gironès

Catedral

Entry to City Wall

Museu d'Història de Girona

Museu d'Art de Girona

Jardins dels Alemanys

EL CALL

Museu d'Història dels Jueus

PL SANT DOMÈNEC

Museu del Cinema

Passeig Arqueològic (City Wall)

Mercat del Lleó

Train Station (1km) & Bus Station (3km)

Airport (13km)

Riu Onyar

N

0   150
metres

those at Granada. Despite the name, they date from the thirteenth century, a couple of hundred years after the Moors' occupation of Girona had ended, and they're a very graceful blend of Romanesque and Moorish elements, albeit probably built by Moorish craftsmen. It only takes fifteen minutes or so to explore the three principal rooms, each designed for different temperatures, with an underfloor heating system.

Museu d'Història de Girona

C/de la Força 27 • May–Sept Tues–Sat 10.30am–6.30pm, Sun 10.30am–1.30pm; Oct–April Tues–Sat 10.30am–5.30pm, Sun 10.30am–1.30pm • Charge, under-16s free • ⓦ www.girona.cat/museuhistoria

Girona's excellent history museum, the **Museu d'Història de Girona**, a couple of streets down from the cathedral, traces the city's story from its origins as Parva Gerunda up to the Franco era. Its most beautiful exhibits are unquestionably its Roman mosaics, but there's an especially interesting room devoted to the trades practised in the medieval city. The museum staff can offer suggestions on historical walking tours around the city.

Museu Arqueològic

Monestir de Sant Pere de Galligants, C/Santa Llúcia 8 • May–Sept Tues–Sat 10am–7pm, Sun 10am–2pm; Oct–April Tues–Sat 10am–6pm, Sun 10am–2pm • Charge, free for under-8s; free entry 1st Sun of the month • ⓦ macgirona.cat

From the cathedral square, the main street, Pujada Rei Martí, leads downhill to the Riu Galligants, a small tributary of the Onyar. The **Museu Arqueològic** stands on the far bank in the former monastic church of Sant Pere de Galligants, a harmonious setting for displays of Roman statuary, sarcophagi and mosaics. The beautiful Romanesque cloisters contain heavier medieval relics, such as inscribed tablets and stones, including some bearing Jewish inscriptions.

Passeig Arqueològic

Daily 8am–10pm • Free

Near the archeological museum, steps up through landscaped grounds lead onto the walls of the old city. You can walk right around their perimeter on the **Passeig Arqueològic**, or archeological route, and enjoy views out over the rooftops and the cathedral. There are endless little diversions along the way, into old watchtowers, ramparts, down blind dead ends and around crumpled sections of masonry.

The Jewish quarter

Quite apart from its Roman remains and Arab influences, Girona also contains one of the most intact **Jewish quarters** in Western Europe, El Call, on and around C/de la Força. At its height it was home to around three hundred people who formed a sort of independent town within Girona, protected by the king in return for payment. From the eleventh century onwards, however, the Jewish community suffered systematic persecution and, until the expulsion of the Jews from Spain in 1492, the quarter was effectively a ghetto, its residents restricted to its limits and forced to wear distinguishing clothing if they did leave.

Museu d'Història dels Jueus

C/Força 8 • July & Aug Mon–Sat 10am–7pm, Sun & hols 10am–2pm; Sept–June Mon, Sun & hols 10am–2pm, Tues–Sat 10am–6pm • Charge, under-14s free; free entry 1st Sun of month • ⓦ girona.cat/call

For an impression of the cultural and social life of Girona's medieval Jewish community, visit the **Museu d'Història dels Jueus**, sited up the skinniest of stepped streets. It's a huge, labyrinthine complex, much of it so heavily restored that you'd never be able to tell exactly which of its many rooms, staircases, courtyards and buildings

13

held the synagogue, the butcher's shop, the baths and other community buildings and services, but everything is very beautifully displayed and explained.

Museu d'Art de Girona

Pujada de la Catedral 12 • May–Sept Tues–Sat 10am–7pm, Sun 10am–2pm; Oct–April Tues–Sat 10am–6pm, Sun 10am–1pm • Charge • ⓦ museuart.cat

Trace the history of art and architecture in Girona and Catalonia at this outstanding museum, housed in the grand Palau Episcopal. Exhibitions span the centuries, from Gothic to Baroque, culminating in the nineteenth- and twentieth-century art movements of *modernisme* and *noucentisme*, featuring artists such as Rusiñol, Tàpies and Miró.

Museu del Cinema

C/Sèquia 1 • July & Aug Mon–Sat10am–7pm, Sun 10am–2pm; Sept–June Tues–Sat 10am–6pm, Sun & hols 10am–2pm • Charge, under-14s free; free entry 1st Sun of month • ⓦ museudelcinema.cat

The superb **Museu del Cinema**, based on an extraordinary private collection, is less a museum and more of what the curators call "cinema before cinema", with an utterly intriguing array of the gadgets and artefacts that provided popular entertainment before cinema itself came along, from Indonesian shadow puppets to eighteenth- and nineteenth-century devices like phantasmagoria, fantascopes and magic lanterns. It's all rounded up with movie memorabilia including costumes from *Tootsie* and *Hello Dolly*. The museum also showcases an array of excellent temporary exhibitions, often with a focus on Catalan cinema and filmmakers.

Mercat del Lleó

Plaça Calvet i Rubalcaba • Mon–Thurs & Sat 7am–3pm, Fri 5–8pm • Free • ⓦ mercatlleo.cat

Barcelona has the famous Boqueria; Girona's version is the **Mercat del Lleó**, a lively, colourful, aromatic market that unfolds just east of the river. The sixty-plus stalls reflect the natural diversity of Catalunya – apples and pears from fragrant Girona orchards, mushrooms pulled from Pyrennean soil, pungent goat cheeses and vast displays of still-twitching seafood from the Mediterranean. Take a twirl through the market for a whiff of local flavour, and then refuel over a café at the market bars.

ARRIVAL AND INFORMATION
GIRONA

By plane Regular bus services run from Girona airport, 12km south of the city, to Girona, Barcelona or the Costa Brava (see page 23).

By train Renfe trains (ⓦ renfe.com) run at least hourly between Sants and Pg. de Gràcia stations in Barcelona, and Girona, with high-speed services taking around 35min, and slower trains taking between 1hr 15min and 1hr 40min and costing slightly less. All services arrive at the same station in Girona, across the river in the modern part of the city; the 10min walk to the old town is well signposted, and you can also take a taxi.

Bike hire and tours Girona offers a wide array of bike tours, services and hire, including the top-notch *Eat Sleep*

Cycle (C/Garbí 34, ⓦ eatsleepcycle.com), with a welcoming café, bike shop and tours in and around Girona, and beyond.

Oficina de Turisme Rambla de la Llibertat 1 (April–Oct Mon–Fri 9am–8pm, Sat 9am–2pm & 3–7pm, Sun & hols 9am–2pm; Nov–March Mon–Fri 9am–7pm, Sat 9am–2pm & 3–7pm, Sun & hols 9am–2pm; ⓦ girona.cat/turisme). The *Punt de Benviguda Girona–Gironès* welcome centre (Berenger Carnicer 3, April–Oct Mon–Fri 9–7pm, Sat 9am–5pm, Sun & hols 9am–2pm; Nov–March Mon–Fri 9am–3pm, Sat, Sun & hols 9am–2pm; ☏ 972011 669, ⓦ girona.cat/turisme) is also a good source for information on the city and region, and they offer guided tours, led by the Association of Girona Guides, of the Old Quarter.

EATING
SEE MAP PAGE 164

Girona is a festive city, with myriad spots to enjoy cocktails and cuisine. Cafés and restaurants abound along Rambla

de la Llibertat and the parallel Pl. del Vi, and there's also a group of bars with lovely terraces at the opposite end of the old town, under Sant Feliu church. Another dozen or so restaurants, all with alfresco terraces, stand just over the river in pretty Pl. Independencia. Plus, Girona is home to this restaurant that's on many culinary bucket lists: *El Celler de Can Roca*. Make reservations far in advance, and prepare to indulge – it's worth it.

★ **El Celler de Can Roca** Can Sunyer 48, off Yaialà road 2.5km northwest of the centre ⓦcellercanroca. com. Eat your way across Catalunya at the spectacular, Michelin-starred *El Celler de Can Roca*, which was hailed as the world's best restaurant by *Restaurant* magazine in 2013 and 2015. Founded by the three Roca brothers – head chef Joan, sommelier Josep and dessert master Jordi – the restaurant showcases dishes that celebrate the remarkably fertile region of Girona. Among the 15-plus courses might be a tiny olive tree hung with melting balls of olive-oil ice cream; and langoustine enveloped in a cocoa bean sauce is served in a bowl the shape of a cocoa bean. Reservations are of course essential – your best bet is to book online. €€€€

Divinum C/Albareda 7 ⓦdivinum.cat. Sleek restaurant serving top-notch modern Catalan cuisine, with individual dishes like foie gras with duck sauce and coriander, veal

sweetbreads with mushrooms, or steak tartare. Go for the tasting menu, which best reveals the chef's prowess. €€€

König Sandwiches C/Calderes 16 ⓦkonig.cat. With its pretty *terrassa* under the high walls of Sant Feliu church, this all-day café-bar makes a pleasant stop for a drink. Food is along the lines of salads, tapas, sandwiches and burgers. €

★ **Massana** Bonastruc de Porta 10 ⓦrestaurant massana.com. Embark on a sensory journey through the inventive menu of this graceful family restaurant. Locally sourced, seasonal dishes with Asian hints might include squid and seaweed tartare, hake with a coconut emulsion, or the restaurant speciality, juicy duck magret. €€€

Rocambolesc C/Clara 50 ⓦrocambolesc.com. It doesn't get much better than spooning up ice cream inside a gelateria that looks like a tiny candy factory. This adorable gelateria is run by Jordi Roca, the youngest brother and dessert chef at *El Celler de Can Roca*, along with his wife. Flavours include caramelized apple and cotton candy, and a tangy sorbet of lime, lemon and mint. Next door is *Rocambolesc Confiteria*, with chocolates, candy and other sweet treats. €

Figueres and around

Figueres' most famous resident has passed away – but his legacy lives on, and on, in this provincial town (pop: 45,700) in northern Catalunya. **Salvador Dalí**, who was born in Figueres, founded the eponymous Museu Dalí, which is installed in a building as surreal as the exhibits within. Figueres is a popular day-trip from Barcelona, as ultra-fast trains take less than an hour to make the 135km journey northeast of the city. The museum is very much the main event in town, though it's easy to fill in the rest of the day in the handsome centre. Pavement cafés line the tree-shaded *rambla*, while art galleries, clothes stores and gift shops line the pedestrianized streets and squares. On Tuesday, Thursday and Saturday, you'll coincide with the main **fruit, veg and flower market** – Thursday is best, since there's also a huge **clothes**

SURREAL SALVADOR

Salvador Dalí i Domènech (1904–89) was born in Figueres – you can see the exterior of his **birthplace**, which is marked with a plaque, at C/Monturiol 6, as well as that of the Dalí family's next home, at no. 10. He gave his first exhibition in the town's municipal theatre when he was just 14 and, after a stint at the Royal Academy of Art in Madrid (he was expelled), he made his way to Paris, where he established himself at the forefront of the Surrealist movement. A celebrity artist in the US in the 1940s and 1950s, he returned eventually to Europe where, among other projects, he set about reconstructing the now-defunct theatre. This opened as the Museu Dalí in 1974, which Dalí then fashioned into an inspired repository for his works.

By 1980, Dalí was growing increasingly frail. After suffering severe burns in a fire in 1984, he moved into the **Torre Galatea**, the tower adjacent to the museum, and controversy surrounded his final years. Spanish government officials and friends feared that he was manipulated in his senile condition. Allegations that he signed blank canvases has inevitably led to doubts over the authenticity of some of his later works. Dalí died in Figueres on January 23, 1989. His body now lies behind a simple granite slab inside the museum.

13

market. As Figueres is a "tourist town", shops in the historic centre are allowed to open on Sundays and holidays.

The surrounding **Empordà** wine region (ⓦdoemporda.cat) holds as much allure as Figueres itself. This verdant wine country, which unfolds inland from the Costa Brava, has been producing wine since the fifth century when the Phoenicians first settled in the area. While mainly known for its naturally sweet Garnatxa, the region is undergoing a renaissance, with new, creative small-batch winemakers developing a wide variety of blends. Over fifty wineries fill the region, which is flanked by the Pyrenees on one side and the Mediterranean on the other, extending from Figueres north to the French border, and south through Baix Empordà. Rich soils and a balmy Mediterranean climate ensure a flourishing harvest, but there's also something else that's special to the region: the strong Tramuntana winds, which help protect the vines from disease and frost. The region runs a variety of DO (Denominació d'Origen) **Empordà Wine Routes** (ⓦdoemporda.cat), which feature a range of recommended wineries, hotels and restaurants.

Museu Dalí

Pl. Gala i Salvador Dalí • Jan–June & Oct–Dec Tues–Sat 10.30am–5.15pm; Sept Tues–Sat 9.30am–5.15pm; July–Aug daily 9am–7.15pm; last admission always 45min before closing • Charge • ⓦ salvador-dali.org

The **Museu Dalí** appeals to everyone's innate love of fantasy, absurdity and participation. While it's not a collection of Dalí's greatest hits – those are scattered far and wide – what you do get beggars description, and should not be missed.

The building (a former theatre) is an exhibit in itself, topped by a huge metallic dome and decorated with a line of luminous egg shapes. **Outlandish sculptures** and statues adorn the square and facade, and things get even crazier inside, where the walls of the circular courtyard are ringed by stylized mannequins preparing to dive from the heights. Below sits the famous **Rainy Cadillac**, where you can water the snail-encrusted

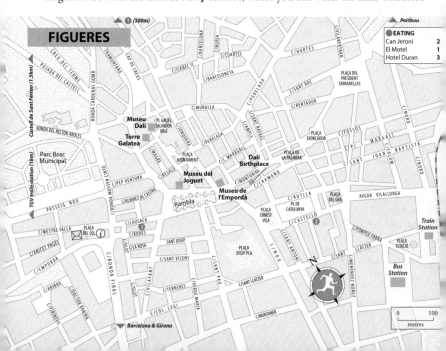

FIGUERES

● EATING
Can Jeroni	2
El Motel	1
Hotel Duran	3

13

occupants of a steamy Cadillac by feeding it with coins. In the **Mae West Room** an unnerving portrait of the actress is revealed by peering through a mirror at giant nostrils, red lips and hanging tresses, while elsewhere you'll find a complete life-sized orchestra, some of Dalí's extraordinary furniture (like the fish-tail bed) and ranks of **Surrealist paintings** – including one room dominated by the ceiling fresco of the huge feet of Dalí and Gala (his Russian wife and muse).

The museum also contains many of Dalí's own collection of works by other artists, from Catalan contemporaries to El Greco, and there are temporary exhibitions, too, while your ticket also allows admission to see the **Dalí-Joies** – a collection of extraordinary jewels, designed in the 1940s for an American millionaire and displayed here with Dalí's original drawings. In the summer, the museum opens for magical *Dalí by Night* visits (generally daily 10pm–1am), when you can enjoy a glass of cava on the terrace; guided tours in Spanish and English (Mon, Wed, Fri & Sun 10.30pm).

ARRIVAL AND INFORMATION · FIGUERES

By train High-speed trains from Barcelona Sants and Pg. de Gràcia take just 53min to reach the Figueres Vilafant TGV station, 1.5km west of the centre; somewhat less frequent slower trains from the same Barcelona stations take up to 2hr and stop at Figueres' original station, 1km east of the centre. Both routes are operated by Renfe (w renfe.com). All trains call at Girona, which is around 15min from Figueres on the fast route, 30–40min on the slower. The "Museu Dalí" is signposted from both Figueres stations.

Oficina de Turisme Pl. del Sol, in front of the post office building (late June to mid-Sept Mon–Sat 9am–8pm, Sun 10am–3pm; mid-Sept to late June Mon–Sat 10am–2pm & 4–7pm, Sun 10am–2pm; t 972 503 155, w visitfigueres.cat).

EATING · SEE MAP PAGE 168

A gaggle of largely missable tourist **restaurants** is crowded into the narrow streets around the Dalí museum, while more cafés and restaurants overlook the *rambla*. Lunch menus everywhere go for €12–15, with the sunniest seats to be found at the top of the *rambla*. Elsewhere, there's a better selection of hidden-away restaurants that are more geared to locals, where the food tends to be more interesting and authentic.

Can Jeroni C/Castelló 36 w canjeroni.com. Locals flock to this tiled tavern opposite the market, with country-style dishes, seafood and grills (roast chicken, meatballs, sausages, cod with garlic). €

★ **El Motel** Avda. Salvador Dalí i Domènech 170 w hotelemporda.com. When famous Catalan chefs talk about inspiration, one restaurant is regularly mentioned: *El Motel*, which is considered the birthplace of modern Catalan cuisine. Josep Mercader opened *El Motel* in 1961 in Figueres, where he brought together the elegance and creamy richness of French cuisine and the natural bounty of Catalunya. Mercader's son-in-law, chef and hotelier Jaume Subirós, now runs this iconic restaurant, serving quietly profound Catalan dishes like a salad of pomegranate, ceps (porcini mushrooms) and pine nuts; and Empordà lamb with anchovies. €€€

Hotel Duran C/Lausaca 5 w hotelduran.com. A top choice in town, known for its excellent regional cuisine, grilled meats, like beef tenderloin with truffle sauce, and fresh fish landed daily from the nearby coast. €€

THE BARCELONETA SEAFRONT

Accommodation

Finding a hotel vacancy in Barcelona at any time of year can be difficult, so it's always best to book in advance. Prices are high for Spain but still pretty reasonable when compared to other big European cities, while stylish rooms on a moderate budget – in this designer style capital – are fairly easy to come by. There's a wide range of overnight options in the city, from youth hostels and budget pensions to glam five-star-plus resort hotels, housed in medieval mansions and *modernista* masterpieces alike. If you're looking for the home-from-home experience then Barcelona also has lots of self-contained apartments for rent, not to mention an increasing number of private "bed-and-breakfast" establishments – some simply the traditional room in someone's house, others very stylish and pricey boutique bolt holes.

Places to stay go under various names – pensión, residència, hostal, hotel – though only **hotels and pensions** are recognized as official categories. These are all star-rated (hotels, one- to five-star; pensions, one- or two-star), but the rating is not necessarily a guide to cost or ambience. Some of the smaller, boutique-style pensions and hotels have services and facilities that belie their star rating; some four- and five-star hotels have disappointingly small rooms and an impersonal feel.

Apartment rentals are an increasingly popular option (see box, page 173). As for **youth hostels**, some traditional backpacker dives survive here and there, but they have largely been superseded by well-equipped, well-run modern hostels with en-suite dorm rooms as well as private rooms. For a more intimate experience there are plenty of **budget pensions** that also have dorms and shared accommodation. A youth hostel, incidentally, is an albergue; hostal is the word for a pensión.

14

ESSENTIALS

ROOM RATES

Prices Rates given in our reviews reflect the usual cost of a double or twin room in high season (basically Easter–Oct, plus Christmas/New Year, major trade fairs, festivals and other events). The cheapest rooms in a simple hotel, sharing a bathroom, cost around €60 (singles from €40), though for private facilities €80–90 a night is more realistic. Places with a bit of boutique styling start at around €120, while for Barcelona's most fashionable hotels, count on €250–400 a night. Studio apartments sleeping two start at around €120, while a hostel dorm bed costs up to €35 a night (but drops to as low as €15 in low season).

Tax A ten-percent tax, IVA, is added to all accommodation bills, though it's sometimes included in the quoted price. An additional "tourist tax" for stays of up to seven nights is also charged on top of your bill – €2.75 to €6.25 (determined by the type of property) per person per night. Under-17s are exempt, though, and most tourist establishments in Barcelona fall into the lowest tax band.

Discounts Book directly online through hotel websites for the best available rates. Some places offer discounts in the off-season months of January, February and November, while others have special rates in August (when business travel is scarce).

Breakfast Breakfast is rarely included; if it is, we mention it in the listings. While many hotels put on a lavish buffet spread, breakfast can be expensive (around €14–20 per person), so if all you want is coffee and a croissant it's better to go out to a café.

RESERVATIONS

Hotels You can reserve hotel accommodation online with the city tourist board (ⓦ barcelonaturisme.com) or make same-day bookings in person only at their tourist offices at Pl. de Catalunya, the airport, Sants train station and elsewhere.

Credit cards Although you may be asked for a credit card number to secure a room, at most hotels your card won't

WHERE TO STAY

If you hanker after a **Rambla** view, you'll pay for the privilege – generally speaking, there are much better deals to be had either side of the famous boulevard, often just a minute's walk away. Alongside some classy boutique choices, most of Barcelona's cheapest accommodation is found in the old town, principally the **Barri Gòtic** and **El Raval** neighbourhoods, which can both still have their rough edges – be careful (without being paranoid) when coming and going after dark. East of the Barri Gòtic, in **Sant Pere** and **La Ribera**, there are a number of safely sited budget, mid-range and boutique options, handy for the Picasso museum and the Born nightlife area. North of Plaça de Catalunya, the **Eixample** – split into Right (**Dreta**) and Left (**Esquerra**) – has some of the city's most fashionable hotels, often housed in converted palaces and mansions and located just a few minutes' walk from the *modernista* architectural masterpieces. Hotels in Sants are convenient for trains, **Montjuïc** and the metro system, and those further north in **Les Corts** for the uptown Avinguda Diagonal shopping district. For waterfront views look at Passeig de Colom and **Port Vell** at the end of La Rambla – while new four- and five-stars abound much further out on the metro/tram at the **Diagonal Mar** conference and events site. If you prefer neighbourhood living, then the northern district of **Gràcia** is the best base, as you're only ever a short walk away from its excellent bars and restaurants.

14

be charged until your stay. However, some smaller *pensions* may take a deposit or charge you in advance. Credit cards are accepted almost everywhere (though American Express isn't always).

While you get cheap or free internet and wi-fi in most hotels and hostels, a few of the swankier hotels still tend to charge a fee for faster internet access.

LA RAMBLA   SEE MAP PAGE 42

★ **Hostal Benidorm** La Rambla 37 ⓦ hostalbenidorm. com; ⓜ Drassanes. Refurbished *pensió* opposite Plaça Reial that offers real value for money, hence the tribes of young tourists. Plain rooms are available for one to four people, all with satellite TV and a/c, bathtubs or showers (some rooms have shared facilities), and a balcony and Rambla view if you're lucky. €€

Hostal Mare Nostrum La Rambla 67, entrance on C/ Sant Pau 2 ⓦ hostalmarenostrum.com; ⓜ Liceu. A cheery Rambla *pensió* whose English-speaking management offers comfortable double, triple and family rooms with satellite TV and a/c. The rooms – all are en suite – are modern and double-glazed against the noise, and some come with balconies and street views. €€€

Hotel Exe Ramblas Boquería La Rambla 91–93 ⓦ exe ramblasboqueria.com; ⓜ Liceu. Snappy little boutique rooms in a small three-star hotel right outside the Boquería market. There's not much space, but all you need is on the doorstep, and the soundproofing is good so you get a street view without the racket. €€€

★ **Hotel H1898** La Rambla 109, entrance on C/Pintor Fortuny ⓦ hotel1898.com; ⓜ Catalunya. The former headquarters of the Philippines Tobacco Company has four grades of room (the standard is "Classic") in deep red, green or black, plus sumptuous suites, some with their own private pool, jacuzzi and garden. Public areas are similarly dramatic, such as the neocolonial hall, lounge and bar,

and the tropics-kissed terrace restaurant *La Isabela*, while other facilities include both outdoor and indoor pools, and a glam spa. €€€€

Hotel Oriente Atiram La Rambla 45 ⓦ atiramhotels. com; ⓜ Liceu. For somewhere on La Rambla that's traditional but not too pricey, this historic three-star is your best bet. Converted from a former convent, its grand public rooms and tastefully updated bedrooms display nineteenth-century style; some of the latter have Rambla views (though the quieter ones face inwards). €€€

Hotel Rivoli Ramblas La Rambla 128 ⓦ hotelserhsrivoli rambla.com; ⓜ Catalunya. The elegant rooms in this stylish four-star hotel near the top of the avenue are imaginatively furnished (Art Deco to avant-garde), and all come with spacious bathrooms, while the front ones have floor-to-ceiling windows with classic Rambla views. There's also a lovely rooftop terrace and bar open during the summer months. €€€

Le Méridien Barcelona Rambla 111 ⓦ lemeridien barcelona.com; ⓜ Catalunya. The five-star *Méridien*, one of the high-end Rambla stalwarts, offers "deluxe" as the norm; bedrooms feature designer leather furniture and marble bathrooms, and amenities include a spa, gym and business centre. You pay a lot more for a Rambla view or any kind of extra space (another €300, for example, gets you a "Grand Terrace" suite with outdoor rain shower), though things are surprisingly democratically priced in the flash *CentOnze* restaurant, which opens right on to La Rambla. €€€€

BARRI GÒTIC   SEE MAP PAGE 48

Hostal Fernando C/Ferran 31 ⓦ hfernando.com; ⓜ Liceu. Rooms at these prices fill quickly around here; that they're also light, modern and well kept by friendly people is a real bonus. All come with a/c and private bathrooms, while straightforward dorm accommodation is available in en-suite rooms that sleep four to six. €€

★ **Hostal Rembrandt** C/Portaferrissa 23 ⓦ hostal rembrandt.com; ⓜ Liceu. A clean, safe, old-town budget pensió that has been smartened up over the years by friendly English-speaking owners, who request "pin-drop silence" after 11pm. Simple tile-floored rooms (a bit cheaper without private bathroom) have a street-side balcony or little patio, while larger rooms are more versatile and can sleep up to four. €€

Hotel Arai C/Avinyó 30 ⓦ hotelarai.com; ⓜ Liceu. Gothic quarter charm meets modern luxury in this renovated eighteenth-century palace turned aparthotel. Original details are preserved and fine art from a private collection lines the walls. The 31 small apartments reveal

ancient bricks and stonework and there is even, perhaps uniquely, a hotel museum. €€€€

Hotel Barcelona Catedral C/Capellans 4 ⓦ barcelona catedral.com; ⓜ Jaume I. Exceptionally friendly modern hotel in an unbeatable location, just a few metres north of the main cathedral square, offering comfortable and stylish contemporary rooms, plus a gym, restaurant, bar and rooftop pool. €€€€

Hotel Cantón C/Nou de Sant Francesc 40 ⓦ hotelcanton barcelona.com; ⓜ Drassanes. A modest one-star hotel that's only two blocks off La Rambla and close to the harbour and Port Vell. The 47 rooms feature uniform blue-and-white trim curtains and bedspreads, central heating and a/c, fridge and wardrobe. A few rooms have balconies (though they don't have much of a view) – all are well insulated against street noise. Breakfast is served in a stone-walled dining room, and room prices drop a good bit out of season. €€

★ **Hotel DO** Pl. Reial 1 ⓦ sonder.com; ⓜ Liceu.

APARTMENT RENTALS

Available by the night or week, prices for apartment rentals can compare well with mid-range hotels, but make sure you're happy with the location (some are out in the suburbs) and understand all the costs – cleaning charges and taxes can push up the attractive quoted figure. Try **Sh Barcelona** (⊛ shbarcelona.com) or **Inside-BCN** (⊛ insidebarcelona.com).

With the advent of online community marketplaces such as **Airbnb** (⊛ airbnb.com) and **9flats** (⊛ 9flats.com), designed to connect travellers with locals who have spaces to rent, a pool of competitively priced – and sometimes unique – lodging has entered the where-to-stay game. Take your pick: from a sailboat in Port Olímpic to a private penthouse overlooking Park Güell. But be aware: the legal status of private-let online services is under constant threat, and Airbnb, as well as various flat owners, are frequently fined huge amounts for licence infractions.

14

Renowned Catalan architect Oriol Bohigas led the renovation of this nineteenth-century Neoclassical building on the city's emblematic Pl. Reial. The result is a gastronomic boutique hotel with eighteen impeccably appointed rooms, most overlooking the square, which seamlessly blends the contemporary with the timeless. On top of this, quite literally, is the rooftop lounge and blue-tiled plunge pool, plus spa with sauna, steam bath and heated bench. Out of season it can be a bargain. **€€€€**

Hotel El Jardí Pl. Sant Josep Oriol 1 ⊛ eljardi-barcelona.com; ⓜ Liceu. The hotel's location, overlooking the charming Pl. del Pi, is what sells this place – and explains the steep-ish prices for quarters that can seem a bit bare and poky. But some rooms (the top ones have terraces or balconies, from €10 extra) look directly onto the square, and there's a range of cheaper internal rooms too. A modest breakfast is included in the price. **€€**

★ **Hotel Neri** C/Sant Sever 5 ⊛ hotelneri.com; ⓜ Liceu/Jaume I. Close to the cathedral, a delightful eighteenth-century palace houses this stunning boutique hotel of just 22 rooms and suites, featuring swags of flowing material, rescued timber, granite-toned bathrooms and lofty proportions. Designers have created eye-catching effects, like a tapestry that falls four floors through the central atrium, while a beamed library and stylish roof terrace provide a tranquil escape. Guests can take their breakfast (€33), which is served as a buffet, either out in the courtyard in summer or in the fine contemporary Mediterranean restaurant. **€€€€**

Hotel Racó del Pi C/Pi 7 ⊛ h10hotels.com; ⓜ Liceu. A stylish little three-star hotel in a great location. Appealing rooms – some with balconies over the street – have wood floors and granite-and-mosaic bathrooms. There's a glass of cava on check-in, and free coffee and snacks during the day in the bar. **€€€**

Itaca Hostel C/Ripoll 21 ⊛ itacahostel.com; ⓜ Jaume I. Bright and breezy converted house close to the cathedral, offering spacious hostel rooms (sleeping six, eight or ten) with balconies. Dorms are mixed, though you can also reserve a private room, and with a hostel capacity of only thirty it rarely feels overcrowded. Free daily walking tours are offered, and there's a kitchen and book-exchange service. Coffee and breakfast available and decent discounts in the low season. **€**

Mercer Hotel C/Lledó 7 ⊛ mercerbarcelona.com; ⓜ Jaume I. When it comes to Old World charm, the beautiful *Mercer* is about as old as it gets. Though the luxurious hotel itself is just a few years old, parts of the building are ancient (the Roman wall that surrounded the ancient city of Barcino makes up the rear facade). Architect Rafael Moneo highlighted a huge mix of architectural styles when restoring the building: medieval arches, wooden coffered ceilings and ornate Gothic columns found in the rooms and public areas marry with contemporary designer furnishings. Rooms are elegant, spacious and silent. Two restaurants, a rooftop bar and pool, a vertical garden of aromatics such as lavender and rosemary and a lovely interior patio offer options for relaxation. **€€€€**

Pensió Alamar C/Comtessa de Sobradiel 1 ⊛ pensio alamar.com; ⓜ Liceu/Jaume I. If you don't mind sharing a bathroom then this simply furnished *pensió* makes a convenient base. There are twelve rooms (singles and

ACCOMMODATION PRICE CODES

Throughout this guide we have given a price code to each accommodation review. The codes are based on the cost of a standard double room for one night in peak season. Outside these times rates can drop considerably, sometimes as much as 50 percent, so check establishments' websites and booking sites for the best current rates. Prices do not include breakfast.

€	under €65
€€	€65–100
€€€	€100–150
€€€€	over €150

14

BALCONIES, VIEWS AND NOISE

Almost all hotels and *pensions* in Barcelona have at least some rooms with a **balcony** over the street or square. These tend to be the brightest rooms in the building and, because of the obvious inherent attraction, they usually cost more than the other rooms. However, it can't be stressed enough that rooms facing on to Barcelona's streets are often noisy. Traffic is a constant presence (including the dawn street-cleaners) and, in a city where people are just getting ready to go out at 10pm, you can be assured of a fair amount of pedestrian noise too, particularly in the old town, and especially at weekends. Soundproofed windows and double-glazing deal partly with the problem, but you tend not to have this luxury in cheaper *pensions* – where throwing open the windows may be the only way to get some air in the height of summer anyway. Bring earplugs if you're at all concerned about having a sleepless night.

Alternatively, ask for an **internal room** (*habitació interior*). It's true that most buildings are built around a central air or lift shaft, and your view could simply be a lime-green wall 1m away and someone's washing line. However, some places are built instead around an internal patio, so your room might overlook a pot-plant terrace or garden – and you shouldn't get any street noise.

doubles), most with little balconies, and while space is tight, there's a friendly welcome, laundry service and use of a kitchen. Requests no noise after midnight, so it suits early birds and sightseers rather than partygoers, but street noise can be a bit of an issue. No credit cards. €

★ **Serras Hotel** Passeig de Colom 9 Ⓦ serrashotel.

com; Ⓜ **Barceloneta**. A breezy, elegant hotel that manages to be smart but relaxed. Rooms feature vast beds and lots of crushed velvet – book a room at the front for a view across the port. The rooftop restaurant is great for a Mediterranean lunch, and you can slide into the small pool afterwards. €€€€

EL RAVAL

SEE MAP PAGE 62

★ **Barceló Raval** Rambla del Raval 17–21 Ⓦ barcelo. com; Ⓜ **Liceu/Sant Antoni**. This glow-in-the-dark tower is the landmark of the neighbourhood; its USP is the 360-degree top-floor terrace with plunge pool and sensational city views. Sophisticated, open-plan rooms have a crisp, space-station-style sheen, plus iPhone docks, espresso machines and other cool comforts, while the slinky lobby *B-Lounge* is the place for everything from tapas to cocktails. €€€

Casa Camper C/Elisabets 11 Ⓦ casacamper.com; Ⓜ **Universitat/Liceu**. Synonymous with creative, comfy shoes, Barcelona-based Camper took a bold step into the hospitality business with this striking hotel. Each of the forty rooms is divided by a corridor: the "sleeping" side (a red-coloured bedroom with bathroom) faces a six-storey-tall vertical garden; the other part is a "mini-lounge" with a flat-screen TV, hammock and street-facing balcony. Breakfast is included, as are the drinks and savoury and sweet treats (salads, sandwiches, cakes) available around the clock in the lobby, and adjacent to the hotel is the Michelin-starred

TOP 5 OLD-WORLD CHARM

Hotel Arai See page 172
Cotton House Hotel See page 177
Mercer Hotel See page 173
Hotel Neri See page 173
Hotel Peninsular See page 175

Dos Palillos (see page 185). To burn off all this good food, there's also a 24hr gym, free for all guests. €€€€

Hostal Cèntric C/Casanova 13 Ⓦ hostalcentric.com; Ⓜ **Universitat**. A good upper-budget choice, a couple of minutes' walk from the Raval. The bright, modern rooms are decorated in a soothing, neutral palette, have private bathrooms, a/c, safes and flat-screen TVs, and some come with a balcony. There's a sunny terrace at the rear. €€€

★ **Hostal Grau** C/Ramelleres 27 Ⓦ hostalgrau.com; Ⓜ **Catalunya**. A really friendly and very attractive pensió that's been updated and adapted over the years. Private bathrooms in the rooms and eco-friendly touches such as handmade, all-natural mattresses. You'll pay €40 more for superior rooms which are very spacious, while two small private apartments in the same building (sleeping two to four, available by the night) offer a bit more independence. Complimentary coffee and home-made cakes are available for breakfast (get there early as they sometimes run out), and there's a café next door. Doubles €€, apartments €€€€

Hotel Curious C/Carme 25 Ⓦ hotelcurious.com; Ⓜ **Liceu**. Stylish budget digs that offer coordinated, elemental room colours and a huge Barcelona photo backdrop behind each bed. Aside from the helpful staff, services are on the light side, but you're only a few steps from La Rambla or from the Raval's restaurants and nightlife. €€€

★ **Hotel España** C/Sant Pau 9–11 Ⓦ hotelespanya. com; Ⓜ **Liceu**. The revamp of the classic *Hotel España* (see box, page 64) as a four-star-plus has been a remarkable success. The sumptuously restored *modernista* icon with its gem-like interior – colourful tiles, bright mosaics, sculpted marble, iron swirls and marine motifs – has no equal in the city. While public areas reboot the *modernista* era, guest rooms are a perfectly judged boutique blend of earth tones and designer style, with rainshowers, iPhone ports and the like. There's a plunge pool and chill-out deck on the roof terrace, while the handsome house restaurant – known as *Fonda España* – offers contemporary Catalan bistro dishes by top chef Martín Berasategui (see page 185). €€€€

Hotel Onix Liceo C/Nou de la Rambla 36 ⓦonixhotels.com/es/onixliceo; ⓜLiceu/Drassanes. Steps from Palau Güell, this four-star hotel features minimalist decor that melds nicely with the building's older architectural elements, such as the grand marble staircase that curves up from the lobby to the second floor. There's a tropical patio and big-for-Barcelona pool on the ground floor and an airy Mozarab-influenced lounge area, plus free refreshments are available throughout the day. €€

Hotel Peninsular C/Sant Pau 34 ⓦhotelpeninsular barcelona.net; ⓜLiceu. This interesting old building originally belonged to a priestly order, which explains the slightly cell-like quality of the rooms. However, there's nothing spartan about the galleried inner courtyard (around which the rooms are ranged), hung with dozens of tumbling houseplants, while breakfast (€7) is served in the

TOP 5 BOUTIQUE HOTELS
Hotel DO See page 172
Hotel España See page 174
Grand Hotel Central See page 175
Hotel H1898 See page 172
Hotel Neri See page 173

arcaded dining room. €€

Hotel Sant Agustí Pl. Sant Agustí 3 ⓦhotelsa.com; ⓜLiceu. Barcelona's oldest hotel occupies a former seventeenth-century convent building, with balconies overlooking a restored square and church. It's of three-star standard, with the best rooms located in the attic, from where there are rooftop views. €€€

★ **Market Hotel** C/Comte Borrell 68, at Ptge. Sant Antoni Abat ⓦhotelmarketbarcelona.com; ⓜSant Antoni. The designer-budget *Market* makes a definite splash with its part-Japanese, part-neocolonial look – think jet-black rooms with hardwood floors and shutters, and boxy wardrobes topped with travel trunks. It's a feel that flows through the building and down into the impressive restaurant, where the food is good value, while the hotel's vintage Asian-style *Bar Rosso* has become a bit of a local hipsters' haunt. €€€

SANT PERE AND LA RIBERA

SEE MAP PAGE 72

★ **Chic & Basic Born** C/Princesa 50 ⓦchicandbasic.com; ⓜJaume I. From the enormous chandelier in the entrance to the open-plan, all-in-white decor, everything here is punchily boutique and in-your-face. The 31 rooms mix glamour and comfort with laugh-aloud conceits like adjustable mood-lighting, sashaying plastic curtains and mirrored walls; larger rooms cost €25 more. Chic, certainly; basic, not at all, though the concept eschews room service, minibars and hordes of staff at your beck and call. There are other *Chic & Basic* outlets in the Raval, one on C/Tallers (near Pl. Universitat), one near the zoo and the other off the bottom of La Rambla (details on the website). €€€

★ **Grand Hotel Central** Via Laietana 30 ⓦgrandhotel central.com; ⓜJaume I. It might be on one of the city's noisiest thoroughfares, but the soundproofing does its job handsomely in this wham-glam designer hotel beloved of all the style mags. Spacious, ever-so-lovely rooms hit all the right buttons – hardwood floors, Egyptian cotton sheets, high-end toiletries – and up on the roof there are amazing views from the sundeck and infinity pool. Tapas and Catalan cuisine are on the menu in the hotel's plush *Bistro Helena*. €€€€

★ **Hostal Nuevo Colón** Avda. del Marquès de l'Argentera 19, 1° ⓦhostalnuevocolon.es; ⓜBarceloneta. In the hands of the same friendly family for decades, this well-kept *pensió* sports 24 simple double and triple rooms, painted yellow and kitted out with directors' chairs and double-

glazing. Sunny front rooms, lounge and terrace all have side views to Ciutadella park. You'll save around €15 in a room with shared facilities. €€

Hotel Ciutat Barcelona C/Princesa 33–35 ⓦciutat barcelona.com; ⓜJaume I. Contemporary comfort at three-star prices in a hotel that's well sited for old-town sightseeing and the Picasso museum. The simply decorated rooms have splashes of colour and are soundproofed against street noise, though a bit tight on space. Unusually for this price range, there's a cute rooftop bar and small pool for lounging about. €€€

K+K Hotel Picasso Pg. de Picasso 26 ⓦkkhotels.com; ⓜJaume I/Barceloneta. A sophisticated four-star hotel offering bright, contemporary rooms with spacious granite bathrooms, a/c, soundproofing and tea- and coffee-making facilities. On the roof, there's a swimming pool and terrace overlooking the verdant Parc de la Ciutadella. A bar and

TOP 5 STYLE ON A BUDGET
Casa Gracia See page 179
Chic & Basic Born See page 175
Hostal Goya See page 177
Market Hotel See page 175
Room-Mate Anna See page 178

14

bistro serves cocktails and tapas, which you can enjoy out on the interior patio. Secure underground parking available. Temporarily closed for renovations. €€€€

Park Hotel Avda. del Marquès de l'Argentera 11 ⓦ park hotelbarcelona.com; ⓜ Barceloneta. The classy update for this elegant, modernist 1950s building starts with the

chic bar and lounge, and runs up the feature period stairway to rooms in fawn and chocolate-brown with parquet floors, marble bathrooms and beds with angular reading lights. It's a bit on the pricey side for a three-star, but there's real retro style here. The tapas restaurant, *Ten's* is overseen by stellar chef Jordi Cruz. €€€

PORT VELL AND BARCELONETA

SEE MAP PAGE 82

H10 Port Vell Pas de Sota Muralla 9 ⓦ h10hotels.com; ⓜ Barceloneta. An elegant hotel set in a restored historic building. On the rooftop there is a lovely terrace with a bar, a swimming pool and a gorgeous view of the port. Light dishes are also available but otherwise it is close to many popular restaurants. €€€

Hotel Duquesa de Cardona Pg. de Colom 12 ⓦ hduquesadecardona.com; ⓜ Drassanes. Step off the busy harbourfront highway into this soothing four-star haven, set in a remodelled sixteenth-century mansion. The rooms are calm and quiet, decorated in earth tones and immaculately appointed. Although not all of them have harbour views, everyone has access to the stylish roof-deck overlooking the harbour. It's great for sundowner drinks and has a diminutive pool. €€€

Sea Hostel Pl. del Mar 1–4 ⓦ seahostelbarcelona.com; ⓜ Barceloneta. The budget beachside choice: neat little modern bunk rooms sleep six or seven, with an en-suite shower-bathroom in each one. The attached café, where you have breakfast, looks right out onto the boardwalk and palm trees. In low season prices fall steeply. Open 24hr. €€

Soho House Barcelona Pl. del Duc de Medinaceli 4

ⓦ sohohousebarcelona.com; ⓜ Drassanes. This offshoot of the swish London members' club also doubles as a hotel. Guests get access to the in-house cinema, gym, rooftop pool and of course the club itself, where Barcelona's creative types meet up to work and play. Like the members, *Soho House*'s interior design works hard to look cool. The attached Cecconi's restaurant is a pleasantly understated affair that serves authentic Italian cuisine to guests and public alike. €€€€

★ **W Barcelona** Pl. de la Rosa dels Vents 1 ⓦ w-barcelona.com; ⓜ Barceloneta. This signature (if controversial) building on the Barceloneta seafront is one of the city's most iconic structures. No one calls it the "W", though – to locals it is the "Vela" (sail) because of its shape. Open-plan designer rooms have fantastic views through floor-to-ceiling windows, and facilities are first-rate: infinity pool, state-of-the-art spa, and "whatever-you-want" concierge service. There's a hip, resort feel, with direct beach access, and famous guest DJs on the see-and-be-seen rooftop lounge. There are five restaurants and bars within the hotel itself, but you can also chill out with cocktails and high-class burgers on the terrace *of Salt Beach Club*. €€€€

PORT OLÍMPIC

SEE MAP PAGE 86

★ **Hotel Arts Barcelona** C/Marina 19–21, Port Olímpic ⓦ hotelartsbarcelona.com; ⓜ Ciutadella-Vila Olímpica. A city benchmark for five-star designer luxury, service and standards: contemporary rooms feature enormous marble bathrooms and fabulous views, while stunning duplex apartments have their own perks (like 24hr butler service and a personal Mini Cooper). The upper floors belong to *The*

Club – an exclusive hotel-within-a-hotel with a luxurious lounge and concierge service. You're only a hop from the beach, but seafront gardens encompass a swimming pool and hot tub. The jaw-dropping spa occupies the top two floors, while dining options include the two-Michelin-starred *Enoteca* by Paco Pérez (see page 189). €€€€

MONTJUÏC

SEE MAP PAGE 92

Hotel Miramar Barcelona Pl. Carlos Ibañez 3 ⓦ hotel miramarbarcelona.com; ⓜ Paral·lel or Funicular de Montjuïc. The remodelled *Miramar* – first built for the 1929 International Exhibition – has 75 super-stylish rooms wrapped around the kernel of the original building, all with views to knock your socks off. From the architecture books

in the soaring lobby to the terrace or balcony that comes with nearly every room, it's clearly designer heaven; the room gadgets and stunning pool, garden and deck come as no surprise. True, you're not in the city centre, but it's only a 10min taxi ride from most downtown destinations. €€€€

DRETA DE L'EIXAMPLE

SEE MAP PAGE 106

BCN Fashion House C/Bruc 13 ⓦ bcnfashionhouse. com; ⓜ Urquinaona. Italian owners have added a touch of chic flair to what was formerly an *atelier* in Barcelona's "garment district", and the seven spacious, high-ceilinged rooms (some with veranda) are lightened with prints,

sculptures and artefacts from their travels. The rooms share three bathrooms and a plant-strewn internal terrace, though a studio-suite has its own facilities, private terrace area and kitchenette. The buffet breakfast is optional, and off-season deals are good value. €€

Casa Bonay Gran Vía de les Corts Catalanes ⓦ casa bonay.com; ⓜ Girona. Calling the project in this renovated, Neoclassical nineteenth-century building a "hotel" is to sell it short, It's also an event space, bookshop, artisanal coffee bar and artists' hang-out. The *Bodega Bonay* restaurant serves serves superb Italo-Catalan dishes and a range of natural wines. There's a rooftop bar, cocktail lounge, DJs, live music – and even some beautifully tasteful, eco-friendly rooms to stay in. The vibe is very much like plugging into the local community. €€€€

Cotton House Hotel Gran Vía de les Corts Catalanes 670, 5° ⓦ hotelcottonhouse.com; ⓜ Passeig de Gràcia. Located in the nineteenth-century former headquarters of the Fundación Textil Algodonera (Cotton Textile Foundation), this addition to Barcelona's luxury hotel scene is a designer masterpiece of mirrors, marble and mahogany, creating an atmosphere of old-fashioned elegance. Guests can live out their *Downton Abbey* fantasies as they swish down spiral staircases, peruse leather-bound books in the library or take tea on the terrace. Bedlinen is, as you'd expect from the name, as good as it gets, and an artisanal tailoring service is available to create made-to-measure garments. €€€€

Hostal Girona C/Girona 24, 1° ⓦ hostalgirona.com; ⓜ Urquinaona. Delightful, family-run *pensió* with cosy, traditional rooms, plus corridors laid with rugs, polished wooden doors, antique paintings and restored furniture. There's a whole range of good-value rooms, some share a bathroom, others have a shower or full bath, while the biggest and best rooms have balconies, though you can expect some noise. €€

★ **Hostal Goya** C/Pau Claris 74, 1° ⓦ hostal-goya. hotelbcn-barcelona.com; ⓜ Urquinaona. Boutique-style *pensió* that offers nineteen crisply furnished, fabulous rooms on two floors of a mansion building. There's a fair range of options, with the best rooms opening on to a balcony or a terrace. Comfortable sitting areas, and free coffee and tea, are available on both floors, while an apartment (sleeping up to six in three bedrooms) offers more space for groups and families. €€€

Hotel Almanac Barcelona Gran Vía de les Corts Catalanes 619–621 ⓦ almanachotels.com/barcelona; ⓜ Passeig de Gràcia. This five-star hotel is a grey-and-gold temple of luxury built around a soaring, oak-slatted atrium with 61 designer rooms and 30 suites featuring details including Ibizan marble bathrooms and antique mirrors. The usual details you'd expect at this level – spas, bars and rooftop pool – are all present and correct. Unusually, the main hotel restaurant serves mostly vegan food, but there's a rooftop restaurant serving the regular hotel light fusion classics. €€€€

Hotel Claris C/Pau Claris 150 ⓦ hotelclaris.com; ⓜ Passeig de Gràcia. Very select grand luxe five-star hotel, from the incense-scented marble lobby complete with authentic Roman mosaics to the hugely appealing rooms

> **TOP 5 VIEWS**
>
> **Gran Hotel La Florida** See page 179
> **Hotel Casa Fuster** See page 179
> **Hotel Majestic** See page 177
> **Hotel Miramar Barcelona** See page 176
> **Serras Hotel** See page 174

14

ranged around a soaring, water-washed atrium. It even has its own private antiquities museum. If there's a gripe, it's that there's not a lot of room space for your euro, but the staff couldn't be more accommodating and there's a swish rooftop terrace pool. The hotel restaurant, *La Terraza*, has fabulous views to go with the Mediterranean cuisine, while downstairs you can tuck into dim sum and other Asian dishes in the chic tapas bar. €€€€

★ **Hotel Condes de Barcelona** Pg. de Gràcia 73–75 ⓦ condesdebarcelona.com; ⓜ Passeig de Gràcia. Straddling two sides of C/Mallorca, the four-star *Condes* is fashioned from two former palaces; the north side has kept its interior marblework and wrought-iron balconies, but there's little difference between the rooms in either building. All 235 are classily turned out in contemporary style, while some have a balcony or a private terrace with views of Gaudí's La Pedrera. There's also a pretty hotel roof-terrace with a plunge pool, plus Alaire, a hip rooftop cocktail bar. €€€

Hotel Majestic Pg. de Gràcia 68 ⓦ hotelmajestic.es; ⓜ Passeig de Gràcia. This traditional *grand-dame* hotel, first opened in 1918, has been refitted in contemporary style and muted colours to provide a tranquil city-centre base. Big-ticket original art adorns the public areas (it's known for its art collection), and the rooms – larger than many in this price range – have been pleasantly refurbished. The absolute clincher is the rooftop spa, pool and deck, with amazing views over to the Sagrada Família. €€€€

★ **Mandarin Oriental** Pg. de Gràcia 38–40 ⓦ mandarin oriental.com/Barcelona; ⓜ Passeig de Gràcia. The latest designer addition to Barcelona's most prestigious avenue is the super-sleek *Mandarin Oriental*, which fills the premises of a former bank building with a soaring white atrium and a serene selection of gorgeously light but extremely thick-walled rooms made from old vaults. The suites, with their stunning bathrooms and private terraces, are among the finest in Barcelona. There are the obligatory super-star restaurants, including *Moments* (see page 191), and a super-cool bar, *Banker's Bar*, which has live music and some of the best cocktails in town. The spa, mimosa garden and rooftop "dipping pool" combine Oriental tranquillity and Euro cool. €€€€

Praktik Bakery C/Provença 279 ⓦ hotelpraktikbakery. com; ⓜ Diagonal. Minimalist, all-white designer rooms and a great location aren't the reason for the queue that

14

TOP 5 MONEY NO OBJECT

Hotel Arts Barcelona See page 176
Mandarin Oriental See page 177
Mercer Hotel See page 173
Sir Victor See page 178
W Barcelona See page 176

constantly stretches out of the hotel's door and on to the street. That would be the in-hotel bakery run by Baluard, makers of some of Barcelona's best bread. Breakfast doesn't get much better than the buffet of butter croissants, cakes, buns and pastries that await you here each morning. €€€
Room-Mate Anna C/d'Aragó 271 ⓦ room-matehotels. com/en/anna; ⓜ Passeig de Gràcia. The Room-Mate chain has cornered the market in affordable mid-range chic and the Anna is one of the most stylish, with bright colours and fantastical wallpaper. Reception can provide you with a smartphone that you can use around town and for free international calls. Other perks unusual in this price range include a small rooftop plunge pool. €€€
Safestay Passeig de Gràcia Pg. de Gràcia 33 ⓦ safestay.com/es/venue/safestay-barcelona-passeig-de-gracia; ⓜ Passeig de Gràcia. The biggest hostel in the city occupies a refurbished *modernista* building in a swish midtown location. Private twins, doubles, triples and quads available, all with shower room, balcony and views, while dorms (all en suite) sleep up to fourteen. Excellent facilities include a spectacular roof terrace with views of the famous boulevard. €
Sir Victor C/del Rosselló 265 ⓦ sirhotels.com/en/victor; ⓜ Diagonal. The latest incarnation of the much-mourned Hotel Omm is an equally designery affair, with bold colours throughout the generously sized rooms and common areas. There is a quiet spa and well-equipped gym, as well as an excellent restaurant, *Mr Porter*, on the ground floor. The rooftop restaurant is a pleasant enough place during the day, but at night caters to more of a party crowd. €€€€

ESQUERRA DE L'EIXAMPLE

SEE MAP PAGE 116

Allegro Barcelona C/Rosselló 205 ⓦ barcelo.com; ⓜ Diagonal. Formerly the Room-Mate Emma, the Allegro now belongs to the Barcelo chain but has stayed much the same – a *Battlestar Galactica*-style lobby, undeniably appealing barebones-chic rooms and suites at realistic uptown prices (particularly in the low season). It has a fresh, fun vibe and an accommodating air, and is off the main tourist track but close to some lively restaurants. €€€
★ **Alternative Creative Youth Home** Ronda de la Universitat 17 ⓦ alternative-barcelona.com; ⓜ Universitat/Catalunya. The hostel hangout for a self-selecting art crowd, who love the laidback vibe, projection lounge, cool music and city-savvy staff. The regular hostel stuff is well designed too, with a walk-in kitchen, lockers and laundry, and a maximum of 24 people spread across three small dorms. €
Hotel Axel C/Aribau 33 ⓦ axelhotels.com; ⓜ Universitat. Central to the self-image of Gaixample, the *Axel*'s snazzy "heterofriendly" boutique stylings are a real hit with LGBTQ+ visitors. It's a hip but relaxed space with designer rooms (featuring eco-friendly toiletries), suites with private terraces, a bar and restaurant that are part of the local scene, plus a fabulous terrace pool and "Skybar", excellent spa and fitness facilities, and a full range of massage and other treatments available. €€€€
Hotel Midmost C/Pelai 14 ⓦ hotelmidmost.com; ⓜ Universitat. The boutique little four-star sister to the Dreta's *Majestic* has an excellent location, harmoniously toned rooms and snazzy bathrooms. Space is at a premium, but some rooms have cute private terraces, others street-side balconies, while best of all is the romantic roof terrace, where you can take a dip in the pool and sip on a cocktail. €€€€
Nobu Hotel Avda. Roma 2–4 ⓦ barcelona.nobuhotels. com; ⓜ Sants Estació. The landmark five-star deluxe hotel outside Sants station features sweeping views from all sides. Breakfast on the 23rd floor is a buzz; there's also a spa with indoor pool, and two superb Japanese restaurants, as you would expect from masterchef Nobu. €€€€
Praktik Rambla Rambla de Catalunya 27 ⓦ hotel praktikrambla.com; ⓜ Passeig de Gràcia. This boutique hotel in a converted *modernista* mansion makes the most of its glorious inheritance by keeping the design touches toned down and letting the architecture do the talking. Big, high-ceilinged rooms (especially the deluxe doubles) look out onto a tranquil terrace, complete with burbling fountain, where you can enjoy the sunshine in peace just yards from the bustling Rambla de Catalunya. €€€
Soho Hotel Gran Via de les Corts Catalanes 543–545 ⓦ hotelsohobarcelona.com; ⓜ Urgell. A smart, modern and no-nonsense hotel, not quite in the thick of things, but a stone's throw away from public transport. There is a small rooftop pool on a wood-decked terrace with superb views. €€€

TOP 5 DORMS AND HOSTELS

Alternative Creative Youth Home See page 178
Barcelona Urbany See page 179
Itaca Hostel See page 173
Safestay Passeig de Gràcia See page 178
Somnio Barcelona See page 179

Somnio Barcelona C/Diputació 251 ☎ 932 725 308; Ⓜ Passeig de Gràcia. Sisters Lauren and Lee from Chicago bring their passion for Barcelona right into their upscale *pensión*, dropping "tips for the day" into your room each morning. Simple but smart rooms with wood-block floors cater for singles, couples and friends. There are four spacious twin rooms, four double rooms (two en suite) and a single. Some have balconies. €€€

SAGRADA FAMÍLIA AND GLÒRIES   SEE MAP PAGE 120

★ **Barcelona Urbany** Avda. Meridiana 97 Ⓦ urbany hostels.com/barcelona; Ⓜ Clot. This huge steel-and-glass four-hundred-bed hostel might be a bit off the beaten track, but it's handy for the metro (it's an easy ride in to Pl. de Catalunya) and airport train, and has terrific views of the landmark Torre Glòries. The rooms are like space-shuttle pods – boxy en suites with pull-down beds (sleeping two to eight), power-showers and key-card lockers – that are just as viable for couples on a budget as backpackers (there are also private rooms). There's a bar and terrace, all sorts of tours and offers available, plus free health club and pool entry in the same building. €

Hotel Eurostars Monumental C/Consell de Cent 498–500 Ⓦ eurostarsmonumental.com; Ⓜ Monumental. A good four-star choice within walking distance of the Sagrada Família; sharply styled, well-equipped standard rooms are real value for money (particularly in the low season), while the top-floor suites have terraces with loungers and views of the Gaudí basilica and distant hills. €€€

GRÀCIA   SEE MAP PAGE 129

★ **Casa Gracia** Pg. de Gràcia 116 Ⓦ casagraciabcn. com; Ⓜ Diagonal. A vibrant and stylish space spread over six floors in a *modernista* building, with comfy leather chairs and large beanbags in the common areas, a huge kitchen in tile and stainless steel, plus bonuses like a concierge, themed dinners, yoga sessions and evening concerts. The crisply decorated rooms (from dorms to doubles to six-bed private rooms) have a/c and are en suite, while the deluxe suite pampers with a spa bath, slippers and bathrobes. Though *Casa Gracia* is technically a hostel, you'll feel like you're staying in a (pretty good) hotel. €€

Generator Hostel and Hotel C/Corsega 373 Ⓦ generatorhostels.com/hostels/barcelona; Ⓜ Diagonal. Big, bright and abuzz with people having fun, the *Generator* lounge frequently features live music, DJ sets and art performances, as well as a pool table and big-screen TV. The clean, modern rooms range from budget dorms up to a penthouse. There's 24hr reception. €

Hotel Casa Fuster Pg. de Gràcia 132 Ⓦ hotelcasafuster. com; Ⓜ Diagonal. *Modernista* architect Lluís Domènech i Montaner's magnificent *Casa Fuster* (1908) is the backdrop for five-star-deluxe luxury with service to match. Rooms are in natural tones, with huge beds and gorgeous bathrooms, while public areas make full use of the architectural heritage, from the magnificent pillared lobby bar, *Cafè Vienès*, to the wonderful panoramic roof terrace and pool – summer nights see the terrace turned over to chill-out lounge bar *Blue View*. There's also a contemporary restaurant, *Aleia* plus fitness centre and 24hr room service. €€€€

PARK GÜELL   SEE MAP PAGE 130

Barcelona Xanascat Pg. de la Mare de Déu del Coll 41–51 Ⓦ xanascat.cat; Ⓜ Vallcarca (follow Avgda. de la República d'Argentina, C/Viaducte de Vallcarca and then signs) or bus #28 from Pl. de Catalunya, plus night buses, stop just across the street. This popular hostel, owned by the regional government, is set in a converted mansion, with a tiled and stained-glass interior, gardens, terrace and great city views – it's a long way out, but close to Park Güell. Dorms sleep six, eight or twelve, and there are all the usual facilities plus meals are provided at low cost (or there's a local restaurant just around the corner). There's a six-night maximum stay. €

TIBIDABO   SEE MAP PAGE 142

★ **ABaC** Avda. Tibidabo 1 Ⓦ abacbarcelona.com; FGC Avda. del Tibidabo. The chic address for intimate, uptown boutique style, the five-star-plus *ABaC* showcases the Michelin-starred talents of celebrity Spanish *Masterchef* presenter Jordi Cruz in a gorgeous designer, glass-and-wood revamp of an old Tibidabo mansion. There are just fifteen rooms – cream and white decor, swishing drapes, sumptuous bathrooms with whirlpool baths and Hermès cosmetics – and services include a spa and lounge bar. €€€€

Gran Hotel La Florida Carretera Vallviderera a Tibidabo 83–93, 7km from the centre Ⓦ hotellaflorida. com. Describing itself as an "urban resort", the five-star, hillside *Gran Hotel La Florida* re-creates the glory days of the 1950s, when it was at the centre of Barcelona high society. Its terraces and garden areas have amazing views, while some of the seventy rooms and suites have private gardens or terraces and Jacuzzis. Jazz sessions in the club are not to be missed. There's also an achingly lovely spa and pool, two restaurants, and a café with panoramic views of the city below. €€€€

14

QUIMET I QUIMET TAPAS BAR

Eating

If you step no further than La Rambla or the streets of the Barri Gòtic, you are not going to experience the best of the city's cuisine – in the main tourist areas food and service can be indifferent and prices high. For the finest food the city has to offer, it pays to be a bit more adventurous and explore the backstreets of neighbourhoods like Sant Pere, La Ribera, El Raval and Poble Sec, where you'll find excellent restaurants, some little more than hole-in-the-wall taverns, others surprisingly chic. Most, but not all, of the big-ticket, destination-dining restaurants are found in the Eixample. Gràcia, further out, is a nice village-like place to spend the evening, with plenty of good mid-range restaurants, while for fish and seafood you're best off in the harbourside Barceloneta district or at the Port Olímpic.

Barcelona's thousands of **cafés** keep the city fuelled from morning to night, and you're rarely more than a step away from a coffee fix or a quick sandwich. Many are classics of their kind – century-old establishments or unique neighbourhood haunts – while others specialize in certain types of food and drink. A **forn** is a bakery, a **pastisseria** a cake and pastry shop, a **xocolateria** specializes in chocolate, while a **granja** (milk bar) offers traditional delights like orxata (horchata, tiger-nut drink) and granissat (granizado, a flavoured crushed-ice drink).

The **tapas** boom, meanwhile, shows no sign of abating, with increasing numbers of bars and restaurants figuring that small is beautiful when it comes to designing new menus. Little dishes are all the rage, and while there are still plenty of old-style, hanging-ham and counter-display tapas bars in town, there's also a real sense of adventure in new-wave places that are deadly serious about their food. You're as likely to get shrimp tempura, a samosa or a yucca chip as a garlic mushroom these days, while a few standout places offer classy, restaurant-standard experiences that are still truly tapas at heart.

Traditional **Catalan and regional Spanish food** remains at the core of many **restaurant** menus, while the city has the usual range of pizza places, curry houses, fast-food joints and the like. But these are exciting times for foodies in Barcelona, as **contemporary Spanish cooking** continues to be a big deal. The minimalist, food-as-chemistry approach, pioneered by best-chef-in-the-world Ferran Adrià (of El Bulli fame), has spawned a thousand followers, many with restaurants in Barcelona (and a fair few now with Michelin stars). The best are reinterpreting classic Catalan dishes in innovative ways, and while prices in these gastro-temples are high there's a trend towards more economic, bistro-style dining even by the hottest chefs. Meanwhile, the current fad obsessing city restaurateurs is the fusion of Mediterranean and Asian flavours – a so-called **"Mediterrasian" cuisine** – that combines local, market-fresh ingredients with more exotic tastes. Sometimes this works, sometimes this doesn't, but eating out in Barcelona has never been more interesting.

15

ESSENTIALS

COSTS AND RESERVATIONS

Prices Overall, eating out in Barcelona is still pretty good value, and you'll be able to dine in a huge variety of restaurants for around €30-40 a head, and a little less if you jump from tapas bar to tapas bar. In fancier, fashionable places you can double this, while "tasting menus" at the current dining hotspots run from €70–150 a head, excluding drinks (still a lot cheaper than equivalents in, say, New York or London).

Getting a good deal Nearly all restaurants offer a weekday (Mon–Fri) three-course menú del dia (menu of the day) at lunchtime, with the cheapest starting at about €12, rising to €20–25 in fancier places. In many restaurants the price also includes a drink, so this can be a real bargain (at night, you might pay three or four times as much to eat dinner in the same restaurant).

Reservations and payment If there's somewhere you'd particularly like to eat – certainly at the more fashionable end of the market – you should reserve a table. Some places are booked solid for days, or weeks, in advance. Credit and debit cards are almost universally accepted in restaurants, traditional tapas bars and the like. Finally, all restaurant

STARTING THE DAY

Unless you're staying somewhere with a decent buffet spread, you may as well pass up the overpriced coffee-and-croissant option in your hotel and join the locals for **breakfast** in one of the city's bars, cafés or patisseries. A few euros will get you a hot drink and a brioche, croissant or sandwich just about anywhere – ensaïmades (pastry spirals) are a popular choice, while xocolata amb xurros (chocolate con churros – long, fried, tubular doughnuts with thick drinking chocolate) is a good cold-weather starter. The traditional country breakfast is pa amb tomàquet (pan con tomate) – bread rubbed with tomato, olive oil and garlic, perhaps topped with some cured ham or sliced cheese. Otherwise, breakfast sandwiches are whatever can be stuffed inside a flauta (thin baguette), from cured ham to a slice of truita (tortilla).

menus should make it clear whether the ten-percent IVA tax is included in the prices or not (it usually is).

OPENING HOURS AND CLOSING DAYS

Opening hours Most cafés are open from 9am until midnight, or much later – so whether it's coffee first thing or a late-night nibble, you'll find somewhere to cater for you. Restaurants are generally open 1 to 4pm and 8.30 to 11pm, though most locals don't eat lunch until at least 2pm and dinner after 9 or even 10pm. However, in tourist zones like La Rambla and Port Olímpic, restaurants tend to stay open all day and serve on request, while many tapas bars are also open all day from morning until night.

Closing days and holidays Many restaurants close on Sunday evening and Monday, and on public holidays, and lots close over Easter and throughout August – check

websites for specific details but expect changes, since many places imaginatively reinterpret their own posted opening days and times.

MENUS

Dishes and specialities To ask for a menu, request *la carta*, though be warned that some cheaper places might not have a written menu, with the waiter merely reeling off the day's dishes at bewildering speed.

A warning Budget meals sometimes come in the form of a garishly photographed *plat combinat* (*plato combinado*), combined plate) of things like eggs, steak or calamari with fries and salad, but generally speaking, pictures of dishes on a menu is not an indicator of great cuisine – especially so in the case of the pre-prepared paellas advertised on boards outside tourist restaurants.

LA RAMBLA SEE MAP PAGE 42

CAFÉS

Cafè de l'Òpera Rambla 74 ⓦ cafeoperabcn.com; ⓜ Liceu. If you're going to pay through the nose for a Rambla seat, it may as well be at one of the bank of sought-after pavement tables at this famous old café-bar opposite the opera house, which retains its *fin-de-siècle* feel. Surprisingly, it's not a complete tourist-fest, and locals pop in day and night for drinks, cakes and tapas. €€

Cafe Zurich Pl. Catalunya 1 ⓣ 933 179 153; ⓜ Catalunya. The most famous meet-and-greet café in town, right at the top of La Rambla underneath El Triangle shopping centre and much changed since it opened in 1920. It's good for croissants and breakfast sandwiches and there's a huge pavement terrace, but sit inside if you don't want to be bothered by endless rounds of buskers and beggars. €€

Escribà Rambla 83 ⓦ escriba.es; ⓜ Liceu. "We don't just make pastries, we create illusions", claims the renowned Escribà family business. Visit their classy, historic *modernista*-designed pastry shop in the Antiga Casa Figueras near the Boqueria market and find out why many rate this as the best pâtisserie in Barcelona. €

TAPAS BARS AND RESTAURANTS

Bar Central La Boqueria Mercat de la Boqueria,

Rambla 91 ⓣ 933 011 098; ⓜ Liceu. This gleaming, chrome stand-up bar in the market's central aisle is the venue for ultra-fresh market produce, served by snazzy staff who work at a fair lick. Breakfast, snack or lunch, it's all the same to them – salmon cutlets, sardines, calamari, razor clams, hake fillets, sausages, pork steaks, asparagus spears and the rest, plunked on the griddle and sprinkled with salt. Breakfast costs just a few euros or it's not much more than that for some tapas or a main dish and a drink. €

CentOnze La Rambla 111 ⓦ centonzerestaurant.com; ⓜ Liceu. Located in the sleek *Le Méridien*, this restaurant boasts great street-level views of La Rambla, and is a perfect place to escape the hustle and bustle while dining on Boqueria-sourced dishes such as salmon and monkfish carpaccio, strawberry gazpacho and *arròs negre* with fresh clams and aioli. €€

Quim de la Boqueria Mercat de la Boqueria, La Rambla 91 ⓦ elquimdelaboqueria.com; ⓜ Catalunya. The beating heart of the Boqueria market is this superb tapas bar. The house speciality is fried eggs with various gourmet options: baby squid, wild mushrooms, prawns cooked in cava and many more. You'll also find oxtail stew, sausage with beans and various other local dishes. Arrive early for a seat at the bar. €€

BARRI GÒTIC SEE MAP PAGE 48

CAFÉS

Bar del Pi Pl. de Sant Josep Oriol 1 ⓦ bardelpi.com; ⓜ Liceu. Located on one of Barcelona's prettiest squares, *Bar del Pi* is best known for its terrace tables. Linger over drinks and sandwiches and let the old town reveal its charms, especially during the weekend artists' market. €

★ **Caelum** C/Palla 8 ⓦ caelumbarcelona.com; ⓜ Liceu. The lovingly packaged confections in this upscale café-

cum-pâtisserie (the name is Latin for "heaven") are made in convents and monasteries across Spain. Choose from *frutas de almendra* (marzipan sweeties) from Seville, Benedictine preserves or Cistercian cookies – or hunker down for cakes and coffee in the atmospheric basement crypt. €

Dulcinea C/Petritxol 2 ⓦ granjadulcinea.com; ⓜ Liceu. One of the old town's age-old treats is to come here for a thick hot chocolate, slathered in cream. Then if you've still

got room, try one of their pastries or perhaps a dish of *mel i mató* (curd cheese with honey). It's a bygone-era kind of place, with dickie-bow-wearing waiters patrolling the beamed and panelled room bearing silver trays. €
Mesón del Café C/Llibreteria 16 ☎933 150 754; ⓜJaume I. An iconic locals' café, opened in 1909 and still full of atmosphere. great for quick coffees, and perhaps a tapa or two. It's tiny and you'll probably have to stand, though there is a sort of cubbyhole at the back with a few tables. €

TAPAS BARS AND RESTAURANTS

Bar Celta Pulpería C/Mercè 16 ⓦbarcelta.com; ⓜDrassanes. This brightly lit, no-nonsense Galician tapas bar specializes in typical dishes like octopus (*pop gallego*) and fried green *pimientos* (peppers), washed down with heady regional wine. You eat at the U-shaped bar or at tables in the back room, and while it's not one for a long, lazy meal, it's just right to kick off a bout of bar-hopping. €€
Bidasoa C/Serra 21 ☎933 818 063; ⓜDrassanes. Tucked away on a narrow street in La Mercè, this third-generation-owned restaurant offers simple and fresh Catalan and Basque-Navarre fare at a good price. Dishes include tapas, soups, salads and tortillas, as well as hearty mains such as garlic chicken and the house speciality (and sure-fire hangover cure) *cocido Bidasoa*, a medley of sausage, tender beef and chickpeas in a savoury broth – all of which are served by jocular staff in a bright, rustic dining room. €€
★ **Bodega La Plata** C/Mercè 28 ⓦbarlaplata.com; ⓜDrassanes. A classic taste of the old town, with a marble counter open to the street and dirt-cheap wine served straight from the barrel. It attracts an enthusiastic local crowd, from businessmen to pre-clubbers, who come for the simple tomato salad, deep-fried sardines and sausages. €
Can Culleretes C/Quintana 5 ⓦculleretes.com; ⓜLiceu. Barcelona's oldest restaurant (founded in 1786) serves straight-up Catalan food (*botifarra* sausage and beans, salt cod, spinach and pine nuts, wild boar stew) in cosy, traditional surroundings. Local families come in droves, especially for celebrations or for Sun lunch, and there are good-value set meals available at both lunch and dinner. €€
Els Quatre Gats C/Montsió 3 ⓦ4gats.com; ⓜLiceu. An absolute gem on the *modernista* route, Els Quatre Gats is also a nice place for a coffee and croissant, sitting at one of the tables where Picasso hung out with his artist friends back in the day. There is an adjoining restaurant but the food is not quite at the level of its surroundings. €€€
El Salón C/Hostal d'en Sol 6–8 ⓦelsalonrestaurant. com; ⓜJaume I. It's easy to fall for the cosy charms of *El Salón*, with its candlelit tables in a Gothic dining room and summer terrace in the nearby square. The menu changes every few months, with inventive salads giving way to things like a confit of cod with spinach, pine nuts and raisins, or lamb with mustard-and-honey sauce. Most mains

EATING OUT PRICE CODES

The price codes used throughout this guide are as follows, and generally refer to two courses, plus one drink and service, for one person:

€	under €25
€€	€25–45
€€€	€45–75
€€€€	over €75

are in the range. €€
Rasoterra C/Palau 5 ⓦrasoterra.cat; ⓜJaume I. A plant-based diet doesn't have to be boring and this lovely bistro has some ingenious recipes to prove it. The vegan and vegetarian options include glazed white asparagus with miso, figs and walnuts and orecchiette with creamy courgette and pepper sauce. *Rasoterra* supports the Slow Food movement, so if you're looking for a place to chill while enjoying some exciting and new tastes – this is where you need to go. €€
Shunka C/Sagristans 5 ⓦkoyshunka.com; ⓜJaume I. The first in the small but mighty Shunka empire, which now numbers four establishments, including one (Koy Shunka) with a Michelin star. Advance reservations are essential, though you might strike lucky if you're prepared to eat early or late. The open kitchen and the bustling staff are half the show, while the food – sushi to udon noodles, Japanese fried chicken to grilled prawns – is really good. You can eat for around €40, though it's easy to spend more. €€€
La Sosenga C/de n'Amargós 1 ⓦlasosenga.cat; ⓜLiceu. With recipes based on those in the Llibre del Sent Soví, the prototype medieval Catalan cookbook, La Sosenga is a welcoming change from the tourist-oriented restaurants that have taken over much of the Barri Gòtic. There's a good fixed-price lunch for €19.50. €€€
Taller de Tapas Pl. de Sant Josep Oriol 9 ⓦtallerde tapas.com; ⓜLiceu. The fashionable "tapas workshop" sucks in tourists with its year-round outdoor terrace and pretty location by the church of Santa María del Pi. The open kitchen turns out reliable market-fresh tapas, with fish a speciality at dinner, from grilled langoustine to seared tuna. There are several other branches around town, though this was the first and has the nicest location. €€

15

TOP 5 CLASSY CAFÉS

Bar del Convent See page 186
Caelum See page 182
Café de les Delícies See page 184
Cafè de l'Òpera See page 182
Dulcinea See page 182

15

NO SUCH THING AS A FREE LUNCH...

… except, once upon a time, in southern Spain. **Tapas** (from *tapar*, to cover) originated as free snacks given away as covers for drinks' glasses, perhaps to keep the flies off in the baking sun. It's still a much more southern, Andalucian thing, though the Basques, Gallegos and other northerners, all with their own tapas traditions, might disagree. In some parts of Spain, tapas still comes for free with drinks – a dish of olives, a bite of omelette, some fried peppers. But in Barcelona you can expect to pay for every mouthful…unless you count the restaurants which kick off proceedings with an *amuse-gueule* shot glass of soup or designer canapé – free to anyone just about to pay €100 for dinner. The classic old-town tapas bars tend to concentrate on specialities from the Spanish regions, like octopus, peppers and seafood from Galicia; cider, cured meats and cheese from Asturias; or the ubiquitous Basque-style *pintxos*, which are bite-sized concoctions on a slice of bread, held together with a cocktail stick (you're charged by the number of sticks on your plate when you've finished). But contemporary tapas bars in Barcelona think nothing of mixing and matching cuisines, so you could just as easily be munching on a cold soba-noodle salad or a pint-sized lamb kebab.

TOP 5 TRADITIONAL TAPAS

Bodega La Plata See page 183
Cal Pep See page 186
Cova Fumada See page 188
Taller de Tapas See page 183
Vaso de Oro See page 189

TOP 5 CONTEMPORARY TAPAS

Doppietta See page 190
Dos Pebrots See page 185
El Bitxo See page 186
Tapas24 See page 192
La Taverna del Clínic See page 193

La Viñatería del Call C/Sant Domènec del Call 9 ⓦla vinateriadelcall.com; ⓜJaume I. The wood-table tavern is principally an eating place – with a long menu of cheese and ham platters, smoked fish, fried peppers and much more – but it's also a great late-night bar, with a serious wine list and jazz and flamenco sounds as a backdrop. If you want to eat, especially at weekends, it's best to reserve a table. €€

EL RAVAL

SEE MAP PAGE 62

CAFÉS

Café de les Delícies Rambla del Raval 47 ☎934 415 714; ⓜLiceu. One of the first off the blocks in this revamped part of the neighbourhood, plonking thrift-shop chairs and tables beneath exposed pipes and girders and coming up with something cute, cosy, mellow and arty. There's breakfast, sandwiches and tapas to share. €€

Federal C/Parlament 39 ⓦfederalcafe.es; ⓜSant Antoni. Sunday brunch is the hottest ticket in town at this effortlessly cool café, squished into a corner townhouse with a great little roof garden on top. Australian owners have imported their own cool vibe, so whether you're looking for a flat white and French toast, a bacon butty and a glass of New Zealand Sauvignon Blanc or a dandelion soy latte, you can guarantee that there's nowhere else quite like this in Barcelona (apart, perhaps, from their second branch at Ptge. de la Pau 11 in the Barri Gòtic). €€

Granja M. Viader C/Xuclà 4–6 ⓦgranjaviader.cat; ⓜLiceu. The oldest traditional *granja* (milk bar) in town is tucked away down a narrow alley just off C/Carme, with a pavement plaque outside for services to the city. The original owner, Sr Viader, was the proud inventor of "Cacaolat" (bottled chocolate milk), but for a taste of the old days you could also try *mel i mató* (curd cheese and honey) or *llet Mallorquina* (fresh milk with cinnamon and lemon rind). €

Kasparo Pl. de Vicenç Martorell 4 ☎933 022 072; ⓜCatalunya. Sited in the arcaded corner of a quiet square, this tiny café and *terrassa* is popular with parents who come to let their kids play in the adjacent playground. There's muesli, Greek yoghurt and toast and jam for early birds, while later in the day sandwiches, tapas and assorted *platos del dia* are on offer – hummus and bread, vegetable quiche, couscous or pasta, for example. €€

TAPAS BARS AND RESTAURANTS

A Tu Bola C/Hospital 78 ⓦatubolarest.com; ⓜLiceu. Israeli chef Shira whips up falafel-like balls of fresh ingredients, to order, in unexpected but delightful flavour combinations. Home-made harissa, sauces and soft drinks bear hallmarks of the obsessive attention to detail that lifts this far above typical "street food" standard. There aren't many seats so expect a wait at busy times, as the bargain prices keep people coming back for more. €

Bar Cañete C/de la Unió 17 ⓦbarcanete.com; ⓜLiceu.

Gleaming mirrors, dark wood furnishings and white-clad waiters set the scene for some of the city's classiest tapas, featuring premium ingredients (and pricetags to match if you don't choose carefully). Take your pick from classic seafood and meat dishes sourced fresh from the local market. €€€

Biocenter C/Pintor Fortuny 25 ⓦrestaurantebiocenter. es; ⓜLiceu. One of the longest-running veggie places in town, with a restaurant-bar across the road from the original health-food store. The fixed-price lunch menu starts with soup and a trawl through the salad bar for a first course, followed by a daily changing choice of mains. For dinner, they dim the lights, add candles and sounds, and turn out a few more exotic dishes, from *seitan* in a white wine sauce to cheese and mushroom *mezzelune*. €€

★ **Ca l'Estevet** C/Valldonzella 46 ⓦrestaurantestevet. com; ⓜUniversitat. An unshifting rock in the fickle seas of foodie fashions, *Ca l'Estevet* has been serving up old-school Catalan cuisine to loyal local customers since 1940 (and, under a different name, for fifty years before that). The practice has made perfect; get a bellyful of the fixed lunch menu or tuck into the likes of grilled sausages, roasted kid or *escudella i carn d'olla* (meat stew), all reasonably priced and under the guidance of a white-tux-wearing waiter. €€€

Cera 23 C/Cera 23 ⓦcera23.com; ⓜSant Antoni. It's always 5 o'clock somewhere, so go ahead and start your meal in this charming Galicia-meets-the-Mediterranean bistro with an effervescent blackberry mojito, and then tuck into market-fresh dishes like grilled duck with apples, a black-rice-and-seafood "volcano" or almond-flavoured beetroot gnocchi in balsamic cream. €€€

★ **Dos Palillos** C/Elisabets 9 ⓦdospalillos.com; ⓜCatalunya. Albert Raurich, former *chef de cuisine* at "world's best restaurant" *El Bulli*, swapped Catalan food for Asian fusion after falling in love with Japan. Attached to the *Casa Camper* (see page 174), his own Michelin-starred two-room restaurant offers a la carte *dim sum* in the front galley bar (steamed dumplings to grilled oysters and stir-fried prawns), and a backroom, counter-style Asian bar where tasting menus (€120 and €140) wade their way through the highlights. The front bar is a playful take on traditional Spanish tapas bars (cushions on upturned beer-crates,

dusty liqueur bottles and steamer baskets); there are no reservations taken for this, though you do have to book for the Asian bar. €€€€

★ **Dos Pebrots** C/Doctor Dou 19 ⓦdospebrots.com; ⓜCatalunya. Around the corner from Dos Palillos is Albert Raurich's love letter to Mediterranean cuisine. The bar here was once a favourite spot for poets and off-duty chefs – including Raurich. Now transformed, it uses historical dishes such as Roman garum (anchovy sauce) as the basis for contemporary tapas and small dishes (€4–9 each). Don't miss the pig's nipples. €€€€

★ **Elisabets** C/Elisabets 2 ⓦelisabets1962; ⓜCatalunya. Catalan home-cooking served at cramped tables in a jovial dining room. Locals breakfast on a sandwich and a glass of wine, the hearty lunchtime *menú del dia* is hard to beat for price or you can just have tapas, sandwiches and drinks at the bar. €€

Fonda España C/Sant Pau 9 ⓦhotelespanya.com/en/fonda-espana-restaurant; ⓜLiceu. The beauty of this nineteenth-century Art Nouveau dining room threatens to distract from the food. Fortunately, the *Fonda* serves Catalan classics by star chef Martín Berasategui – such as potato *trinxat* with poached egg – that live up to the glorious *modernista* surroundings. The set menus are good value at this level. €€€€

Frankie Gallo Cha Cha Cha C/Marquès de Barberà 15 ⓦfrankiegallochachacha.com; ⓜLiceu. A long, jumping pizza joint with a disco aesthetic but a very serious attitude to their artisanal pizzas, which they describe as "transgressive pineapple-free creations". Prices are reasonable, portions large and the approach eco-friendly. €€

Sésamo C/Sant Antoni Abat 52 ☎934 416 411; ⓜSant Antoni. This classy tapas place (with bar at the front and restaurant tables at the back) offers up a chalkboard menu of innovative organic dishes that are either vegetarian or vegan. Small and not-so-small dishes roll out of the open kitchen – think Catalan mushroom croquettes, gnocchi with beetroot and hazelnuts or grilled vegetables with goat cheese and rosemary, all reasonably priced, or you could go for the set tapas menu. The Catalan wines and cheeses are a high point too. €€

15

THE CUP THAT CHEERS

'**Un café**' in Barcelona is simply espresso – also known as a *café sol* (*café solo*). For decaff (*descafeinat*, *descafeinado*), make sure you ask for it *de màquina* ("from the machine") to avoid an instant sachet ("de sobre"). A slightly weaker large black coffee is a *café americano*. A *tallat* (*cortado*) is like a *macchiato*, ie a small strong black coffee with a dash of steamed milk; a larger cup with more hot milk is a *café amb llet* (*café con leche*). Chuck brandy, cognac or whisky into a black coffee and it's a *cigaló* (*carajillo*), or add them to a *tallat* to make a *trifàsic*.

Tea comes without milk unless you ask for it, and is often just a teabag in a cup of hot water. If you do ask for milk, chances are it'll be hot and UHT. Better to try an infusion, like mint (*menta*), camomile (*camomila*) or lime (*tila*).

TOP 5 VEGGIE-FRIENDLY RESTAURANTS

Biocenter See page 185
Green Spot See page 188
Rasoterra See page 183
Sésamo See page 185
Teresa Carles See page 186

★ **Suculent** Rambla de Raval 43 ⓦsuculent.com; ⓜLiceu. Star chef Carles Abellán and talented newcomer Toni Romero have teamed up to refine classic rustic dishes at this bistro. As well as meaning "succulent", the name is a play on the Catalan words "sucar lent" – to dip slowly – and you'll do just that, using the fresh, warm bread to mop up the sauces from dish after lip-smacking dish. The steak tartare on a split, grilled marrowbone (€17) will put hairs on your chest and bring tears of joy to your eyes. €€€

Teresa Carles C/Jovellanos 2 ⓦteresacarles.com; ⓜCatalunya. Stylish vegetarian and vegan cuisine served in a hip – but most certainly not "hippie" – space with soaring ceilings, exposed brick walls and soft, white lighting. The lunch menu is a great bargain, while a la carte offerings like artisanal pastas, a hearty *seitan* burger and vegan *ceviche* don't cost much more. Their second Barcelona outpost, *Flax & Kale*, is located nearby at C/Tallers 74. €€

CAFÉS

★ **Bar del Convent** Centre Cívic Convent de Sant Agustí, Pl. de l'Acadèmia, C/Comerç 36, Sant Pere ⓦbardelconvent.com; ⓜJaume I. The cloister café-bar in the converted old convent, now cultural centre, is a bargain for lunch and light meals, with soups, stir-fries, lasagne and couscous, served indoors or on a child-friendly terrace. In its latest reincarnation it is run by an organization that helps people into the workplace. €

La Masala C/Mònec 6 ⓦinstagram.com/la_masala_cafe; ⓜUrquinaona. Named after the masala chai tea they serve, the actual speciality here is excellent coffee. There's a short, simple list of breakfast dishes and home-made cakes. La Masala is hidden down a narrow sidestreet and is mostly beautifully quiet. €

Pim Pam Burger C/Sabateret 4, La Ribera ☏933 152 093; ⓜJaume I. The go-to choice for a quick bite, *Pim Pam Burger* is the place for takeaway burgers, fries, franks and sandwiches. There are a few stools and tables if you'd rather not eat on the hoof, but it does get busy by about 8pm. €

TAPAS BARS AND RESTAURANTS

El Bitxo C/Verdaguer i Callís 9, Sant Pere ⓦelbitxo.es; ⓜUrquinaona. This is a great find for drinks and tapas, very close to the Palau de la Música Catalana. It's tiny (four small wooden tables and a line of bar stools) but there's a friendly welcome, and the food is good, especially the cured and smoked meats and sausages and regional cheeses. €€

TOP 5 CHEAP EATS

Cal Boter See page 193
Can Maño See page 188
Elisabets See page 185
Le Cucine Mandarosso See page 186
Quimet I Quimet See page 191

★ **Cal Pep** Pl. de les Olles 8, La Ribera ⓦcalpep.com; ⓜBarceloneta. There's no equal in town for fresh-off-the-boat and -from-the-market tapas. You will have to queue (there are no reservations for the bar), and prices are high for what's effectively a bar meal (up to €50 a head), but it's definitely worth it for the likes of impeccably fried shrimp, grilled sea bass, Catalan sausage and beans, and baby squid and chickpeas. There's also a small dining room and a handful of tables outside. €€€

Carmina C/Argenteria 37 ⓦcarminarestaurante.com; ⓜJaume I. A gorgeous renovation of an eighteenth-century building has been artfully blended with neon, artsy ceramics and oversized lamps and is now the home of Carmina. The speciality is superb Italian food with nods to Spanish cuisine, such as oxtail croquettes with pecorino. The pasta dishes are especially good. €€

Casa Delfín Pg. del Born 36, La Ribera ⓦcasadelfin restaurant.com; ⓜJaume I. There are many reasons to like this bubbly, updated taverna, not least its sunny *terrassa* outside the old market. It's a slick operation, inside and out, with a long menu that takes a loving look at traditional Catalan dishes, from grilled farmhouse sausage and white beans to crispy artichoke hearts with *romesco* sauce. It's served tapas-style, so you don't have to come for a full meal, but if you've got room don't miss English owner Kate's signature pudding, Eton Mess. €€

Casa Mari y Rufo C/Freixures 11, Sant Pere ☏933 197 302; ⓜJaume I. A great place for no-frills but high-quality market cooking, with a busy family at a smoky range turning out platters of seafood, grilled Catalan sausage, stewed oxtail, steak, chips and the like – or ask what's good from the Mercat de Santa Caterina fish stalls that day. Expect whitewashed walls, bare light bulbs and chipped tiles, but prices that reflect the quality of the food on offer. €€€

Le Cucine Mandarosso C/Verdaguer i Callís 4, Sant Pere ⓦlecucinemandarosso.com; ⓜUrquinaona. Naples meets Barcelona in this tiny space near the Via Laietana. It's crowded

CATALAN FOOD AND DISHES

Traditional Catalan food places heavy emphasis on meat, olive oil, garlic, fruit and salad. The cuisine is typified by a willingness to mix flavours, so savoury dishes cooked with nuts or fruit are common, as are salads using both cooked and raw ingredients.

Meat is usually grilled and served with a few fried potatoes or salad, though Catalan sausage served with a pool of haricot beans is a classic menu item. Stewed veal and other casseroles are common, while poultry is sometimes mixed with seafood (known as *mar i muntanya* – "sea and mountain") or fruit for tastes very definitely out of the Spanish mainstream. In season, **game** is also available, especially partridge, hare, rabbit and boar.

As for **fish and seafood**, you'll be offered hake, tuna, squid or cuttlefish, while the local anchovies are superb. Cod is often salted and turns up in *esquiexada*, a summer salad of salt cod, tomatoes, onions and olives. Fish stews are a local speciality, though the mainstays of seafood restaurants are the rice- and noodle-based dishes. **Paella** comes originally from Valencia, but as that region was historically part of Catalunya, the dish has been enthusiastically adopted as Catalunya's own. More certainly Catalan is **fideuà**, thin noodles served with seafood – you stir in the fiery *all i olli* (garlic mayonnaise) provided. **Arròs negre** (black rice, cooked with squid ink) is another local delicacy.

Vegetables rarely amount to more than a few French fries or boiled potatoes, though there are some authentic Catalan vegetable dishes, like spinach tossed with raisins and pine nuts, or *samfaina*, a ratatouille-like stew. Spring is the season for **calçots**, huge spring onions, which are roasted whole and eaten with a spicy *romesco* dipping sauce. Autumn sees the arrival of **wild mushrooms**, mixed with rice, omelettes, salads or scrambled eggs. In winter, a dish of **stewed beans or lentils** is also a popular starter, almost always flavoured with bits of sausage, meat and fat.

For **dessert**, apart from fresh fruit, there's always crème caramel (*flan* in Catalan) – fantastic when home-made – though *crema catalana* is the local choice, more like a crème brûlée, with a caramelized sugar coating. Or you might be offered *músic*, nuts and dried fruit served with a glass of sweet *moscatel* wine.

15

and cramped but the top-value southern Italian comfort food here is the real deal (the home-made cakes are so good you'll buy more to take away). There are no reservations at lunchtimes so expect to queue with the locals. €€

Cuines Santa Caterina Mercat de Santa Caterina, Avda. de Francesc Cambó 16, Sant Pere ⓦ grupotragaluz. com; ⓜ Jaume I. The handsome neighbourhood market has a ravishing open-plan restaurant, with tables set under soaring wooden rafters. Food in the restaurant touches all bases – pasta to sushi, Catalan rice to Thai chicken – with most things costing €10–16. Or you can just drink and munch superior tapas at the horseshoe bar. €€

Euskal Etxea Pl. de Montcada 1–3, La Ribera ⓦ gruposa gardi.com; ⓜ Jaume I. The bar at the front of the local Basque community centre is great for *pintxos* – pint-sized tapas, held together by a toothpick. Just point to what you want (and keep the toothpicks so that the bill can be tallied at the end – most things are a couple of euros each). There's a pricier restaurant out back with more Basque specialities. €€

Flora Passeig Pujades 21 ⓦ instagram.com/floracafe bcn; ⓜ Arc de Triomf. Start the day wandering around Barcelona's loveliest park with brunch at one of Flora's terrace tables. Eggs Benedict, avocado toast and all the breakfast favourites are available, along with freshly squeezed juices, excellent coffee and fun, friendly waiters. €

Llamber C/Fusina 5, La Ribera ⓦ llamber.com; ⓜ Jaume I. In a former industrial warehouse facing the Mercat del Born cultural centre, renowned Asturian chef Francisco Heras has created a modern factory of first-rate tapas. Open 365 days a year, *Llamber* is a stylish "gastronomic tavern" with a wood-and-brick aesthetic that makes the most of the building's heritage. There are full dishes, such as quail with garlic and octopus with creamed potato, but the emphasis is very much on shared eating and drinking in groups. €€

Mosquito C/Carders 46, Sant Pere ⓦ mosquitotapas.com; ⓜ Jaume 1. Happy indeed are the locals for whom this is their neighbourhood drink-and-chow joint. The Asian tapas bar, festooned with hanging paper lanterns, pours artisan beers and offers an authentic, made-to-order dim sum menu (dishes €3–5), from shrimp dumplings to tofu rolls. The pho (only served at lunchtime) is highly recommended. €

★ **NAP (Neapolitan Authentic Pizza)** Avda. Francesc Cambó 30, Sant Pere ⓦ napofficial.com; ⓜ Jaume I. Italian staff. Italian ingredients. Italian pizza. Specifically, Neapolitan thin-base pizza. Like the best pizza places in Naples itself, *N.A.P.* is loud, chaotic, crowded and cheap.

TOP 5 FOR PAELLA & RICE DISHES

L'Arrosseria Xàtiva See page 193
La Mar Salada See page 189
Pez Vela See page 189
Set Portes See page 188
Xiringuito Escribà See page 190

You'll have to queue, then wait as the small wood-fired oven struggles to deal with the workload. But the result is probably the best pizza in town, with the possible exception of *NAP*'s second, less-crowded branch on C/Baluard, in Barceloneta. €̄

Set Portes Pg. d'Isabel II 14, La Ribera ⓦ 7portes.com;

Ⓜ Barceloneta. A wood-panelled classic with the names of its famous clientele much to the fore – they've all eaten here, from Errol Flynn to Yoko Ono. The decor in the "Seven Doors" has barely changed in almost two hundred years and, while very elegant, it's not exclusive – you should book ahead, though, as the queues can be horrendous. The renowned rice dishes are fairly reasonably priced (€21–26), but for a full meal prices can rack up. €̄€̄€̄

El Xampanyet C/Montcada 22, La Ribera ⓦ el xampanyet.es; Ⓜ Jaume I. Traditional blue-tiled bar doing a roaring trade in basic cava, cider and tapas – anchovies are the speciality, but there's also marinated tuna, spicy mussels, sun-dried tomatoes, sliced meats and cheese. As is often the way, the drinks are cheap and the tapas turn out to be rather pricey (€5–9 each, and portions aren't generous), but there's usually a good buzz. Be prepared to queue. €̄€̄

PORT VELL AND BARCELONETA

SEE MAP PAGE 82

CAFÉ

Vioko Pg. de Joan de Borbó 74, Barceloneta ⓦ vioko. es; Ⓜ Barceloneta. Quite simply, the slinkiest, swishiest ice-cream and chocolate shop in town – *Vioko*'s minimalist white curves serve as the backdrop for artisan *gelati* in flavours such as banana split or pomelo and jasmine, gourmet chocolates and coffee, rainbows of airy macaroons, ready to take away on a stroll along the marina. €̄

TAPAS BARS AND RESTAURANTS

1881 Per Sagardi Pl. de Pau Vila 3, Barceloneta ⓦ gruposagardi.com; Ⓜ Barceloneta. Ride the escalators to the roof of the waterfront Museu d'Història de Catalunya and you'll be met with the smell of wood smoke. A huge grill dominates the glass-walled *1881 per Sagardi*, churning out Basque dishes like magnificent *txuletón* steaks and Catalan dishes like artichokes with *romesco* sauce. Main courses are about €22–26 each, but it's worth paying just to sit on the terrace, which also serves a mean Martini, and watch the yachts sailing in and out of the harbour. €̄€̄€̄

★ **Can Maño** C/Baluard 12, Barceloneta ☎ 933 193 082; Ⓜ Barceloneta. This old-fashioned diner is packed with noisy locals around formica tables. Basically, your choice is fried or grilled fish, such as sardines, mullet or calamari, supplemented by a few daily seafood specials and basic meat dishes. Expect rough house wine and absolutely no frills, but it's an authentic experience, which is likely to cost you less than €18 a head. €̄

★ **Cova Fumada** C/Baluard 56, Barceloneta ☎ 932 214 061; Ⓜ Barceloneta. Behind brown wooden doors on Barceloneta's market square (there's no sign) is this rough-and-ready tavern with battered marble tables and antique barrels. It might not look like much but the food's great, with ingredients straight from the market, from griddled prawns to fried artichokes. €̄€̄

Green Spot C/de la Reina Cristina 12, Barceloneta ⓦ encompania delobos.com/the-green-spot; Ⓜ Barceloneta. Vegetarian and vegan restaurants good enough to keep omnivores happy too are rare in Barcelona. *Green Spot* fits the bill, even though its fun, fresh, international dishes, embracing all the latest trends, aren't quite as refined as its oak-panelled decor. €̄€̄

Jai-Ca C/Ginebra 9 & 13, Barceloneta ⓦ barjaica.com; Ⓜ Barceloneta. Always a winning choice for seafood tapas, with bundles of razor clams, plump anchovies, stuffed mussels and other platters piled high on the bar. Meanwhile,

---

BARCELONA'S BEST BURGERS

Take one financial crisis, add locals looking for value-for-money dining and the current rage for burger bars becomes more understandable. These range from the stylish to the unpretentious-but-good, such as the cheerful **Pim Pam Burger** (see page 186). More and more bars are starting to serve great burgers, which in, **Betty Ford's** (see page 197) come with excellent fries. **Makamaka Beach Burger Cafe** (see page 189) in La Barceloneta earns top marks for its juicy burgers, ample outdoor seating and – if you like that sort of thing, cocktails. Poble Sec's **De Paula** (see page 191) makes a strong case to be considered the king of them all, with a winning combo of top quality, charm and relative cheapness.

IT TAKES TWO

You want a seafood paella or an *arròs negre* (black rice, with squid ink), or maybe a garlicky *fideuà* (noodles with seafood). Of course you do. Problem is, you're on your own and virtually every restaurant that offers these classic Barcelona dishes does so for a minimum of two people (often you don't find out until you examine the menu small print). Solution? Ask the waiter upfront, as sometimes the kitchen will oblige single diners, or look for the dishes on a *menú del dia* (especially on Thursdays, traditionally rice day), when there should be no minimum. Probably best not to grab a stranger off the street to share a paella, however desperate you are.

the fryers in the kitchen work over-time, turning out crisp baby squid, fried shrimp and little green peppers scattered with rock salt. Take your haul to a tile-topped cane table, or outside onto the tiny street-corner patio. The second location at no. 9 also has a patio and serves the same menu. €

★ **Makamaka Beach Burger Cafe** Pg. de Joan de Borbó 76, Barceloneta ⓦ makamaka.es; ⓜ Barceloneta. You really can't ask for more: creative cocktails and some of the city's finest burgers served on a large *terrassa* steps from the beach. It's Hawaii-meets-Barcelona – laidback, late night and lots of fun. €

★ **La Mar Salada** Pg. de Joan de Borbó 58, Barceloneta, ⓦ lamarsalada.cat; ⓜ Barceloneta. While many of the classic fish restaurants in Barceloneta have let standards slip under the groaning weight of tourist numbers, the young team at *La Mar Salada* have instead raised the bar. Buying freshly landed fish straight from the dock directly opposite, they offer refined, creative variations of great seafood dishes at bargain prices. The €18 lunchtime *menú del dia* is outrageously good value, and there's even a

sunny terrace to eat it on. €€€

Pez Vela Pg. del Mare Nostrum 19/21 ⓦ grupotragaluz. com; ⓜ Barceloneta. At the base of the towering *W* hotel this restaurant styled on a "*chiringuito*" (beach bar) serves excellent paella and rice dishes, plus seafood such as clams and Galician-style octopus, from its sunny terrace. It's hard to beat for simple waterfront dining, and main courses are reasonably priced given the swish location. €€€

Porch Pas de Sota Muralla 1 ⓦ instagram.com/ porchbcn; ⓜ Barceloneta. A cocktail and tapas bar catering to a young and predominantly foreign crowd, who fill its leafy terrace on the way back from the beach. A short list of tapas, salads and pinsas (small pizzas) provide a good excuse to linger awhile. €€

★ **Vaso de Oro** C/Balboa 6, Barceloneta ☎ 933 193 098; ⓜ Barceloneta. If you can get in this corridor of a bar you're doing well – Sunday lunch is particularly busy – and there's no menu, but standard bites include *patatas bravas*, fried sausage and tuna salad, with fancier shellfish dishes and meat grills available too (most tapas €5–15). €

PORT OLÍMPIC AND POBLENOU SEE MAP PAGE 86

CAFÉ

El Tío Ché Rambla del Poblenou 44–46, Poblenou ⓦ eltioche.es; ⓜ Poblenou, or bus #36 from ⓜ Barceloneta. A down-to-earth classic on this newly hip boulevard, run by the same family for four generations. The specialities are orange or lemon *granissat* (crushed ice) and their famous *orxata* (tiger-nut drink), but there are also *torrons* (almond fudge), hot chocolate, coffee, croissants and sandwiches. It's a bit off the beaten track, though you can stroll up easily enough from Bogatell beach (15min) or down the *rambla* from Poblenou metro (10min). €

TAPAS BARS AND RESTAURANTS

Agua Pg. Marítim 30, Port Olímpic ⓦ somosesencia. es; ⓜ Ciutadella-Vila Olímpica. Much the nicest boardwalk restaurant on the beach-front strip, perfect for brunch, though if the weather's iffy you can opt for the sleek, split-level dining room. The menu is contemporary Mediterranean – grills, *risotti*, pasta, salads and tapas – and the prices are pretty fair for such a prime spot (most dishes

€15–25), so it's usually busy. €€

Enoteca Hotel Arts Barcelona C/Marina 19–21, Port Olímpic ⓦ enotecapacoperez.com; ⓜ Ciutadella-Vila Olímpica. A contender for the crown of Barcelona's best fine-dining restaurant, *Enoteca* contributes two Michelin stars to the five-star constellation of chef Paco Pérez. Everything here from the all-white dining room to the wine list and service is appropriately stellar. The food? A creative *tour de force* of modern Catalan cooking that will put a smile on your face – and a hole in your bank account (a tasting menu of the chef's greatest hits goes for €220). €€€€

Koh C/Pujades 133, Poblenou ☎ 938 289 240; ⓜ Llacuna. This relaxed little restaurant draws influences from all over Asia, so you might find massaman curry, chicken tikka masala, cod tempura with beetroot tzatziki or a banh mi made with spiced lamb. Get there early for one of the handful of tables outside. €€

★ **Els Pescadors** Pl. de Prim 1, Poblenou ⓦ els pescadors.com; ⓜ Poblenou. The best top-class fish restaurant in Barcelona? It's a tough call, but many would

15

choose this hideaway place in a pretty square with gnarled trees in the back alleys of Rambla de Poblenou. Lunch outside on a sunny day just can't be beaten (reservations advised). The menu offers daily changing fresh fish dishes, and plenty more involving rice, noodles or salt cod (try the latter with *samfaina*, like a Catalan ratatouille). Most dishes cost €18–35 and if you don't go mad with the wine list you'll escape for around €60 a head. €€€

Xiringuito Escribà Ronda del Litoral 42, Platja Bogatell ⓦ xiringuitoescriba.com; ⓜ Ciutadella-Vila Olímpica. Beachfront restaurant (really a glorified beach shack) that's enough off the beaten track (a 15min walk from Port Olímpic) to mark you out as in the know. High points are paellas and daily fish specials (around €26), followed by sensational cakes and pastries from the Escribà family patisserie. €€€

MONTJÜIC SEE MAP PAGE 92

TAPAS BARS AND RESTAURANTS

Casa de Tapas Cañota C/Lleida 7 ⓦ casadetapas.com; ⓜ Poble Sec. This colourful, family-friendly tapas bar is an ideal spot to refuel over-tired children after a visit to Montjüic's Magic Fountain. Adults can unwind with a fresh, cold beer pulled from pressurized copper tanks. The tapas are above average in both quality and price (tapas are in the €5–15 range). €€

Espai Kru C/Lleida 7 ⓦ espaikru.com; ⓜ Poble Sec. Annexed to Cañota and upstairs from traditional – and extremely expensive – seafood restaurant *Rías de Galicia*, this creative restaurant gives deep-sea delicacies a more contemporary context. Expect cocktails, oysters and first-rate sashimi plus a handful of equally impressive meat dishes. €€€€

POBLE SEC SEE MAP PAGE 102

TAPAS BARS AND RESTAURANTS

Bella Napoli C/Margarit 14 ⓦ labellanapoli.es; ⓜ Poble Sec. Authentic Neapolitan pizzeria, right down to the cheery waiters and cheesy pop music. The pizzas come straight from the depths of a beehive-shaped oven, or there's a big range of pastas, *risotti* and veal *scaloppine*, with almost everything priced between €11 and €21. €€

Benzina Passatge de Pere Calders 6 ⓦ benzina.es; ⓜ Poble Sec. Down a wide pedestrianised alleyway off the hipster drag of C/del Parlament is this industrially chic Italian restaurant, serving some of the best food around. The convivial atmosphere and upbeat seventies and eighties soundtrack provide a joyful backdrop to linguine *aglio e olio*

with lobster and avocado, a heavenly carbonara and much more. €€€

Casa Xica C/França Xica 20 ⓦ casa-xica.es; ⓜ Poble Sec. This unassuming and slightly scruffy little neighbourhood joint surprises with a range of excellent Spanish-infused Asian dishes from squid tartar with coconut and lime *ajo blanco* (a garlicky Andalucian soup) to glazed Iberian pork bao, served with a choice of natural wines. Be warned the portions are quite small and order accordingly. €€

Doppietta Passatge de Pere Calders 4 ⓦ doppietta. es; ⓜ Poble Sec. The people behind *Benzina* have more recently opened this classy cocktail bar and *salumeria* next door. It's a homage to all things Italian, but particularly the

WHAT'S COOKING?

The man behind the reimagining of modern cuisine – the foams, the essences, the vapours, the taste explosions, the deconstructed, laboratory-tested dishes – is Catalan chef **Ferran Adrià**, whose world-famous, triple-Michelin-starred restaurant *El Bulli*, on the Costa Brava, set the benchmark for creative contemporary cooking. *El Bulli* closed as a restaurant in 2011 – it is now a cookery foundation (ⓦ elbullifoundation.com) and "centre for creativity" – though Adrià and his brother Albert have also had a high-profile presence on the Barcelona dining scene over the last few years, with various projects including their new-wave tapas bar, *Tickets*, traditional vermut bar, *Bodega 1900*, and modern takes on Japanese cuisine (*Pakta*) and Mexican (*Hoja Santa* and *Niño Viejo*). Their most theatrical project yet, *Enigma*, opened early in 2017 and features a secret entrance code, an otherworldly, cloud-like interior, and a €220, forty-course tasting menu. Meanwhile, the Adrià effect has spawned a generation of regional chefs – many of them alumni of the *El Bulli* kitchens – who have helped put contemporary Spanish cuisine on the map. Talents like Jordi Vilà, Carles Abellán, Ramón Freixa and the trio behind *Disfrutar* (see page 192) are cooking right now in Barcelona, so it's time to brush up on your chemistry and educate your tastebuds.

Mille Miglia motor race, black-and-white photos of which plaster the walls (*doppietta* refers to a gear shift). The cocktails are first-class, the perfect accompaniment to some superb antipasti and sharing plates. €€

★ **De Paula** C/Creu dels Molers 65 ⓦ depaula.cat; ⓜ Poble Sec. This little burger joint might just be the best in town. Charcoal grill? Check. Hand-chopped, quality Brazilian meat? Check. Artisanal bread? Check. The burgers are posh but the prices (€8–11) and serving sizes will suit everyone. The only downside is the size of the premises, despite a recent expansion. Try the local beers when you're

in there – if you can get a table. €€

★ **Quimet i Quimet** C/Poeta Cabanyes 25 ⓣ quimetiquimet.com; ⓜ Paral·lel. Poble Sec's cosiest tapas bar is a foodie place of pilgrimage and at busy times everyone has to breathe in to squeeze another punter through the door. The wine bottles are stacked five shelves high (there's a chalkboard menu of wines by the glass), while little plates of classy finger food are served reverently from the minuscule counter – things like roast onions, marinated mushrooms, stuffed cherry tomatoes, grilled aubergine, anchovy-wrapped olives and a terrific range of regional cheeses. €€

DRETA DE L'EIXAMPLE

SEE MAP PAGE 106

15

CAFÉS

Café del Centre C/Girona 69 ⓦ cafedelcentre.com; ⓜ Girona. This beautiful old bar has been here since 1873 (a plaque outside honours its service to the city) and, despite new ownership and a complete overhaul, has retained many of its *modernista* features. Not as sleepy as it once was, it now attracts a younger, more energetic crowd at night. €€

Laie Llibreria Café C/Pau Claris 85 ⓦ laie.es; ⓜ Passeig de Gràcia. The city's first and best bookshop-café (buy a book downstairs and take it to the café to read) is known for its popular weekday buffet breakfast spread, set lunch deals and a la carte dining. It's also a comfortable place to work, and you'll see plenty of people tapping at laptops. €€

TAPAS BARS AND RESTAURANTS

2254 C/Consell de Cent 335 ⓦ 2254restaurant.com; ⓜ Passeig de Gràcia. The name of the restaurant stands for the number of kilometres between Barcelona and Palermo – the birthplace of the restaurant owner and chef, Nuncio Cona. Creative, tasty dishes influenced by not just Spanish cuisine, but also Italian, French and from further afield. Try the gyoza stuffed with oxtail or the lamb shank with mustard, mint and yoghurt. €€€

La Bodegueta Rambla de Catalunya 100 ⓦ labodegueta rambla.com; ⓜ Diagonal. This long-established basement *bodega* serves cava by the glass, a serious range of other wines and good ham, cheese, anchovies and other tapas to soak it all up. For most of the year you can sit outside at tables on the city's second, less touristy, *rambla*. €€

Ciutat Comtal Rambla de Catalunya 18 ⓦ ciudadcondal. cat; ⓜ Passeig de Gràcia. The best of the large uptown tapas-hall-style places is a handy city-centre pit stop that caters for all needs. Breakfast sees the bar groan under the weight of a dozen types of crispy baguette sandwich, plus croissants and pastries, while the daily changing tapas selection ranges far and wide, from *patatas bravas* to octopus. It can be standing room only at lunchtime (and not much of that either), so get there early. €€

Embat C/Mallorca 304 ⓦ embatrestaurant.com; ⓜ Verdaguer. Hidden a few streets away from the tourist

traffic, this modern Catalan bistro has won the loyalty of locals over the past ten years by serving refined, first-class food at affordable prices – the weekday three-course lunch is especially good value at €23.50. It's a small, white, minimalist space where the money is spent on ingredients not interior designers. Many of the dishes are close to Michelin-star standard. €€

★ **Lasarte** C/Mallorca 259 ⓦ restaurantlasarte.com; ⓜ Diagonal. Quite simply, one of the best restaurants in Spain, with three Michelin stars to prove it. Basque gastronomic superstar Martín Berasategui has his name on the door but it's Paolo Casagrande who runs the kitchen, turning out a €305 tasting menu (there's a €205 version at lunchtime) that's strong on perfectionism and clean flavours. Send a message of apology to your bank manager before you reach for the wine list. €€€€

★ **Moments** Hotel Mandarin Oriental, Pg. de Gràcia 38–40 ⓦ mandarinoriental.com/Barcelona; ⓜ Passseig de Gràcia. The two-star *Moments*, run by Raul Balam and his mother, fêted chef Carme Ruscalleda, is a majestic experience. You'll pay €215 for a mind- and budget-blowing tasting menu of exquisite beauty and refinement, set in an appropriately luxurious gold dining room. €€€€

Mordisco Pg. de la Concepció 10 ⓦ gmordisco.com; ⓜ Diagonal. A Barcelona favourite since the '80s, *Mordisco* serves fresh, rustic stuff straight from the charcoal grill, with excellent steak and seasonal mushroom dishes. You can even shop for fresh vegetables and deli ingredients here. That's not to say that style takes a back seat: this former high-end jeweller's is a palace of white columns with a gorgeous glass-covered courtyard, and the upper floor has been converted into a relaxed cocktail bar. Expect to pay €15–19 for main courses. €€

★ **El Nacional BCN** Pg. de Gràcia, 24 ⓦ elnacionalbcn. com; ⓜ Passseig de Gràcia. This massive 2600-square-metre food court offers a one-stop-shop for Spanish cuisine. In its gorgeous, high-ceilinged space you find a fish restaurant, grill, tapas bar, snack bar, oyster bar, wine bar, cocktail bar and most other bars you can think of. Quality across the board is very high; prices aren't low either, but

15

TOP 5 MONEY NO OBJECT

Cinc Sentits See page 192
Disfrutar See page 192
Enoteca See page 189
Lasarte See page 191
Moments See page 191

not bad by Pg. de Gràcia standards. Check it out on the cheap with a quick snack for a few euros or go for broke with a massive €112/kg extra-aged rib-steak cooked on a wood grill. There are no bookings, so be prepared to wait or pick a different section at busy times. €€€

★ **Tapas24** C/Diputació 269 ⓦ carlesabellan.com; ⓜ Passeig de Gràcia. Star chef Carles Abellan gets back to

his roots at this basement tapas bar. There's a reassuringly traditional feel that's echoed in the menu – *patatas bravas*, Andalucian-style fried fish, meatballs, chorizo sausage and fried eggs. But the kitchen updates the classics too, so there's also *calamares romana* (fried squid) dyed black with squid ink or a burger with foie gras. Sharing plates cost from €12 to €22. There's always a rush and a bustle at mealtimes, so be aware you might have to queue. €€

Tragaluz Ptge. de la Concepció 5 ⓦ grupotragaluz. com/; ⓜ Diagonal. This place attracts beautiful people by the score, and the classy Mediterranean-with-knobs-on cooking, served under a glass roof (*tragaluz* means "skylight"), doesn't disappoint. Mains include steak tartare, slow-roasted pork with pineapple and pasta with truffles, and cost €16–26. It's a relaxing stop for those fresh off the *modernista* trail (La Pedrera is just across the way). €€€

ESQUERRA DE L'EIXAMPLE

SEE MAP PAGE 116

TAPAS BARS AND RESTAURANTS

Cerveseria Catalana C/Mallorca 236 ⓦ cerveceria catalana.com; ⓜ Passeig de Gràcia. An uptown beer-and-tapas joint where the counters are piled high with elaborately assembled dishes, supplemented by a blackboard list of daily specials like bacon, cheese and date skewers and mushroom risotto (most tapas €2–10). It gets busy after work and at mealtimes, and you might have to wait for a table. €

Cinc Sentits C/Aribau 58 ⓦ cincsentits.com; ⓜ Universitat. Jordi Artal's "Five Senses" wows diners with his contemporary Catalan cuisine – and it has two Michelin stars to boot, so you'll need to book well in advance. Two tasting menus (€159 and €189, wine pairings available) use rigorously sourced ingredients – wild fish, mountain lamb, seasonal vegetables, farmhouse cheeses – in elegant, pared-down dishes that are all about flavour. €€€€

Compartir C/València 225 ⓦ disfrutarbarcelona.com; ⓜ Passeig de Gràcia. The more affordable little sister of the divine *Disfrutar* has the same culinary geniuses behind it and a similar approach to creative and stunning dishes (the pickled sardine dish with purple carrots, particularly, is a work of art). The bold and eclectic décor, and unfussy service, make this a more informal experience than is usually paired with this level of cooking. €€€

Coure Ptge. del Marimon 20 ☎ 932 007 532; ⓜ Hospital Clinic/Diagonal. *Coure's* ground-floor tapas bar is always packed with an afterwork crowd; the main dining room is in the basement, beyond the swaying copper curtains. There's no view, as you'd imagine, but the outstanding creative Catalan cooking and friendly service ensure the atmosphere is always sunny. €€€

★ **Disfrutar** C/Villaroel 163 ⓦ disfrutarbarcelona. com; ⓜ Hospital Clinic. The hottest restaurant in Barcelona currently belongs to three former head chefs of the now-closed *El Bulli*, for many years considered the best in the world. The creativity here is off the charts. Tasting menus (€175) are an endless procession of tiny delights that will make you groan with pleasure, at least until the bill arrives. €€€€

★ **La Flauta** C/Aribau 23 ☎ 933 237 038; ⓜ Universitat. One of the city's best-value lunch menus sees diners queuing for tables early – get there before 2pm to avoid the rush. It's a handsome bar-restaurant of dark wood and deep colours, and while the name is a nod to the house speciality gourmet sandwiches (a *flauta* is a thin baguette), there are also meals served tapas-style, day and night (dishes €4–12), based on local market produce, from wild mushrooms to locally landed fish. €

★ **Gresca** C/Provença 230 ☎ 934 516 193; ⓜ Diagonal. It is a long-running source of bemusement among food writers that *Gresca's* Rafa Penya does not have a Michelin star. But what's bad news for him is good news for diners: you get to keep eating his superb food at prices that are much cheaper than they really ought to be. The €24 lunchtime *menú del dia* is a great bargain as is the adjoining *Gresca Bar*. It's a touch more informal, and serves superb tapas accompanied by a selection of natural wines. €€€

Hisop Ptge. del Marimon 9 ⓦ hisop.com; ⓜ Hospital Clinic/Diagonal. This tiny alleyway has always housed a clutch of great little restaurants. *Hisop* is the little restaurant that could: a tiny eatery that has long held a Michelin star despite its unstylish decor, cramped dimensions, and refusal to use unpaid interns. Chef/owner Oriol Ivern somehow keeps prices low too — *Hisop's* €85 tasting menu is considerably cheaper than those of some of its starred competition. €€€€

Igueldo C/Rosselló 186 ⓦ restauranteigueldo.com; ⓜ Diagonal. Basque co-owners Ana and Gonzalo have imported their regional cuisine, polished by years of practice in some of Spain's finest restaurants. There's a focus on excellent ingredients and an effort to keep prices accessible

(mains €19–26). Don't miss the steak tartare. €€€
Manteca C/Aribau 23 ⓦ manteca-restaurante.
negocio.site; ⓜ Rocafort. A welcome addition to a quiet
corner of the Eixample, with tables outside on the newly
pedestrianised Carrer de Consell de Cent. Sharing plates
range from patatas bravas and chicken goujons to roast
aubergine with citrus tahini, tomato and honey, and the
atmosphere is cheerfully relaxed. €€
La Taverna del Clínic C/Rosselló 155 ⓦ latavernadel

clinic.com; ⓜ Hospital Clínic. This sleek taverna, named
for the hospital over the road, is a gourmet tapas spot
that concentrates on rigorously sourced regional produce.
Chef Toni Simôes was proclaimed young chef of the year
in 2014, when the restaurant was expanded to cope with
its burgeoning popularity. Dishes (most cost between €15
and €30) are accompanied by artisan-made olive oil and a
high-class wine list, and include crispy suckling pig and sea
urchins artfully arranged on mounds of sea salt. €€

SAGRADA FAMÍLIA AND GLÒRIES SEE MAP PAGE 120

TAPAS BARS AND RESTAURANTS
★ **Bardeni** C/Valencia 454 ⓦ bardeni.es; ⓜ Sagrada
Família. This "meat bar" specializes in carnivore-centric
snacks, such as oxtail cannelloni and tacos (all priced around
€7) made with specific kinds of beef, such as Nebraska Black
Angus and Charolais. Chef/owner Dani Lechuga (whose
surname ironically means "lettuce") is from a family of
butchers and meat experts so the (sometimes literally) raw
materials here are first-rate. No reservations. €€
Casa Rafols Ronda de Sant Pere 74 ⓦ casarafols.com;
ⓜ Arc de Triomf. For over a century, Rafols was a celebrated
ferreteria (ironmonger's), and still has the elaborate
wrought-iron facade to show it. These days it's a slick
combination of art deco cocktail bar and lively restaurant,
serving Mediterranean dishes in a high-ceilinged space or
at tables outside on the pavement. €€€
Firo Tast Avda Gaudí 83 ⓦ grupfiro.com; ⓜ Sant Pau
Dos de Maig. Three *Firo* food businesses cluster together
here; the superb Chocofiro chocolatiers is flanked by *El
Petit Firo* (a quality tapas bar) and *Firo Tast*, a sit-down
restaurant. Together they form a bright spot in a street full
of mediocre tourist restaurants. *Firo Tast* serves a solid set
menu of Catalan classics for €16. €€
Gorria C/Diputació 421 ⓦ restaurantegorria.com;
ⓜ Monumental. This traditional family-owned restaurant

serves simply cooked Basque cuisine, like *pochas de
Sanguesa* (a sort of white-bean stew), wood-grilled
lamb, clams in salsa verde or monkfish stuffed with
smoked salmon. Prices are on the high side (€70 a head
and upwards), and it can feel a little dated, but this is good-
quality regional Spanish cooking. €€€
Granja Petitbo Passeig de Sant Joan 82 ⓦ granjapetitbo.
com; ⓜ Tetuan. The long, tree-lined Passeig de Sant Joan is
now a hub of cool cafés and restaurants, but Granja Petitbo
was one of the first to herald a turnaround in the fortunes of
this neighbourhood – a friendly, shabby-chic place for coffee,
brunch or lunch, with a handful of tables outside. €€
Parking Pizza Passeig de Sant Joan 56 ⓦ parkingpizza.
com; ⓜ Tetuan. Housed in a former garage (hence the
name) this is a vast operation, packed every night, with long
communal tables and elbow-to-elbow dining. The pizzas,
though, are truly excellent, as are the starters and salads (the
red quinoa with avocado and a poached egg is a favourite). €
La Taquería Ptge. del Font 5 ⓦ lataqueria.eu;
ⓜ Sagrada Família. When it comes to Mexican food in
Europe, throwing the word "authentic" around can get
you in trouble with the purists, but in this case, it's an apt
description for this fun little restaurant's offerings: the
tangy *tacos al pastor*, savoury *sopa Azteca* and fresh-made
guacamole are all hits (€7–11). €

GRÀCIA SEE MAP PAGE 129

CAFÉS
Deliziosa Gelateria Italiana Pl. de la Revolució 2
ⓦ gelateriaitalianadeliziosa.com; ⓜ Fontana. The place
to go for real handmade Italian ice cream, and a stroll
around a pretty square in the sun – expect queues at peak
times and then more waiting as you struggle to choose from
the twenty-odd flavours. €
★ **La Nena** C/Ramon y Cajal 36 ⓦ la-nena-chocolate-
café.business.site; ⓜ Fontana. First and foremost, it's the
food at "the little girl" that's the main attraction – lovely
home-made cakes, plus waffles, quiches, organic ice cream,
squeezed juices and the like. But parents love it too, as it's
very child-friendly, from the changing mats in the loos to
the little seats, games and puzzles. €€

TAPAS BARS AND RESTAURANTS
L'Arrosseria Xàtiva C/Torrent d'en Vidalet 26 ⓦ grup
xativa.com; ⓜ Joanic. Rice done right is hard to find. The
microwaved and burnt offerings that pass for paella in most
city restaurants enrage proud Valencians, who hate to see
their heritage abused in the name of profit margins. For the
real thing, try one of the two *Xàtiva* restaurants (the other is
in Les Corts). There's also the full range of Catalan rice dishes
including creamy *arròs melós*, all made with fresh stock and
organic vegetables. The *menú del dia* (€22) is a great way to
fill up before exploring the area. €€€
★ **Cal Boter** C/Tordera 62 ⓦ restaurantcalboter.com;
ⓜ Verdaguer. This old-school neighbourhood bistro is
perpetually packed with people of every age. Survive the

15

TOP 5 DATE NIGHTS

Carmina See page 186
El Salón See page 183
Fonda España See page 185
Els Pescadors See page 189
La Viñatería del Call See page 184

queue (or arrive when it opens) and you'll be rewarded with rib-sticking stews, meatballs, snails and other classic dishes at knockdown prices. The lunch menu is €15 and a la carte main courses range from €8 to €16. Decades of customers' letters on the walls are evidence of *Cal Boter*'s beloved local status. €€

Flash Flash C/Granada del Penedès 25 ⓦflashflash barcelona.com; ⓂDiagonal. A classic 1970s survivor, *Flash Flash* does *tortillas* (€8–10) served any time you like, any way you like, from plain and simple to elaborately stuffed, with sweet ones for dessert. If that doesn't grab you, there's a menu of salads, steaks, burgers and fish. Either way, you'll love the original white leatherette booths and monotone "models-with-cameras" cutouts – very Austin Powers. €

Goliard C/Progrés ⓦgoliard.cat; ⓂDiagonal. Smart but casual *Goliard* offers a pared-down dining experience in a contemporary foodie bistro that looks like it should cost three times as much. Dishes are of-the-moment – shitake

croquetas with wasabi mayonnaise, grilled octopus with pancetta and creamed potato. The weekday lunch is a really good deal too (€17.80). €€

Nou Candanchu Pl. Vila de Gràcia 9 ☎932 377 362; ⓂFontana. Good for lunch on a sunny day or a leisurely night out on a budget, when you can sit beneath the clocktower in the ever-entertaining local square. There's a wide menu – tapas and hot sandwiches, but also steak and eggs, steamed clams and mussels, or cod and hake cooked plenty of different ways. It's managed by an affable bunch of young guys, and there's lots of choice for €12–18. €€

La Pepita C/Còrsega 343 ⓦlapepitabcn.com; ⓂDiagonal/Verdaguer. There's usually a queue out the door, and deservedly so. The tapas, such as carabinero prawn croquettes with romesco sauce or smoked aubergine fritters with goat's cheese, honey and apples, are fantastic, and the atmosphere is chatty and convivial. Hundreds of "love notes" scrawled by customers on the white-tiled walls hint at its popularity. €€

San Kil C/Legalitat 22 ⓦinstagram.com/restaurante_san_kil; ⓂJoanic. There's no shortage of Korean restaurants in Barcelona, but *San Kil* has a place in the hearts of locals as the original. Family-run and super friendly, it's a no-nonsense affair, but the bulgogi (spicy beef wrapped in lettuce leaves), dumplings and seafood omelette are all excellent. €€

LES CORTS, PEDRALBES AND SARRIÀ-SANT GERVASI   SEE MAP PAGE 134

TAPAS BARS AND RESTAURANTS

★ **Bar Tomás** C/Major de Sarrià 49, Sarrià ⓦeltomas desarria.com; FGC Sarrià. The best *patatas bravas* in the city? Everyone points you here, to this utterly unassuming, white-formica-table bar in the 'burbs (12min by train from Pl. Catalunya FGC station) for a taste of their spicy fried potatoes with garlic mayo and *salsa picante*. €

Can Punyetes C/Marià Cubí 189, Sant Gervasi ⓦcan punyetes.com; FGC Muntaner. Traditional – well, since 1981 anyway – grillhouse-tavern that offers slick city diners a taste of older times. There are simple salads and tapas, and open grills turning out sausage, lamb chops, chicken and pork, accompanied by grilled country bread, white beans and chargrilled potato halves. Prices are very reasonable

(almost everything is under €10) and locals love it. €

Casa Fernández C/Santaló 46, Sant Gervasi ⓦcasa fernandez.com; FGC Muntaner. The long kitchen hours are a boon for the bar-crawlers in this neck of the woods. It's a contemporary place featuring elegant tapas such as tuna tartare as well as market cuisine. Most dishes are in the range €12 to €20. €€

★ **Fragments Cafè** Pl. de la Concórdia 12 ⓦfragments cafe.com; ⓂLes Corts. A classy yet casual bistro popular with locals for its fresh, classic food (*patatas bravas* are a speciality) that's served in the charming dining room or in the shaded garden. Main courses include salmon tartar, grilled sea bass and glazed beef cheek, and there's a list of hot and cold tapas. €€

TIBIDABO   SEE MAP PAGE 142

RESTAURANT

★ **El Asador de Aranda** Avda. del Tibidabo 31 ⓦasador dearanda.com; FGC Avgda. Tibidabo. There are a number of *Asadors* in town but this is the crown jewel. A multilevel

modernista mansion with an opulent interior is the setting for simple but succulent rare-breed lamb roasted in clay ovens. Wash it down with a bottle of good red wine then have a coffee on the rooftop terrace with views over the city. €€€

A CAFÉ IN BARCELONA

Drinking and nightlife

Whatever you're looking for from a night out, you'll find it somewhere in
Barcelona – bohemian boozer, underground club, cocktail bar, summer dance
palace, techno temple, Irish pub or designer bar, you name it. Some of the finest
places for a drink are cafés and tapas bars (see page 181), and undoubtedly
one of the city's greatest pleasures is to pull up a pavement seat and watch
the world go by. However, the bar scene proper operates at a different pace,
and with a different set of rules. Specialist bars in Barcelona include *cellers/
bodegas* (specializing in wine), *cerveseries* (beer), *xampanyeries* (champagne
and cava) and *cocteleries* (cocktails). Best known of the city's nightlife haunts
are its hip designer bars, while there's a stylish club and music scene fuelled by
a potent mix of resident and guest DJs, local bands and visiting superstars.

Generally, the bars and clubs in the old town are a mixture of traditional tourist haunts, party-time Irish bars, local drinking places and fashionista hangouts. In the **Barri Gòtic**, it's the streets around Plaça Reial and Plaça George Orwell that see most of the action, while in **La Ribera**, Passeig del Born is the main focus, though a hip scene is developing in the neighbouring *barri* of **Sant Pere** too. **El Raval has seen a proliferation of bars in recent years** – the coolest places are found in the upper part of the neighbourhood near the MACBA (especially along C/Joaquín Costa). You can still find tradition (and sleaze) further south, closer to the port, in the surviving bars of the old Barri Xinès, while over in the newly touristed neighbourhood of **Poble Sec** there's an increasing number of mellow bars, music venues and late-night haunts and clubs. **Port Olímpic** used to be a mainstream summer-night playground for raucous tourists, with scores of bars, but recent attempts to make the area more dignified mean many have been closed down, with just a handful of seaside clubs remaining. Up in **Gràcia**, there's a lively bar scene and several offbeat music joints. Meanwhile, the bulk of the big-name warehouse and designer venues are in peripheral areas such as **Poblenou** and **Les Corts**, while also high on the list of any seasoned clubber is La Terrrazza in the tourist fantasy village of **Poble Espanyol** in Montjuïc.

As for music, major bands include Barcelona on their tours, playing either at sports stadium venues or at the city's bigger clubs. The city's pretty hot on **jazz**, **Latin** and **blues**, while **folk**, **roots** and **world music** aficionados need to scour the club gig lists for home-grown and touring talent alike. All sorts of city venues, museums, galleries and institutions have **live music programmes** too – CaixaForum is particularly well regarded, while the books-and-music chain **FNAC** (⊚fnac.es) sponsors small gigs and events at its stores at Plaça de Catalunya, L'Illa Diagonal and Glòries.

ESSENTIALS

What's on Local listings magazine *Time Out Barcelona* (⊚timeout.cat) covers current openings, hours and club nights, and most bars, cafés, boutiques and music stores carry flyers and free magazines containing news and reviews. For the Barcelona music scene, check out the website ⊚atiza.com.

Tickets Tickets for major gigs are available from the main ticket agencies (see page 38); in addition, there's a concert ticket desk in the Pl. Catalunya FNAC store (⊚Catalunya), while the music shops along C/Tallers (just off La Rambla; ⊚Catalunya) also sell gig tickets.

Opening hours Most bars stay open until 2am, or 3am at weekends, while clubs tend not to open much before midnight, only barely getting started by 2am and staying open until 5am, or even later at weekends. Unlike restaurants, bars and clubs generally stay open throughout August.

Admission charges Some clubs are free before a certain time, usually around midnight. Otherwise, expect to pay €10–20 for club admission, though this usually includes your first drink (if there is free entry, don't be surprised to find that there's a minimum drinks charge of anything up to €10). Tickets for gigs run from €20 to €50, depending on the act, though there are cheaper gigs (€5–20) almost every night of the year at a variety of smaller clubs and bars.

LA RAMBLA SEE MAP PAGE 42

BARS

Boadas Cocktails C/Tallers 1 ⊚boadascocktails. com; ⊚Catalunya. Inside Barcelona's oldest cocktail bar, tuxedoed bartenders shake, stir and pour classic drinks for a well-dressed crowd against an Art Deco background. It's a timeless place that's a perfect start for a sophisticated night on the town.

Bosc de les Fades Ptge. de la Banca 5 ⊚museocerabcn. com; ⊚Drassanes. Tucked away in an alley off La Rambla, beside the entrance to the wax museum, the "Forest of the Fairies" is festooned with gnarled plaster tree trunks, hanging branches, fountains and stalactites. It's a bit cheesy and the service isn't the best, but tourists love to huddle in the grottoes with a cocktail or two.

La Cazalla La Rambla 25 ⊚lacazalla.com; ⊚Drassanes. A historic remnant of the old days, the hole-in-the-wall *Cazalla* (under the arch, at the beginning of C/Arc del Teatre) first opened its hatch in 1912. It was closed for some years, but it's now back in business offering stand-up coffees, beers and shots to an assorted clientele of locals, cops, streetwalkers and the occasional stray tourist.

BARRI GÒTIC

SEE MAP PAGE 48

BARS

★ **L'Ascensor** C/Bellafila 3 ❼933 185 347; ⓜ Jaume I. Sliding, antique wooden elevator doors announce the entrance to "The Lift", but it's no theme bar – just an easy-going local hangout, great for a late-night drink.

Milans Cocktail Bar C/Milans 7 ❼639 426 613; ⓜ Drassanes. Hidden down a bendy alley, this isn't much more than a hacked-out room in an old Gothic Quarter building, cocktail bar inside, couple of sofas outside, but it works – helped by some wacky art displays, a great soundtrack (Siouxsie to Roxy Music) and one-offs like pop-up vintage clothes sales.

★ **Milk** C/Gignàs 21 ⓦ milkbarcelona.com; ⓜ Jaume I. Irish-owned bar and bistro that's carved a real niche as a welcoming neighbourhood hangout. Decor is that of a millionaire's drawing room, with its sofas, cushions and antique chandeliers. Get there any time before 4pm for the famously relaxed brunch, or there's dinner (and cocktails every night to a cool soundtrack).

Oviso C/Arai 5, Pl. George Orwell ❼933 043 726; ⓜ Drassanes. Holding a mirror on to the neighbourhood, the *Oviso* fits right in with the scruffy urban square outside – a shabby-chic mural-clad café-bar, formerly an adult cinema. There's a sunny *terrassa*, and the salads and sandwiches are good too, available from breakfast onwards.

★ **Zim** C/Dagueria 20 ❼934 126 548; ⓜ Jaume I. Katherine and co-owner Francesc offer up this tiny, hole-in-the-wall tasting bar for selected wines from boutique Spanish producers. For a soothing glass or two accompanied by farmhouse cheese, wonderful cured meats from the Pyrenees and artisan-made bread, you really can't beat it – and closing time is often somewhat flexible if you're in the mood for more wine.

CLUBS AND LIVE MUSIC

★ **Harlem Jazz Club** C/Comtessa de Sobradiel 8 ⓦ harlemjazzclub.es; ⓜ Jaume I. For many years *the* hot place for jazz, where every style gets an airing, from African and gypsy to flamenco and fusion. There are two shows a night; it's best to get advance tickets for the second spot.

Jamboree Pl. Reial 17 ⓦ masimas.com/jamboree; ⓜ Liceu. They don't get the big jazz names here that they used to, but the nightly gig still pull in the crowds, while the wild Monday night WTF jazz, funk and hip-hop jam session (from 8pm) is a city fixture. Stay on for the club, which kicks in after midnight and you get funky sounds until the small hours.

Karma Pl. Reial 10 ⓦ karmadisco.com; ⓜ Liceu. A stalwart of the scene since 1978, this old-school studenty basement place can get claustrophobic at times. Sounds are indie, Britpop and US college, while a lively crowd gathers at the square-side bar and *terrassa* which is open from 6pm.

La Macarena C/Nou de Sant Francesc 5 ⓦ macarenaclub. com; ⓜ Drassanes. Once a place where flamenco tunes were offered up to La Macarena, the Virgin of Seville – now a tiny, heaving temple to all things electro.

★ **Sidecar** Pl. Reial 7 ⓦ sidecar.es; ⓜ Liceu. The hippest concert space in the old town – pronounced "See-day-car" – has nightly gigs and DJs that champion rock, indie, roots, electronica and fusion acts.

16

EL RAVAL

SEE MAP PAGE 62

BARS

Betty Ford's C/Joaquín Costa 56 ⓦ bettyfordsbcn.com; ⓜ Universitat. With a vibe somewhere between a student lounge and a beach bar, *Betty's* is a bouncy place full of youngsters sipping colourful cocktails and cold Australian beer. Deal with the late-night munchies by getting to grips with their famed burger menu.

★ **Casa Almirall** C/Joaquín Costa 33 ⓦ casaalmirall. com; ⓜ Universitat. Dating from 1860, Barcelona's oldest bar is a *modernista* design classic – check out the doors, counter and stupendous glittering bar. Not too young, not too loud, and always good for a late-night drink.

La Confitería C/Sant Pau 128 ⓦ confiteria.cat; ⓜ Paral·lel. This one-time bakery and confectioner's – featuring a carved wood bar, faded tile floor, murals, antique chandeliers and mirrored cabinets – is now a popular bar and meeting point. It's a handy stop-off on the way to a night out in Poble Sec.

Fàbrica Moritz Ronda de Sant Antoni 41 ⓦ moritz.com; ⓜ Sant Antoni/Universitat. Cultural centre, *cervesería*, museum and more all come together in French architect Jean Nouvel's gorgeous revamp of the Catalan brewer's nineteenth-century factory. An on-site microbrewery supplies the beer, while star chef Jordi Vilà directs the various gastronomic spaces here.

La Llibertària C/Tallers 48 ⓦ tabernaycafetin.es/la-llibertaria; ⓜ Universitat. Run by an anthropologist and historian, *La Llibertària* is part bar, part museum, its walls covered in memorabilia from the Spanish Civil War and the

TOP 5 HISTORIC BARS

Casa Almirall See page 197
La Confitería See page 197
Dry Martini See page 200
Marsella See page 198
Velódromo See page 201

HERE FOR THE BEER?

Until recently, **beer** (*cervesa* in Catalan, *cerveza* in Spanish) in Barcelona meant lager, and only lager, but a growing interest in artisan beers, craft brews and foreign imports means many bars now offer a wider choice and there's been a surge in microbreweries. Beer is brewed on the premises in **Garage Beer Co.** in the Eixample (see page 200), and in Gràcia at **La Cervesera Artesana** (see page 201), Barcelona's original brew-pub. Another top spot is the absolutely stunning microbrewery **Fàbrica Moritz** (see page 197) in Raval. For thirty taps of local and international beers plus quality tapas and burgers, try **BierCaB** (see page 200). There are also a few pioneering bars serving a decent handcrafted beer – standouts are the Asian tapas joint **Mosquito** (see page 187) and **Ale&Hop** (see page 198) in Sant Pere, and Poble Sec's beer-and-music bar **Cervecería Jazz** (see page 200). The city is also home to some excellent artisan beer festivals, including the **Barcelona Beer Festival** (ⓦ barcelonabeerfestival.com), held over three days each March (the venue varies from year to year), which has proved wildly popular and now attracts thousands of visitors and brewers, and **La Fira del Poblenou** (ⓦ lafiradelpoblenou.com) in July.

anarchist Barcelona of the 1920s and '30s. Service is friendly and the tapas are good.

Marmalade C/Riera Alta 4–6 ⓦ marmaladebarcelona.com; ⓜ Sant Antoni. A hugely glam face-lift for the old Muebles Navarro furniture store has gone for big, church-like spaces and a backlit Art Deco bar that resembles a high altar. Cocktails, bistro meals and gourmet burgers pull in a relaxed dine-and-lounge crowd, and there's a popular weekend brunch too. If you like the style, give the more informal Barri Gòtic sister bar, *Milk* (see page 197), a whirl as well.

★ **Marsella** C/Sant Pau 65 ⓦ facebook.com/pesca saladabar; ⓜ Liceu. Authentic, atmospheric 1930s bar – named after the French port of Marseilles – where absinthe is the drink of choice. It featured in Woody Allen's *Vicky Cristina Barcelona*, so expect a spirited mix of film fans, oddball locals and young dudes, all looking for a slice of the old Barri Xinès.

★ **Pesca Salada** C/Cera 32 ☎ 686 265 309; ⓜ Sant Antoni. This former fish market turned gin haven turns up the charm with a cleverly executed (and just subtle enough) under-the-sea theme. It's an intimate corner spot with good music, lovingly crafted cocktails and nibbles like *montaditos* (helpful for maintaining one's sea legs as the night goes on).

Resolis C/Riera Baixa 22 ⓦ resolisbar.com; ⓜ Sant

Antoni. A decaying, century-old bar turned into a cool hangout with decent tapas. The owners didn't do much – a lick of paint, polish the panelling, patch up the brickwork – but now punters spill out of the door on to a street famous for secondhand clothes shops and a good time is had by all.

CLUBS AND LIVE MUSIC

23 Robadors C/Robador 23 ⓦ facebook.com/robadors23; ⓜ Liceu. The tapas are lukewarm but the live jazz, blues and flamenco performances in this underground bar are red hot. Listen free from the bar or pay to sit near the stage. It gets packed quickly, so arrive early or sharpen your elbows.

La Concha C/Guàrdia 14 ⓦ laconchadelraval.com; ⓜ Drassanes. The Arab–flamenco fusion throws up a great atmosphere, worth braving the slightly dodgy area for. It's a kitsch, LGBTQ+-friendly joint, dedicated to the "incandescent presence" of Sara Montiel, queen of song and cinema (and icon of the Spanish LGBTQ+ community), with uninhibited dancing by tourists and locals alike.

★ **Moog** C/l'Arc del Teatre 3 ⓦ masimas.com/moog; ⓜ Drassanes. It's tiny, but one of the most influential clubs around for electronic sounds, playing techno, electro, drum'n' bass and trance to a cool but up-for-it crowd. The bigger-name international DJs tend to play Wednesday nights.

SANT PERE AND LA RIBERA

SEE MAP PAGE 70

BARS

★ **Ale&Hop** C/Basses de Sant Pere 10, Sant Pere ⓦ facebook.com/aleandhop; ⓜ Urquinaona. Consider yourself a beer geek? Then *Ale&Hop* (pronounced "Al-eh-UP") is your kind of bar. Ten rotating taps pour artisanal beers in all styles (porters, stouts, lagers, gluten free) with names like "Dark Alliance" and "Sex-A-Pils". There's also a large selection of bottled beer, and some they've brewed themselves).

★ **Casa Paco** C/Allada Vermell 10, Sant Pere ☎ 935 073

719; ⓜ Jaume I. Sant Pere's signature bar is this tiny bar with ample tables under the trees, and if you can't get a table here try one of several other alfresco bars down the traffic-free boulevard. Meanwhile, a list of tapas, along with the associated *Pizza Paco* across the way (also with its own terrace) means you don't have to go anywhere else for dinner.

Collage C/Consellers 4 ⓦ collagecocktailbar.com; ⓜ Jaume I. A stylish vintage place with a relaxed, pleasant atmosphere. The knowledgeable bartenders will mix you a creative drink and offer insightful advice on mixing. If that piques your interest you can even go to their cocktail-making class for a well-spent afternoon.

Marlowe C/Rec 24 ⓦ marlowe.bar; ⓜ Barceloneta. There's a slightly noir atmosphere in this small, elegant cocktail bar – yes, the bar is named after the famous Chandlerian character. There is no set drink menu, just talk to the creative bartenders and their professional hands will mix something just for you.

Mudanzas C/Vidrería 15, La Ribera ⓦ barmudanzas. com; ⓜ Barceloneta. A recent change in ownership means that this much beloved local haunt is now popular with a young, international, cocktail crowd but during the day it's still a relatively peaceful place for a beer off the main drag.

La Vinya del Senyor Pl. de Santa María 5, La Ribera ⓦ lavinyadelsenyor.es; ⓜ Jaume I. A great wine bar with front-row seats on to the lovely church of Santa María del Mar. The wine list is really good – with a score available by the glass – and there are oysters, smoked salmon and other

> ## TOP 5 MUSIC BARS
> **El Col·lectionista** See page 202
> **Heliogàbal** See page 202
> **JazzMan** See page 201
> **La Garrafa dels Beatles** See page 202
> **Tinta Roja** See page 200
> **Vinilo** See page 201

classy tapas available.

CLUB
Magic Pg. Picasso 40 ⓦ magic-club.net; ⓜ Barceloneta. A Barcelona classic that's been rocking out since the mid-1970s. While first and foremost a rock 'n' roll club, *Magic* doesn't take itself too seriously. The usual suspects (Ramones, AC/DC and Iggy Pop) are played alongside hits from the likes of the Beastie Boys, the Violent Femmes and more.

PORT VELL AND BARCELONETA   SEE MAP PAGE 82

BAR
★ **Can Paixano (La Xampanyeria)** C/Reina Cristina 7, Port Vell ⓦ canpaixano.com; ⓜ Barceloneta. A must on everyone's itinerary is this backstreet joint with attached shop where the drink of choice – all right, the only drink – is cava (Catalan champagne). Don't go thinking sophistication

– it might come in traditional champagne saucers (the sort of thing Dean Martin used to stack in a pyramid and then pour wine over), but this is a counter-only joint where there's fizz, tapas and sausage butties and that's your lot. Who could want more?

16

PORT OLÍMPIC AND POBLENOU   SEE MAP PAGE 86

BAR
Balius C/Pujades 196 ⓦ baliusbar.com; ⓜ Poblenou. The amount of drinking and eating options in Poblenou has not kept pace with the area's sudden popularity among young loft-dwelling types, and consequently *Balius* is rammed every night. Set in a converted pharmacy, it's a handsome space for cocktails and craft beer.

CLUBS AND LIVE MUSIC
CDLC Pg. Marítim 32, Port Olímpic ⓦ cdlcbarcelona. com; ⓜ Ciutadella-Vila Olímpica. With a clientele of A-list

celebs, football players, well-heeled tourists and local rich kids, this beautiful-person lounge-club hangout is for those who want to dine, dance and kick back in like-minded company.

Sala Razzmatazz C/Pamplona 88, Poblenou ⓦ sala razzmatazz.com; ⓜ Bogatell. *Razzmatazz* hosts the biggest in-town rock gigs (the concert hall capacity is 3,000), while at weekends the former warehouse turns into "five clubs in one", spinning indie, rock, pop, techno, electro, retro and more in variously named music bars like "The Loft", "Pop Bar" or "Lolita".

MONTJUÏC   SEE MAP PAGE 92

BAR
La Caseta del Migdia Mirador del Migdia ⓦ lacaseta. org; cable car (Telefèric de Montjuïc) or bus #150 to Castell de Montjuïc, then follow signs to "Mirador" (15min walk). It's cooler in every sense up on the heights of Montjuïc, as a welcome summer breeze and chill-out sounds entice visitors to the panoramic, open-air bar of *La Caseta*, in the woods around the back of the castle.

CLUB
La Terrrazza Poble Espanyol, Avgda. Francesc Ferrer i Guàrdia ⓦ laterrrazza.com; ⓜ Espanya. Open-air summer club that's *the* place to be in Barcelona. Non-stop dance, house and techno, though don't get there until at least 3am, and be prepared for the style police.

POBLE SEC
SEE MAP PAGE 102

BARS

Celler Cal Marino C/Margarit 54 ⓦcalmarino.com; ⓜPoble Sec. The wines in the barrels are to take away at knockdown prices, and you can drink a *copa* for around two euros, but there's also a more sophisticated wine selection available in this cavernous, stone-walled tavern. Add cheap tapas and a jolly neighbourhood crowd, and there are more than enough reasons to stop by.

Cervecería Jazz C/Margarit 43 ⓦcerveceriajazz.com; ⓜPoble Sec. Grab a stool at the carved bar and shoot the breeze over a Catalan craft beer. It's an amiable joint with great music, jazz to reggae, and locals swear that the burgers are the best in town.

La Tieta C/Blai 1 ⓦbodegalatieta.com; ⓜParal·lel. Small but perfectly formed, "The Aunt" is a cool drinks and tapas place, with selected wines served by the glass, an open window on to the street and just enough room inside for a dozen or so good friends.

★**Xixbar** C/Rocafort 19 ⓦxixbar.com; ⓜPoble Sec. "Chicks" is an old *granja* (milk bar) – which explains the milk pail and big cow photos – turned candlelit, but completely unstuffy, cocktail bar. Gin's the big drink here (they claim over one hundred varieties), and they mix stonking gin cocktails and even have their own specialist gin shop on site, with tasting courses and other activities.

CLUBS AND LIVE MUSIC

★**Maumau** C/Fontrodona 33 ⓦmaumauunderground. com; ⓜParal·lel. If you're really in the know, then *Maumau* is one of your first weekend ports of call – a great underground lounge-club, cultural centre and chill-out space with comfy sofas, nightly film and video projections, exhibitions and a roster of guest DJs playing deep, soulful grooves. Strictly speaking it's a private club, but they tend to let foreign visitors in for free – if you do join, the "Carnet Maumau" (Maumau Card) gives you all sorts of discounts and deals at hot venues right across the city.

Sala Apolo C/Nou de la Rambla 113 ⓦsala-apolo.com; ⓜParal·lel. Old-time ballroom turned hip concert venue with gigs on two stages (local acts to big names) and an eclectic series of club nights with names to reckon with (Nasty Mondays, Crappy Tuesdays etc). Sounds range far and wide, from punk or Catalan rumba to the weekend's long-running techno/electro Nitsa Club (ⓦnitsa.com). "CupCake Night" on Thursdays is highly camp, with an Abba- and Village People-heavy playlist.

Tinta Roja C/Creu dels Molers 17 ⓦtintaroja.cat; ⓜPoble Sec. More of an experience than most bars, this highly theatrical tango bar features a succession of over-the-top crimson rooms leading to a stage at the back. There's cabaret and live music (folk, rock, world music) – often free – a couple of nights a week.

DRETA DE L'EIXAMPLE
SEE MAP PAGE 106

BAR

★**Nits d'estiu: Jazz a la Pedrera** La Pedrera, Pg. de Gràcia 92, ⓦlapedrera.com; ⓜDiagonal. The city's most exciting pop-up bar has a regular summer season on the extraordinary Gaudí roof terrace at La Pedrera (see page 111). Performers range from jazz trios to chamber ensembles.

CLUB

City Hall Rambla de Catalunya 2–4 ⓦcityhallbarcelona. com; ⓜCatalunya. This medium-sized club, just off the Plaça Catalunya, thrums to techno and electronica most nights of the week, attracting a decent roster of local and international DJs. Earlier in the evening there are live flamenco shows (ⓦflamencobarcelonacity.com).

ESQUERRA DE L'EIXAMPLE
SEE MAP PAGE 116

BARS

Aire Chicas C/Diputació 233 ⓦarenadisco.com; ⓜPasseig de Gràcia. The hottest, most stylish lesbian bar in town is a relaxed place for a drink and a dance to pop, house and retro sounds. Gay men are welcome too.

BierCaB C/Muntaner 55 ⓦbiercab.com; ⓜUniversitat. Thirty international craft beers on tap, updated constantly, means that there's an ale to slake all thirsts here. The staff are all enthusiastic and well informed, and happy to let you try before you buy. Soak it all up with some of the hearty Wagyu beef burgers or tapas and pick up a bottle of your favourite to take home from the adjoining shop.

★**Dry Martini** C/Aribau 166 ⓦdrymartiniorg.com; ⓜProvença. White-jacketed bartenders, dark wood and brass fittings, a self-satisfied air – it could only be the city's legendary uptown cocktail bar, regularly ranked among the best in the world. To be fair, though, no one mixes drinks better and the regulars aren't the one-dimensional business types you might expect. There's also a mysterious hideaway back-room restaurant, *Speakeasy*, where you can play at being Al Capone.

★**Garage Beer Co.** C/Consell de Cent 261 ⓦgarage beer.co; ⓜUniversitat. This friendly brewpub was an early fixture on Barcelona's "beer mile" – the craft beer bar-filled area that's boomed in recent years. There are no frills, just great ales, simple snacks, wooden benches and a glass wall onto the microbrewery out back.

★ **Velódromo** C/Muntaner 213 🌐 barvelodromo.com; Ⓜ Hospital Clinic. This Art Deco gem, with a lofty, *Parisien* feel, a swooping staircase and a gleaming bar, is ideal for swish drinks and cocktails. There is an almost round-the-clock menu of excellent tapas and bistro dishes, making it a favourite of early risers – and late-to-bedders – in search of quality snacks.

TOP 5 WINE BARS

Can Paixano See page 199
Celler Cal Marino See page 200
La Tieta See page 200
La Vinya del Senyor See page 199
Zim See page 197

CLUBS AND LIVE MUSIC

Antilla BCN Latin Club C/Aragó 141 🌐 antillasalsa. com; Ⓜ Hospital CliniC/Urgell. Latin and Caribbean tunes galore – rumba, son, salsa, merengue, mambo, you name it – for out-and-out good-time dancing. There are live bands, killer cocktails and dance classes most nights.

Luz de Gas C/Muntaner 246 🌐 luzdegas.com; Ⓜ Diagonal. Former ballroom venue popular with a slightly older crowd, with live music (rock, blues, soul, jazz and covers) every night around midnight. Foreign acts appear regularly, too, mainly jazz-blues types but also old soul acts and up-and-coming rockers.

Quilombo C/Aribau 149 🌐 quilombo.com; Ⓜ Diagonal. Unpretentious music bar – just a bare box of a room really – that's rolled the years since 1971, featuring live guitarists, Latin American bands and a clientele that joins in enthusiastically, maracas in hand.

SAGRADA FAMÍLIA & GLORÌES SEE MAP PAGE 120

CLUBS AND LIVE MUSIC

JazzMan C/Roger de Flor 238, 🌐 jazzmanbcn.com; Ⓜ Verdaguer. Everything you'd want from a cosy jazz club: low lights, free live music, good drinks and an intimate vibe. When there's no-one on stage, expect to hear classics from JazzMan's impeccable vinyl and CD collection.

Pipa Club C/Santa Eulàlia 21 🌐 bpipaclub.wixsite.com/ bpipaclub3; Ⓜ Verdaguer. Barcelona's pipe-smokers' club abandoned its clandestine-but-known-to-everyone home in Plaça Reial in 2015. Its new, wood-panelled home is less crowded but even more classy; there is, as you'd expect, a pipe-smoking room, but also cultural events and live jazz, blues, soul, swing and world music sessions around the Sherlock Holmes bar.

GRÀCIA SEE MAP PAGE 129

BARS

Bobby Gin C/Francisco Giner 47 🌐 bobbygin.com; Ⓜ Diagonal. The sign near the bar says "*El gintonic perfecto no existe*" (the perfect gin and tonic does not exist). Perhaps. But the sizeable G&Ts here come very, very close.

Café del Sol Pl. del Sol 16, ☎ 932 371 448; Ⓜ Fontana. The grandaddy of the Pl. del Sol scene sees action day and night. On summer evenings, when the square is packed, there's not an outdoor table to be had, but even in winter this is a popular drinking den – the pub-like interior has a backroom and gallery, often rammed to the rafters.

★ **Canigó** Pl. de la Revolució 10 🌐 barcanigo.com; Ⓜ Fontana. Family-run neighbourhood bar now entering its third generation and second century. It's not much to look at, but the drinks are cheap and it's a real Gràcia institution, packed out at weekends with a young, hip and largely local crowd.

La Cervesera Artesana C/Sant Agustí 14 🌐 lacervesera. net; Ⓜ Diagonal. A score of identikit Irish pubs in town serve Guinness and other imported beers, but for real ale, Catalan style – including an own-brew stout – the city's original microbrewery is well worth a visit.

Elephanta C/Torrent d'En Vidalet 37 🌐 elephanta.cat; Ⓜ Joanic. This relaxed hideout with flea-market chairs and menus made from old album covers serves crisp mixed drinks (gin is the main attraction) in a chilled-out space that feels just like home.

★ **Vinilo** C/Matilde 2, 🌐 instagram.com/bar_vinil; Ⓜ Diagonal. A 1912 gramophone greets you at the entrance of this dimly lit music bar, but the playlist – all on vinyl as the name suggests – is a little more contemporary. Expect to hear anything from Massive Attack to Edith Piaf as you rub shoulders with local musicians, touring indie stars and hipsters.

Virreina Pl. de la Virreina 1 ☎ 934 153 209; Ⓜ Fontana. Another real Gràcia favourite, on one of the neighbourhood's prettiest squares, with a very popular summer *terrassa*. It's one of those places where you drop by for a quick drink and find yourself staying for hours.

CLUBS AND LIVE MUSIC

★ **Centre Artesà Tradicionàrius (CAT)** Trav. de Sant Antoni 6–8 🌐 tradicionarius.cat; Ⓜ Fontana. The best place in town for folk, traditional and world music by Catalan, Spanish and visiting performers, including some occasional big names. You can expect anything from

16

THE GIN AND TONIC CRAZE

In Barcelona, they don't let anything come between their gin and their tonic – not even the word "and". The *gintonic*, as it's known, has always been a favourite drink, but in recent years there's been a surge in bars specializing in the classic cocktail and its star ingredient, *ginebra*. **Bobby Gin** in Gràcia has some sixty varieties, **Pesca Salada** in El Raval stocks 54 kinds and **Xixbar**, which claims to be the first Barcelona bar specializing in gin, mixes it up with more than a hundred types. And the tonic component has not been forgotten, with bars pouring a dizzying array of premium varieties, from the regionally produced Tònica Catalana to those from Argentina, the UK and beyond. It's a refreshing trend worthy of glass-clinking ¡salut!

Basque bagpipes to Brazilian singers. There are also music and instrument workshops, while *CAT* sponsors all sorts of outreach concerts and festivals, including an annual international folk and traditional dance festival (Jan–April). Concerts usually at 9.30 or 10pm.

El Col·lectionista Torrent de les Flors 46 ⓜ Joanic. "The collector" offers 60s, 70s, 80s and 90s pop-and-rock nostalgia, in a cosy Gràcia setting. The live music is varied and there's room to dance if you get into the groove.

★ **Heliogàbal** C/Ramon y Cajal 80 ⓦ heliogabal.com; ⓜ Joanic. Not much more than a boiler room given a lick of paint, but filled with a cool, twenty-something crowd

here for the live poetry and music. Recent licensing issues have meant that they have only been able to host small, acoustic sessions, usually in the afternoons or early evening, but these are always special, intimate events. Admission is usually €3–10, depending on the act, and drinks aren't expensive.

Otto Zutz C/Lincoln 15 ⓦ ottozutz.com; FGC Gràcia. It first opened as a club in 1985 and has since lost some of its glam cachet, but this three-storey former textile factory still has a shedload of pretensions. The sounds are basically hip-hop, r'n'b and house, and with the right clothes and face, you're in.

LES CORTS, PEDRALBES AND SARRIÀ-SANT GERVASI   SEE MAP PAGE 134

BAR

Gimlet C/Santaló 46, Sant Gervasi ⓦ gimletbcn.com; FGC Muntaner. This favoured cocktail joint is especially popular in summertime, when the street-side tables offer a great vantage point for watching the party unfold. There are also two or three other late-opening bars on the same stretch.

CLUBS AND LIVE MUSIC

★ **Bikini** Avda. Diagonal 547, Les Corts ⓦ bikinibcn. com; ⓜ Les Corts/María Cristina. This traditional landmark of Barcelona nightlife (behind L'Illa shopping centre) offers

a regular diet of great indie, rock, roots and world gigs, followed by club sounds from house to Brazilian, according to the night.

La Garrafa dels Beatles C/Joan Güell 150, Les Corts ⓦ lagarrafadelsbeatles.com; ⓜ Plaça del Centre. Get back to the classics of 60s rock at Barcelona's only Beatles-themed pub. Locals and day-trippers come together to twist and shout along to the Fab Four's greatest hits, played live from 12.30pm onwards by co-owners Joan and Ricky. Check the website for other live shows here, which run (almost) eight days a week.

TIBIDABO   SEE MAP PAGE 142

BAR

Mirablau Pl. del Dr Andreu, Avda. Tibidabo ⓦ mirablau bcn.cat; FGC Avda. del Tibidabo then Tramvia Blau, or

taxi. This chic bar by the tram and funicular terminus has unbelievable city views. By day it's a great place for drinks, while at night it's more of an upmarket tapas and music joint.

PALAU DE LA MÚSICA CATALANA

Arts and culture

As you would expect from a city of its size, Barcelona has a busy arts and culture calendar – there will always be something worth catching, whether it's a contemporary dance performance, cabaret show or night at the opera. Classical and contemporary music, in particular, gets an airing in some stunning auditoriums, and while local theatre is less accessible for non-Catalan or -Spanish speakers, many cinemas show films in their original language. The city boasts a long tradition of innovative street and performance art, right down to the human statues plying their trade on La Rambla. Barcelona excels in the visual arts, too – from traditional exhibitions of paintings to contemporary photography or installation works – and dozens of arts centres and galleries put on varied shows throughout the year.

17

ESSENTIALS

Tickets and information A useful first stop for tickets and information is the Palau de la Virreina, La Rambla 99 (ticket counter daily noon–8pm; Ⓦbcn.cat/cultura; ⓂLiceu). Ticketmaster (Ⓦticketmaster.es), BCN Shop (Ⓦbcnshop. barcelonaturisme.com) and Eventbrite (Ⓦeventbrite.es) are the main advance booking agencies for music, theatre, cinema and exhibition tickets.

What's on The city council's Institute of Culture website, Ⓦlameva.barcelona.cat/barcelonacultura, is invaluable – it covers every aspect of art and culture in the city, with links to daily updated arts stories and a comprehensive calendar of events. Otherwise, the best listings magazine is *Time Out Barcelona* (Ⓦtimeout.cat), online or found in cafés, restaurants and around town.

CLASSICAL, CONTEMPORARY AND OPERA

Most of Barcelona's **classical** music concerts take place in the *modernista* Palau de la Música Catalana or at the purpose-built, contemporary L'Auditori, while **opera** is performed at its traditional home, the Gran Teatre del Liceu on La Rambla. Many of the city's churches, including the cathedral and Santa María del Mar, also host concerts and recitals, while other interesting venues holding concerts include the Palau Robert, FNAC Triangle at Pl. de Catalunya, CaixaForum, the Fundació Joan Miró and CCCB (these last two particularly for **contemporary** music). Notable **festivals** include the Festival de Barcelona Grec (July) and the Festa de la Música (June 21), while there are free concerts in Barcelona's parks each summer, the so-called Música als Parcs.

VENUES

★ **Ateneu Barcelonès** C/Canuda 6, Barri Gòtic Ⓦateneubcn.org; ⓂCatalunya. The 150-year-old Ateneu cultural association and library presents a variety of intellectually stimulating fare throughout the year, including conferences, film screenings and workshops, as well as concerts and recitals (from Baroque to contemporary), some of which take place in its verdant garden. Many events are for members only.

L'Auditori C/Lepant 150, Glòries Ⓦauditori.cat; ⓂMarina/Glòries. The city's main contemporary concert hall is home to the Orquestra Simfònica de Barcelona i Nacional de Catalunya (OBC), whose weekend concert season runs Oct–June. L'Auditori also puts on other orchestral and chamber works, jazz and world gigs and music for children and families, while it's the main venue for the annual Early Music festival. Under-26s with ID are eligible for discounts of up to fifty percent on tickets.

Casa Elizalde C/València 302, Dreta de l'Eixample Ⓦcasaelizalde.com; ⓂPasseig de Gràcia. Small-scale classical concerts and recitals, plus more offbeat

---

THE SARDANA – DANCING WITH CATALANS

If you're intrigued by what looks like a mass dance flash mob outside the cathedral, La Seu, chances are you've stumbled upon a performance of the Catalan national dance – the **sardana**. Its origins are obscure, though similar folk dances in the Mediterranean date back hundreds, if not thousands, of years. It was established in its present form during the mid-nineteenth-century Renaixença (Renaissance), when Catalan arts and culture flourished, and was so identified with expressions of national identity that public dancing of *sardanes* was banned under the Franco regime. Sometimes mocked elsewhere in Spain, Catalans claim it to be truly democratic – a circle-dance open to all, danced in ordinary clothes (though some wear espadrilles) with no restriction in age or number. The dancers join hands, heads held high, arms raised, and though it looks deceptively simple and sedate it follows a precise pattern of steps, with shifts in pace and rhythm signalled by the accompanying *cobla* (band) of brass and wind instruments. This features typically Catalan instruments like the *flabiol* (a type of flute), and both tenor and soprano oboes, providing the characteristic high-pitched music. A strict etiquette applies to prevent the circle being broken in the wrong place, or a breakdown in the steps, and some of the more serious adherents may not welcome an intrusion into their circle by well-meaning first-timers. But usually visitors are encouraged to join the dance, especially at festival times, when the *sardana* breaks out spontaneously in the city's squares and parks.

There are regular *sardana* dances held outside La Seu, in Plaça de la Seu (ⓂJaume I), every Sunday at 11.15am from February to July, and in the Plaça del Tibidabo every Saturday at 6pm from February to July. The **Federació Sardanista de Catalunya** (Ⓦportalsardanista.cat) also publishes a calendar of dances and events on its website.

contemporary performances, are held at the cultural centre, usually with free entry.

Gran Teatre del Liceu Ramblas 51–59 ⓦliceu barcelona.cat; ⓜLiceu. One of Europe's finest opera houses hosts a wide-ranging programme of opera and dance productions, plus other concerts and recitals. The season runs Sept–June. Make bookings well in advance by phone or online – sales for the next season go on general sale in mid-July.

★ **Palau de la Música Catalana** C/Palau de la Música 4-6, off C/Sant Pere Més Alt, Sant Pere ⓦpalaumusica. cat; ⓜUrquinaona. The extravagantly decorated Catalan concert hall is home to the Orfeó Català choral group and

TOP 5 CULTURE ON A BUDGET 17

L'Antic Teatre See page 207
Casa Elizalde See page 204
FilmoTeca See page 205
Sala Montjuïc See page 206
Tarantos See page 205

venue for concerts by the Orquestra Ciutat de Barcelona, among others, though there's a broad remit here – over a season you can catch anything, from *sardanes* to pop concerts. Concert season Sept–June.

DANCE

Barcelona is very much a contemporary dance city, with its own dedicated dance venue, Mercat de les Flors, as well as regular performances by regional, national and international artists and companies at theatre venues (see page 206) like the TNC, Teatre Lliure and Institut del Teatre – the latter, the city's theatre and dance school, has its own youth dance company, IT Dansa. Although its home is indisputably Andalucía, flamenco also has deep roots in and around Barcelona, courtesy of its *andaluz* immigrants – unless you're looking for a showy night out, the pricey, tourist-oriented *tablaos* (flamenco and dinner shows) are best passed up in favour of the smaller clubs and restaurants that put on performances. If you're here at the end of April, don't miss the wild flamenco shows and parties of the Feria de Abril de Catalunya, a ten-day **festival** held down at the Fòrum site (see page 213), and the De Cajón (see page 214) festival in winter (Jan–March).

DANCE VENUE

Mercat de les Flors C/Lleida 59, Montjuïc ⓦmercatflors.

cat; ⓜPoble Sec. The city's old flower market serves as the "national centre for movement arts", with dance the central focus of its varied programme – from Asian performance art to European contemporary dance.

FLAMENCO CLUBS

El Tablao de Carmen Poble Espanyol, Montjuïc ⓦtablao decarmen.com; ⓜEspanya. Despite the shamelessly touristy environs, the long-standing *tablao* in the Poble Espanyol is the real deal, sited in a replica Andalucian street and featuring a variety of flamenco styles from both seasoned performers and new talent. Deals include a drink or dinner, and advance reservations are essential.

★ **Tarantos** Pl. Reial 17, Barri Gòtic ⓦmasimas.com/ tarantos; ⓜLiceu. Some purists are sniffy about the experience, but for a cheap flamenco taster you can't beat *Tarantos* – a couple of rows of seats and a small bar in front of a stage where young singers, dancers and guitarists perform nightly. It's the sister club to jazz/dance club *Jamboree*, at the same address.

FILM

At most of the larger cinemas and multiplexes films are usually shown dubbed into Spanish or Catalan. However, several cinemas do show mostly **original-language** (*versión original* or V.O.) foreign films; the best are listed below. Tickets cost around €7–9, and most cinemas have one night (usually Mon or Wed) when entry is **discounted**, usually to around €5-6. Many cinemas also feature **late-night** screenings (*matinades o sessions golfo*) on Friday and Saturday nights, which begin at 12.30 or 1am. The city hosts several small film **festivals** throughout the year, including an international festival of independent short films, plus festivals devoted specifically to children, music, gastronomy, sports, animation, women, and gay and lesbian film. The Generalitat's FilmoTeca is often the venue for festival screenings. The sci-fi, horror and fantasy fest that is the Festival Internacional de Cinema de Fantàstic (ⓦsitgesfilmfestival.com) is held down the coast in nearby Sitges in October.

CINEMAS

★ **Cinema Maldà** C/Pi 5, Barri Gòtic ⓦcinemamalda. com, ⓜLiceu. Hidden away in a little shopping centre just up from Pl. del Pi, the Maldà is a great place for independent movies and festival winners (all in V.O.).

FilmoTeca Pl. Salvador Seguí 1–9, El Raval ⓦfilmoteca. cat; ⓜLiceu. Run by the Catalan government, the FilmoTeca shows two to five different films (often foreign language, and usually in V.O.) every day – the programme changes every couple of weeks, and themed seasons, classic films, retrospectives and obscure world cinema releases are its stock in trade. Tickets are just €4 per film, or there's a €20 pass allowing entry to ten films in one calendar year.

★ **Phenomena Experience** C/Sant Antoni María Claret, Sagrada Família & Glòries ⓦphenomena-experience.com; ⓜSant Pau/Dos de Maig. This independent cinema run by and for fans puts the magic

17

ON LOCATION

You can fall in love with Barcelona all over again with a stack of DVDs and a giant bucket of popcorn. The major movie event of recent years for the city was Woody Allen's extended homage to its photogenic landmarks in **Vicky Cristina Barcelona** (2008), a frothy love triangle – partly financed by the city administration, who definitely got their money's worth – that bounced from the Barri Gòtic to the Sagrada Família. Iñárritu's *Biutiful* (2010) is its antithesis, portraying Barcelona as dark, seamy and desperately lonely. Film buffs point back to 1975 and Michelangelo Antonioni's **The Passenger** as the first major film to showcase the city's attractions, as Jack Nicholson negotiates Gaudí rooftops and cable cars in a cryptic case of stolen identity. Madrid's inimitable Pedro Almodóvar gave his own seedy, oddball take on Barcelona in **All About My Mother** (1999) – an Oscar winner for Best Foreign Language Film – while in Tom Tykwer's **Perfume** (2006), the city's atmospheric old town stood in for eighteenth-century Paris in the adaptation of Patrick Süskind's cult novel. However, the two most arresting Barcelona movies to date show not a single colourful landmark or famous sight, being set entirely within the confines of a Rambla de Catalunya mansion block. All you glean of the city from Jaume Balagueró and Paco Plaza's zombie-virus-shockers **Rec** (2007) and **Rec 2** (2009) is never to join the Barcelona fire brigade, and never to take a hand-held camera (*rec* = record) into a locked-down apartment building…

back into watching movies. Fall in love again with the great movies of the 1970s, 80s and 90s (in V.O.) and occasional recent favourites, with state-of-the art sound and one of the biggest screens in the country.
Renoir Floridablanca C/Floridablanca 135, El Raval ⓦ cinesrenoir.com; ⓜ Sant Antoni. Seven screens in smallish auditoriums showing a mix of independent films and blockbusters. Membership is especially good value at €15 a year, and includes two free tickets.
Verdi/Verdi Park Verdi C/Verdi 32, Gràcia; Verdi Park, C/Torrijos 49, Gràcia ⓦ cines-verdi.com; ⓜ Fontana. Gràcia's popular sister cinemas are in adjacent streets, showing independent, art-house and V.O. movies from around the world on nine screens.

THEATRE AND CABARET

The **Teatre Nacional de Catalunya** (Catalan National Theatre) was specifically conceived as a venue to promote Catalan productions, and features a repertory programme of translated classics (such as Shakespeare in Catalan), original works and productions by guest companies from Europe. The other big local theatrical project is the **Ciutat del Teatre** (Theatre City) on Montjuïc, which incorporates the fringe-style Mercat de les Flors, the progressive Teatre Lliure and the Institut del Teatre theatre and dance school. The centre for commercial theatre is on and off La Rambla and along Avda. Paral·lel and the nearby streets. There are a few options for **children's theatre** (see page 230). Some theatres draw on the city's strong **cabaret** tradition – particularly burlesque, music-hall entertainment – which is far more accessible to non-Catalan or -Spanish speakers than straight theatre. **Tickets** are available from theatre box offices, or the usual agency outlets, while for last-

OPEN-AIR CINEMA

Sala Montjuïc Castell de Montjuïc ⓦ salamontjuic.org; cable car (Telefèric de Montjuïc) or cinema bus (normal tickets and passes valid) from Pl. d'Espanya (ⓜ Espanya), departures from 8.15pm, returns when film finishes. Every July there's a giant-screen open-air cinema established on the grass under the walls at Montjuïc castle) – you're encouraged to bring a picnic and deckchairs are available to hire. Screenings are in the original language, with Spanish subtitles, and range from current art-house hits to film-club stalwarts like *Some Like it Hot*. The films usually start at 10pm, with live music first from 8.45pm, but with space limited to 2,000 it's best to get there at opening time (8.30pm). Tickets sell out quickly – buy in advance through the website.

minute tickets visit the counter at the Palau de la Virreina (see page 43), which offers same-day half-price tickets from three hours before the start of the show. The summer **Festival de Barcelona Grec** always has a strong theatre and dance programme; many performances are at the open-air Teatre Grec on Montjuïc (see box, page 97).

THEATRES

Institut del Teatre Pl. de Margarida Xirgu, Montjuïc ⓦ institutdelteatre.cat; ⓜ Poble Sec. The school for dramatic arts and dance has a regular programme of events scheduled at its two theatres, where you can catch performances by the current crop of students.
Teatre Lliure Pl. de Margarida Xirgu 1, Montjuïc ⓦ teatrelliure.com; ⓜ Poble Sec. The "Free Theatre" performs the work of contemporary Catalan and Spanish playwrights, as well as reworkings of the classics, from

Shakespeare to Samuel Beckett (some productions have English surtitles). It also hosts visiting dance companies, concerts and recitals. The original theatre, a smaller auditorium in Gràcia, also has a full programme.

Teatre Nacional de Catalunya (TNC) Pl. de les Arts 1, Glòries ⓦtnc.cat; ⓜGlòries. Intended to foster Catalan works, the national theatre – built as a modern emulation of an ancient Greek temple – features major productions by Catalan, Spanish and European companies, as well as smaller-scale plays, experimental works and dance productions.

Teatre Poliorama La Rambla 115, El Raval ⓦteatrepoliorama.com; ⓜCatalunya. Specializes in modern drama (Catalan and translation) and musicals, often utilizing the talents of offbeat companies like Dagoll Dagom (see box, page 207).

Teatre Romea C/Hospital 51, El Raval ⓦteatreromea.com; ⓜLiceu. Has an emphasis on contemporary Catalan and Spanish playwrights and pan-European productions, and gives space to new theatre groups and radical directors.

CABARET AND OTHER VENUES

L'Antic Teatre C/Verdaguer i Callís 12, Sant Pere ⓦlanticteatre.com; ⓜUrquinaona. A small, independent theatre with a wildly original programme of events, many free, from video shows and art exhibitions to offbeat cabaret performances, modern dance and leftfield music.

TOP 5 BIG NIGHTS OUT

L'Auditori See page 204
Gran Teatre del Liceu See page 205
El Molino See page 207
Palau de la Música Catalana See page 205
Teatre Nacional de Catalunya See page 206

In the end, though, the best bit may just be the scruffy bar (daily 4pm–midnight) and the garden *terrassa*.

★ **Café Teatre Llantiol** C/Riereta 7, El Raval ⓦllantiol.com; ⓜSant Antoni. Idiosyncratic cabaret café-theatre whose varied shows feature a mix of mime, song, clowning, magic and dance, and sometimes there's English-language stand-up comedy by local and visiting acts. Shows normally begin at 8.30pm & 10.30pm, with late-night specials on Friday and Saturday.

El Molino C/Vila i Vilà 99, Avda. Paral·lel, Poble Sec ⓦelmolinobcn.com; ⓜParal·lel. One of Barcelona's most famous old cabaret theatres reopened in 2010 after many years in mothballs, and the self-styled "Little Moulin Rouge" has a classy new look for its traditional burlesque and music stage shows. It also hosts the city's annual burlesque festival in June, and there are regular jazz nights and concerts, too.

VISUAL ARTS

Barcelona has dozens of **private art galleries** and exhibition halls in addition to the temporary displays on show in its art centres, museums and galleries. Major venues with regularly changing art exhibitions include CaixaForum, CCCB, MACBA and Fundació Antoni Tàpies for contemporary art; Espai 13 at Fundacío Joan Miró for young experimental artists; MNAC and La Pedrera for blockbuster international art shows; Disseny Hub for industrial and graphic art, design, craft and architecture; and Arts Santa Mònica for contemporary Catalan art and photography. **Commercial galleries** cluster together in the Barri Gòtic on C/Palla and C/Petritxol near the church of Santa María del Pi; in La Ribera on C/Montcada and Pg. del Born; in El Raval on C/Àngels and C/Doctor Dou near the MACBA; and in the Eixample on Pg. de Gràcia, C/Consell de Cent and Rambla Catalunya. Note that most commercial galleries are closed on Sundays, Mondays and in August. The the Associació de Galeries d'Art Contemporani (ⓦartbarcelona.es) have gallery listings and exhibition news. A map showing some of Barcelona's best-known art galleries is available at tourist information centres.

CATALAN THEATRE COMPANIES

Els Comediants (ⓦcomediants.com) – a travelling collective of actors, musicians and artists, established in 1971, who use any open space as a stage to celebrate "the festive spirit of human existence".

La Cubana (ⓦlacubana.es) is a highly original company that started life as a street theatre group, though it has since moved into television and theatre proper. It still hits the streets occasionally, taking on the role of market traders in the Boqueria or cleaning cars in the street in full evening dress.

Dagoll Dagom (ⓦdagolldagom.com) specializes in hugely theatrical, over-the-top musicals.

La Fura del Baus ("The Ferret from Els Baus"; ⓦlafura.com) are performance artists who aim to shock and lend a new meaning to audience participation. They've subsequently taken on opera, cabaret, film and installations, lending each a wild, challenging perspective.

17

ART AND CULTURAL CENTRES

La Capella C/Hospital 56, El Raval ⓦlacapella.bcn.cat; ⓜLiceu. This space in the medieval Hospital de la Santa Creu promotes contemporary art of all kinds, though is often a platform for work by young Barcelona artists.

Fundació Foto Colectania Pg. Picasso 14, Born ⓦfotocolectania.org; ⓜFontana. A private foundation that puts on exhibitions culled from the work of more than sixty Spanish and Portuguese photographers, with works from the 1950s onwards.

Miscelänea C/Doctor Dou 16, El Raval ⓦmiscelanea.info; ⓜDrassanes. This nonprofit cultural association promotes the work of up-and-coming artists, mounting ten to fifteen shows a year that have included collections of collages, Polaroid photographs and illustrated skateboard decks. Closed Aug.

Palau Robert Pg. de Gràcia 107, Dreta de l'Eixample ⓦpalaurobert.gencat.cat; ⓜDiagonal. The Catalan government's information office and gallery space sponsors a wide range of shows, all with a Catalan connection.

Palau de la Virreina Ramblas 99, Barri Gòtic ⓦajuntament.barcelona.cat/lavirreina; ⓜLiceu. Changing shows at the city council's cultural headquarters concentrate on contemporary culture, social studies and photography.

Sala d'Art Jove de la Generalitat C/Calàbria 147, Esquerra de l'Eixample ⓦsaladartjove.cat; ⓜRocafort. The Generalitat's youth art space is for artists under 30 – expect anything from formal portraiture to one-off installations. Closed Aug.

COMMERCIAL GALLERIES

Galeria Joan Prats Rambla de Catalunya 54, Dreta de l'Eixample ⓦgaleriajoanprats.com; ⓜPasseig de Gràcia. One of the city's best-regarded galleries for the works of contemporary Catalan artists and photographers. Closed Aug.

H2O C/Verdi 152, Gràcia ⓦh2o.es; ⓜFontana/Lesseps. Independent gallery working in the fields of architecture, design, photography and contemporary art.

Sala Parés C/Petritxol 5–8, Barri Gòtic ⓦsalapares. com; ⓜLiceu. Possibly the most famous gallery in the city, established in the mid-nineteenth century, Sala Parés hosted Picasso's first show. It still deals exclusively in nineteenth- and twentieth-century Catalan art, putting on around twenty exhibitions a year, including its annual "Famous Paintings" exhibition of works by some of the best-known Spanish and Catalan names.

LGBTQ+ Barcelona

There's a vibrant LGBTQ+ scene in Barcelona, backed up by an established organizational infrastructure and a generally supportive city council. Information about the scene – known in Spanish as *el ambiente*, "the atmosphere" – is pretty easy to come by, while locals and tourists alike are well aware of the lure of Sitges, mainland Spain's biggest LGBTQ+ resort, just forty minutes south by train. Bars, clubs, restaurants and hotels aimed specifically at LGBTQ+ clientele are scattered across Barcelona, though there's a particular concentration in the so-called Gaixample, the "Gay Eixample", an area of a few square blocks just northwest of the university in the Esquerra de l'Eixample. But you'll also be well received at plenty of other nominally straight dance bars and clubs in a city that's generally welcoming to its LGBTQ+ visitors.

18

PARTY TIME

The biggest LGBTQ+ event of the year – in the country's biggest gay-friendly resort – is **Carnival** in Sitges (see page 148), while the main city bash is Barcelona's annual **Pride** festival (ⓦpridebarcelona.org), which has events running over three days in July, from street parades and stiletto races to Tibidabo fun-fair parties. Barcelona is also often the venue of choice for other international gatherings – in the past, the city has hosted the **Eurogames** (the European Gay and Lesbian Sports Championships), while the gay and lesbian **Circuit** festival (ⓦcircuitfestival.net) is a Barcelona stalwart. For movie buffs there's the annual **Barcelona International Gay and Lesbian Film Festival** (ⓦmostrafire.com), usually in July, while the appearance of the sun also sees the city's **Mar Bella** beach come into its own as Barcelona's own gay summer beach zone.

ESSENTIALS

Accommodation Finding sympathetic accommodation in the city isn't a problem, as there's any number of chic, boutique properties with a gay-friendly vibe. Barcelona also has two out-and-out LGBTQ+ hotels, the very cool "hetero-friendly" *Hotel Axel* (see page 178), which is right in the middle of the Gaixample district, and its nearby little sister *TwoHotel* (ⓦaxelhotels.com).

Information For up-to-date information and other advice on the LGBTQ+ scene, you can call any of the organizations listed below.

What's on Aside from *Time Out Barcelona* (ⓦtimeout.cat, in English), you'll find info on ⓦtravelgay.com/destination/gay-spain/gay-barcelona. Also worth a look is Patroc (ⓦpatroc.com), a guide for LGBTQ+ travellers to European destinations including Barcelona and Sitges.

USEFUL CONTACTS

Antinous C/Casanova 72, Esquerra de L'Eixample, ⓦantinouslibros.com; ⓜDrassanes. LGBTQ+ bookshop with useful contacts and information board.

Ca la Dona C/Ripoll 25, Barri Gòtic ⓦcaladona.org; ⓜUrquinaona. A women's centre with library and bar, used for meetings by various feminist and lesbian organizations; information available to callers.

Casal Lambda C/Comte Borrell 22, Poble Sec ⓦlambda.cat; ⓜUrquinaona. An LGBTQ+ centre with a wide range of social, cultural and educational events.

DRINKING AND NIGHTLIFE

CAFÉS & BARS

Aire Chicas C/Diputació 23, Esquerra de l'Eixample ⓦarenadisco.com; ⓜPasseig de Gràcia; map page 116. The hottest, most stylish lesbian bar in town is a relaxed place for a drink and a dance to pop, house and retro sounds. Gay men are welcome too.

La Casa de la Pradera C/Carretes 57, El Raval ⓦinstagram.com/lacasadelapraderaraval; ⓜSant Antoni; map page 62. No gimmicks here (well, except that every drink comes with a tapa). Just a scruffy and friendly bar that's a great starting – or ending – point to a night out, with occasional drag shows, talks and live music.

La Chapelle C/Muntaner 67, Esquerra de l'Eixample

TOP 5 LGBTQ+-FRIENDLY BARS

Betty Ford's See page 197
La Casa de la Pradera See page 210
La Concha See page 198
La Federica See page 210
Velódromo See page 201

☎934 533 076; ⓜUniversitat; map page 116. Decorated with masses of tongue-in-cheek religious imagery, this long, narrow bar attracts a laidback crowd of well-dressed professionals, gym bunnies and local hipsters. It's a quiet spot for the first drink of the night but after midnight it's standing room only.

La Federica C/Salvà 3, Poble Sec ⓦinstagram.com/barlafederica; ⓜParal·lel; map page 102. A colourful, lively spot with singalong film screenings, queer flamenco nights and more. There's also a short list of tapas.

Madame Jasmine Rambla de Raval 22, Raval ⓦinstagram.com/madamejasminebar ⓜParal·lel; map page 62. The decor is part nineteenth-century bordello and part 1960s B-movie, but somehow it works. A mellow spot for a coffee during the day, things get fairly wild, with a trans-friendly crowd, as the night wears on. Free tarot readings on Thursday nights.

Punto BCN C/Muntaner 63–65, Esquerra de l'Eixample ⓦgrupoarena.com; ⓜUniversitat; map page 116. A Gaixample classic that attracts a lively crowd for drinks, chat and music. Wednesday happy hour is a blast, while Friday night is party night.

CALVACADA DELS REIS

Festivals and events

Almost any month you visit Barcelona you'll coincide with a saint's day, festival or holiday, and it's hard to beat the experience of arriving to streets decked out with flags and streamers, bands playing and the entire population out celebrating. Traditionally, each neighbourhood celebrates with its own festa, though the major ones – like Sants' and Gràcia's Festa Majors and the Mercè – have become city institutions, complete with music, dancing, traditional parades and firework displays. The religious calendar has its annual highlights too, with Carnival, Easter and Christmas popular times for festivities. Meanwhile, the biggest and best of the annual arts and music events are the Festival de Barcelona Grec, the ever-expanding Sónar extravaganza of electronic music and multimedia art, and the rock and indie fest that is Primavera Sound.

Not all **public holidays** coincide with a festival, but many do (see page 37). In addition, saints' day festivals – indeed, all Catalan celebrations – can vary in date, often being observed over the weekend closest to the dates given. For more information about what's going on at any given time, call into the cultural information office at the **Palau de la Virreina** (see page 43) or check out the Ajuntament's useful **website** (ⓦlameva.barcelona.cat/barcelonacultura).

JANUARY

Cap d'Any New Year's Eve. Street and club parties, and mass gatherings in Pl. de Catalunya and other main squares. You're supposed to eat twelve grapes in the last twelve seconds of the year for twelve months of good luck. The next day, Jan 1, is a public holiday.

Cavalcada dels Reis Jan 5. The Three Kings (who distribute Christmas gifts to Spanish children) arrive by sea at the port and ride into town, throwing sweets as they go. The parade begins at about 5pm; the 6th is a public holiday.

Festa dels Tres Tombs Jan 17. The first big festival of the year is the costumed horseback parade through the Sant Antoni neighbourhood, with local saint's day festivities to follow. *Tomb* is the Catalan word for a circuit, or tour, so the riders make three processional turns of the neighbourhood.

Barnasants Dates vary, Jan–May ⓦbarnasants.com. A singer-songwriter festival (Catalan/Spanish, plus Brazilian and Latin American artists), with more than a hundred gigs held over three months in city clubs and concert venues.

FEBRUARY

Festes de Santa Eulàlia Feb 12 ⓦlameva.barcelona. cat/santaeulalia. Eulàlia, the young Barcelona girl who suffered a beastly martyrdom by the Romans, is a revered patron of the city. Celebrations around her saint's day focus on children and families – parades of giants, *sardanes*, dances, concerts, *castellers* (see box, page 212) and fireworks. Lots of historic buildings and museums are also open for free on the day.

Carnaval/Carnestoltes Week before Lent, sometimes in March. Costumed parades – where you're encouraged to don a mask and join in – dances, concerts, open-air barbecues and other traditional carnival events take place in every city neighbourhood.

GuitarBCN Feb–April ⓦguitarbcn.com. A spring-season perennial, the annual guitar festival showcases all sorts of musical styles – jazz and Latin, blues and fusion – with some big names playing every year. Gigs are at concert halls across the city.

MARCH/APRIL

Festes de Sant Medir de Gràcia First week in March ⓦsantmedir.org. A horse-and-carriage parade around Gràcia, which then heads to the Sant Medir hermitage in the Collserola hills. Later, the procession returns to Gràcia, where thousands of sweets are thrown to children along the route, and there's plenty of traditional dancing and feasting.

Setmana Santa Easter, Holy Week. Religious celebrations and services at churches throughout the city. Special services are on Thursday and Friday in Holy Week at 7–8pm, Saturday at 10pm; there's a procession from the church of Sant Agustí on C/Hospital (El Raval) to La Seu,

starting at around 4pm on Good Friday; and Palm Sunday sees the blessing of the palms at La Seu. Public holidays on Good Friday and Easter Monday.

Dia de Sant Jordi St George's Day, April 23. St George's Day, dedicated to Catalunya's dragon-slaying patron saint, is a day of national identity – the Catalan flag appears everywhere and red roses (the colour of the dragon's blood) are the bloom of choice, with the two coming together at the Palau de la Generalitat, the home of the Catalan government. The saint's day has been entwined over the years with two other occasions, so that it's also a

---

CASTLES IN THE SKY

Guaranteed to draw crowds at every festival are the teams of **castellers** – castle-makers – who pile person upon person, feet on shoulders, to see who can construct the highest, most aesthetically pleasing tower. It's an art that goes back over two hundred years, combining individual strength with mutual cooperation – perhaps this is why it was discouraged as an activity under Franco. There's a real skill to assembling the *castell*, with operations directed by the *cap de colla* (society head) – the strongest members form the crowd at the base, known as the *pinya*, with the whole edifice topped by an agile child, the *anxaneta*, who lifts their palm above their head to "crown" the castle. Ten human storeys is the record. For more, see ⓦcastellersdebarcelona.cat.

CELEBRATING CATALAN-STYLE

Central to any Catalan festival is the parade of **gegants**, the overblown 5m-high giants with a costumed frame (to allow them to be carried) and papier-mâché or fibreglass heads. Barcelona has its own official city *gegants* of King Jaume and his queen (there's more at ⓦgegantsbcn.cat), while each neighbourhood cherishes its own traditional figures, from elegant noblewomen to turban-clad sultans – the Barri Gòtic's church of Santa María del Pi has some of the most renowned. Come festival time they congregate in the city's squares, dancing cumbersomely to the sound of flutes and drums, and accompanied by smaller, more nimble figures known as **capgrossos** (bigheads) and by outsized lions and dragons. Also typically Catalan is the **correfoc** (fire-running), where brigades of drummers, fire-breathing dragons and demons with firework-flaring tridents cavort in the streets. It's as devilishly dangerous as it sounds, with intrepid onlookers attempting to stop the dragons passing, as firecrackers explode all around – approach with caution.

19

kind of local Valentine's Day (traditionally, men give their sweethearts a rose…) and International Book Day (…and receive a book in return).

Feria de Abril de Catalunya Last week in April ⓦfecac.com. The region's biggest Andalucian festival, with ten days of food, drink and flamenco. All the action goes down at the big marquees erected at the Parc del Fòrum plaza (Diagonal Mar).

Còmic Barcelona Dates vary, April or May ⓦficomic.com. The international comic fair takes place over three days, with stalls, drawing workshops and children's activities at one of the city's exhibition halls.

MAY

Dia del Treball May 1. May Day/Labour Day is a public holiday, with union parades along main city thoroughfares.

Dia de Sant Ponç May 11. A traditional saint's day, celebrated by a market running along C/Hospital in the Raval, with fresh herbs, flowers, aromatic oils, honey and sweets.

Barcelona Poesia Second or third week ⓦlameva. barcelona.cat/barcelonapoesia. Week-long poetry festival with readings and recitals in venues across the city. It incorporates the Jocs Floral (Floral Games), while Spanish and foreign poets converge for the International Poetry Festival at the Palau de la Música Catalana.

Dia Internacional dels Museus May 18. On International Museum Day, there's free entrance to all city-run museums – local press have details of participating museums, opening hours and special events.

Corpus Christi Late May/early June. See box, page 52.

Primavera Sound Usually last week ⓦprimaverasound. com. The city's hottest music festival heralds a massive five-day bash down at the Parc del Fòrum (Diagonal Mar), attracting superstar names in the rock, indie and electronica world. It's extended into the city and Poble Espanyol too, with club gigs and free street gigs now part of the scene.

JUNE

Sónar Usually second or third week ⓦsonar.es. The International Festival of Advanced Music and Multimedia Art is Europe's biggest and most cutting-edge electronic music, multimedia and urban art festival, attracting more than 100,000 visitors for three days of brilliant noise and spectacle. Sónar by day centres on events at Fira Montjuïc; by night the action shifts to L'Hospitalet, with all-night buses running from the city to the Sónar bars and clubs.

Festa de la Música June 21. Every year on this day scores of free concerts are held in squares, parks, civic centres and museums in every neighbourhood across the city – from buskers to orchestras, folk to techno.

Revetlla/Dia de Sant Joan June 23–24. The "eve" and "day" of St John herald probably the wildest celebrations in the city, with a "night of fire" of bonfires and fireworks across Barcelona. The traditional place to end the night is on the beach, watching the sun come up.

Música als Parcs June–Aug. More than two dozen parks become venues for evenings of free classical and jazz concerts and performances by the Municipal Orchestra.

JULY

Festival de Barcelona Grec July 1–31 ⓦlameva. barcelona.cat/grec. Since the 1970s, the summer's foremost arts and music festival has centred its performances on Montjuïc's open-air 'Greek' (*grec*) amphitheatre (see page 97) – a dramatic location for cutting-edge Shakespearean productions or events by Catalan avant-garde performance artists, while music ranges from the likes of Philip Glass to African rap. There are also concerts, plays and dance productions at the CCCB and city theatres – in total, nearly eighty different events held over a five-week period.

SOME THINGS YOU MIGHT HAVE MISSED...

If you look beyond the big-name acts and the major annual celebrations, there's a whole world of off-the-radar festive fun in Barcelona. March's **Minifestival** (Ⓦminibarcelona. wordpress.com), for example, provides a neat suburban counterpoint to the bigger city music fests, highlighting international indie acts that you've definitely never heard of. In May/ June, **Loop** (Ⓦloop-barcelona.com), the international fair and festival for video art, attracts hundreds of artists from dozens of countries. In July, **Festival Matsuri BCN** (Ⓦmatsuri-bcn. com) has displays of traditional Japanese music and dance, as well as workshops and plenty of Japanese street food stalls. By October/November, digi-heads and Second Lifers are ready for **Artfutura** (Ⓦartfutura.org), the digital culture and creativity festival; while alternative Christmas shopping is best done at **Drap-Art** (Ⓦdrap-art.org), the Festival of Creative Recycling, which puts on its annual bash and market at the CCCB.

19

AUGUST

Festa Major de Gràcia Mid-Aug Ⓦfestamajordegracia. cat. What was once a local village festival is now an annual week-long city highlight, with banging music, boisterous dancing, wackily decorated floats and streets transformed into magical scenes, plus the usual noisy fireworks, parades of giants and devils and *castellers*.

Festa Major de Sants Last week of Aug. Another week's worth of traditional festivities in an untouristed neighbourhood, in the streets behind Barcelona Sants station.

Mas i Mas Festival Ⓦmasimasfestival.com/festival. The quietest summer month gets a shot in the arm with a music festival by promoters Mas i Mas that crosses genres, hip-hop to classical jazz, at a variety of venues across the city.

SEPTEMBER

Diada Nacional Sept 11. Catalan national day, commemorating the eighteenth-century defeat at the hands of the Bourbons. It's a public holiday in Barcelona; the last few years have seen huge gatherings on the city streets, demanding the right to vote on independence from Spain. Things can get heated.

Festes de la Mercè Sept 24 Ⓦlameva.barcelona.cat/ merce. The biggest annual festival (a public holiday) is dedicated to Our Lady of Mercy, co-patroness of the city, whose image is paraded from the church of la Mercè near the port. It's an excuse for a week of merrymaking, including costumed giants, fireworks and *castellers* – not to mention outdoor concerts, bicycle races, children's events and free admission to city museums and galleries on the saint's day. During the week, the concurrent alternative music festival, known as BAM (Ⓦlameva.barcelona.cat/bam), puts on free rock, world and fusion gigs at emblematic old-town locations and at Parc del Fòrum.

Festa Major de Sant Miquel Last week. Traditional festivities on the waterfront as Barceloneta celebrates its saint's day with fireworks, parades, *castellers* and dancing.

OCTOBER

48H Open House BCN Oct (varies) Ⓦ48hopenhouse barcelona.org. Architectural gems, including those that are usually closed to the public, open their doors for one weekend.

LEM Throughout Oct Ⓦgracia-territori.com. Experimental and electronic music and art festival organized by the Gràcia Territori Sonor collective, with free or cheap concerts, events and happenings held in Gràcia's bars, cafés and galleries.

Festival Internacional de Jazz Last week in Oct and through Nov Ⓦjazz.barcelona. The biggest annual jazz festival in town has been going for more than four decades and attracts superstar solo artists and bands to the clubs and concert halls, as well as putting on smaller-scale street concerts.

NOVEMBER

Tots Sants All Saints' Day, Nov 1. The day when the Spanish remember their dead with cemetery visits and special meals. It's traditional to eat roast chestnuts (*castanyes*), sold by street vendors, sweet potatoes and *panellets* (almond-based sweets). It's also a public holiday.

De Cajón! Nov-Dec Ⓦtheproject.es. Big-name flamenco stars perform a series of one-off concerts in major city concert halls.

Ciutat Flamenco Oct-Nov Ⓦciutatflamenco.com, Ⓦtallerdemusics.com. Annual old-town flamenco bash, organized by the Taller de Músics (music workshop) and Mercat de les Flors. Nine days of guitar recitals, singing and dancing, plus DJ sessions and chill-out zone, and lectures and conferences on all matters flamenco.

DECEMBER

Fira de Santa Llúcia Dec 1–22. For more than two hundred years the Christmas season has seen a special market and crafts fair outside the cathedral. Browse for gifts or watch the locals snapping up Christmas trees, Nativity figures and traditional decorations.

Nadal/Sant Esteve Dec 25–26 ⓦ barcelona.cat/ca/nadal. Christmas Day and St Stephen's Day are both public holidays, which Catalans tend to spend at home – the traditional gift-giving is on Twelfth Night (Jan 6). Each year, there's a Christmas Nativity scene erected in Pl. de Sant Jaume, Barri Gòtic, which stays there for the whole of December and the first week in January.

CROWD AT THE CAMP NOU STADIUM

Sports and outdoor activities

Barcelona is well placed for access to the sea and mountains, which is one of the reasons it was picked for the 1992 Olympics – the event that really put the modern city on the map. A spin-off from the games was an increased provision of top-quality sports and leisure facilities throughout Catalunya, which have attracted an increasing number of major games events, such as the European Athletics Championships, the IAAF World Junior Championships, the World Swimming Championships and the UEFA Champions League finals. The Americas Cup will be held in Barcelona in 2024. In addition, there are scores of sports centres and swimming pools in Barcelona, though. most visitors are content to relax on the city beaches or take off for a hike or jog in the surrounding hills of the Parc del Collserola.

ESSENTIALS

Information Servei d'informació Esportiva (☎010, ⓦajuntament.barcelona.cat/esports/ca), the city council's sports information service, is the main source of information about municipal sports facilities. It also has a drop-in office (Direcció d'Esports) on Montjuïc at Avda. de l'Estadi 40 (ⓜEspanya), at the side of the Picornell swimming pool (Piscines B. Picornell).

Tickets Tickets for all major sporting events can be bought from the agencies, Eventbrite (ⓦeventbrite.es) or Ticketmaster (ⓦticketmaster.es).

BASKETBALL

Second only to football in popularity in Catalunya, basketball has been played in Barcelona since the 1920s. Games are usually played September to June at weekends, with most interest in the city's two main teams. **Club Joventut de Badalona**, founded in 1930, were European champions in 1994, while **FC Barcelona Bàsquet**, founded 1926, finished runners-up five times before finally becoming European champions in 2003, a title they regained in 2010. It's easiest to go and watch FC Barcelona, as Badalona is out in the sticks. The team plays at the Palau Blaugrana, adjacent to the Camp Nou in Les Corts. **Tickets** to games are fairly inexpensive, and you can either buy tickets online (ⓦfcbarcelona.com) or go to the stadium (the day before the game).

CYCLING

Cycling is being heavily promoted by the city authorities as a means of transport. There's a successful **bike-sharing scheme** (known as Bicing), while around 270km of cycle paths traverse the city. Not all locals have embraced the bike, and some cycle paths are still ignored by cars or are clogged with pedestrians, indignantly reluctant to give way to two-wheelers. But, on the whole, cycling around Barcelona is not the completely hairy experience it was. The nicest place to get off the road is the **Parc del Collserola**, where there are bike trails for varying abilities through the woods and hills. **Montjuïc** is another popular place for mountain-biking. Bikes are allowed on the metro, on FGC trains and on the Montjuïc and Vallvidrera funiculars.

Bike tours and rental The best way to see the city by bike – certainly as a first-time visitor – is to take a bike tour (see page 30), for which bikes and equipment will be provided; or to rent a bike (see page 29).

Maps You might want to pick up the map detailing current cycle paths. It's available from the tourist office, or on the city council's website ⓦajuntament.barcelona.cat/bicicleta.

Races and festivals The city hosts a variety of annual cycling events, including the main regional race, the Volta a Catalunya (ⓦvoltacatalunya.cat) every March. June/July sees the Ajuntament's annual Festa de la Bici (Bicycle Fiesta), while September is another big month, with races during the Mercè festival and a day during the city's "Mobility Week" dedicated to cycling.

Amics de la Bici C/Demóstenes 19, Sants ⓦamicsde labici.org; ⓜPlaça de Sants. The "Friends of the Bike" organize a full range of events and activities, from rides to bike-mechanic courses.

20

FOOTBALL

To be honest, there's only one sport in Barcelona and that's football, as played by local heroes **FC** (Futbol Club) **Barcelona**. The team is worshipped at the Camp Nou stadium in the north of the city and, even if you don't coincide with a game, the stadium's football museum and tour alone is worth the trip (see page 136). The other local team – though not to be compared – is **RCD** (Reial Club Deportiu) **Espanyol**, whose games are played at their 40,000-seater stadium at Cornellà, west of the city centre. The season runs from late August until May, with games usually played on Sundays (though live broadcasts on TV now mean that games are also frequently played on Fridays, Saturdays and

BYE-BYE BULLS

Bullfights are an integral part of many southern Spanish festivals, and while Catalunya too has had a long, if less renowned, bullfighting tradition, the more progressive city of Barcelona has always stood somewhat apart. One bullring, the **Plaza de Toros Monumental**, Gran Via de les Corts Catalanes 749 (ⓜMonumental) – site, incidentally, of the Beatles' only ever concert in Barcelona, in 1965 – lasted, with the dwindling support of local aficionados and tourists, until 2011 when bullfighting was banned by the Catalan parliament – a ruling being contested by Spain's constitutional court but upheld by the city council. The future of the building is still undecided, but it may meet a similar fate to the ring in Plaça Espanya, which retained its Moorish facade but was transformed inside into the stylish Arenas de Barcelona shopping centre (see page 118).

TOP 5 GREATEST EVER BARCELONA PLAYERS

Carles Rexach (1965–81)
Johan Cruyff (1973–78)
Ronaldinho (2003–08)
Xavi (1998–2015)
Lionel Messi (2004–2021)

TEAM CONTACTS

FC Barcelona Camp Nou, Avda. Aristides Maillol, Les Corts ⓦ fcbarcelona.com; ⓜ Collblanc/Palau Reial. Tickets go on general sale (online or at the stadium) a week or more before each match, or try Ticketmaster. Season-ticket holders who aren't attending the match put their seats up for sale through the club, right up until kick-off time, so it's not advised to buy tickets from touts at the ground. For a typical league game you're likely to pay from €50 (and be seated *very* high up), though prices run as high as €245.

Mondays). You'll have little problem getting a ticket to see an Espanyol game – you can usually just turn up on the day – and, perhaps surprisingly, it's also fairly straightforward to get tickets for FC Barcelona. The Camp Nou seats 99,000, which means it's only really full for big games against rivals like Real Madrid, or for major European ties.

RCD Espanyol Avda. Baix Llobregat 100, Cornellà de Llobregat ⓦ rcdespanyol.com; ⓜ Cornellà Centre, then 20min walk. Most tickets cost €40–90; you can buy online and pick your tickets up on the day.

HORSERIDING

Escola Municipal d'Hípica La Foixarda Avgda. Montanyans 1, Montjuïc ⓦ hipicalafoixarda.es; ⓜ Espanya, then bus #150. The municipal riding school on Montjuïc offers lessons and courses for adults (beginners especially welcome), children and disabled people, with prices averaging around €230 for ten classes.

ICE SKATING

There are a couple of ice rinks in the city, including one at FC Barcelona's Camp Nou stadium, and a seasonal rink at Pl. Catalunya over Christmas and New Year. It's a good idea to check hours and restrictions before you go, as weekends and holidays especially can see the rinks inundated with children. Note that gloves are compulsory for all skaters and helmets for under-12s, and both can be rented at the rinks.

ICE RINKS

Pavelló Pista Gel Camp Nou, C/Aristides Maillol 12, Les Corts ⓦ fcbarcelona.com; ⓜ Collblanc/Palau Reial. Morning and afternoon skating sessions daily throughout the year, times vary; closed Aug. Also a skating school, for classes of all ages and levels.

ROLLERBLADING, SKATING AND SKATEBOARDING

The Passeig Marítim and Port Olímpic area (ⓜ Ciutadella-Vila Olímpica) see heavy **skate and blade** traffic, while other popular runs include Arc de Triomf (ⓜ Arc de Triomf), Parc Joan Miró (ⓜ Tarragona) and Barceloneta, next to the Palau del Mar (ⓜ Barceloneta). The Fòrum site down at Diagonal Mar (ⓜ El Maresme Fòrum) has acres of wide, open space, and there's a skatepark behind Mar Bella beach. You're supposed to keep off all marked cycle paths. Meanwhile, *the* place for **skateboarders** is the piazza outside MACBA, the contemporary art gallery in the Raval.

RUNNING AND JOGGING

The **Passeig Marítim** (ⓜ Ciutadella-Vila Olímpica) is the best place for a seafront run – there's a 5km promenade from Barceloneta all the way to the River Besòs, with a fitness circuit on the way at Mar Bella beach. To get off the beaten track, you'll need to head for the heights of Montjuïc or the Parc del Collserola.

FOLLOW THAT CAR

Catalunya's motor racing circuit, the **Circuit de Catalunya** (ⓦ circuitcat.com), hosts the annual Formula 1 Spanish Grand Prix in April/May, as well as a whole series of other Spanish and Catalan bike and motor races throughout the year, from truck-racing to endurance rallies. The track, which you can tour (€16, pre-purchase tickets online), is out near Granollers, north of the city (trains from Sants/Pg. de Gràcia), a twenty-minute walk from Montmeló station, but during the Grand Prix there are also shuttle-bus services and direct buses from Barcelona. For Formula 1, you need to sort out tickets well in advance (they go on sale the previous Aug; check the website), while sports travel companies can offer special race packages.

SURFIN' BCN

If you've experienced Barcelona's beaches in the summer, you might find it hard to believe that those glass-smooth waters could ever be surf-worthy. However, from September to April, the Mediterranean picks up enough steam to send waves to Barcelona's sandy doorstep. On rare occasions (maybe twice a year), there's enough power to push the waves toward the 2–3m marks, but for the most part, the soft-breaking waves are knee- to waist-high, making the city's beaches – as one local surf instructor put it – a "paradise for beginners". If you're a newbie looking to get your feet wet or are a more experienced surfer in need of gear, try **Pukas Surf Eskola** (Pg. de Joan de Borbó 93, Barceloneta; ⓦpukassurf.com/schools) or **Box Barcelona** (C/Pontevedra 51–53, Barceloneta; ⓦboxbarcelona.com) – both offer rentals and lessons.

Races and festivals There's a half-marathon (Mitja Marató de Barcelona) held in the city every February or March, while the full Barcelona Marathon (Marató Barcelona; application forms and details on ⓦzurichmaratobarcelona.com) takes place in March. There are more road races during the September Mercè festival, while La Cursa (ⓦcursaelcorteingles.cat; April), the annual 11km run organized by El Corte Inglés department store, attracts over 50,000 fun-runners onto the streets. It's one of the longest-established city runs, held since 1979, and the 1994 event, attracting 110,000 runners, won the Guinness world record for number of participants.

SPORTS CENTRES

Every city neighbourhood has a sports centre, most with swimming pools but also offering a variety of other sports, games and activities. Schedules and prices vary, so it's best to contact the centres directly for any sport you might be interested in. Most have a general daily admission fee (€15–20) if all you want is a swim and use of the gym. For a full rundown call ☎010 (within Barcelona) or consult the sports section database on ⓦbcn.cat.

CEM Frontó Colom La Rambla 18, Barri Gòtic ⓦfrontocolom.com; ⓜDrassanes. Centrally situated sports centre with pool and gym, where you can see traditional Spanish *frontón* (handball) or Basque *jai alai*, reputedly the fastest sport in the world.

CEM Marítim Pg. Marítim 33, Vila Olímpica ⓦclaror.cat; ⓜCiutadella-Vila Olímpica. Large complex by the Port Olímpic with a pool, gym and sauna, plus a wide range of organized activities, games and treatments, from aerobics, dance and yoga to indoor biking, beach tennis and hydrotherapy. Check the website for the other three centres they have in the city.

SWIMMING

The city **beaches** are safe, clean and green-flagged but sometimes very crowded. Better swimming can be found at the region's coastal beaches; Sitges is popular, but the very fine sand there will still be in your ears weeks later, while Caldetes (Caldes d'Estrach) is probably the best. Barcelona also has scores of municipal **pools** – we've picked out three of the best. You may be required to show your passport before being allowed in, and you'll need to wear a swimming cap. If you're hardy enough, the annual Christmas Swimming Cup involves diving into the port on December 25 and racing other like-minded fools.

SWIMMING POOLS

Club Natació Atlètic Barceloneta Pl. del Mar, Barceloneta ⓦcnab.cat; ⓜCiutadella-Vila Olímpica. One indoor pool, two outdoor, plus bar, restaurant and gym facilities.

Piscina Municipal de Montjuïc Avda. Miramar 31, Montjuïc Funicular de Montjuïc. The city's most beautiful outdoor pool, low on facilities but high on Montjuïc with spectacular views – it was built to look good on TV for the Olympic diving competitions.

Piscines Picornell Avda. de l'Estadi 30–38, Montjuïc ☎934 234 041, ⓦpicornell.cat; ⓜEspanya, then bus #150. Remodelled and expanded for the Olympics, the 50m indoor pool is open all year, while the outdoor pool is open to the public from June to Sept. Nudist sessions all year on Sat night, plus Sun pm Oct–May. Admission includes gym and sauna.

TENNIS

Municipal tennis courts, including Vall d'Hebron, are listed on the city council website ⓦbcn.cat or the English-language ⓦbarcelona-tennis.com, while for private clubs consult the website of the Federació Catalana de Tennis (ⓦfctennis.cat). One of these, the Reial Club de Tennis Barcelona-1899 (ⓦrctb1899.es), hosts the **Barcelona Open** every April.

20

TENNIS COURTS
Centre Municipal de Tenis Pg. Vall d'Hebron 178–196, Vall d'Hebron ⓦinstagram.com/cmtvallhebron; ⓂMontbau. The main municipal tennis centre at Vall d'Hebron, in the northeastern suburbs, is the best place to play. Unlike many clubs in the city, you can rent courts by the hour without being a member. There are asphalt and clay courts, costing around €20–25 an hour, plus a pool, gym and café. Rackets are available for rent. Check out the special deals after 3pm on Sundays.

WATERSPORTS

Base Nàutica Municipal Avda. Litoral, Platja Mar Bella ⓦbasenautica.org (Catalan only); ⓂCiutadella-Vila Olímpica, then bus #41. You can rent kayaks and windsurfers, and there's a popular bar here as well. Prices vary considerably, but you can expect to pay from around €60 for a couple of hours' windsurfer rental or €250 for a three-day (three sessions of four hours) elementary sailing course.

Centre Municipal de Vela Moll de Gregal, Port Olímpic ⓦvelabarcelona.com (Catalan only); ⓂCiutadella-Vila Olímpica. Port Olímpic's sailing club has courses and instruction in catamaran and Laser sailing, kayaking and windsurfing, from two hours to two days. Prices are much the same as at Base Nàutica Municipal.

20

LA BOQUERIA

Shopping

Barcelona is one of the world's most stylish cities – architecture, fashion and decoration are thoroughly permeated by Catalan *disseny* (design). All of this makes for great shopping, whether you're looking for unique clothing by a hot local designer or something stylish for the home. Traditional arts and crafts have a place here too, from basketwork to ceramics, and many artists and craftworkers have workshops that are open to the public. Antiques and curios abound, while souvenirs range from the gloriously tacky to the outrageously wacky – a walk down La Rambla and through the Barri Gòtic alone throws up anything from Picasso T-shirts to Peruvian bangles, not to mention Barcelona football scarves, handmade soap, carnival masks, designer chocolates and vintage dresses.

21

The best **general shopping area** for clothes, souvenirs, arts and crafts is the Barri Gòtic, particularly between the upper part of La Rambla and Avinguda Portal de l'Àngel. Established designer and **high-street fashion** is at home in the Eixample, along Passeig de Gràcia, Rambla de Catalunya and Carrer de Pelai, as well as along Avinguda Diagonal in Les Corts. Hot **new designers and boutiques** – including shoe, street- and skatewear specialists – can be found in La Ribera, around Passeig del Born (C/Flassaders, C/Rec, C/Calders, C/Espartería, C/Vidrería, C/Bonaire), but also down C/Avinyó in the Barri Gòtic, between C/Carme and MACBA in El Raval, and along C/Verdi in Gràcia. In recent years, the Sant Antoni neighbourhood (adjacent to Poble Sec) has also been transformed into a hip shopping area, particularly along C/Parlament. For **secondhand and vintage clothing**, stores line the whole of C/Riera Baixa (El Raval), with others nearby on C/Carme and C/Hospital, and on Saturdays there's a street market here. More bargains are in the **remainder stores, wholesalers and discount outlets** found along C/Girona in the Eixample, between the Gran Via and Ronda Sant Pere.

For **antiques** – books, furniture, paintings and artefacts – you need to trawl C/Palla, C/Banys Nous and surrounding streets in the Barri Gòtic, best combined with the antique market on Thursdays in front of the cathedral. **Delis and specialist food shops** tend to be concentrated around the Passeig del Born in La Ribera. Independent **music and CD stores** are found on and around C/Tallers (El Raval), just off the top of La Rambla. And don't forget the city's **museums and galleries**, where you'll find reasonably priced items ranging from postcards to wall-hangings.

ESSENTIALS

Opening hours Shop opening hours are typically Mon– Sat 10am–1.30/2pm & 4.30–7.30/8pm, though all the bigger shops stay open over lunchtime, while smaller shops close on Saturday afternoons and/or may vary their hours in other ways. Major department stores and shopping malls open Mon–Sat 10am–10pm, though the cafés, restaurants and leisure outlets in malls are usually open on Sunday too. Barcelona's daily food markets, all in covered halls, are generally open Mon–Sat 8am–3pm & 5–8pm (seasonalvariations apply), though the most famous, La Boqueria on La Rambla, opens throughout the day. Most fish stalls, however, are closed on Mondays.

Sales The annual sales (*rebaixes*, *rebajas*) follow the main fashion seasons – mid-January until the end of February, and June–July.

Tax refunds Non-EU residents can get an IVA (ie VAT) refund on each purchase over the value of €90.16; if there's a "Tax-Free Shopping" sticker displayed at the store (ⓦpremiertaxfree.com), ask for the voucher and claim the refund at the airport before leaving.

ANTIQUES

★ **L'Arca** C/Banys Nous 20, Barri Gòtic ⓦlarca.es; ⓂLiceu; map page 48. Catalan brides used to fill up

---

CRAFT WORKSHOPS

Crafts have always been central to Barcelona's industry, with a history dating back to the Middle Ages. Many of the street names in the Born (ⓂJaume I/Barceloneta), particularly, refer to the crafts once practised there; eg C/Argentería, silversmith's street, C/Mirallers, the street where they used to make mirrors, C/Vidriería, glassmakers' street, or C/Sombrerers, where hats (*sombreros*) were made. Over the last couple of decades, neighbourhoods like the Born, El Raval and Poblenou have once again become craft centres as empty buildings and warehouses have been opened up as workshops. Some artists work behind closed doors, while others have a space at the front where they sell their limited series or unique pieces.

A good way to see the Ciutat Vella (old town) workshops is to coincide with the **Tallers Oberts**, or open workshops (ⓦtallersobertsbarcelona.cat), usually held over the last two weekends of May, when there are studio visits, exhibitions, children's workshops, guided tours and lots of other events. Or contact Barcelona tour agency My Favourite Things (ⓦmyft.net), who can organize a workshop tour on request, introducing you directly to selected artists.

their nuptial trunk (*arca*) with embroidered bedlinen and lace, and this shop is a treasure trove of vintage and antique textiles. Period (eighteenth to early twentieth century) costumes can be rented or purchased as well – one of Kate Winslet's *Titanic* costumes came from here.

Bulevard dels Antiquaris Pg. de Gràcia 55–57, Dreta de l'Eixample Ⓦ bulevarddelsantiquaris.com; Ⓜ Passeig de Gràcia; map page 106. An arcade with over seventy shops full of antiques of all kinds, from toys and dolls to Spanish ceramics and African art.

Mercantic C/Rius i Taulet 120, Sant Cugat del Vallès Ⓦ mercantic.com; FGC Volpalleres (15min on line S2 from Plaça Catalunya in central Barcelona, then a 5min walk). This permanent antiques and collectables market is out in the suburbs but makes a great trip for casual browsers and serious collectors alike. You'll find everything from furniture to farm machinery, old radios to vintage jewellery, postcards to erotic drawings, plus an outdoor flea market (Sun until 3pm), weekly lot auctions (Sat) and trade markets (1st Sun of each month). Tues–Fri 10am–7pm, Sat & Sun 10am–3pm; closed three weeks in Aug.

ARTS, CRAFTS AND GIFTS

Artesanía Catalunya C/Banys Nous 11, Barri Gòtic Ⓦ bcncrafts.com; Ⓜ Liceu; map page 48. It's always worth a look in the "Emprentes de Catalunya" showroom of the local government's arts and crafts promotion board. Exhibitions change, but most of the work is contemporary in style, from basketwork to glassware, though traditional methods are still very much encouraged. They also have an online shop: Ⓦ bcncrafts.com.

Cerería Subirà Bxda. de la Llibreria 7, Barri Gòtic Ⓦ cereriasubira.cat; Ⓜ Jaume I; map page 48. Barcelona's oldest shop (it's been here since 1760) has a beautiful interior, and sells unique handcrafted candles.

Estanc Duaso C/Balmes 116, Esquerra de l'Eixample Ⓦ duaso.com; Ⓜ Diagonal/FGC Provença; map page 116. Owned and run by Jordi Duaso, president of Barcelona's Tobacconist's Guild, this cigar-smoker's paradise features a huge walk-in humidor, expert advice and regular workshops by international cigar-makers, who roll stogies in-store by hand.

★ **Fantastik** C/Joaquín Costa 62, El Raval ☎ 933 013 068, Ⓦ fantastik.es; Ⓜ Universitat; map page 62. Beguiling gifts, crafts and covetable objects from four continents. You'll never know how you lived without them, whether it's Chinese robots, African baskets, Russian domino sets or Vietnamese kitchen scales.

Papirum Bxda. de la Llibreria 2, Barri Gòtic ☎ 933 105 242; Ⓜ Jaume I; map page 48. For all your writing needs – hand-painted paper, draughtsman's pens, leather-bound notebooks, calligraphy sets and more.

Teranyina C/Notariat 10, El Raval Ⓦ textilteranyina. com; Ⓜ Catalunya; map page 62. Teresa Rosa Aguayo opened her Raval textile workshop in 1987, and continues to weave striking contemporary carpets, rugs and wall-hangings, and make textile jewellery and other objects. You can call in any time to see the design work being carried out, or sign up for one of the courses.

Vuelasola C/Zamora 103-105, Poblenou Ⓦ vuelasola. com; Ⓜ Jaume I; map page 70. A shop-cum-workshop tucked away on one of La Ribera's quietest streets, this is a great place for an unusual gift, with stylish bowls and serving dishes, mugs, mobiles and hand-painted ceramic fish in cream and pastel shades. You can see the artists at work and join in one of their regular ceramic workshops if you'd like to have a go yourself.

BOOKS

GENERAL

Casa del Llibre Pg. de Gràcia 62, Dreta de l'Eixample Ⓦ casadellibro.com; Ⓜ Passeig de Gràcia; map page 106. Barcelona's biggest book emporium, strong on literature, humanities and travel, with plenty of English-language titles and Catalan literature in translation.

★ **La Central del Raval** C/Elisabets 6, El Raval Ⓦ la central.com; Ⓜ Catalunya; map page 62. Occupying a unique space in the former Misericordia chapel, La Central is a fantastically stocked arts and humanities treasure trove, with books piled high in every nook and cranny. There's a big English-language section (and other European languages too), while other La Central outlets are found in MACBA (contemporary art museum) and MUHBA (Barcelona History Museum).

Come In C/Balmes 129, Esquerra de l'Eixample Ⓦ libreriainglesa.com; Ⓜ Diagonal; map page 116. Stocks only English-language books and literature, and is also a good place for language-learning and teaching aids.

Laie C/Pau Claris 85, Dreta de l'Eixample Ⓦ laie.es; Ⓜ Passeig de Gràcia; map page 106. This has been one of Barcelona's favourite bookshops for years, though probably just as much for its café-restaurant, which is a good place to unwind. Other speciality Laie arts outlets are found in galleries like CaixaForum, CCCB, La Pedrera, Museu Picasso and the Liceu.

ART, DESIGN AND PHOTOGRAPHY

Museu Nacional d'Art de Catalunya Palau Nacional, Montjuïc Ⓦ museunacional.cat; Ⓜ Espanya; map page 92. The MNAC bookshop has the city's widest selection of books on Catalan art, architecture, design and style.

21

COMICS AND GRAPHIC BOOKS

Norma Comics Pg. de Sant Joan 9, Sagrada Família/Glòries Ⓦnormacomics.com; ⓂArc de Triomf; map page 120. Spain's best comic and graphic-novel shop, for everything from manga to the Caped Crusader, plus DVDs and all kinds of related gear and gizmos.

SECONDHAND

★**Hibernian Books** C/Montseny 17, Gràcia Ⓦhibernianbooks.com; ⓂFontana; map page 129. Barcelona's best secondhand English bookshop has around 40,000 titles in stock. It's not especially cheap, but there are occasional bargains. There are new titles available as well and you can part-exchange or exchange for credit.

TRAVEL, GUIDES AND MAPS

★**Altaïr** Gran Via de les Corts Catalanes 616, Esquerra de l'Eixample Ⓦaltair.es; ⓂUniversitat; map page 116. This travel superstore has a massive selection of travel books, guides, maps and world music, plus a programme of travel-related talks and exhibitions.

Espai Quera C/Petritxol 2, Barri Gòtic Ⓦespaiquera.com; ⓂLiceu; map page 48. The most knowledgeable place in town for Catalan and Pyrenean maps and trekking guides, plus anything else to do with the great outdoors. Going strong for over a century, this much-loved bookshop has recently transitioned to become part café.

CLOTHES, SHOES AND ACCESSORIES

DESIGNER FASHION

Antonio Miró C/Enric Granados 46, Esquerra de l'Eixample Ⓦantoniomiro.com; ⓂPasseig de Gràcia; map page 116. The showcase for Barcelona's most innovative designer, Antonio Miró – especially good for classy suits, though now also stocks accessories and household design items.

La Comercial C/Rec 73, La Ribera Ⓦlacomercial.info; ⓂJaume I; map page 70. Three Comercial boutiques clustered around C/Rec – comprise this one for menswear, another for women and one stocking Paul Smith. The homeware shop recently closed but a few lines live on in the clothes stores.

Custo Barcelona Pl. de les Olles 7, La Ribera Ⓦcusto.com; ⓂBarceloneta; map page 70; Pl. del Pi 2, Barri Gòtic ☎933 042 753; ⓂLiceu; map page 48. Selling hugely colourful designer tops and sweaters for men and women, this is where the stars get their T-shirts. Last season's gear gets another whirl at the Pl. del Pi discount outlet in the Barri Gòtic.

Desigual Pl. Catalunya 9, Dreta de l'Eixample Ⓦdesigual.com; ⓂCatalunya; map page 106. The flagship store for Barcelona's best-known international label offers three floors of bright patchwork and printed clothes for men, women and kids, plus equally colourful home decor. There are other stores around the city.

Jean-Pierre Bua Avda. Diagonal 469, Esquerra de l'Eixample Ⓦjeanpierrebua.com; ⓂHospital Clinic; map page 116. The city's high temple for fashion victims: a postmodern shrine for Yamamoto, Gaultier, Miyake, McQueen, McCartney, Westwood and other international stars.

★**Natalie Capell** Atelier de Moda C/Banys Vells 4, entrance at C/Carassa 2, La Ribera Ⓦnataliecapell.com; ⓂJaume I; map page 70. Where "each dress carries a story". The boutique stocks Natalie Capell's own very elegant designs, in 1920s- and 1930s-style, every one sewn and colour-dyed by hand.

Petit Gegant C/Parlament 65, Sant Antoni Ⓦpetitgegant.com; ⓂPoble Sec; map page 102. On what is currently Barcelona's coolest street, this small boutique, hung with bunting and balloons, is a stylish mummy's dream. Kit out your tot in colourful designs (age range from 0 to 8), with funky T-shirts, sleepsuits and leggings, plus bibs, muslins and organic lotions.

Purificación García C/Provença 292, Dreta de l'Eixample Ⓦpurificaciongarcia.es; ⓂPasseig de Gràcia; map page 106. A hot designer with an eye for fabrics – García's first job was in a textile factory. She's also designed clothes for films, theatre and TV, and her costumes were seen at the opening ceremony of the Barcelona Olympics. The eponymous shop's a beauty, with the more casual items and accessories not particularly stratospherically priced.

HIGH-STREET FASHION

Mango Pg. de Gràcia 36, Dreta de l'Eixample ☎932 157 530; Ⓦmango.com; ⓂPasseig de Gràcia; map page 106. Now available worldwide, Barcelona is where Mango began, and prices here are generally a bit cheaper than in North America or other European countries. This is the flagship store, but there are branches all over the city.

Zara Pg. de Gràcia 16, Dreta de l'Eixample Ⓦzara.com; ⓂPasseig de Gràcia; map page 106. Trendy but cheap seasonal fashion for men, women and children from the Spanish chain. The Pg. de Gràcia branch is the flagship store, but you'll find outlets right across the city.

JEWELLERY, TEXTILES AND ACCESSORIES

★**Almacenes del Pilar** C/Boqueria 43, Barri Gòtic Ⓦadelpilar.com; ⓂLiceu; map page 48. A world of frills, lace, cloth and materials used in the making of Spain's traditional regional costumes. You can pick up a decorated fan for just a few euros, though high-quality items go for a whole lot more.

Alonso C/Santa Anna 27, Barri Gòtic ⓦguanteria-alonso.com; ⓜLiceu; map page 48. An emblematic Gòtic shop, resplendent with its wooden *modernista* facade since 1973. The speciality is beautifully soft gloves for men and women, and a huge range of fans. You'll also find handkerchiefs, shawls and veils.

Iriarte Iriarte C/Cotoners 12, La Ribera ⓦiriarteiriarte.com; ⓜJaume I; map page 70. Atelier-showroom for sumptuous handmade leather bags and belts. The alley (off C/Cotoners) has several other interesting craft workshops and galleries to browse.

Obach Sombrería C/Call 2, Barri Gòtic ⓦsombreria obach.com; ⓜLiceu; map page 48. For traditional hats of all kinds, hats and caps to berets and Stetsons, this venerable store has been open since 1924.

SECONDHAND, VINTAGE AND DISCOUNT OUTLETS

Flamingos Vintage Kilo C/Tallers 31, El Raval ⓦvintagekilo.com ⓜCatalunya; map page 62. Trendy second-hand vintage clothing from the 70s and 80s sold by the kilo, ranging from biker jackets to Hawaiian shirts. The stock is varied, stylish and carefully selected with a lot of North American gems.

Holala! Plaza Pl. de Castella 2, El Raval ⓦholala-ibiza.com; ⓜUniversitat; map page 62. Vintage heaven in a warehouse setting (up past CCCB) for denim, flying jackets, Hawaiian shirts, baseball gear and much, much more.

Mango Outlet C/Girona 37, Dreta de l'Eixample ⓦmangooutlet.com; ⓜGirona; map page 106. Last season's Mango gear at unbeatable prices, with items starting at just a few euros. The shop is in the city's

"garment district" and there are other outlet stores in the same neighbourhood.

La Roca Village La Roca del Vallès ⓦlarocavillage.com. The out-of-town outlet mall is one for serious designer discount-hounds, with a hundred stores selling designer gear at up to sixty percent off normal prices. It's half an hour from the city centre and you can get there directly by bus – there are full transport details on the website.

SHOES

Camper Passeig de Gràcia 4, Dreta de l'Eixample, ⓦcamper.com; ⓜCatalunya; map page 106. Spain's favourite shoe store opened its first shop in Barcelona in 1981. Providing hip, well-made, casual city footwear at a good price has been the cornerstone of its success – there's a store seemingly on every corner and in every mall, including this one, at the bottom of the Passeig de Gràcia.

★**La Manual Alpargatera** C/Avinyó 7, Barri Gòtic ⓦlamanualal.com; ⓜLiceu; map page 48. In this traditional workshop they make and sell *alpargates* (espadrilles) to order, as well as producing other items using straw, rope- and basketwork.

DEPARTMENT STORES AND SHOPPING MALLS

Arenas de Barcelona Gran Via de les Corts Catalanes 373–385, Esquerra de l'Eixample ⓦarenasdebarcelona.com; ⓜEspanya; map page 116. This designer mall is a glam refit of a former bullring, and while it's bigger on leisure facilities than shops and boutiques, you won't want to miss the view from the circular rooftop promenade.

El Corte Inglés Pl. de Catalunya 14, La Rambla ⓦelcorteingles.es; ⓜCatalunya; map page 40; Av. del Portal de l'Àngel 19–21, Barri Gòtic ⓦelcorteingles.es; ⓜCatalunya; map page 48. The city's largest department store – visit the flagship Pl. de Catalunya branch for nine floors of clothes, accessories, cosmetics, household goods, toys and top-floor café. For music, books, computers and sports gear, head for the Portal de l'Àngel branch.

Diagonal Mar Avda. Diagonal 3, Diagonal Mar ⓦdiagonalmarcentre.es; ⓜMaresme Fòrum or T4 tram; map page 88. Home to nearly 200 shops, this mall anchors the Diagonal Mar zone, and features the usual high-street suspects (El Corte Inglés, H&M, Zara, Mango, Primark

and Sephora) plus designer clothes and accessories, cafés, and restaurants.

L'Illa Avda. Diagonal 557, Les Corts ⓦlilla.com; ⓜMaría Cristina; map page 134. The landmark uptown shopping mall is stuffed full of designer fashion (including locals Beatriz Furest and Javier Simorra), plus Camper (shoes), FNAC (music, film and books), Rituals (home and body, cosmetics), Decathlon (sports), El Corte Inglés (department store), Caprabo (supermarket), gourmet food hall and much more.

El Triangle Pl. de Catalunya 4 ⓦeltriangle.es; ⓜCatalunya; map page 40. Shopping centre at the top of La Rambla, dominated by the flagship FNAC store, which specializes in books (good English-language selection), music, film and computer stuff. Also a Camper (for shoes), and Sephora (cosmetics), plus lots of boutiques, and a café on the ground floor next to the extensive newspaper and magazine section.

Westfield Glòries Avda. Diagonal 208 at Pl. de les Glòries Catalanes, Glòries ⓦlesglories.com; ⓜGlòries;

map page 120. Huge mall with all the national high-street fashion names (H&M, Zara, Bershka, Mango and FNAC) as well as a big Carrefour supermarket, children's wear, toys and games, ice-cream parlours, a dozen bars, cafés and restaurants and a seven-screen cinema complex.

DESIGN, DECORATIVE ART AND HOUSEHOLD GOODS

Cubiña C/Mallorca 291, Dreta de l'Eixample ☎ 934 765 721, ⓦ cubinya.es; ⓜ Verdaguer; map page 106. The building itself is stupendous – Domènech i Montaner's *modernista* Casa Thomas – while the inside holds the very latest in household design, from slinky CD racks to €5,000 dining tables.

Ganivetería Roca Pl. del Pi 3, Barri Gòtic ⓦ ganiveteria roca.cat; ⓜ Liceu; map page 48. Handsome old shop dating from 1911, selling a big range of knives, cutlery, corkscrews and other household goods, including a fine array of gentlemen's shaving gear.

Ici et Là Ptge Sert 5, Sant Pere, ⓦ icietla.com; ⓜ Urquinaona; map page 70. A showroom for covetable pieces from a range of local designers and artists. You'll find furniture, lampshades, cushions, sculptures and artworks in an airy space on the pretty little Passatge del Sert.

FOOD AND DRINK

There's a full list of city **markets** at ⓦ ajuntament. barcelona.cat/mercats. The main local **supermarket** chain is Caprabo (ⓦ caprabo.com), which has a useful branch in the Mercat de la Barceloneta, though most other branches are located in residential neighbourhoods, away from the tourist sights. The most downtown supermarkets with long hours are those in the basement of El Corte Inglés (Pl. de Catalunya), and the Carrefour Markets at La Rambla 113 and Via Laietana 48.

★ **La Botifarreria de Santa María** C/Santa María 4, La Ribera ⓦ labotifarreria.com; ⓜ Jaume I; map page 70. If you ever doubted the power of the humble Catalan pork sausage, drop by this designer temple-deli where otherwise beautifully behaved locals jostle at the counter for the day's home-made *botifarra*, plus rigorously sourced hams, cheeses, pâtés and salamis. True disciples can even buy the T-shirt.

Bubó C/Caputxes 10, La Ribera ⓦ bubo.es; ⓜ Jaume I; map page 70. There are chocolates and then there are Bubó chocolates – jewel-like creations and playful desserts by pastry maestro Carles Mampel. There's also a coffee machine and a handful of seats if you want to sample the cakes in-store.

La Campana C/Princesa 36, La Ribera ⓦ lacampana desde1890.com; ⓜ Jaume I; map page 70. This gorgeous shop from 1890 stocks handmade pralines and truffles, but it's best known for its beautifully packaged squares and slabs of *torró*, traditional Catalan nougat.

Casa Carot C/Dagueria 16, Barri Gòtic ⓦ instagram. com/casacarot; ⓜ Jaume I; map page 48. Set in an old dairy building, Casa Carot sells a variety of farmhouse cheeses from independent producers around Catalunya, focusing on small producers and those that guarantee the best animal welfare.

★ **Casa Gispert** C/Sombrerers 23, La Ribera ⓦ casa gispert.com; ⓜ Jaume I; map page 70. Roasters of nuts, coffee and spices for over 170 years, Casa Gispert have a truly delectable store of wooden boxes, baskets, stacked shelves and tantalizing smells. There are organic nuts and dried fruit, teas and gourmet deli items available too.

★ **A Casa Portuguesa** C/Or 8, Gràcia; ⓦ acasa portuguesa.com; ⓜ Fontana; map page 129. This inviting café and deli is a showcase for the food, wine and culture of Portugal. Call in for a break while trawling the designer and streetwear stores of nearby C/Verdi – they make Portuguese specialities daily (including the famous *pasteis de Belém*, little custard tarts), and have a full programme of wine tastings, food festivals and other events.

La Colmena Plaça de l'Àngel 12, Barri Gòtic ⓦ pastisserialacolmena.com; ⓜ Jaume I; map page 48. Established in 1849, "the hive" has a huge range of traditional Catalan cakes, pastries and sweets prettily displayed in wooden cabinets in its carefully preserved interior. In autumn, try the *panellets* (marzipan balls, often covered with pine nuts) or choose a bag of the prettily wrapped sweets that have been handmade to the same recipe for well over a century.

★ **Entre Latas** C/Torrijos 16, Gràcia ⓦ entrelatas-bcn. com; ⓜ Joanic; map page 102. A truly charming shop, with beautifully arranged displays of stylishly packed gourmet tinned goods, from smoked sardines from Riga to razor clams from Galicia. To go with them, pick up a box of gourmet crackers and a bottle of vermouth, all equally attractively packaged.

Forn Baluard C/Baluard 38–40, Barceloneta ⓦ baluard barceloneta.com; ⓜ Barceloneta; map page 82. There are scores of bakeries in Barcelona and every neighbourhood has its favourite, but when push comes to shove, foodies pick the *Baluard*, right next to Barceloneta market, where the passion for artisan bread, cakes and pastries knows no bounds.

Papabubble C/Banys Nous 3, Barri Gòtic ⓦ papabubble. com; ⓜ Liceu; map page 48. Groovy young things rolling out home-made candy to a chill-out soundtrack. Come and watch them at work, sample a sweetie, and take home a gorgeously wrapped gift.

Reserva Ibérica Rambla de Catalunya 61, Dreta de l'Eixample ⓦ reservaiberica.com; ⓜ Passeig de Gràcia;

21

DAILY FOOD MARKETS

Mercat de la Barceloneta Pl. de la Font, Barceloneta; ⓜ Barceloneta. See page 86

Mercat de la Concepció C/Valencia, Dreta de l'Eixample; ⓜ Passeig de Gràcia. See page 111

Mercat de Galvany C/Santaló 65, Sant Gervasi; ⓜ María Cristina. See page 136

Mercat de la Llibertat Pl. de la Llibertat, Gràcia; ⓜ Fontana. See page 129

Mercat del Ninot C/Mallorca 133, Esquerra de l'Eixample; ⓜ Hospital Clinic. See page 115

Mercat de Sant Antoni Ronda de Sant Antoni, El Raval; ⓜ Sant Antoni. See page 67

Mercat Sant Josep/La Boqueria Ramblas; ⓜ Liceu. See page 44

Mercat Santa Caterina Avgda. Francesc Cambó, Sant Pere; ⓜ Jaume I. See page 71

---

map page 106. A ham wonderland specializing in "jamón ibérico de bellota", the finest of all of the Spanish cured hams, which comes from acorn-fed pigs. Pick up pre-packaged samplers or tuck into a plate of paper-thin slices at one of the marble-topped tables.

Vila Viniteca C/Agullers 7, La Ribera ⓦ vilaviniteca.es; ⓜ Barceloneta; map page 70. A very knowledgeable specialist in Catalan and Spanish wines. Pick your vintage and then nip over the road for the gourmet deli part of the operation.

MARKETS

Antiques Avda. de la Catedral, Barri Gòtic; ⓦ mercat goticbcn.com; ⓜ Jaume I; harbourside, Port Vell ⓦ port vellbcn.cat/ca/portfolio-item/mercat-de-brocanteria-mercat-de-colom; ⓜ Barceloneta. The weekly antiques market outside the cathedral is quite a spectacle but attracts high prices. Better for bargains is the weekend market on the Port Vell harbourside. Cathedral market from 10am, days vary (see website); harbourside market Sat & Sun from 10am.

Art Pl. Sant Josep Oriol, Barri Gòtic; ⓜ Liceu. The square is filled with stalls and easels every weekend from 11am, with local artists banging out still-lifes, harbour views, and so on.

Christmas Avda. de la Catedral and surrounding streets, Barri Gòtic; ⓜ Jaume I. Traditional decorations, gifts, Christmas trees and more at the annual Fira de Santa Llúcia (ⓦ firadesantallucia.cat). Dec 1–22 daily 10.30am–8.30pm (until 9.30pm Sat & Sun).

Coins, books and postcards Mercat de Sant Antoni, Ronda de Sant Antoni, El Raval ⓦ mercatdominicalde santantoni.com; ⓜ Sant Antoni. The rare coin and secondhand/antiquarian book stalls around Sant Antoni market are also good for posters, trading cards and comic collectables. Sun 8.30am–2pm.

Coins and stamps Pl. Reial, Barri Gòtic; ⓜ Liceu. Specialist coin and stamp dealers and collectors do regular weekend battle under the arcades of Barcelona's most emblematic old-town square. Sun 9am–2.30pm.

Farmers' market Pl. del Pi, Barri Gòtic; ⓜ Liceu. Specializes in honey, cheese, cakes and other produce. Also takes place during the Festa de la Mercè (Sept), and the Festa de Sant Ponç in C/Hospital (May 11). First and third Fri–Sun of the month.

Flea market Els Encants, Avda. Meridiana 69, Glòries ⓦ encantsbarcelona.com; ⓜ Glòries/Encants. The most entertaining place to trawl through old clothes, jewellery, antiques, junk and furniture is the city's oldest flea market (see box, page 125), in its shiny home on the southwest side of Pl. de les Glòries Catalanes. Every Mon, Wed, Fri & Sat 9am–8pm, plus Dec 1–Jan 5 Sun 9am–3pm.

Flowers La Rambla, between Pl. de Catalunya and Mercat de la Boqueria; ⓜ Liceu; Mercat de la Concepció, C/Valencia, Dreta de l'Eixample, ⓜ Passeig de Gràcia. La Rambla flower stalls always put on a pretty show, but locals are more likely to do serious flower and plant shopping at Flores Navarro (ⓦ floresnavarro.com) inside the Mercat de la Concepció.

MUSEUMS, GALLERIES AND ATTRACTIONS

L'Aquàrium Moll d'Espanya, Port Vell ⓦ aquariumbcn. com; ⓜ Drassanes or Barceloneta; map page 82. A fish-related extravaganza, from the mundane (T-shirts, stationery, posters, games, toiletries) to cult must-haves (Mariscal-designed bathroom transfers).

CosmoCaixa C/Issac Newton 26, Tibidabo ⓦ cosmo caixa.com; FGC Avda. del Tibidabo; map page 142. The shop in the science museum is the place to buy space jigsaws, planet mobiles, model lunar-rovers, dinosaur kits,

star charts and natural history books.

Fundació Joan Miró Parc Montjuïc, Montjuïc ⓦ miro shop.com; ⓜ Espanya; map page 92. The artist's mark is on almost everything, from bibs and beakers to watches and necklaces.

Museu d'Art Contemporani de Barcelona Pl. dels Àngels, El Raval ⓦ macba.cat; ⓜ Universitat; map page 62. Designer aprons, espresso cups, T-shirts, posters, gifts and toys, plus art and design books.

21

MADE IN BARCELONA

The world owes Barcelona, big time. For a start, in the fashion world there are the global brands **Mango** (women's clothes), **Camper** (shoes) and **Custo** (designer T-shirts), each of which started out in the city. Suitably togged up, you don't just drink a beer here, it's an **Estrella Damm** (tagline, the "beer of Barcelona"), a brew that sponsors everything from the Primavera Sound rock festival to America's Cup yacht racing. And then there are **Chupa Chups** (from the Spanish *chupar*, to lick), the lolly on a stick invented by one Enric Bernat in 1958 – Salvador Dalí, no less, designed the company logo. Kojak in the 1970s TV series wouldn't be seen without one, and Chupa Chups even made it aboard the *Mir* space station. Meanwhile, radical poet, publisher and inventor Alejandro Finisterre (admittedly, born in Galicia) was convalescing outside Barcelona after a bomb injury suffered during the Civil War, when he first came up with the idea for the game of **table football** (*bar football, foosball*). He took out a patent in Barcelona in 1937 and, though there are competing claims, is often regarded as the man subsequently responsible for endless hours wasted in bars worldwide.

MUSIC

Casa Beethoven La Rambla 97 ⓦ instagram.com/casa beethovenbarcelona; ⓜ Liceu; map page 42. Wonderful old shop selling sheet music, CDs and music reference books – classical, but also rock, jazz and flamenco.

Discos Paradiso C/Ferlandina 39, El Raval ⓦ discos paradiso.com; ⓜ Universitat; map page 62. A vinyl-lover's paradise, especially for those with a penchant for electronic music. Techno, dubstep and house aside, there are plenty of offerings for indie, funk and world music fans as well.

Revólver Records C/Tallers 11, El Raval ⓦ revolver records.es; ⓜ Catalunya; map page 62. Revólver sells the city's best selection of vinyl at the lowest prices. Defiantly old-school, it's a record shop like they used to make them. Next door to its near-identically named but separately run sister shop, Discos Revólver.

★ **Wah Wah Discos** C/Riera Baixa 14, El Raval ⓦ wah-wahsupersonic.com; ⓜ Liceu; map page 62. Vinyl heaven for record collectors – rock, indie, garage, 1970s punk, electronica, blues, folk, prog, jazz, soul and rarities of all kinds.

SPORTS

Botiga del Barça FC Barcelona, Camp Nou, Les Corts ⓦ fcbarcelona.es; ⓜ Collblanc/Palau Reial; map page 134. For official merchandise the stadium megastore has it all – including that all-important lettering service for the back of the shirt that elevates you to the squad.

Decathlon C/Canuda 20, at Pl. Vila de Madrid, Barri Gòtic ⓦ decathlon.es; ⓜ Catalunya; map page 48. They've got clothes and equipment for 63 sports in the old-town megastore, so you're bound to find what you want. Also bike rental and repair.

TOYS, MAGIC, COSTUME AND PARTY WEAR

★ **Almacen Marabi** C/Flassaders 31, La Ribera ⓦ almacenmarabi.blogspot.com; ⓜ Jaume I; map page 70. Mariela Marabi, originally from Argentina, makes handmade felt finger-dolls, mobiles, puppets and animals of extraordinary invention. She's often at work at the back, while her workshop also has limited-edition pieces by other selected artists and designers.

Marionetas Travi C/Amargós 4, Barri Gòtic ⓦ marionetastravi.com; ⓜ Urquinaona; map page 48.

Exquisite handmade puppets and marionettes. Owner Teresa Travieso trained in the dramatic arts and makes pieces for the theatre when she's not creating for the public.

El Rey de la Màgia C/Princesa 11, Sant Pere ⓦ elreydela magia.com; ⓜ Jaume I; map page 70. Spain's oldest magic shop contains all the tricks of the trade, from rubber chickens to Dracula capes. They also have an associated magic school and theatre, with events and performances posted on the website.

FELIX THE ROBOT, COSMOCAIXA SCIENCE MUSEUM

Children's Barcelona

Taking your children to Barcelona doesn't pose insurmountable travel problems. On the whole, once you're happily ensconced, and have cracked the transport system, you'll find that your children will be given a warm welcome almost everywhere you go. There's plenty to do, whether it's a day at the beach or a daredevil cable-car ride, while if you coincide with one of Barcelona's festivals, you'll be able to join in with the local celebrations, from sweet-tossing and puppet shows to fireworks and human castles. "Children's attractions" rounds up the best of the options for keeping everybody happy; sporting events and outdoor activities might also appeal (see page 216). For plenty more ideas, check out the English-language site ⓦbarcelonacolours.com, which is packed with information on fun activities, child-friendly restaurants and so on.

22

PUBLIC TRANSPORT

The metro and FGC Public transport has vastly improved of late for those with very young children and pushchairs and most metro stations are now also accessible via lifts and ramps. Most FGC stations have lifts to the platforms, too, including Espanya (for Montserrat trains) and Avda. del Tibidabo (for Tibidabo).

Buses All city buses have been adapted for wheelchair access and so have room to handle a buggy.

Tickets Children under four travel free on public transport, while there are reduced prices for tickets on the sightseeing Bus Turístic and the cable cars.

PRODUCTS, CLOTHES AND SERVICES

Products Disposable nappies (diapers), baby food, formula milk and other standard items are widely available in pharmacies and supermarkets, though not necessarily with the same range or brands that you will be used to at home. Organic baby food is getting easier to come by, though it's best to look in health-food stores rather than supermarkets – and most Spanish non-organic baby foods contain small amounts of sugar or salt.

Clothing For relatively cheap, well-made babies' and children's clothing, Prénatal (W prenatal.es) has an excellent range, and has a branch at Ronda Sant Pere 5. Chicco (in La Maquinista shopping centre; W chicco.es) is the place for baby and toddler clothes and gear. Or go to El Corte Inglés

(see page 225) for more children's and babies' clothes.

Services Most establishments are baby-friendly in the sense that you'll be made very welcome if you turn up with a child in tow. Many museum cloakrooms, for example, will be happy to look after your pushchair as you carry your child around the building, while restaurants will make a fuss of your little one. However, specific facilities are not as widespread as they are in the UK or US. Baby-changing areas are relatively rare, except in department stores and shopping centres, and even where they do exist they are not always up to scratch. By far the best is at El Corte Inglés, though major shopping centres now have pull-down changing tables in their public toilets.

RESTAURANTS, ACCOMMODATION AND BABYSITTING

Restaurants Local restaurants tend not to offer children's menus (though they will try to accommodate specific requests), highchairs are not always provided and restaurants open relatively late for lunch and dinner. Despite best intentions, you might find yourself eating in one of the international franchise restaurants, which tend to be open throughout the day.

Accommodation Suitable accommodation is easy to find, and most hotels and *pensions* will be welcoming. However, bear in mind that much of the city's budget accommodation

is located in buildings without lifts. If you want a cot provided, or baby-listening and -sitting services, the larger hotels may be better – though always check in advance about facilities. Renting an apartment is often a good idea as you'll get a kitchen and a bit more space for the kids to play in.

Babysitting You'll pay from around €25–30/hr for babysitting if arranged through your hotel; or contact Barcelona Babysitter (from €25/hr; enquiries Mon–Sat 9am–9pm; ☎ 647 845 935, W bcnbabysitter.com), who can provide English-speaking nannies and babysitters.

CHILDREN'S ATTRACTIONS

If you've spent too much time already in the showpiece museums, galleries and churches, any of the suggestions below should head off a children's revolt. **Admission charges** are almost always reduced for children, though the cut-off age varies from attraction to attraction. At most municipally run museums, admission is free to under-18s.

CINEMA, SHOWS AND THEATRE

Cinema Children's film sessions are held at the FilmoTeca (see page 205), Sat & Sun 5pm, admission €2. These are mostly dubbed into Catalan, but there are often cartoons without dialogue. Phenomena Experience (see page 205) also regularly shows classic kids' movies in English.

Font Màgica The sound-and-light show in front of the Palau Nacional on Montjuïc (see page 94) is always a hit, though it only starts after dark, and at the time of writing was suspended during city-wide water restrictions.

Magic shows The magic shop, El Rey de la Màgia (see

page 228), organizes regular magic shows at its theatre (C/ Jonqueres 15, El Raval, ☎ 933 187 192, W elreydelamagia. com). Prices are usually in the €20–30 range.

Theatre There are often children's puppet shows, music, mime and clowns at the Fundació Joan Miró (see page 99), usually at weekends and holidays. Jove Teatre Regina (C/Sèneca 22, Gràcia; ☎ 932 181 512, W jtregina.com; M Diagonal) also puts on music and comedy productions for children (Sat & Sun 5.30pm; adult admission €12, includes children), though these are usually in Catalan. Children's activities are also held at the Pati Llimona on C/ Regomir near the Town Hall (Ajuntament) in Pl. Sant Jaume (W patillimona.net).

MUSEUMS, GALLERIES AND ATTRACTIONS

L'Aquàrium Adults might find the Aquarium disappointing, but there's no denying its popularity with children. Under-3s get in free, and there are discounts for

4- to 10-year-olds and families (see page 84).

Museums Most of the major museums and galleries run children's activity programmes, especially in school holidays. These range from art and craft workshops at the Fundació Joan Miró and MACBA to chocolate-making at the Museu de la Xocolata. Museums with a special interest for children include Museu Blau (see page 90), CosmoCaixa science museum (see page 141), Museu del Futbol, FC Barcelona (see page 136), Museu d'Història de Barcelona (see page 53), Museu de Cera, wax museum (see page 46), and Museu Marítim (see page 83).

Parc Zoològic All the usual suspects, plus children's zoo; free for under-3s, discounts for under-12s (see page 79).

Poble Espanyol Open-air "museum" of Spanish buildings, craft demonstrations, gift shops and restaurants. Free for under-4s and a family ticket is available (see page 95).

PARKS AND GARDENS

Gardens Top choice is the Parc del Laberint in Horta (see page 132), where the hillside gardens, maze and playground provide a great day out.

Parks Parc de la Ciutadella has the best range of attractions, with a boating lake and a zoo. Older children will love the bizarre gardens and buildings of Gaudí's Park Güell, while the Parc del Collserola is a good target for a walk in the hills and a picnic. At Parc del Castell de l'Oreneta (daily 10am–dusk), behind Pedralbes monastery, there are miniature train rides and pony rides on Sundays and public holidays (not Aug); it's at the end of C/Montevideo (take bus #V3 from the Maria Cristina metro stop).

Playgrounds Most city kids use the squares as playgrounds, under parental supervision. In Gràcia, Pl. de la Virreina and Pl. de Rius i Taulet are handsome traffic-free spaces with good bars with attached *terrasses*. In the old town, the nicest traffic-free playground is in Pl. de Vicenç Martorell, in El Raval, where there are some fenced-off swings in front of a great café, *Kasparo* (see page 184). In the Born is another good playground on a wide pedestrian street, C/Allada Vermell, where parents can sit at a café terrace. Parc del Fòrum, at Diagonal Mar, also has a good children's playground and lots of other child-oriented attractions.

RIDES AND VIEWS

Cable cars The two best rides in the city are the cross-

harbour cable car from Barceloneta to Montjuïc (see page 93), and the Telefèric de Montjuïc (see page 93), which then takes you up to the castle at the top of Montjuïc. Neither is for the faint-hearted.

Las Golondrinas Sightseeing boat rides around the port and local coast (see page 30).

Mirador de Colom See the city from the top of the Columbus statue at the bottom of La Rambla (see page 81).

Torre de Collserola Stunning views from the telecommunications tower near Tibidabo. Under-3s go free (see page 143).

THEME PARKS

Catalunya en Miniatura Torrelles de Llobregat, 17km southwest of Barcelona (A2 highway, exit 5) Ⓦ catalunyaen miniatura.com. A theme park with 147 Catalan monuments in miniature, plus mini-train rides, children's shows, playground and an adventure circuit.

Illa Fantasia Vilassar de Dalt, 25km north of Barcelona, just short of Mataró (exit 92 on the main highway) ☎ 937 514 553, Ⓦ illafantasia.com. A huge water park with 22 slides, plus splash pools, swimming pools, water games and picnic areas. Buy a combined ticket (*billete combinado*) at Barcelona Sants station and you can travel free on the train to Premià de Mar, and then take the free connecting bus to the park.

PortAventura World 1hr south of Barcelona, near Salou and La Pineda (exit 35 on A7) Ⓦ portaventura. es. This massive theme park is based on five different cultures – Mexico, the Wild West, Polynesia, China and the Mediterranean – and also features the Costa Caribe water adventure park and Ferrari Land (16 rides related to the Italian team). There are several on-site hotels, a beach club, shops, restaurants and shows, as well as fairground rides (including the highest and fastest rollercoaster in Europe). Tickets are available for one, two or three parks over one, two, three or four days Renfe trains from Pg. de Gràcia/Barcelona Sants run directly to Port Aventura's own station (1hr 25min; Ⓦ renfe.com), or the park is just 15min from Reus airport.

Tibidabo Dubbed "La Muntanya Màgica", the rides and shows in the mountain-top amusement park (see page 141) are unbeatable as far as location goes, though tame compared with those at PortAventura.

KING FERDINAND, QUEEN ISABEL AND CHRISTOPHER COLUMBUS

Contexts

History

Catalan cultural identity can be traced back as far as the ninth century, when a powerful dynastic entity, dominated by Barcelona and commonly known as the Crown of Aragón, emerged from the quilt of independent polities of the eastern Pyrenees. It developed over the next six hundred years, before its merger with Castile-León in the late 1400s led to eventual inclusion in the new Spanish empire of the sixteenth century – which marked the decline of Catalan independence and its eventual subjugation to Madrid. Catalunya has rarely been a willing subject, and regional yearning for social and cultural divorce from the rest of Spain remains deeply ingrained.

Early civilizations

During the **Upper Paleolithic** period (35,000–10,000 BC), cave-dwelling hunter-gatherers lived in parts of the Pyrenees; some **dolmens**, or stone burial chambers, from around 5000 BC still survive. Although no habitations from this period have been discovered, huts of some sort were erected, and farming had certainly begun. By the start of the **Bronze Age** (around 2000 BC), the Pyrenean people had started to move into fortified villages in the coastal lowlands.

The first of many successive **invasions** of the region came some time after 1000 BC, when the Celtic "urnfield people" crossed the Pyrenees and settled in the river valleys. These people lived side by side with indigenous Iberians, and the two groups are commonly, if erroneously, referred to as **Celtiberians**.

The foundation of Barcelona

The **Greeks** had established Mediterranean trading posts at Roses and Empúries by around 550 BC. Two centuries later, though, the coast and the rest of the peninsula were conquered by the North African **Carthaginians**, who founded **Barcino** (later Barcelona) in around 230 BC, probably on the heights of Montjuïc. The Carthaginians' famous commander, Hannibal, went on to cross the Pyrenees in 214 BC and attempted to invade Italy. However, the Second Punic War (218–201 BC) – much of which was fought in Catalunya – resulted in the expulsion of the Carthaginians from the Iberian peninsula in favour of the **Romans**, who made their new base at the former Carthaginian stronghold of Tarraco (Tarragona).

Roman Catalunya

The Roman colonization of the Iberian peninsula was far more intense than anything previously experienced and met with great resistance from the Celtic and Iberian tribes. It took almost two centuries for the conquest to be complete, by which time Spain

c.230 BC	218–201 BC	304 AD
Carthaginians found the settlement of "Barcino", probably on the heights of Montjuïc	Romans expel Carthaginians from Iberian peninsula in Second Punic War. Roman Barcino is established around today's Barri Gòtic	Santa Eulàlia – the city's patron saint – is martyred by Romans for refusing to renounce Christianity

> ### BARCINO – TARRAGONA'S LITTLE SISTER
>
> Barcelona does its best to champion its Roman remains, and the sketchy ruins of **Barcino** – or Colonia Julia Augusta Faventia Pia, as it was dubbed in 15 BC by the emperor Augustus – can be traced today in a walk around the Barri Gòtic, centred on the cathedral area (see box, page 49). However, Roman Barcino was always second best to the provincial capital of **Tarraco**, whose extremely fine monuments can still be seen in and around today's Tarragona. Imperial Tarraco (see page 157) was home for two years to Augustus himself, and boasted two forums, a theatre and a circus, plus temples and necropolises, not to mention an infrastructure of roads, bridges and aqueducts – much of which remained in use well into modern times.

had become the most important centre of the Roman Empire after Italy. During the first two centuries AD, the Spanish mines and the granaries of Andalucía brought unprecedented wealth, and **Roman Spain** enjoyed a period of stable prosperity in which Catalunya played an influential part. In Tarraco, Barcino and the other Roman towns, the inhabitants were granted full Roman citizenship; the former Greek settlements on the Costa Brava had meanwhile accepted Roman rule without difficulty, and experienced little interference in their day-to-day life.

By the third century AD, the Roman political framework was showing signs of decadence and corruption, and it became increasingly vulnerable to **barbarian invasions** from northern Europe. The Franks and the Suevi swept across the Pyrenees, sacking Tarraco in 262 and destroying Barcelona. Within two centuries Roman rule had ended, forced on the defensive by new waves of Suevi, Alans and Vandals, and finally superseded by the **Visigoths** from Gaul, former allies of Rome.

Visigothic Spain

The **Visigoths** established their first Spanish capital at Barcelona in 415. They went on to base themselves further south at Toledo, and build a kingdom that encompassed most of what is now Spain and southwestern France. Their triumph, however, was relatively short-lived. Ruling initially as a caste apart from the local people, with a distinct status and laws, the Visigoths lived largely as a warrior elite, and were further separated by their adherence to Arian Christianity, which was considered heretical by the Catholic Church. Under their domination, the economy and the quality of life in the former Roman towns declined, while plots and rivalries within their ranks pitted members of the ruling elite against each other.

Moorish conquest

Divisions within the Visigothic kingdom coincided with Islamic expansion in North Africa, which reached the shores of the Atlantic in the late seventh century. In 711, Tariq ibn Ziyad, governor of Tangier, led a force of several thousand troops across the Straits of Gibraltar and routed the Visigothic nobility. With no one to resist, the stage was set for the **Moorish conquest of Spain**. Within ten years, the Muslim Moors had advanced far to the north, destroying Tarragona and forcing Barcelona to surrender – although the more

c.350	415	711
Roman city walls built as threat of invasion grows	Visigoths sweep across Spain and establish temporary capital in Barcino	Moorish conquest of Spain. Barcelona eventually forced to surrender (719)

inaccessible parts of the Pyrenees retained their independence. In most places, the local population were granted limited autonomy in exchange for payment of tribute. There was no forced conversion to Islam, and Jews and Christians lived securely as second-class citizens. In areas of the peninsula that remained under direct Muslim power during the ninth century, a new ethnic group emerged: the **Mozarabs**, Christians who lived under Muslim rule, and adopted Arabic language, dress and social customs.

The Spanish Marches

Moorish raiding parties reached beyond the Pyrenees as far as Poitiers, where Charles Martel, the de facto ruler of Merovingian France, dealt them a minor defeat in 732 that convinced them to withdraw. Both Martel's son Pepin, and his famous grandson **Charlemagne** (768–814), pushed the invaders further back, with Charlemagne's empire including the southern slopes of the Pyrenees and much of Catalunya. After being ambushed and defeated by the Basques at Roncesvalles in 778, Charlemagne switched his attention to the Mediterranean side of the Pyrenees, attempting to defend his empire against the Muslims. He took Girona in 785 and his son Louis directed the successful siege of Barcelona in 801. With the capture of Barcelona, the Frankish counties of Catalunya became a sort of buffer zone, known as the **Spanish Marches**. Separate territories were established, each ruled by a count and theoretically owing allegiance to the Frankish king or emperor.

The birth of Catalunya

As the Frankish empire of Charlemagne disintegrated in the wake of his death, the counties of the Marches enjoyed greater independence, which was formalized in 878 by Guifré el Pelós – **Wilfred the Hairy**. Wilfred was count of Urgell and the Cerdagne and, after adding Barcelona to his holdings, named himself its first count, founding a dynastic line that was to rule until the 1400s. In the wake of the Muslim withdrawal from the area, **Christian outposts** had been established throughout Catalunya. Wilfred continued the process, founding Benedictine monasteries at Ripoll (about 880) and Sant Joan de les Abadesses (888), where his daughter was the first abbess.

Wilfred was followed by a succession of rulers who attempted to consolidate his gains. Early counts, like **Ramon Berenguer I** (1035–76), concentrated on establishing their superiority over the other local counts, which was bitterly resisted. **Ramon Berenguer III** (1144–66) added considerable territory to his realms with his marriage in 1113 to a Provençal heiress, and made alliances and commercial treaties with Muslim and Christian powers around the western Mediterranean.

The most important stage in Catalunya's development, however, came in 1137 with the marriage of **Ramon Berenguer IV** to Petronella, the 2-year-old daughter of King Ramiro II of Aragón. This led to the **dynastic union of Catalunya and Aragón**. Although this remained a loose and tenuous federation – the regions retained their own parliaments and customs – it provided the platform for rapid expansion over the next three centuries. Ramon also managed to force most of the other counts to recognize his superior status, and subsequently issued the **Usatges de Barcelona**, a code of laws and customs defining feudal duties, rights and authorities. To make them appear older than

801	878	985
Barcelona retaken by Louis the Pious, son of Charlemagne. Frankish counties of Catalunya become a buffer zone, known as the Spanish Marches	Guifré el Pelós (Wilfred the Hairy) declared first Count of Barcelona, founding a dynastic line that rules until 1410	Moorish sacking of city. Sant Pau del Camp – city's oldest surviving church – built after this date

---

CATALAN ROOTS

During the ninth century, conflicting loyalties in the territories of the Spanish Marches sparked the construction of many local fortifications to protect and control the population. That led to the term *catlá* ("lord of the castle") being used to refer to the people of the area – the root of today's "**Catalan**" (Castilian has an analogous root). At around the same time, spoken Latin had taken on geographical particularities, as happened across much of the former Roman Empire, and the "Romance" languages, including Catalan, had begun to develop. A document from 839 recording the consecration of the cathedral at La Seu d'Urgell in the Pyrenees is seen as the first Catalan-language historical document.

---

they were, he sneakily put Ramon I's name on them. He also captured Muslim Tortosa and Lleida in 1148–49, which mark the limits of the modern region of Catalunya. Now, however, the region began to look east for its future, across the Mediterranean.

The Kingdom of Catalunya and Aragón

Ramon Berenguer IV was no more than a count, but his son **Alfons I**, who succeeded to the throne in 1162, also inherited the title of King of Aragón (where he was Alfonso II), and became the first count-king of what historians later came to call the **Crown of Aragón**. To his territories he added Roussillon and much of southern France, becoming known as "Emperor of the Pyrenees".

Alfons's son in turn, Pere (Peter) the Catholic, gained glory as one of the military leaders in the decisive defeat of Muslim forces at the **Battle of Las Navas de Tolosa** in 1212. Through his ties of lordship to the French counts of Toulouse, however, Pere found himself on the wrong side in the Albigensian wars (the Catholic Church's crusade against the Cathar heresy), and he was killed a year later. These were uncertain times in Catalunya, but a golden age was about to dawn.

Jaume I

Pere was succeeded by his 5-year-old son, **Jaume I** (1213–76), whose extraordinary reign started unpromisingly when he was initially entrusted to the care of the Knights Templar while his crown was disputed by rival counts. Shrugging off the tutelage of his Templar masters at the age of 13, Jaume personally took to the field to tame his rebellious nobles, before embarking on a series of campaigns of conquest, which brought him Muslim Mallorca in 1229, Menorca in 1231 and Ibiza in 1235. Next he turned south and conquered the city of Valencia in 1238, establishing a new kingdom of which he was also ruler. Recognizing that Catalunya's future lay in **Mediterranean expansion**, Jaume signed the **Treaty of Corbeil** in 1258, renouncing his rights in France (except for Montpellier, the Cerdagne and Roussillon), in return for the French king Louis' renunciation of claims in Catalunya.

Catalan expansion

On Jaume's death, his kingdom was divided between his sons, one of whom, **Pere II** ("the Great"), took Catalunya, Aragón and Valencia. Connected through

1137	1213–76	1282–1387	1348
Dynastic union of Catalunya and Aragón established	Reign of Jaume I, "the Conqueror", expansion of empire and beginning of Catalan golden age	Barcelona at centre of a Mediterranean empire. Successive rulers construct most of Barcelona's best-known Gothic buildings	Black Death strikes, killing half of Barcelona's population

marriage to the Sicilian Crown, Pere used the 1282 "Sicilian Vespers" rising against Charles of Anjou to press his claim to the island. In August that year, Pere was crowned in Palermo, and Sicily became the base for Catalan exploits throughout the Mediterranean. Catalan mercenaries, the **almogávares**, took Athens and Neopatras between 1302 and 1311, and famous sea-leaders-cum-pirates such as Roger de Flor and Roger de Llúria fought in the name of the Catalan-Aragónese Crown. Malta (1283), Corsica (1323), Sardinia (1324) and Naples (1423) all fell under the influence of successive count-kings.

Barcelona's medieval mercantile class were quick to see the possibilities of Mediterranean commerce. Maritime customs were codified in the so-called *Llibre del Consolat de Mar*, trade relations were established with North Africa and the Middle East, and Catalan became used as a trading language throughout the Mediterranean.

Catalunya in the golden age

Catalunya's first parliament, the **Corts** – one of the earliest such bodies in Europe – was established during Jaume I's reign, while in 1249, the first governors of Barcelona were elected, nominating councillors to help them who became known as the Consell de Cent. The year 1289 saw the first recorded meeting of a body that became known as the **Generalitat**, a sort of committee of the Corts. Within it were represented each of the three traditional estates – commons, nobility and clergy – and the Generalitat gradually became responsible for administering public order, justice and defence of the realm.

By the mid-fourteenth century Catalunya was at its economic peak. Barcelona had impressive new buildings to match its status as a regional superpower – the cathedral, the church of Santa María del Mar, the Generalitat building, the Ajuntament (with its Consell de Cent meeting room) and the Drassanes shipyards all testify to Barcelona's wealth in this period. Catalan became established as a **literary language**, and Catalan works are recognized as precursors of much of the great medieval literature of Europe: Ramon Llull's romance *Blanquerna* was written a century before Chaucer's *Canterbury Tales*. **Architecture** progressed from Romanesque to Gothic styles, with churches displaying features that have become known as Catalan-Gothic, including spacious naves, hexagonal belfries and a lack of flying buttresses.

The rise of Castile

The last of Wilfred the Hairy's dynasty of Catalan count-kings, Martin the Humane (Martí el Humà), died in 1410 without an heir. After nearly five hundred years of continuity, there were six claimants to the succession, and in 1412 nine specially appointed counsellors elevated Ferdinand (Ferran) de Antequera, son of a Catalan princess, to the vacant throne.

Ferdinand ruled for only four years, but his reign and that of his son, Alfons, and grandson, John (Joan) II, spelled the end of Catalunya's influence in the Mediterranean. The Castilian rulers were soon in dispute with the Consell de Cent, and non-Catalans started to be appointed to key positions in the Church, state offices and the armed forces. In 1469 John's son, Prince Ferdinand (Ferran), who was born in Aragón, married Isabel of Castile, a union that would eventually finish off Catalan

1391	1410	1469	1479
Pogrom against the city's Jewish population	Death of Martí el Humà (Martin the Humane), last of Catalan count-kings. Beginning of the end of Catalan influence in the Mediterranean	Marriage of Ferdinand of Aragón and Isabel of Castile	Ferdinand succeeds to Catalan-Aragónese Crown. Inquisition introduced to Barcelona, leading to forced flight of the Jews

THE INQUISITION IN CATALUNYA

The Catholic monarchs, Ferdinand and Isabel, shared in the religious bigotry of their contemporaries, although Isabel, under the influence of her personal confessor, Tomás de Torquemada, was the more reactionary of the two. In Catalunya, the **Inquisition** was established in 1487, and aimed to purify the Catholic faith by rooting out heresy. It was directed mainly at the secret **Jews**, most of whom had been converted to Christianity by force after the pogrom of 1391. Their descendants, known as **New Christians**, were suspected of practising their former faith in secret, and in 1492, an edict forced some seventy thousand Jews to flee the country. The Jewish population in Barcelona was completely eradicated in this way, while communities elsewhere – principally in Girona, Tarragona and Lleida – were massively reduced, and those who remained were forced to convert to Christianity.

independence. Both came into their inheritances quickly, Isabel taking Castile in 1474 and the Catalan-Aragónese Crown coming to Ferdinand in 1479.

Ferdinand and Isabel

Under **Ferdinand and Isabel**, the two largest kingdoms in Spain were united under a ruling pair known as "**Los Reyes Católicos**" ("Els Reis Catòlics" in Catalan) – the Catholic monarchs. Devoting their energies to the reconquest and unification of Spain, they finally took back Granada from the Moors in 1492, and initiated a wave of Christian fervour with the **Inquisition** at its heart.

In 1493, the final shift in Catalunya's outlook occurred with the triumphal return of **Christopher Columbus** from the New World, to be received in Barcelona by Ferdinand and Isabel. Castile, like Portugal, looked away from the Mediterranean to the Americas for trade and conquest, and the exploration and exploitation of the New World was spearheaded by the Andalucían city of Seville. Meanwhile, Ferdinand gave the Supreme Council of Aragón control over Catalan affairs in 1494. The Aragonese nobility, who had always resented the success of the Catalan maritime adventurers, now saw the chance to complete their control of Catalunya by taking over its ecclesiastical institutions; Catalan monks were thrown out of the great monasteries of Poblet and Montserrat.

Habsburg rule

Charles I, a **Habsburg**, came to the throne in 1516 as a beneficiary of the marriage alliances made by the Catholic monarchs. Five years later he was elected emperor of the **Holy Roman Empire** (as Charles V), inheriting not only Castile, Aragón and Catalunya, but also Flanders, the Netherlands, Artois, the Franche-Comté and all the American colonies. With such responsibilities, attention was inevitably diverted from Spain, whose chief function became to sustain the Holy Roman Empire with gold and silver from the Americas. It was during this era that Madrid was established as capital city of the Spanish empire, and the long rivalry between Madrid and Barcelona began.

1493	1516	1640–52
Christopher Columbus received in Barcelona after triumphant return from New World	Spanish Crown passes to Habsburgs and Madrid is established as capital of Spanish empire	Uprising known as "War of the Reapers" declares Catalunya an independent republic. Barcelona besieged and surrenders to Spanish army

Throughout the **sixteenth century**, Catalunya continued to suffer under the Inquisition. Deprived of trading opportunities in the Americas, it became impoverished. Habsburg wars wasted the lives of Catalan soldiers, banditry increased, and the poverty of the mass of the population was a source of perpetual tension.

With Spain and France at war in 1635, the Catalans took advantage of the situation to revolt, declaring themselves an **independent republic** under the protection of the French King Louis XIII. This, the **War of the Reapers** – after the marching song *Els Segadors* ("The Reapers"), later the Catalan national anthem – ended in 1652 with the surrender of Barcelona to the Spanish army. The **Treaty of the Pyrenees** in 1659 finally split the historical lands of Catalunya, as the Spanish lost control of Roussillon and part of the Cerdagne to France.

Bourbon repression

In 1700, when the Habsburg king Charles II died heirless, France's Louis XIV saw an opportunity to fulfil his longtime ambition of putting a **Bourbon** (*Borbón* in Castilian, *Borbó* in Catalan) on the Spanish throne. He secured the succession of his grandson, Philippe d'Anjou, on the condition that Philippe renounced his rights to the throne of France. This deal put a Bourbon on the throne of Spain, but led to war with the other claimant, Archduke Charles of Austria: the resulting **War of the Spanish Succession** lasted thirteen years from 1701, with Catalunya lining up on the Austrian side (along with England) in an attempt to regain its ancient rights.

However, the **Treaty of Utrecht** in 1714 gave the throne to the Bourbon Philippe, now **Philip V** of Spain, and initiated a fresh period of repression from which the Catalans took a century to recover. Barcelona lay under siege for over a year, and with its eventual capitulation a fortress was built at Ciutadella to subdue the city's inhabitants – the final defeat, on September 11, is still mourned every year on Catalunya's National Day, known as **La Diada**. The university at Barcelona was closed, the Catalan language was banned, the Consell de Cent and Generalitat were abolished. In short, Catalunya was finished as even a partially autonomous region.

Napoleonic and Peninsular wars

When neighbouring France became aggressively expansionist following the Revolution of 1789, Spain was a natural target, first for the Revolutionary armies and later for the machinations of Napoleon. In 1805, during the **Napoleonic Wars**, the French fleet (along with the Spanish who had been forced into an alliance) was defeated at Trafalgar. Charles IV was forced to abdicate shortly afterwards, and Napoleon installed his brother Joseph on the throne three years later.

Attempting to broaden his appeal among Spain's subjects, the French emperor proclaimed a separate government of Catalunya – independent of Joseph's rule – with Catalan as its official language. The region's response was an indication of how far Catalunya had become integrated into Spain during the Bourbon period – despite their history the Catalans supported the Bourbon cause solidly during the ensuing **Peninsular War** (1808–14), ignoring Napoleon's blandishments. Girona was defended heroically from the French in a seven-month siege, while Napoleon did his cause no

1714	1755	1778	1814
After War of Spanish Succession, Spanish throne passes to Bourbons. Barcelona finally subdued on September 11 (now Catalan National Day); Ciutadella fortress built	Barceloneta district laid out – gridded layout is early example of urban planning	Steady increase in trade with America; Barcelona's economy improves	After Peninsular War, French finally driven out, with Barcelona the last city to fall

good at all by attacking and sacking the holy shrine and monastery at Montserrat. Fierce local resistance was eventually backed by the muscle of a British army, and the French were at last driven out.

The slow Catalan revival

Despite the political emasculation of Catalunya, the eighteenth century had seen signs of **economic revival**, not least as (from 1778) Catalunya was allowed to trade with the Americas for the first time. In this way, the shipping industry received a boost and Catalunya was able to export its textiles to a broader market.

After the Napoleonic Wars, Catalunya experienced **industrialization** on a scale like nowhere else in Spain. In the mid-nineteenth century, the country's first **railway** was built from Barcelona to Mataró, later to be extended south to Tarragona and north to Girona and the French border. **Manufacturing** industries encouraged a population shift from the land to the towns; Catalan olive oil production helped supply the whole country; and previously local industries flourished on a wider scale – for example, cava production was introduced in the late nineteenth century, supported closely by the age-old cork industry of the Catalan forests. From 1890, hydroelectric power was harnessed from the Pyrenees, and by the end of the century Barcelona was the fastest-growing city in Spain – one of only six with more than 100,000 inhabitants.

Cultural renaissance

The first stirrings of what became known as the **Renaixença** (Renaissance) came in the mid-nineteenth century. Despite being banned in official use and public life, the Catalan **language** had never died out. Books started to appear again in Catalan, and the language was revived among the bourgeoisie and intellectuals as a means of making subtle nationalist and political points. Catalan **poetry** became popular, and the late medieval **Jocs Florals** (Floral Games), a sort of literary competition, were revived in 1859 in Barcelona: one winner was the great Catalan poet, Jacint Verdaguer (1845–1902). Catalan **drama** developed (although even in the late nineteenth century there were still restrictions on performing wholly Catalan plays), led mainly by the dramatist Pitarra.

Prosperity led to the rapid **expansion of Barcelona**, particularly the mid-nineteenth-century addition to the city of the planned Eixample district. Encouraged by wealthy patrons and merchants, architects such as Josep Puig i Cadafalch, Lluís Domènech i Montaner and Antoni Gaudí i Cornet were in the vanguard of the *modernista* movement that changed the face of the city. Culture and business came together with the **Universal Exhibition** of 1888, based around the *modernista* buildings of the Parc de la Ciutadella, and later the **International Exhibition** on Montjuïc in 1929.

The seeds of civil war

In 1814, the repressive Ferdinand VII had been restored to the Spanish throne. Despite the Catalan contribution to the defeat of the French, he stamped out the least hint of liberalism in the region, abolishing virtually all Catalunya's remaining privileges. On his

1848	1850	1859	1882
Rapid expansion and industrialization	Plaça Reial – emblematic old-town square – is laid out	Old city walls demolished and Eixample district built to accommodate growing population	Work begins on Sagrada Família; Antoni Gaudí takes charge two years later

death, the crown was claimed both by his daughter Isabel II, with liberal support, and by his brother Charles, backed by the Church and the conservatives. The ensuing **First Carlist War** (1833–39) ended in victory for Isabel, who came of age in 1843. Her reign was a long record of scandal, political crisis and constitutional compromise, until liberal army generals under the leadership of General Prim eventually effected a coup in 1868, forcing Isabel to abdicate. However, the experimental **First Republic** (1873–75) failed, and following the **Second Carlist War** the throne passed to Isabel's son, Alfonso XII.

Against this unstable background, Catalan dissatisfaction increased and the years preceding World War I saw a growth in working-class **political movements**. Barcelona's textile workers organized a branch affiliated to the Communist First International, founded by Karl Marx, and the region's wine growers also banded together to seek greater security. Tension was further heightened by the **loss of Cuba** in 1898, which added to local economic problems, with returning soldiers seeking employment in cities where there was none.

Conflict in Barcelona

A call-up for army reserves to fight in Morocco in 1909 provoked a general strike and, at the end of July, a solid week of rioting in Barcelona, and then throughout Catalunya, in which over one hundred people died. Working-class Catalans objected violently to the suggestion that they should fight abroad for a state that did little for them at home, and Barcelona's streets saw the widespread burning of churches and other religious institutions – symbols of the power of the state that dominated their lives. Battle lines were drawn in the very name given to the disturbances – what to the rioters was a glorious "July revolution" came to be known by the nervous bourgeoisie as the **Tragic Week** (Setmana Tràgica). Mass arrests, executions and repression followed, as the rioters were put down, but seeds were sown as Catalan workers realized the need to be better organized. One direct result was the establishment of the Confederación Nacional del Trabajo – the **CNT** – in 1911, which included many previously unconnected Catalan working-class organizations.

World War I and the start of dictatorship

During **World War I** Spain was neutral, though inwardly turbulent since soaring inflation and the cessation of exports following the German blockade of the North Atlantic hit the country hard. As rumblings grew among the workers and political organizations, the army moved decisively, crushing a general strike in 1917. However, the situation did not improve. Violent strikes and assassinations plagued Barcelona, while the CNT and the union of the socialists, the CGT, both saw huge increases in membership.

In 1923, **General Primo de Rivera**, the captain-general of Catalunya, overthrew the national government in a military coup that had the full backing of the Catalan middle class, and established a dictatorship that at first enjoyed economic success. The general resigned in 1930, dying a few months later, but the hopes of some for the restoration of the monarchy's political powers were short-lived. The success of anti-monarchist parties in the municipal elections of 1931 led to the abdication of the king and the foundation of the **Second Republic**.

1888	1893	1900	1909
Universal Exhibition held at Parc de la Ciutadella. *Modernista* architects start to make their mark	First stirrings of anarchist unrest. Liceu opera house bombed	Pablo Picasso's first public exhibition held at *Els Quatre Gats* tavern	Setmana Tràgica (Tragic Week) of rioting. Many churches destroyed

The Second Republic

In 1931, Catalunya, under Francesc Macià, leader of the Republican Left, declared itself to be an **independent republic**, and the Republican flag was raised over the Ajuntament in Barcelona. Madrid refused to accept the declaration, though a statute of limited autonomy was granted in 1932. Despite initial optimism, the government failed to satisfy raised local expectations. **Anarchism** in particular gained adherents among the frustrated middle classes as well as among workers and peasantry. The **Communist Party** and the left-wing **socialists**, driven into alliance by their mutual distrust of the "moderate" socialists in government, were also forming a growing bloc. On the Right, the **Falangists** (founded in 1923 by José Antonio Primo de Rivera, son of the dictator) made uneasy bedfellows with conservative traditionalists and dissident elements in the army upset by modernizing reforms.

In this atmosphere of growing confusion, the left-wing **Popular Front** alliance, including the Catalan Republican Left, won the general election of January 1936 by a narrow margin, and an all-Republican government was formed. In Catalunya, **Lluís Companys** became president of the Generalitat. But with the economy crippled by strikes, the government singularly failed to exert its authority over anyone.

Finally, on July 17, 1936, the military garrison in Morocco rebelled under the leadership of **General Francisco Franco**, to be followed by uprisings at military garrisons throughout the country. Much of the south and west quickly fell into the hands of Franco's Nationalists, but Madrid and the industrialized northeast remained loyal to the Republican government. In Barcelona, although the military garrison supported Franco, it was soon subdued by local Civil Guards and workers, while local leaders set up militias in preparation for the coming fight.

In October 1936, Franco was declared military commander and head of state; fascist Germany and Italy recognized his regime as the legitimate government of Spain in November. The Civil War was on.

Civil War

The **Spanish Civil War** (1936–39) was one of the most bitter and bloody the world has seen. Both sides visited violent reprisals on their enemies – the Republicans shooting priests and local landowners wholesale, and burning churches and cathedrals; the Nationalists carrying out mass slaughter of the population of almost every town they took. This was also the first modern war – Franco's German allies demonstrated their ability to inflict terror on civilian populations with bombing raids on Gernika and Durango, while radio became an important propaganda weapon, with Nationalists offering starving Republicans the "white bread of Franco".

Despite sporadic help from Russia and the 35,000 volunteers of the **International Brigades**, the Republic could never compete with the professional armies and the massive assistance from fascist Italy and Nazi Germany that the Nationalists enjoyed. Eventually, the nonintervention of other European governments effectively handed victory to the Nationalists. The Republican government fled Madrid first for Valencia, and then moved on to base itself at Barcelona in 1937. The **Battle of the Ebro** around Tortosa saw massive casualties on both sides; Nationalist troops advanced on Valencia in 1938, and from the west were also approaching Catalunya from

1922	1926	1929	1936–39
Park Güell opens to the public	Antoni Gaudí run over by a tram; Barcelona stops en masse for his funeral	International Exhibition held at Montjuïc	Spanish Civil War. Barcelona at heart of Republican cause, with George Orwell and other volunteers arriving to fight. City eventually falls to Nationalists in January 1939

their bases in Navarre. When Bilbao was taken by the Nationalists, the Republicans' fight on the **Aragón front** was lost. The final Republican hope, that war in Europe over Czechoslovakia would draw the Allies into a war against fascism, evaporated in September 1938 with the British Prime Minister Chamberlain's capitulation to Hitler at Munich. Instead, Franco was able to call on new arms and other supplies from Germany for a final offensive against Catalunya.

The **fall of Barcelona** came on January 25, 1939 – the Republican parliament held its last meeting at Figueres a few days later. Republican soldiers, cut off in the valleys of the Pyrenees, made their way across the high passes into France, joined by women and children fearful of a fascist victory. Among the refugees and escapees was **Lluís Companys**, president of the Generalitat, who was later captured in France by the Germans, and handed back to Spain. Under orders from Franco, he was shot at the castle prison on Montjuïc in 1940.

Catalunya in Franco's Spain

Although the Civil War left more than half a million dead, destroyed a quarter of a million homes and sent a third of a million people (including 100,000 Catalans) into exile, Franco was in no mood for reconciliation. With his government recognized by Allied powers, including Britain and France, he set up **war tribunals** that ordered executions and created concentration camps in which upwards of two million people were held until "order" had been established by authoritarian means.

The **Catalan language** was banned again, in schools, churches, the press and in public life; only one party was permitted; and censorship was rigorously enforced. The economy was in ruins, and Franco did everything possible to further the cause of Madrid against Catalunya, starving the region of investment and new industry. After **World War II**, during which the country was too weak to be anything but neutral, Spain was economically and politically isolated.

What saved Franco was the acceptance of **American aid**, offered on the condition that he provide land for US air bases. Prosperity increased after this, fuelled in the 1960s and 1970s by a growing tourist industry, but Catalunya (along with the Basque Country, another thorn in Franco's side) remained economically backward. Absentee landlords took much of the local revenue, a situation exacerbated by Franco's policy of encouraging emigration to Catalunya from other parts of Spain, and granting the immigrants land, in an attempt to dilute regional differences.

Despite the **cultural and political repression**, the distinct Catalan identity was never obliterated. The Catalan Church retained a feisty independence, while Barcelona emerged as the most important publishing centre in Spain. Clandestine language and history classes were conducted, and artists and writers continued to produce work in defiance of the authorities. Nationalism in Catalunya, however, did not take the same course as the Basque separatist movement. There was little violence against the state in Catalunya, and no serious counterpart emerged to the Basque terrorist organization ETA. The Catalan approach was subtler: an audience at the Palau de la Música sang the unofficial Catalan anthem when Franco visited in 1960; a massive petition against language restrictions was raised in 1963; and a sit-in by Catalan intellectuals at Montserrat was organized in protest against repression in the Basque Country.

1939–75	1975	1977
Spain under Franco. Generalitat president Lluís Companys executed, Catalan language banned and Catalan identity threatened by Madrid	Death of General Franco, who is succeeded as head of state by King Juan Carlos	First democratic Spanish elections for forty years

Franco's death and the new democracy

When Franco died in 1975, **King Juan Carlos** – approved by the powerful army and groomed for the succession by Franco himself – was officially designated to succeed as head of state. The king's initial moves were cautious in the extreme, though to his credit, Juan Carlos recognized that some real break with the past was inevitable, and, accepting the resignation of his prime minister, set in motion the process of **democratization**. His newly appointed prime minister, Adolfo Suárez, steered through a Political Reform Act, which allowed for a two-chamber parliament and a referendum in favour of democracy, and also legitimized the Socialist Party (the PSOE) and the Communists.

In the elections of 1977, the first since 1936, the **Pacte Democratico per Catalunya** – an alliance of pro-Catalan parties – gained ten seats in the lower house of the Spanish parliament, which was otherwise dominated by Suárez' own centre-right UCD party but also had a strong Socialist presence. In a spirit of consensus, it was announced that Catalunya was to be granted a degree of autonomy, and a million people turned out on the streets of Barcelona to witness the re-establishment of the Generalitat and welcome home its president-in-exile, **Josep Tarradellas**.

A new Spanish constitution of 1978 allowed for a sort of devolution within a unitary state, and the **Statute of Autonomy** for Catalunya was approved in 1979, with the first regional elections taking place in March 1980. The conservative **Jordi Pujol i Soley** and his coalition party **Convergència i Unió** (CiU) gained regional power – and proceeded to dominate the Catalan parliament for the next quarter of a century. In a way, the pro-conservative vote made it easy for the central government to deal with Catalunya, since Catalan demands for autonomy did not have the extreme political dimension seen in the Basque Country.

The 1980s and 1990s

Felipe González' PSOE was elected in 1982 with a massive swing to the left in a country that had for 43 years remained firmly in the hands of the political right; they were given a renewed mandate in 1986, the same year Spain joined the **European Community**. The country also decided by referendum to stay in NATO and boasted one of the fastest-growing economies in western Europe. Barcelona's successful hosting of the **1992 Olympic Games** brought the city to a global audience, galvanizing tourism and sparking development projects including the radical restoration of the old town and port areas. Narrow victories in two more elections kept the Socialists in power, but they failed to win an overall majority in 1993 and were forced to rely on the support of the Catalan nationalist coalition, CiU, to retain power. That state of affairs enabled Jordi Pujol to pursue long-cherished nationalist aims, in particular the right to retain a proportion of Catalunya's own income-tax revenue.

In the wake of allegations of sleaze and the disclosure of the existence of a secret "dirty war" against the Basque terrorists, it was no surprise that the PSOE lost the general election of 1996 to the conservative Partido Popular (PP), under **José María Aznar**. However, the PP came in well short of an outright majority, and Aznar was left with the same problem as his predecessor, relying on the Catalan nationalists and other smaller regionalist parties to maintain his party in power. A resounding victory in the national elections of 2000 finally enabled the PP to govern unconstrained by other

1978–80	1992	1995
Generalitat re-established and Statute of Autonomy approved. Socialist mayor and municipal government elected (1979); Conservative nationalist government elected (1980)	Olympics held in Barcelona. Massive rebuilding projects transform Montjuïc and the waterfront	MACBA (contemporary art museum) opens, signalling regeneration of El Raval district

> **NO NUDES PLEASE, WE'RE CATALAN**
>
> Barcelona is one of Europe's most popular city-break destinations, but tourism has brought its own problems, as Barcelona has acquired a not-always-welcome reputation as a beach resort and party town. The roaming stag parties and antisocial late-night behaviour by visitors causes much hand-wringing at City Hall (and much street-hosing early each morning), while certain old-town areas are now virtual tourist-only zones for much of the year. The city council has banned resort-style behaviour on Barcelona's streets – you can take your shirt off, or walk around in swimwear on the beach or the beach promenade, but strolling up and down La Rambla as if you're on the Costa del Sol is not tolerated by police.

parties, but Aznar swiftly lost his way, with ninety percent of Spaniards opposing his support for US and British **military action in Iraq** in 2003.

The tables turned once again in 2004, when the PSOE were unexpectedly victorious in a general election shaped by the deaths of two hundred people in the Madrid **train bombings** that March. The Socialists took power in a minority administration led by PSOE prime minister **José Luis Rodríguez Zapatero**, forced to rely on parliamentary support from Catalan separatists and other regional parties. Spectacular economic growth ensued, and Zapatero and the PSOE were re-elected in 2008, though not quite enjoying an absolute majority.

The irresistible rise of Catalan nationalism

The current high profile of the campaign for **Catalan independence** owes much to the impact of the worldwide **economic recession** on Spain as a whole, from 2008 onwards. With his government's **austerity measures** growing increasingly unpopular, Zapatero called time on his leadership in April 2011, and the PP won a resounding victory in the snap election that followed. In its wake, PP prime minister Mariano Rajoy largely abandoned any pretence of seeking political accommodation with Catalunya, and growing numbers of Catalans have lost faith in a future within Spain.

Nationalist fervour has swept across the political spectrum, with those who support independence as a matter of political principle or historical identity finding common cause with those who believe the national austerity programme to have damaged social and economic justice in Catalunya, and others who feel the rest of Spain to be a financial drain on what might otherwise be a prosperous Catalunya.

After Rajoy rejected a request from Catalan president Artur Mas for a referendum on independence, Catalunya staged a non-binding referendum in November 2014, and the majority of those who turned out supported the proposition that Catalunya should be a separate, independent nation. The Spanish government reacted by condemning the poll as unconstitutional, and charging Mas with perverting the course of justice, misuse of public funds and abuse of power. Mas was ultimately found guilty in a Barcelona court in 2017 – by which time he had been replaced as Catalan president by Carlos Puigdemont. After a second unofficial independence referendum in October 2017, Spain was gripped by its greatest constitutional crisis since the death of Franco. The Spanish government had not only declared the referendum to be illegal, but had

2004	2010	2015	2017
Diagonal Mar hosts Universal Forum of Cultures, heralding transformation of Poblenou district	Catalan parliament bans bullfighting; Catalunya becomes first region in mainland Spain to do so	Anti-eviction campaigner Ada Colau becomes Barcelona's first female mayor	Thirteen international visitors die when a driver deliberately targets pedestrians on La Rambla

violently disrupted it, while Puigdemont was insisting that despite a turnout of well under fifty percent of voters, he had a mandate to declare Catalunya independent. With massive demonstrations both for and against independence filling the streets of Barcelona, the government in Madrid was on the point of suspending the Catalan parliament and revoking Catalan autonomy altogether, reviving local memories of how often in Barcelona's history Spain has played the role of an occupying power.

Since then, and with the arrival of a Socialist Party government under prime minister Pedro Sánchez, the nationalist fervour has quieted somewhat. At the time of writing – after an inconclusive general election in the summer of 2023 – Sánchez was considering offering an amnesty to the architects of the 2017 insurrection if Catalan separatist parties lent their support to return him to power.

A new era

Meanwhile, following municipal elections in May 2015, **Ada Colau**, representing a left-wing citizens' coalition known as Barcelona en Comú and supported by the national anti-austerity movement Podemos, became Barcelona's first female mayor. Colau declared her determination not to "sacrifice Barcelona on the altar of mass tourism". Barcelona has become the fourth most visited city in Europe, receiving almost ten million overnight visitors each year. There's a growing consensus that the social cost has come to outweigh the economic benefits. In particular, the "black economy" of illegal tourist accommodation – there are an estimated fifty thousand illegal rooms in the city, let through the likes of Airbnb – has priced locals out of affordable city-centre rental accommodation. Entire residential blocks no longer house permanent inhabitants, and some have even been demolished and replaced with short-term lets.

Colau's powers to act were limited, but, as well as a crackdown on illegal lets, no new tourist apartments are being licensed, and a moratorium has been declared on further hotel building. As part of an ongoing attempt to control overcrowding, Segway tours were also banned from the old town and waterfront in 2017, and in 2023, limits were placed on cruise ships.

The summer of 2017 also saw Barcelona experience a devastating terror attack, when a 22-year-old man deliberately drove a van into pedestrians on La Rambla, killing thirteen and seriously wounding well over a hundred others. The tragedy prompted a rare moment of national unity, in which the king and prime minister of Spain joined Catalan president Carlos Puigdemont for a march through Barcelona that attracted over half a million participants.

In the municipal elections of 2023, Socialist candidate **Jaume Collboni** emerged the victor (with support from Colau, who did not gain enough votes to win outright). It was a blow for the separatists, who had been confident of winning, and a blow for environmentalists, who were sceptical of Collboni's dedication to the pedestrianisation and greening of Barcelona that become a hallmark of Colau's rule.

2017	2023
In a referendum deemed illegal and violently suppressed, Catalans vote in favour of independence. The Catalan parliament declares independence and is dissolved by the Spanish government, which then calls for new regional elections, won again by pro-independence parties.	General election, no majority vote. At time of writing, both major parties were still negotiating.

Books

The selection of books reviewed below provides useful background on Barcelona's history, people and institutions. Despite its long pedigree, Catalan literature is hard to find in translation, though novels set in the city by (mostly foreign) authors provide a feel of Barcelona past and present. Most of the major local bookshops (see page 223) carry English-language guides and titles about the city; or look in relevant museum bookshops for books on art, design and architecture. There's plenty in the archive of online literary magazine ⓦbarcelonareview.com on Spanish and Catalan writers, art, culture and life, while the very useful Lletra (ⓦlletra.uoc/edu/en) makes an excellent online resource (in English) for Catalan literature.

HISTORY

BARCELONA

★ **Jimmy Burns** *Barça: A People's Passion*. On one level, it's simply an informative history of the city's famous football team, alma mater of Cruyff, Lineker, Maradona, Ronaldinho et al. However, like the club itself, the book is so much more than that, as Burns examines Catalan pride and nationalism through the prism of sport.

Liz Castro (ed) *What's Up With Catalonia?* Excellent anthology of 36 short and very readable essays discussing various political, economic, cultural and historical aspects of the campaign for Catalan independence.

Felipe Fernàndez-Armesto *Barcelona: A Thousand Years of the City's Past*. An expertly written appraisal of what the author sees as the formative years of the city's history, from the tenth to the early twentieth century.

★ **Robert Hughes** *Barcelona*. The renowned art critic casts his accomplished eye over two thousand years of Barcelona's history and culture, with special emphasis on the nineteenth and early twentieth centuries – explaining, in his own words, "the zeitgeist of the place and the connective tissue between the cultural icons".

★ **Matthew Stewart** *Monturiol's Dream*. A witty and engaging account of the life of Narcís Monturiol, nineteenth-century Catalan utopian visionary, revolutionary and inventor of the first true submarine. Ever at the centre of Barcelona's social and political turmoil, Monturiol printed seditious magazines, manned the barricades in the 1850s, and fled into exile.

Colm Tóibín *Homage to Barcelona*. Echoing Orwell, the Irish writer pays his own homage to the city, tracing Barcelona's history through its artists, architects, personalities, organizations and rulers.

Richard Wright *Pagan Spain*. In his eye-opening account of visiting Spain in the late 1950s, the celebrated African-American writer provides an astonishing insight into quite how much Barcelona has changed since the Franco era.

SPAIN

Michael Reid *Spain: The Trials and Triumphs of a Modern European Country*. Published in 2023, this is a much-needed account of Spain's political and economic trajectory since Franco's death, dispelling various myths of the country's "otherness" and looking at what might come next in the context of its place in Europe.

Hugh Thomas *Rivers of Gold: The Rise of the Spanish Empire*. Thomas's scholarly but eminently accessible history provides a fascinating snapshot of Spain's most glorious period – the meteoric imperial rise in the late fifteenth and early sixteenth centuries, when characters such as Ferdinand and Isabel, and Columbus and Magellan, shaped the country's outlook for the next three hundred years.

Nigel Townson *The Penguin History of Modern Spain*. A thorough history of twentieth-century Spain, with particular emphasis on the Spanish Civil War and the events leading up to it.

★ **Giles Tremlett** *Ghosts of Spain*. In this warts-and-all look at contemporary Spain, the Madrid-based journalist finds the dark days of the Civil War never very far from the surface, even now.

THE CIVIL WAR

Gerald Brenan *The Spanish Labyrinth*. Published in 1943, this record of the background to the Civil War is tinged by personal experience, yet impressively rounded.

★ **George Orwell** *Homage to Catalonia*. Stirring account of the Civil War fight on the Aragón front and Orwell's participation in the early exhilaration of revolution in Barcelona. A forthright, honest and entertaining tale, covering Orwell's injury and subsequent flight from factional infighting in Republican Spain.

Paul Preston *A Concise History of the Spanish Civil War; Franco; The Spanish Holocaust*. From the leading historian of twentieth-century Spain, *Civil War* is an easily accessible introduction to the subject, while *Franco* offers a penetrating, monumental biography of Franco and his regime. *The Spanish Holocaust* is a controversial account of the murders and massacres that took place in Spain during and after the Civil War – violence that still engenders dark passions on both sides of the argument in contemporary Spain.

Hugh Thomas *The Spanish Civil War*. This exhaustive political study is still the best single telling of the convoluted story of the Civil War.

ART AND ARCHITECTURE

★ **Gijs van Hensbergen** *Gaudí: The Biography*. A worthy biography of "arguably the world's most famous architect". Van Hensbergen places his work firmly in context, as Spain lost its empire and Catalunya slowly flexed its nationalist muscles.

John Richardson *A Life of Picasso*. The definitive multi-volume biography. Volume 1, covering the period 1881–1906, is an extremely readable account of the artist's early years, covering the entire seminal period that he spent in Barcelona.

Philippe Thiébaut *Gaudí: Builder of Visions*. Read van Hensbergen for the life, but pick up this pocket-sized volume for its excellent photographic coverage – not just Gaudí buildings and interiors, but sketches, historical photographs and architectural insights that add up to a useful gateway to his work in the city and surroundings.

FOOD AND WINE

★ **Colman Andrews** *Catalan Cuisine*. The best available English-language book dealing with Spain's most adventurous regional cuisine. Full of historical and anecdotal detail, it's a pleasure to read, let alone cook from (no pictures, though).

Penelope Casas *The Foods and Wines of Spain*. Casas roams across every region of Spain in this classic Spanish cookery book, including the best dishes that Catalunya has to offer. Her *Paella* and *Tapas: The Little Dishes of Spain* covers the rest of the bases.

Jan Read *Wines of Spain*. All you need to know to sort out your Penedès from your Priorat – an explanation of regions and producers, plus tasting notes and tips for wine tourists.

NOVELS SET IN BARCELONA

John Bryson *To the Death, Amic*. Barcelona, under siege during the Civil War, is the backdrop for a coming-of-age novel recounting the adventures of 10-year-old twins Enric and Josep.

Miguel Cervantes *Don Quixote*. Barcelona is the only city to which Cervantes gives its real name in his picaresque classic – in the Barcelona chapters, Don Quixote and Sancho Panza see the ocean for the first time, and Quixote fights a duel on Barceloneta beach against the Knight of the White Moon.

Ildefonso Falcones *Cathedral of the Sea*. Barcelona lawyer Falcones set his award-winning first novel in the expansionist years of the fourteenth century, where work is under way on the building of the city's most magnificent church, Santa María del Mar. His highly realistic, excitingly plotted tale lifts the skirts of medieval Barcelona to show an authentic picture of a city on the make.

Juan Marsé *Lizard Tails* and *Shanghai Nights*. Marsé spent his formative years in a Barcelona scarred by the Civil War, and ruptured childhood and family hardship are recurrent themes. *Lizard Tails* is an evocation of post-Civil War childhood, while *Shanghai Nights* – again, Barcelona and war to the fore – is billed as "a tale of the human spirit".

★ **Eduardo Mendoza** *City of Marvels, The Truth About the Savolta Case* and *The Year of the Flood*. Mendoza's first and best novel, *City of Marvels*, is set in the expanding Barcelona of 1880–1920, full of rich underworld characters and riddled with anarchic and comic turns. The milieu is reused with flair in *The Truth About the Savolta Case*, while *The Year of the Flood* adds a light touch to an unusual amorous entanglement in 1950s Barcelona.

Raul Nuñez *The Lonely Hearts Club*. A parade of grotesque and hard-bitten characters haunts the city in this oddball but likeable romantic comedy.

Merce Redoreda *In Diamond Square*. A mesmerizing close-up vision of everyday life in Barcelona during and after the Civil War.

Colm Tóibín *The South*. Barcelona provided the background for Tóibín's first novel, about an Irish woman looking for a new life.

Carlos Ruiz Zafón *The Shadow of the Wind*. A Gothic literary thriller set after the Civil War, full of atmospheric Barcelona locations. It generated rave reviews and sold over fifteen million copies worldwide. Zafón followed up with a similarly intricate and successful prequel, *The Angel's Game*.

THRILLERS AND CRIME NOVELS

Bernado Atxaga *The Lone Man*. The noted Basque writer set his well-received psychological thriller during the 1982 World Cup, when two ETA gunmen hole up in a Barcelona hotel.

★ **Manuel Vázquez Montalbán** *Murder in the Central Committee, Southern Seas, The Angst-Ridden Executive, An Olympic Death, Offside, The Man of My Life* and *Tattoo*. Montalbán's greatest creation, the fast-living gourmand-detective Pepe Carvalho, ex-Communist and CIA agent, first appeared in print in 1972, and went on to investigate foul deeds in the city in a series of wry and racy Chandler-

CATALAN LITERATURE AND WRITERS

Catalan was established as a literary language as early as the thirteenth century, and the **golden age** of medieval Catalan literature lasted until the mid-sixteenth century, with another cultural and literary flowering in the nineteenth century known as the **Renaixença** (Renaissance). However, with the rise of Castile and later Bourbon rule, the Catalan language was eclipsed and then suppressed, and similarly under Franco, when there was a ban on Catalan books and publications. Post-Civil War, there was some relaxation of the ban, but only since the return of democracy to Spain has Catalan literature once again flourished.

Catalan and Spanish speakers and readers are best served by the literature, since there's little still in translation. The vernacular works of mystic and philosopher **Ramon Llull** (1233–1316) mark the onset of a true Catalan literature – his *Blanquerna* was one of the first books to be written in any Romance language, while the later chivalric epic *Tirant lo Blanc* (*The White Tyrant*) by **Joanot Martorell** (1413–68) represents a high point of the golden age. None of the works of the leading lights of the nineteenth-century Renaixença is readily available in translation, so look to *Solitud* (*Solitude*) by **Victor Català** (1869–1966) for the most important pre-Civil War Catalan novel. This tragic tale of a woman's life and sexual passions in a Catalan mountain village was published pseudonymously in 1905 by **Caterina Albert i Paradís**, who lived most of her life in rural northern Catalunya.

During and after the Civil War, many authors found themselves under forcible or self-imposed exile, including perhaps Spain's most important modern novelist, **Juan Goytisolo** (1931–2017), a bitter enemy of the Franco regime (which banned his books). Goytisolo spent most of his life abroad and his great trilogy – *Marks of Identity*, *Count Julian* and *Juan the Landless* – confronted the whole ambivalent idea of Spain and Spanishness. Other notable exiles included **Pere Calders i Rossinyol** (1912–94), best known for his short stories, and **Mercè Rodoreda i Gurguí** (1909–83), whose *Plaça del Diamant* (*In Diamond Square*), *El Carrer de les Camèlies* (*Camelia Street*) and *La Meva Cristina i Altres Contes* (*My Cristina and Other Tales*) can be readily found in translation. The works of **Maria Antònia Oliver i Cabrer** (born 1946), novelist, children's author and short-story writer born in Mallorca, were influenced by her birthplace, but her *Estudi en Lila* (*Study in Lilac*) and *Antipodes* introduce fictional Barcelona private eye Lonia Guiu. More detectives – this time, oddball twins Eduard and Pep – comb the city in the work of contemporary Catalan novelist **Teresa Solana** (born 1962).

Some Catalan writers write in Spanish rather than Catalan, including perhaps the best-known of all, **Manuel Vázquez Montalbán** (1939–2003), crime writer *par excellence*, and novelist, poet, journalist, political commentator and committed Communist to boot. His Pepe Carvalho books did much to expose the shortcomings of the new Spanish democracy in fast-changing Barcelona. Montalbán's contemporary **Juan Marsé** (born 1933) uses the post-Civil War dictatorship as the background for many of his Barcelona-set novels, and the same period spawned the Barcelona blockbuster *The Shadow of the Wind* by **Carlos Ruiz Zafón** (born 1964), and its prequel *The Angel's Game*. For other new Catalan writers, such as **Albert Sánchez Piñol** (born 1965), nationality seems incidental at best – his well-regarded first novel, *Cold Skin*, is a creepy psychological sci-fi tale of solitude on an Antarctic island, while literary adventure story *Pandora in the Congo* starts in the dark heart of the African jungle.

esque thrillers. *Murder in the Central Committee* is a good place to start, as Carvalho confronts his Communist past. *Southern Seas* won the Planeta, Spain's biggest literary prize, while the city's businesses, institutions and events come under typical scrutiny in *The Angst-Ridden Executive*, *An Olympic Death* and *Offside*. Twenty-first-century Catalan politics come under the spotlight in the last Carvalho novel, *The Man of My Life*, while the early *Tattoo* plunges readers right back into "sex, death and food in 1970s Barcelona".

Teresa Solana *A Not So Perfect Crime; A Shortcut to Paradise*. In her first two Barcelona noir novels, Solana introduces bumbling detective twins Eduard and Pep – they don't look alike and they don't solve cases, but they do skewer contemporary high society, whether in politics (*A Not So Perfect Crime*) or literary circles (*A Shortcut to Paradise*).

Barbara Ellen Wilson *Gaudí Afternoon*. Pacy feminist thriller making good use of Gaudí's architecture as a backdrop for deception and skulduggery.

Language

In Barcelona, Catalan (català) has more or less taken over from Castilian Spanish (castellano) as the language on street signs, maps, official buildings and notices, and so on. On paper, it looks like a cross between French and Spanish, and is generally easy to read if you know those two. Spoken Catalan is harder to come to grips with, as the language itself is not phonetic, and accents vary from region to region.

Few visitors realize how important Catalan is to those who speak it: never commit the error of calling it a dialect. However, despite the ubiquity of the Catalan language, you'll get by perfectly well in Spanish, as long as you can learn to understand Catalan in timetables, on menus, and the like. You'll find some basic pronunciation rules below, for both Spanish and Catalan, and a selection of words and phrases in both languages. Spanish is certainly easier to pronounce, but don't be afraid to try Catalan, especially in the more out-of-the-way places – you'll generally get a good reception if you at least try communicating in the local language.

Numerous **phrasebooks** are available, not least the *Spanish Rough Guide Phrasebook*, in print and digital formats, laid out dictionary-style, and featuring 24 typical travel scenarios that can also be downloaded as audio files. In Barcelona, *Parla Català* (Pia) is the only readily available English–Catalan phrasebook, though more extensive Catalan–English dictionaries and teach-yourself Catalan guides are available online.

PRONUNCIATION

CASTILIAN (SPANISH)

Unless there's an accent, words ending in "D", "L", "R" or "Z" are **stressed** on the last syllable, all others on the second last. All **vowels** are pure and short; combinations have predictable results.

A somewhere between the "A" sound of "back" and that of "father".

E as in "get".

I as in "police".

O as in "hot".

U as in "rule".

C is lisped before "E" and "I", hard otherwise: "cerca" is pronounced "thairka".

G works the same way, a guttural "H" sound (like the "ch" in "loch") before "E" or "I", a hard "G" elsewhere – "gigante" becomes "higantay".

H is always silent.

J the same sound as a guttural "G": "jamón" is pronounced "hamon".

LL sounds like an English "Y": "tortilla" is pronounced "torteeya".

N is as in English unless it has a tilde (accent) over it, when it becomes "NY": "mañana" sounds like "man-yaana".

QU is pronounced like an English "K".

R is rolled, "RR" doubly so.

V sounds more like "B", "vino" becoming "beano".

X has an "S" sound before consonants, normal "X" before vowels.

Z is the same as a soft "C", so "cerveza" becomes "thairbaitha".

CATALAN

With Catalan, don't be tempted to use the few rules of Spanish pronunciation you may know – in particular the soft Spanish "Z" and "C" don't apply, so unlike in the rest of Spain the city is not "Barthelona" but "Barcelona", as in English.

A as in "hat" if stressed, as in "alone" when unstressed.

E varies, but usually as in "get".

I as in "police".

IG sounds like the "tch" in the English scratch; "lleig" (ugly) is pronounced "yeah-tch".

O a round full sound, when stressed, otherwise like a soft "U" sound.

U somewhere between the "U" of "put" and "rule".

Ç sounds like an English "S"; "plaça" is pronounced "plassa".

C followed by an "E" or "I" is soft; otherwise hard.

G followed by "E" or "I" is like the "zh" in "Zhivago"; otherwise hard.

H is always silent.

J as in the French "Jean".

TALKING THE TALK

Catalan (català) is a Romance language, stemming directly from Latin, and closely resembling the language of Occitan, spoken in southern France. Catalan is spoken by over ten million people in total, in Barcelona and Catalunya, part of Aragón, much of Valencia, the Balearic islands, Andorra and parts of the French Pyrenees – and its use is thus much more widespread than, say, Danish, Finnish or Norwegian. Other Spaniards tend to belittle it by saying that to get a Catalan word you just cut a Castilian one in half, but in fact the grammar is more complicated and it has eight vowel sounds compared with Castilian's five. Catalan was banned from the radio, TV, daily press and schools during the Franco era, so many older people cannot read or write it, even if they speak it all the time. Virtually every Catalan is bilingual, but most regard Catalan as their mother tongue and it's estimated to be the dominant language in around half of Catalunya's households.

L.L is best pronounced (for foreigners) as a single "L" sound; but for Catalan speakers it has two distinct "L" sounds.

LL sounds like an English "Y" or "LY", like the "yuh" sound in "million".

N as in English, though before "F" or "V" it sometimes sounds like an "M".

NY corresponds to the Castilian "Ñ".

QU before "E" or "I" sounds like "K", unless the "U" has an umlaut (Ü), in which case, and before "A" or "O", as in "quit".

R is rolled, but only at the start of a word; at the end, it's often silent.

T is pronounced as in English, though sometimes it sounds like a "D", as in "viatge" or "dotze".

V at the start of a word sounds like "B"; in all other positions it's a soft "F" sound.

W is pronounced like a "B/V".

X is like "SH" or "CH" in most words, though in some, like "exit", it sounds like an "X".

Z is like the English "Z" in "zoo".

USEFUL WORDS AND PHRASES

Words and phrases below are given in the following order: **English** – Spanish – *Catalan*.

BASICS

Yes, No, OK Sí, No, Vale *Si, No, Val*
Please, Thank you Por favor, Gracias *Si us plau, Gràcies*
Where? When? Dónde? Cuando? *On? Quan?*
What? How much? Qué? Cuánto? *Què? Quant?*
Here, There Aquí, Allí/Allá *Aquí, Allí/Allà*
This, That Esto, Eso *Això, Allò*
Now, Later Ahora, Más tarde *Ara, Mès tard*
Open, Closed Abierto/a, Cerrado/a *Obert, Tancat*
With, Without Con, Sin *Amb, Sense*
Good, Bad Bueno/a, Malo/a *Bo(na), Dolent(a)*
Big, Small Gran(de), Pequeño/a *Gran, Petit(a)*
Cheap, Expensive Barato, Caro *Barat(a), Car(a)*
Hot, Cold Caliente, Frío *Calent(a), Fred(a)*
More, Less Más, Menos *Mes, Menys*
I want Quiero *Vull (pronounced "vwee")*
I'd like Quisiera *Voldria*
Do you know? ¿Sabe? *Vostès saben?*
I don't know No sé *No sé*
There is (is there?) (¿)Hay(?) *Hi ha(?)*
What's that? ¿Qué es eso? *Què és això?*
Give me (one like that) Deme (uno así) (a bit brusque) *Doneu-me*

Do you have? ¿Tiene? *Té ...?*
The time La hora *L'hora*
Today, Tomorrow Hoy, Mañana *Avui, Demà*
Yesterday Ayer *Ahir*
Day before yesterday Ante ayer *Abans-d'ahir*
Next week La semana que viene *La setmana que ve*
Next month El mes que viene *El mes que ve*

GREETINGS AND RESPONSES

Hello, Goodbye Hola, Adiós *Hola, Adéu*
Good morning Buenos días *Bon dia*
Good afternoon/night Buenas tardes/noches *Bona tarde/nit*
See you later Hasta luego *Fins després*
Sorry Lo siento/Disculpéme *Ho sento*
Excuse me Con permiso/Perdón *Perdoni*
How are you? ¿Cómo está (usted)? *Com va?*
I (don't) understand (No) Entiendo *(No) Ho entenc*
Not at all/You're welcome De nada *De res*
Do you speak English? ¿Habla (usted) inglés? *Parleu anglès?*
I (don't) speak Spanish/Catalan (No) Hablo español *(No) Parlo Català*
My name is ... Me llamo ... *Em dic ...*
What's your name? ¿Como se llama usted? *Com es diu?*
I am English Soy inglés(a) *Sóc anglès(a)*

... **Scottish** ... escocés(a) ... *escocès(a)*
... **Australian** ... australiano(a) ... *australian(a)*
... **Canadian** ... canadiense(a) ... *canadenc(a)*
... **American** ... americano(a) ... *americà (a)*
... **Irish** ... irlandes(a) ... *irlandès (a)*

FINDING ACCOMMODATION

Do you have a room? ¿Tiene una habitación? *Té alguna habitació? ... amb*
... **with two beds/double bed** ... con dos camas/cama *dos llits/llit per dues persones*
... **with shower/bath** matrimonial ... con ducha/baño *... amb dutxa/bany*
It's for one person (two people) Es para una persona (dos personas) *Per a una persona (dues persones)*
For one night (one week) Para una noche (una semana) *Per una nit (una setmana)*
It's fine, how much is it? ¿Está bien, cuánto es? *Esta bé, quant és?*
It's too expensive Es demasiado caro *És massa car*
Don't you have anything cheaper? ¿No tiene algo más barato? *En té de mé sbon preu?*

DIRECTIONS AND TRANSPORT

How do I get to ...? ¿Por donde se va a ...? *Per anar a ...?*
Left, right, straight on Izquierda, derecha, todo recto *A la dreta, a l'esquerra, tot recte*
Where is ...? ¿Dónde está ...? *On és ......?*
... **the bus station** ... la estación de autobuses ... *l'estació de autobuses*
... **the train station** ... la estación de ferrocarril ... *l'estació*
... **the nearest bank** ... el banco más cercano ... *el banc més a prop*
... **the post office** ... el correos/la oficina de correos ... *l'oficina de correus*
... **the toilet** ... el baño/servicio ... *el lavabo*
It's not very far No está muy lejos *No és gaire lluny*
Where does the bus to ... leave from? ¿De dónde sale el autobús para ...? *De on surt el autobús a ...?*
Is this the train for Barcelona? ¿Es este el tren para Barcelona? *Aquest tren va a Barcelona?*
I'd like a (return) ticket to ... Quisiera un billete (de ida y vuelta) para *Voldria un bitllet (d'anar i tornar) a*
What time does it leave (arrive in)? ¿A qué hora sale (llega)? *A quina hora surt (arriba a)?*

NUMBERS

1 un/uno/una *un(a)*
2 dos *dos (dues)*
3 tres *tres*
4 cuatro *quatre*
5 cinco *cinc*
6 seis *sis*
7 siete *set*
8 ocho *vuit*
9 nueve *nou*
10 diez *deu*
11 once *onze*
12 doce *dotze*
13 trece *tretze*
14 catorce *catorze*
15 quince *quinze*
16 dieciseis *setze*
17 diecisiete *disset*
18 dieciocho *divuit*
19 diecinueve *dinou*
20 veinte *vint*
21 veintiuno *vint-i-un*
30 treinta *trenta*
40 cuarenta *quaranta*
50 cincuenta *cinquanta*
60 sesenta *seixanta*
70 setenta *setanta*
80 ochenta *vuitanta*
90 noventa *novanta*
100 cien(to) *cent*
101 ciento uno *cent un*
102 ciento dos *cent dos (dues)*
200 doscientos *dos-cents (dues-centes)*
500 quinientos *cinc-cents*
1000 mil *mil*
2000 dos mil *dos mil*

DAYS AND MONTHS

Monday lunes *dilluns*
Tuesday martes *dimarts*
Wednesday miércoles *dimecres*
Thursday jueves *dijous*
Friday viernes *divendres*
Saturday sábado *dissabte*
Sunday domingo *diumenge*
January enero *gener*
February febrero *febrer*
March marzo *març*
April abril *abril*
May mayo *maig*
June junio *juny*
July julio *juliol*
August agosto *agost*
September septiembre *setembre*
October octubre *octobre*
November noviembre *novembre*
December diciembre *desembre*

FOOD AND DRINK

Words and phrases below are given in the following
order: **English** – Spanish – *Catalan*.

SOME BASIC WORDS
To have breakfast Desayunar *Esmorzar*
To have lunch Comer *Dinar*
To have dinner Cenar *Sopar*
The bill La cuenta *El compte*
I'm a vegetarian Soy vegetariano/a *Sóc vegetarià/
vegetariana*
Knife Cuchillo *Ganivet*
Fork Tenedor *Forquilla*
Spoon Cuchara *Cullera*
Table Mesa *Taula*
Bottle Botella *Ampolla*
Glass Vaso *Got*
Menu Carta *Carta*
Soup Sopa *Sopa*
Salad Ensalada *Amanida*
Hors d'oeuvres Entremeses *Entremesos*
Omelette Tortilla *Truita*
Sandwich Bocadillo *Entrepà*
Toast Tostadas *Torrades*
Tapas Tapes *Tapes*
Butter Mantequilla *Mantega*
Eggs Huevos *Ous*
Bread Pan *Pa*
Olives Aceitunas *Olives*
Oil Aceite *Oli*
Vinegar Vinagre *Vinagre*
Salt Sal *Sal*
Pepper Pimienta *Pebre*
Sugar Azucar *Sucre*

GENERAL MENU TERMS
Assorted Surtido/variado *Assortit*
Baked Al horno *Al forn*
Char-grilled A la brasa *A la brasa*
Fresh Fresco *Fresc*
Fried Frito *Fregit*
Fried in batter A la romana *A la romana*
Garlic mayonnaise Alioli *All i oli*
Grilled A la plancha *A la plantxa*
Pickled En escabeche *En escabetx*
Roast Asado *Rostit*
Sauce Salsa *Salsa*
Sautéed Salteado *Saltat*
Scrambled Revuelto *Remenat*
Seasonal Del tiempo *Del temps*
Smoked Ahumado *Fumat*
Spit-roasted Al ast *A l'ast*
Steamed Al vapor *Al vapor*
Stewed Guisado *Guisat*
Stuffed Relleno *Farcit*

FISH AND SEAFOOD/PESCADO Y MARISCOS/PEIX I MARISC
Anchovies Anchoas/Boquerones *Anxoves/Seitons*
Baby squid Chipirones *Calamarsets*
Bream Besugo *Besuc*
Clams Almejas *Cloïsses*
Crab Cangrejo *Cranc*
Cuttlefish Sepia *Sipia*
Eels Anguilas *Anguiles*
Hake Merluza *Lluç*
Langoustines Langostinos *Llagostins*
Lobster Langosta *Llagosta*
Monkfish Rape *Rap*
Mussels Mejillones *Musclos*
Octopus Pulpo *Pop*
Oysters Ostras *Ostres*
Perch Mero *Mero*
Prawns Gambas *Gambes*
Razor clams Navajas *Navalles*
Red mullet Salmonete *Moll*
Salmon Salmón *Salmó*
Salt cod Bacalao *Bacallà*
Sardines Sardinas *Sardines*
Scallops Vieiras *Vieires*
Sea bass Lubina *Llobarro*
Sole Lenguado *Llenguado*
Squid Calamares *Calamars*
Swordfish Pez espada *Peix espasa*
Trout Trucha *Truita (de riu)*
Tuna Atún *Tonyina*
Whitebait Chanquete *Xanguet*

MEAT AND POULTRY/CARNE Y AVES/CARN I AVIRAM
Beef Buey *Bou*
Boar Jabalí *Senglar*
Charcuterie Embutidos *Embotits*
Chicken Pollo *Pollastre*
Chorizo sausage Chorizo *Xoriço*
Cured ham Jamón serrano *Pernil serrà*
Cured pork sausage Longaniza *Llonganissa*
Cutlets/Chops Chuletas *Costelles*
Duck Pato *Ànec*
Ham Jamón York *Pernil dolç*
Hare Liebre *Llebre*
Kid/goat Cabrito *Cabrit*
Kidneys Riñones *Ronyons*
Lamb Cordero *Xai/Be*
Liver Hígado *Fetge*
Loin of pork Lomo *Llom*
Meatballs Albóndigas *Mandonguilles*

Partridge Perdiz *Perdiu*
Pigs' trotters Pies de cerdo *Peus de porc*
Pork Cerdo *Porc*
Rabbit Conejo *Conill*
Sausages Salchichas *Salsitxes*
Snails Caracoles *Cargols*
Steak Bistec *Bistec*
Tongue Lengua *Llengua*
Veal Ternera *Vedella*

VEGETABLES AND PULSES/VERDURAS Y LEGUMBRES/VERDURES I LLEGUMS

Artichokes Alcachofas *Carxofes*
Asparagus Esparragos *Esparrecs*
Aubergine Berenjena *Albergínia*
Avocado Aguacate *Alvocat*
Broad/lima beans Habes *Faves*
Cabbage Col *Col*
Carrots Zanahorias *Pastanagues*
Cauliflower Coliflor *Col-i-flor*
Chickpeas Garbanzos *Cigrons*
Courgette Calabacín *Carbassó*
Cucumber Pepino *Cogombre*
Garlic Ajo *All*
Haricot beans Judías blancas *Mongetes*
Herbs Hierbas *Herbes*
Leeks Puerros *Porros*
Lentils Lentejas *Llenties*
Mushrooms Champiñones *Xampinyons*
Onion Cebolla *Ceba*
Peas Guisantes *Pèsols*
Peppers Pimientos *Pebrots*
Potatoes Patatas *Patates*
Spinach Espinacas *Espinacs*
Tomatoes Tomates *Tomàquets*
Turnips Nabos *Naps*
Wild mushrooms Setas *Bolets*

FRUIT/FRUTA/FRUITA

Apple Manzana *Poma*
Apricot Albaricoque *Albercoc*
Banana Plátano *Plàtan*
Cherries Cerezas *Cireres*
Figs Higos *Figues*
Grapes Uvas *Raïm*
Melon Melón *Meló*
Orange Naranja *Taronja*
Peach Melocotón *Pressec*
Pear Pera *Pera*
Pineapple Piña *Pinya*
Strawberries Fresas *Maduixes*

DESSERTS/POSTRES/POSTRES

Cake Pastel *Pastís*

Cheese Queso *Formatge*
Crème caramel Flan *Flam*
Fruit salad Macedonia *Macedonia*
Ice cream Helado *Gelat*
Rice pudding Arroz con leche *Arròs amb llet*
Tart Tarta *Tarta*
Yoghurt Yogur *Yogur*

CATALAN SPECIALITIES

Amanida catalana Salad served with sliced meats (sometimes cheese)
Ànec amb peres Duck with pears
Arròs a banda Rice with seafood, the rice served separately
Arròs a la cubana Rice with fried egg and home-made tomato sauce
Arròs a la marinera Paella: rice with seafood and saffron
Arròs negre "Black rice", cooked – risotto-style – in squid ink
Bacallà a la llauna Salt cod baked with garlic, tomato and paprika
Bacallà amb mongetes Salt cod with stewed haricot beans
Botifarra (amb mongetes) Grilled Catalan pork sausage (with stewed haricot beans)
Bunyols Fritters, which can be sweet (like little doughnuts, with sugar) or savoury (salt cod or wild mushroom)
Calçots Large chargrilled spring onions, eaten with romesco sauce (available Feb–March)
Canelons Cannelloni
Conill all i oli Rabbit with garlic mayonnaise
Conill amb cargols Rabbit with snails
Crema catalana Crème caramel, with caramelized sugar topping
Entremesos Hors d'oeuvres of mixed meat and cheese
Escalivada Grilled aubergine, pepper and onion
Escudella i carn d'olla A winter dish of stewed mixed meat and vegetables, served broth first, meat and veg second
Espinacs a la Catalana Spinach cooked with raisins and pine nuts
Esqueixada Salad of salt cod with peppers, tomatoes, onions and olives – a summer dish
Estofat de vedella Veal stew
Faves a la Catalana Stewed broad beans, with bacon and botifarra – a regional classic
Fideuà Short, thin noodles (the width of vermicelli) served with seafood, accompanied by all i oli
Fideus a la cassola Short, thin noodles baked with meat
Fricandó (amb bolets) Braised veal (with wild mushrooms)
Fuet Catalan salami

Llagosta amb pollastre Lobster with chicken in a rich sauce
Llenties guisades Stewed lentils
Mel i mató Curd cheese and honey – a typical dessert
Oca amb naps Goose with turnips
Pa amb tomàquet Bread (often grilled), rubbed with tomato, garlic and olive oil
Panellets Marzipan cakes – served for All Saints' Day
Perdiu a la vinagreta Partridge in vinegar gravy
Perdiu amb col Partridge with cabbage dumplings
Pollastre al cava Chicken with cava (champagne) sauce
Pollastre amb gambes Chicken with prawns
Postres de músic Cake of dried fruit and nuts
Rap amb all cremat Monkfish with creamed garlic sauce
Salsa romesco Spicy sauce (with chillis, ground almonds, hazelnuts, garlic, tomato and wine), often served with grilled fish
Samfaina Ratatouille-like stew (onions, peppers, aubergine, tomato), served with salt cod or chicken
Sarsuela Fish and shellfish stew
Sípia amb mandonguilles Cuttlefish with meatballs
Sopa d'all Garlic soup, often with egg and bread
Suquet de peix Fish and potato casserole

Xató Mixed salad of olives, salt cod, preserved tuna, anchovies and onions

DRINKS

Beer Cerveza *Cervesa*
Wine Vino *Vi*
Champagne Champán *Xampany*
Sherry Jerez *Xerès*
Coffee Café *Cafè*
Espresso Café solo *Cafè sol*
Large black coffee Café americano *Cafè americà*
Large white coffee Café con leche *Cafè amb llet*
Small white coffee Café cortado *Cafè tallat*
Decaff Descafeinado *Descafeinat*
Tea Té *Te*
Drinking chocolate Chocolate *Xocolata*
Juice Zumo *Suc*
Crushed ice drink Granizado *Granissat*
Milk Leche *Llet*
Tiger nut drink Horchata *Orxata*
Water Agua *Aigua*
Mineral water Agua mineral *Aigua mineral*
… (sparkling) … (con gas) … *(amb gas)*
… (still) … (sin gas) … *(sense gas)*

A GLOSSARY OF CATALAN WORDS

Ajuntament Town hall (city council)
Avinguda Avenue
Barcino Roman name for Barcelona
Barri Neighbourhood
Bodega Cellar, wine bar or warehouse
Caixa Savings bank
Call Jewish quarter
Camí Path
Capella Chapel
Carrer Street
Casa House
Castell Castle
Cava Catalan "champagne"
Comarca County
Correus Post office
Església Church
Estació Station
Estany Lake
Festa Festival
Font Fountain
Forn Bakery
Generalitat Catalan government
Gòtic Gothic (eg Barri Gòtic, Gothic Quarter)
Granja Milk bar/café

Guiri Foreigner (pej.)
Llotja Stock exchange building
Mercat Market
Modernisme Catalan Art Nouveau
Monestir Monastery or convent
Museu Museum
Palau Aristocratic mansion/palace
Passatge Alley
Passeig Promenade/boulevard; also the evening stroll thereon
Pastisseria Cake/pastry shop
Pati Inner courtyard
Plaça Square
Platja Beach
Pont Bridge
Porta Gateway
Rambla Boulevard
Renaixença Renaissance
Ríu River
Sant/a Saint
Sardana Catalunya's national folk dance
Serra Mountain range
Seu Cathedral
Terrassa Outdoor terrace

Small print and index

A ROUGH GUIDE TO ROUGH GUIDES

Published in 1982, the first Rough Guide – to Greece – was a student scheme that became a publishing phenomenon. Mark Ellingham, a recent graduate in English from Bristol University, had been travelling in Greece the previous summer and couldn't find the right guidebook. With a small group of friends he wrote his own guide, combining a contemporary, journalistic style with a thoroughly practical approach to travellers' needs.

The immediate success of the book spawned a series that rapidly covered dozens of destinations. And, in addition to impecunious backpackers, Rough Guides soon acquired a much broader readership that relished the guides' wit and inquisitiveness as much as their enthusiastic, critical approach and value-for-money ethos. These days, Rough Guides include recommendations from budget to luxury and cover more than 120 destinations around the globe, from Amsterdam to Zanzibar, all regularly updated by our team of roaming writers.

Browse all our latest guides, read inspirational features and book your trip at **roughguides.com**.

Rough Guide credits

Editor: Rachel Lawrence
Cartography: Katie Bennett
Picture Editor: Piotr Kala
Picture Manager: Tom Smyth

Layout: Pradeep Thapliyal
Head of DTP and Pre-Press: Rebeka Davies
Head of Publishing: Sarah Clark

Publishing information

Thirteenth edition 2024

Distribution

UK, Ireland and Europe
Apa Publications (UK) Ltd; sales@roughguides.com
United States and Canada
Ingram Publisher Services; ips@ingramcontent.com
Australia and New Zealand
Booktopia; retailer@booktopia.com.au
Worldwide
Apa Publications (UK) Ltd; sales@roughguides.com

Special Sales, Content Licensing and CoPublishing

Rough Guides can be purchased in bulk quantities
at discounted prices. We can create special editions,
personalised jackets and corporate imprints tailored to
your needs. sales@roughguides.com.
roughguides.com

Printed in Czech Republic

This book was produced using **Typefi** automated
publishing software.

A catalogue record for this book is available from the
British Library

The publishers and authors have done their best to ensure
the accuracy and currency of all the information in **The
Rough Guide to Barcelona**, however, they can accept
no responsibility for any loss, injury, or inconvenience
sustained by any traveller as a result of information or
advice contained in the guide.

Help us update

We've gone to a lot of effort to ensure that this edition of
The Rough Guide to Barcelona is accurate and up-to-
date. However, things change – places get "discovered",
transport routes are altered, restaurants and hotels raise
prices or lower standards, and businesses cease trading. If
you feel we've got it wrong or left something out, we'd like
to know, and if you can direct us to the web address, so
much the better.

Please send your comments with the subject
line "**Rough Guide Barcelona Update**" to mail@
uk.roughguides.com. We'll acknowledge all contributions
and send a copy of the next edition (or any other Rough
Guide if you prefer) for the very best emails.

Acknowledgements

Sally Davies Enormous thanks to the indefatigable Mary Ann Gallagher for her research assistance, and to Rachel
Lawrence for endless patience. Thanks, too, to Tess O'Donovan for tolerating my absences with good grace.
AnneLise Sorensen Thanks to all who invited me in, wined and dined me and shared information, travel tips and lively
evenings, including: Maite, as always, for her splendid hospitality and knowledge of Spain; my ever-entertaining Catalan
family, including all my wonderful cousins and tiets and tietas; and Claire (and family) for being such a special best friend.
A hearty thank you to my talented editor and co-author, as well as to dear friends and travel colleagues in New York and
California for their support and cheery emails. Finally, a big gracias, mange tak and thank you to Papa, the best companion
a travel writer could ask for, and to Mama, who both inspired my lifelong love of exploring the world

ABOUT THE AUTHORS

Sally Davies settled in Barcelona in 2001 after stints living in Madrid and Seville. She has
written guidebooks to most regions of Spain, along with a book on Spanish cuisine. Her work
as a journalist leads her all over the country, seeking out culinary and cultural experiences of
every stripe – but Barcelona will always be home.

AnneLise Sorensen is a travel writer and editor with Catalan-Danish roots. She has penned
(and wine-tasted) her way across Spain, reporting for guidebooks, magazines, newspapers,
radio, podcasts and more. AnneLise divides her time between New York, California and
Europe, sustained by *cafés con leche* on both sides of the Atlantic. She also regularly covers
Scandinavia, Central America, New York, California and beyond.

Photo credits

(Key: T-top; C-centre; B-bottom; L-left; R-right)

Index

Map symbols

The symbols below are used on maps throughout the book

── ··	International boundary	⚹	Viewpoint	⊠	Post office		Building
━━━	Railway	⊙	Statue	✚	Hospital		Church/cathedral/c
═══	Road	ⓘ	Information office	✡	Synagogue		Market
▬▬	Motorway	🅿	Parking	✈	Airport		Park/garden
▬▬	Pedestrian road	⚲	Swimming pool	Ⓜ	Metro station		Forest
●----●	Cable car	─Ⓣ─	Tram line & stop	ⓕ	FGC station		Beach
━━━	Wall	⊥	Gardens	⊠	Gate		Cemetery
▭▭▭	Steps						

Listings key

■ Accommodation

● Eating

■ Drinking/nightlife

● Shopping

City plan

The **city plan** on the pages that follow is divided as shown:

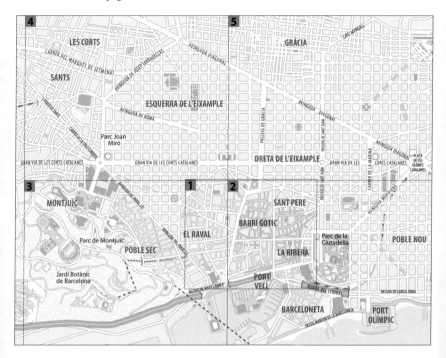

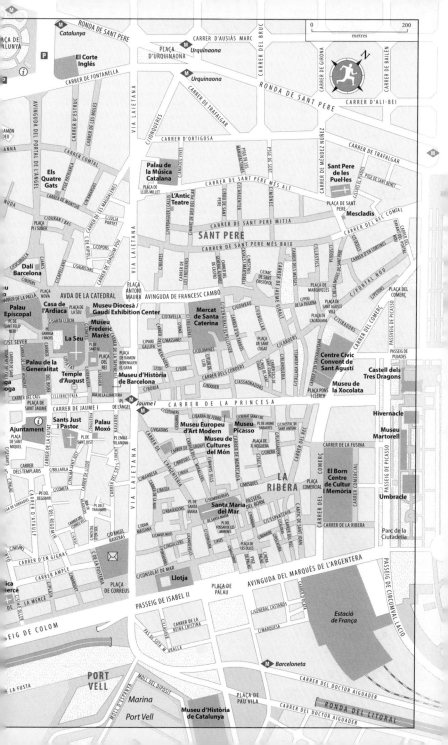

CRER D'AUSIAS MARC
CARRER DE SICILIA
CARRER DE RIBES
CARRER DE LEPANT
L'Auditori
PLAÇA DE LES ARTS
CARRER DE PADILLA
CARRER DE BOLIVIA

CARRER DE NAPOLS
CARRER D'ALI-BEI
CARRER DE LA MARINA
AVINGUDA MERIDIANA
CARRER DE TANGER

Barcelona Nord
(Bus Station)
CARRER DE SANCHO DE ÁVILA
TGE DE RIBES

Parc de l'Estacio del Nord
CARRER DE SARDENYA

RRER DELS ALMOGÀVERS
Marina
CARRER DELS ALMOGÀVERS
CARRER D'ALABA
CARRER D'ÀVILA
CARRER DE BADAJOZ

ER DE BUENAVENTURA MUÑOZ
CARRER DE WELLINGTON
CARRER DE PALLARS

SEIG DE PUJADES
CTRA ANTIGA DE MATARO
CARRER DE JOAN D'ÀUSTRIA
CARRER DE PERE IV
Bogatell
CARRER DE ZAMORA
CARRER DE PUJADES

Cascada
AVINGUDA DEL BOGATELL
CARRER DE PAMPLONA
CARRER DE LLULL

arc de la
iutadella
CARRER DE LA MARINA
CARRER DE RAMÓN TURRÓ
POBLENOU
PTGE DE MAS DE RODA

arlament
Catalunya
CARRER DE JOAN MIRÓ
CARRER DE DOCTOR TRUETA
Cementiri
de Poblenou

de
ona
CARRER DE RAMON TRIAS FARGAS
CARRER DE MOSCOU
ROSA SENSAT
PTGE DEL GENERAL BASSOLS
CARRER DE L'ARQUITECTE SERT
C/JAUME VICENS I VIVES
C/BISBE I CLIMENT

Ciutadella–
Vila Olímpica
AVINGUDA D'ICÀRIA
CARRER DE
Yelmo-Icaria
Cinema
C/FREDERIC MOMPOU
C/JOAN OLIVER
C/CARMEN AMAYA

PASSEIG DE GARCIA FARIA
C/SALVADOR ESPRIU

ER DEL DOCTOR AIGUADER
PLAÇA DELS VOLUNTARIS OLÍMPICS
Parc del Port Olímpic
AVINGUDA DEL LITORAL

PRBB
C/TELAWNEY
CAR.TRIAS FARGAS
Hotel
Arts
Torre
Mapfre
PASSEIG MARÍTIM DEL BOGATELL

spital
l Mar
Frank
Gehry Fish
PASSEIG MARÍTIM DEL PORT OLÍMPIC

Casino
MOLL DE MESTRAL

Centre de
la Platja
PORT OLÍMPIC
MOLL DE LLEVANT

MOLL DE XALOC
Centre
Municipal
de Vela

N

0   200
metres

3

Avda Francesc Ferrer i Guàrdia

Carrer dels Morabos

C/ Montfar

C/ Campsega

Caixa Forum

Carrer de l'Exèr

Avinguda de la Reina Maria Cristina

Fira de Barcelona

Avinguda dels Marques de Comillas

Poble Espanyol

Pavelló Mies van der Rohe

Palau de Congressos

Avinguda de Rius i Taulet

Font Màgica

Plaça de Carles Buïgas

Avinguda dels Montanyans

Carrer del Polvorí

Carrer de la Fontà

Carrer dels Jocs del 92

Carrer de Lleida

MONTJUÏC

Avinguda de l'Estadi

C/ Cigales

La Franç

Mercat de les Flors

Institu del Teat

Museu Nacional d'Art de Catalunya (MNAC)

Plaça de Margarida Xirgu

C/ Conco

LA CI DEL TE

Parc de Montjuïc

Museu Etnològic

Teatre Lliure

Piscines Bernat Picornell

Passeig de Santa Madrona

Museu d'Arqueologia de Catalunya

Jard Amar

Carrer dels Jocs del 92

Jardins de Joan Maragall

Passeig de Santa Madrona

Passeig de Santa Madrona

Teatre Grec

Carrer de Pierre de Coubertin

Jardins de Laribal

Palau Sant Jordi

Fundació Joan Mir

Estadi Olímpic Lluís Companys

Museo Olímpic i de L'Esport

Avinguda de Mirama

Passeig Olímpic

Carrer del Doctor Font i Quer

Jardins de Mossèn Cinto Verdaguer

Passeig del Migdia

Carrer de Cavallero

Jardí Botànic de Barcelona

Carrer dels Tabongers

Passeig del Migdia

Avinguda del Castell

Cementiri del Sud-Oest

Castell de Montjuïc

Mirador del Migdia

Camí Del Mar

Ronda del Litoral

Passeig de Cantunis

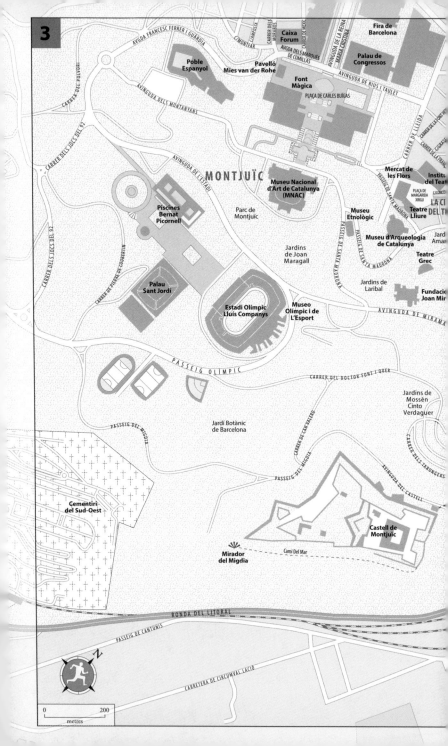

Carretera de Circumval·lació

0   200

metres

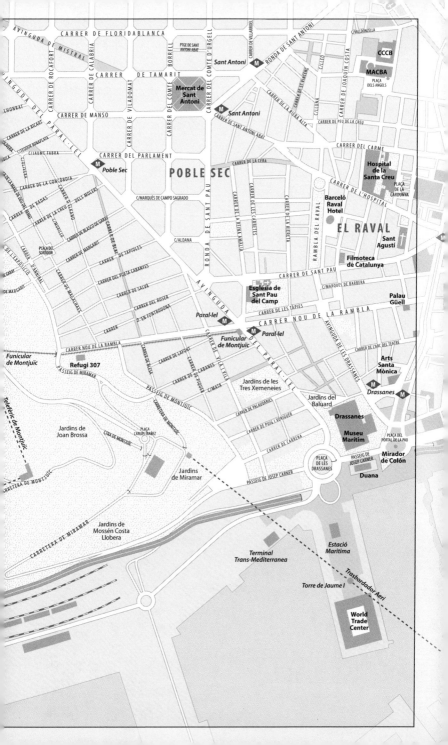

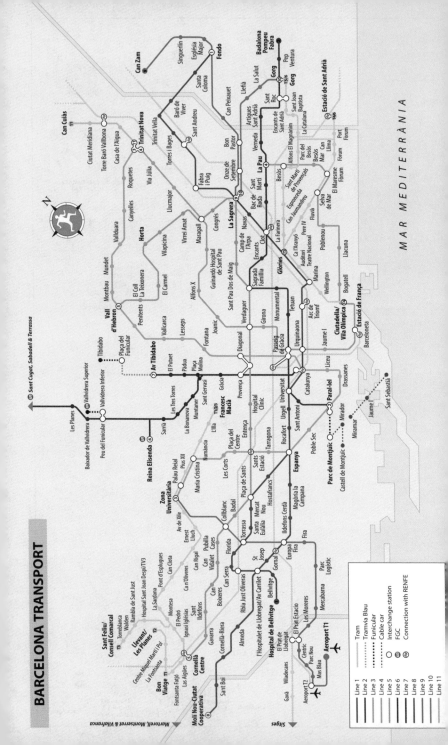